The Evolving Constitution

Essays by

Arthur J. Goldberg

J. Skelly Wright

Elbert P. Tuttle

Abe Fortas

Thurgood Marshall

Irving R. Kaufman

David L. Bazelon

Shirley M. Hufstedler

James L. Oakes

John Paul Stevens

Wilfred Feinberg

Harry A. Blackmun

William J. Brennan, Jr.

The Evolving Constitution

*Essays on the Bill of Rights
and the
U.S. Supreme Court*

Edited and with a Foreword by
Norman Dorsen

Introduction by
Archibald Cox

Wesleyan University Press
Middletown, Connecticut

Library of Congress Cataloging in Publication Data

The Evolving Constitution.

Bibliography: p.
Includes index.
1. Civil rights—United States. 2. United States.
Supreme Court. 3. Political questions and judicial
power—United States. I. Dorsen, Norman.
KF4749.A2E96   1987   342.73′085   87-15182
347.30285
ISBN 0-8195-5178-3 (alk. paper)

All inquiries and permissions requests should be addressed to the Publisher,
Wesleyan University Press, 110 Mt. Vernon Street, Middletown, Connecticut
06457.

Distributed by Harper & Row Publishers, Keystone Industrial Park, Scranton, Pennsylvania 18512.

Manufactured in the United States of America

FIRST EDITION

Contents

Contents   vii

Norman Dorsen

Foreword

The American political system is built upon two fundamental ideas. The first is the idea of majority rule through electoral democracy. This principle is firmly established in our culture. The second is less established, less understood, and much more fragile: the idea that even in a democracy the majority must be limited in order to assure individual liberty.

The Bill of Rights—the first ten amendments to the Constitution— is the primary source of the legal boundaries on what the majority, acting through government, can do to individuals. Such limits are for the benefit of everyone, but in practice they often serve to protect dissenters and unpopular minorities from official wrongdoing and assist them to share in the advantages of a free society. John Locke, whose ideas permeate our Constitution, recognized that these goals are the highest purpose of organized government. "However it may be mistaken," he wrote, "the end of law is not to abolish or restrain, but to preserve and enlarge freedom."

The James Madison Lectures by federal appellate judges were inaugurated at the New York University School of Law in 1960 "to enhance the appreciation of civil liberty and strengthen the national purpose." The first four lectures were published in book form in 1963, in *The Great Rights*,* edited by the first director of the series, Edmond Cahn. It contained lectures by Supreme Court Justice Hugo Black, Justice William J. Brennan, Jr., Chief Justice Earl Warren, and Justice William O. Douglas on the general philosophy of constitutional liberty. It also included a perceptive essay on "The Madison Heritage," by the historian Irving Brant, which reminded us of Madison's many contributions to the principles of liberty, including the drafting of the Bill of Rights itself.

* The James Madison Lectures that have been published in *The Great Rights* and in this book have all appeared in the *New York University Law Review*, to which grateful acknowledgment is made for permission to republish.

The thirteen lectures published in this volume were delivered in almost equal number by justices of the Supreme Court and judges of the United States Courts of Appeals.* They present several themes, all closely related to the objectives of a free society as ensured by a properly functioning Bill of Rights.

The essays by Justices Arthur Goldberg and Abe Fortas and Judges Elbert P. Tuttle and J. Skelly Wright focus on equality, and particularly the vast injustices and implications, not by any means exhausted today, of American segregation and discrimination practiced against blacks. The 1960s, when these lectures were delivered, was the occasion for the nation's sad recollection that the Constitution explicitly countenanced slavery, although it avoided mentioning the odious term. It was also an occasion to recall the failed hopes of the constitutional amendments ratified after the Civil War that were designed to bring former slaves into full equality in the United States. The insights and analysis of these four lectures are still relevant to the ongoing struggle to fulfill in fact the formal assumption that (in de Tocqueville's words) "Americans are all of the same estate" before the law.

Since these lectures were delivered, new conceptions have stirred the nation. Popular movements support equality for women, the elderly, homosexuals, the physically handicapped, and other groups. The constitutional issues these movements have spawned should also be the subject of James Madison Lectures, and I hope that they soon will be.

The second principal theme addressed in these lectures concerns the administration of justice. How the federal courts are run and the nature of their jurisdiction are not technical sideshows. Far from it. When a court has power to resolve a dispute, when it must defer to state tribunals or refrain from decision altogether, which sorts of plaintiffs are authorized to sue, and whether "efficiency" outweighs the importance of having the leisure for reflection and composition are all questions of the highest moment. Justice Thurgood Marshall and Judges David L. Bazelon and Shirley M. Hufstedler address

---

* The James Madison Lectures delivered by Justice Tom Clark in 1968 and Judge A. Leon Higginbotham, Jr. in 1986 are not included here. Justice Clark's article was inappropriate for this collection, and Judge Higginbotham's article will be published as part of a larger work that he is writing. It is hoped that the lecture scheduled for November 1987 by Judge Frank M. Coffin will be published in due course in a third volume of these lectures.

themselves imaginatively to these and other issues of judicial administration and reform.

The remaining six articles fit no clear pattern as they consider a series of topical questions. The essay by Justice John Paul Stevens on the relationship between adherence to precedent and the pivotal rule that permits four justices of the Supreme Court to accept a case for review would fit comfortably within the rubric of judicial administration. The same might be said about Justice Harry A. Blackmun's careful exploration of the proper scope of the most important federal statute that protects constitutional rights, 42 U.S.C. § 1983.

The essays by Justice William J. Brennan, Jr., and Judge James L. Oakes make a natural pair, both reminiscent of the articles on the general philosophy of the Constitution that were published in *The Great Rights*. In 1986, Justice Brennan became the only person to deliver a second James Madison Lecture when, a quarter century after his first appearance, he discussed state constitutions as guardians of individual rights. Judge Oakes, in an extensive analysis, examines the central role of the federal courts in enforcing the Bill of Rights.

The other two articles are by a former and the present chief judge of the Court of Appeals for the Second Circuit. Judge Irving R. Kaufman's article on the relationship between the "message" of speech and the "medium" through which it is conveyed illuminates a perplexing area of First Amendment jurisprudence. Judge Wilfred Feinberg focuses on recent legislative attempts, all fortunately unsuccessful, to limit the jurisdiction of the federal courts. In a sense, his essay probes the pathology of the system, when political reaction to unpopular rulings on behalf of minority rights spawns efforts to restrict judicial authority to hear controversial constitutional issues.

The James Madison Lectures contained in this book span twenty-two years, from Arthur Goldberg's 1964 lecture to William Brennan's in 1986. They reflect enduring principles of constitutional law and policy.* The ideas are of direct contemporary relevance to current debates on the role that the federal courts, and particularly the Supreme Court, should play in our system of government.

This book, through its title, acknowledges the evolving nature of the American Constitution. It was recognized from the beginning that the document was not frozen in time. In an oft-quoted passage, Chief

---

* Where particular developments since the delivery of a lecture seem important to an understanding of the subject, they are indicated by an editor's note.

Justice John Marshall said that the Constitution is an instrument "intended to endure for ages to come and, consequently, to be adapted to the various crises of human affairs." This insight has been almost universally accepted. For example, in 1910 in *Weems v. United States* the Court discussed the meaning of the clause that prohibits "cruel and unusual punishments":

Time works changes, brings into existence new conditions and purposes. Therefore, a principle to be vital must be capable of wider application than the mischief which gave it birth. This is peculiarly true of constitutions. They are not ephemeral enactments, designed to meet passing occasions.

In 1934, Chief Justice Charles Evans Hughes forcefully rejected the proposition that "the great clauses of the Constitution must be confined to the interpretation which the framers, with the conditions and outlook of their time, would have placed upon them."

This understanding of the Constitution was virtually common ground until Attorney General Edwin Meese, in a series of speeches, expressed what he called a "Jurisprudence of Original Intention" that would, as he said to the American Bar Association in July 1985, "endeavor to resurrect the original meaning of constitutional provisions and statutes as the *only* reliable guide for judgment" (emphasis added).

The torrent of reply to Mr. Meese explained why his approach to the Constitution is simplistic. In many if not most controversies in which "the great generalities of the Constitution"—freedom of speech and religion, due process, equal protection of the laws—are open to interpretation, it is not possible to ascertain the "original meaning." Some current issues were not foreseen, others were never discussed, and still others saw conflicting "intentions." Beyond these problems, it is not easy to decipher the eighteenth-century mind when it is being juxtaposed to twentieth-century problems. This is especially the case when it is a group "intention" that is being sought, and still further when it is several groups whose intention is of concern—the members of the Constitutional Convention, the First Congress (which proposed the Bill of Rights), and the ratifying conventions of the states that at different times approved the original document and the amendments.

An exclusive inquiry into "original intention" is thus neither practicable as a matter of interpretation nor consistent with the underlying philosophy of a document designed to meet the exigencies of future generations.

This is not to say that text and history are unimportant to constitutional interpretation. To the contrary, they must be starting points of analysis. But, in the effort to apply constitutional principles to contemporary problems, text and history must be supplemented by an understanding of the purposes of particular provisions, the values that underlie them, and the judicial interpretation that the Constitution has received over two centuries.

This is one of the many lines of thought contained in Archibald Cox's masterful Introduction, "Storm Over the Supreme Court." Professor Cox examines previous controversies that enveloped the Court, discusses the changes in doctrine and role that took place over the past generation beginning with *Brown v. Board of Education* in 1954, and relates these events and ideas—always with reference to particular cases—to the disputes swirling around the present Court. This analysis will assist the reader to grasp more fully the arguments and themes of the lectures that follow, just as Irving Brant's essay performed this function for the lectures contained in *The Great Rights*.

The celebration of the bicentennial of the Constitution and Bill of Rights, if properly conducted, will rededicate the people to the principles of liberty that are the bedrock of our national identity. That these principles have often been ignored or flouted over the years, while a cause for regret and outrage, should not be discouraging. Rather, it should steel us to what Edmond Cahn identified as the "personal commitment, costly risk, and constant effort" needed for the cultivation of civil liberty. The James Madison Lectures in this book are offered with the hope that they will contribute to that noble goal.

Acknowledgments

I thank Norman Redlich, dean of the Law School and for several years my predecessor as director of the James Madison Lectures, for his support.

I thank Bobbie Glover, director of special occasions at the School of Law, for her many contributions to the administration of the James Madison Lectures.

I thank Holly Thompson, my assistant and secretary, and Thomas Viles, a senior at the Law School, for their excellent help in regard to my editorial chores.

All of us thank our late colleague, Professor Edmond Cahn, for conceiving the James Madison Lecture series, and the late Louis Schweitzer for endowing them.

Norman Dorsen
New York University School of Law

May 1987

List of Contributors

Editor

Norman Dorsen is Stokes Professor of Law at New York University School of Law, where he directs the Arthur Garfield Hays Civil Liberties Program. During military service, he was an assistant to Joseph Welch in the 1954 Army-McCarthy Hearings. In 1957–58 he was law clerk to Supreme Court Justice John Marshall Harlan. Among books he has written or edited are *Frontiers of Civil Liberties*, *The Rights of Americans*, and *Our Endangered Rights*. Dorsen was president of the Society of American Law Teachers from 1973 to 1975. He has been president of the American Civil Liberties Union since 1976.

Contributors

Archibald Cox, Carl M. Loeb University Professor Emeritus at Harvard University, served as solicitor general of the United States in the Kennedy and Johnson administrations and, in 1973, was the first director of the Watergate Special Prosecution Force. He is the author of *The Warren Court*, *The Role of the Supreme Court in American Government*, and *Freedom of Expression*. He is chairman of Common Cause.

Arthur J. Goldberg was an associate justice of the United States Supreme Court from 1962 to 1965. He also served as secretary of labor and as United States ambassador to the United Nations. He is a recipient of the Presidential Medal of Freedom.

J. Skelly Wright was a judge of the United States Court of Appeals for the District of Columbia Circuit for twenty-five years, including a period as chief judge from 1979 to 1981. He previously served as the United States attorney and United States district judge for the Eastern District of Louisiana.

Elbert P. Tuttle has been a judge of the United States Court of Appeals for the Fifth Circuit since 1954. He served as chief judge from 1961 to 1967. He was chairman of the Advisory Committee on Civil Rules of the United States Judicial Conference and is a recipient of the Presidential Medal of Freedom.

Abe Fortas was an associate justice of the United States Supreme Court from 1965 to 1969. For many years he was a senior partner of Arnold, Fortas and Porter in Washington, D.C. He served as an adviser to the first United States delegation to the United Nations.

Thurgood Marshall has been an associate justice of the United States Supreme Court since 1967. He served for many years as special counsel to the NAACP. From 1961 to 1965 he was a judge on the United States Court of Appeals for the Second Circuit and from 1965 to 1967 he served as solicitor general of the United States.

Irving R. Kaufman is a judge of the United States Court of Appeals for the Second Circuit; he was chief judge from 1973 to 1980. Before that, he was a judge of the United States District Court for the Southern District of New York.

David L. Bazelon has been a judge of the United States Court of Appeals for the District of Columbia Circuit since 1949. He was chief judge from 1962 to 1978.

Shirley M. Hufstedler is a member of the Los Angeles law firm of Hufstedler, Miller, Carlson & Beardsly. She has served as a judge in the California courts, as a judge of the United States Court of Appeals for the Ninth Circuit, and as United States secretary of education.

James L. Oakes is a judge of the United States Court of Appeals for the Second Circuit. He has also served as a Vermont state senator, Vermont attorney general, and a United States district judge for the District of Vermont.

John Paul Stevens has been an associate justice of the United States Supreme Court since 1975. Before his appointment, he was a judge of the United States Court of Appeals for the Seventh Circuit.

Wilfred Feinberg is chief judge of the United States Court of Appeals for the Second Circuit. He has been a circuit judge since 1966. Before that, he was a judge of the United States District Court for the Southern District of New York.

Harry A. Blackmun has been an associate justice for the United States Supreme Court since 1970. For more than a decade before that, he was a judge of the United States Court of Appeals for the Eighth Circuit.

William J. Brennan, Jr., has been an associate justice of the United States Supreme Court since 1956 and the senior associate justice since 1975. Before his appointment, he was a New Jersey state court judge for many years.

The Evolving Constitution

Archibald Cox

Storm Over the Supreme Court

Controversy has surrounded the Supreme Court of the United States throughout our history. The Jeffersonian Republicans sought to dominate the Court by impeachment. President Franklin D. Roosevelt was so frustrated by the Court's decisions that he proposed to increase the size of the Court in order to pack it with supporters of the New Deal.

Today, the controversy seems louder and more intense than at any time since 1937. The president and the attorney general lambaste the Court for disregarding the intent of the framers of the Constitution in order to impose upon the country social experiments flowing from the justices' personal values. They speak as if they would fill the federal bench with judges committed to undoing the recent past by reading their personal philosophy into the Constitution, perhaps in the name of "original intent." From the liberals comes loud political reaction. The Court's own opinions show the justices to be deeply divided. At least two of them, Justices Brennan and Stevens, have temporarily put aside their judicial robes to make speeches seeming to enter into political debate with the attorney general.

Beneath the surface, behind the rulings upon school prayer and abortion, lie more fundamental questions concerning the role of the Supreme Court in American government and, more particularly, the way in which the justices do and should go about reaching decisions. Thomas Jefferson argued that to recognize the Court as the final arbiter of constitutional questions would place us "under the despotism of an oligarchy." Whether Jefferson was right depends upon how the justices go about making their decisions. Jefferson would be largely right if the justices are to decide as a small policy-making or political

Archibald Cox's introduction was delivered as the Albert H. Blumenthal Memorial Lecture at Hunter College of The City University of New York on February 13, 1986. We are grateful to the College for permission to reproduce it here.

body free, like a legislature, to make and change the law as a majority thinks wise. How far the Court is to act as an unconstrained policy-maker the justices will decide, but the people's understanding of the Court and respect for its authority will also be greatly influenced by the president's selection of justices and judges, by the way in which he and the attorney general present the Court and questions concerning its role, and by our expectations as citizens.

My fear is that excessive politicization of the whole process of constitutional interpretation, to some extent inside but especially outside the Court, is doing great harm to the institution and may erode the very foundation of our constitutionalism and the rule of law.

I

What is the Supreme Court for? The kinds of constitutional problems with which we expect the Court to deal are easily identified. In the beginning the questions, What may be regulated by Congress? and What powers are reserved to the states? provided the great constitutional issues. Since 1937 the powers of Congress have been interpreted so broadly that the distribution of power in the federal system has become largely a legislative or political, rather than justiciable, constitutional question. Working out the relations between state and federal law and state and federal courts remains a regular part of the Court's docket but is no longer the stuff of high controversy.

At the moment disputes over the separation of powers—over the respective functions of the Congress and the president—command the spotlight because of the litigation challenging the constitutionality of the Gramm-Rudman Act. Even though a change may be in the wind, such questions too are not at present a regular part of the main work of the Court.

Today the Court's prime and most controversial role is as the protector of individual and minority rights against government, whether state or federal. The role is a response to the ancient and deep-seated human conviction that there are fundamental individual liberties, chiefly in the realm of the spirit, that should be beyond the reach of government. The United Nations charter speaks of human rights. In the seventeenth and eighteenth centuries the longing found eloquent expression in the writings of John Locke and Jean Jacques Rousseau concerning "natural law," "natural rights," and the "rights of man." From the Magna Carta wrested from King John at Runnymede there also came the tradition that even the king, the government, is subject to "the law of the land." In America, in the years following independence, the idea gradually emerged that important individual liberties ("natural rights") could be protected by three steps: *First*, let the fundamental human rights to be put beyond the reach of government be written down in a constitution. *Second*, treat the constitution as law to be interpreted and applied by courts in the same fashion as any other law, but make the constitution supreme so that in case of conflict between the constitution and any other law, the constitution shall prevail. *Third*, make the judiciary impartial and independent. James Madison put it in a nutshell when he said in proposing the Bill of Rights: "[I]ndependent tribunals of justice will consider themselves in a peculiar manner the guardians of those rights; they will be an impenetrable bulwark against every assumption of power in the Legislative or Executive."

The original Bill of Rights restricted only the federal government. In 1868, however, we adopted the Fourteenth Amendment. Section 1 forbids any state to "deprive any person of life, liberty or property without due process of law" or to "deny any person . . . the equal protection of the laws." The obvious intention was to provide national constitutional protection of some fundamental individual rights against invasion by a state.

So much is clear. The question, What is the Court for? now becomes one of judicial method: How is the Court to decide what rights the Constitution protects? How is the Court to determine the scope of the protected rights and the justifications for invading them?

"Read the Constitution," one might reply. The Bill of Rights does list some rights with some degree of particularity: freedom of speech, no laws respecting an establishment of religion, trial by jury, freedom from unreasonable searches and seizures, and so forth. But even these phrases are imprecise. Not every spoken or written word is part of the freedom of speech. Which words are, and which are not? And what is a law "respecting an establishment of religion"? Where should the Court look for the answers to such questions of interpretation?

The problem becomes a great deal more difficult when we turn to the open-ended guarantees forbidding a state to "deprive any person of life, liberty or property without due process of law," and to deny any person "the equal protection of the laws." The phrases have a hard core of historic meaning, but give no answers in many cases. Is freedom to refuse vaccination against smallpox a "liberty" secured by the Fourteenth Amendment? Freedom to employ a man who wishes to work a 60-hour week? Freedom to terminate a pregnancy? Freedom to engage in private in homosexual relations?

Few individual rights are absolute. Even freedom of speech may sometimes be limited for sufficient reason. Incitement to immediate riot is a crime. Consequently, the basic question concerning the proper method of constitutional interpretation sometimes becomes, How is the Court to know whether or when the legislative or executive branch has sufficient justification for violating what might otherwise be a protected constitutional right?

II

Such questions first became prominent about a century ago. State legislatures were responding to the political pressure for laws limiting the economic power of large-scale business enterprises by enacting legislation regulating certain occupations, fixing maximum· hours of work and minimum wages, protecting the formation of labor unions, and, in some areas, imposing price controls. The legislation conflicted with the traditional ideals of sturdy individualism in a land of unfettered economic activity and deep belief in *laissez faire*. The business enterprises that lost the battles in the political forums carried the war to the courts. Minimum-wage and maximum-hours laws were held to take liberty and property without due process of law because they excessively curtailed liberty of contract. So were laws prohibiting employers from discharging employees who joined a labor union. The decision in *Lochner v. New York*, holding unconstitutional a statute making it a crime to employ a man to work more than ten hours a day in a bakery, symbolized the era. The resulting constitutional debate developed jurisprudential themes that influence the debate today.

One criticism was that the Court erred in reading into the general words of the Fourteenth Amendment protection for a liberty of contract that the Constitution never mentions. Instead of enforcing the Constitution, the critics said, the conservative majority was simply imposing its values and economic philosophy upon society without support in the words of the Constitution. The parallel criticism of the abortion rulings is that the modern Court read into those same phrases a right of privacy or "freedom of choice" without warrant in the words and so imposed its permissive values upon society. In effect, the critics were saying that in identifying constitutional rights for protection against legislative regulations enforced through fair procedures, the courts should not go beyond the specific words of the Constitution itself.

The majority in the old cases could at least respond that freedom to pursue economic advantage, to contract, and to acquire and use property, were old and cherished rights not only in Anglo-American law but according to John Locke and the other seventeenth and eighteenth century philosophers of liberty who profoundly influenced the framers. The Court then found its law—its values—in the past, in precedent and tradition. In this sense, the Court was giving effect to the basic ideas and the original intent of the framers.

The response raised a second issue important today. The critics argued that the Court had failed to keep pace with the times. Possibly there was a time and place, the critics said, in which it could fairly be said that the right of a person to sell his labor upon such terms as he saw fit was the same as the right of the employer to prescribe the terms on which he would offer employment. Perhaps any law that disturbed that equality, when there was equality, was an arbitrary interference with liberty. But there is no such equality of bargaining power in the modern industrial world, the argument ran; the concept has now become a sterile abstraction. To adhere to the verbal dogma after new conditions have changed its practical impact is to distort the true intention.

A third criticism—a plea for majoritarianism and judicial deference both to legislative determinations and to the value of state autonomy—was the most telling. The Constitution predicates popular sovereignty. Why should the Court rather than the elected representatives of the people have the final word in determining whether legislation limiting the bargaining power (the freedom of contract) of corporate employers is of sufficient public benefit to outweigh the sacrifice of liberty and so constitutes due process of law? The Constitution also predicates a federal system in which the states may make laws according to their local needs. Why should a national court in Washington interfere with what the state has decided? To be specific, why should nine men appointed for life have the final word in appraising the dangers of long hours of work in a bakery and then weighing the dangers against the invasion of liberty, after a state legislature has already performed that very function?

In the 1930s the criticisms began to take hold, aided by the Great Depression and the New Deal. President Roosevelt lambasted the

Court for applying rules outmoded since the horse and buggy days. President Reagan borrows the Rooseveltian phrases in lambasting the Court for leaving the horse and buggy behind. In 1937, in the face of political, social, and economic realities and a flood tide of legal criticism, the Court retreated. All three criticisms became part of the stream of constitutional law.

Some justices, notably Justice Hugo Black, espoused the view that no individual rights should be recognized as deserving constitutional protection under the general phrase "life, liberty or property" unless specifically mentioned elsewhere in the Constitution, as in the cases of the freedom of speech and trial by jury. Probably, a majority never accepted this view, but there was reluctance to create new constitutional rights.

The majorities of 1937 and subsequent years were "activist" in the sense that they engaged in bringing the law up to date by overruling earlier precedents based upon concepts that industrialization had deprived of reality.

The philosophy of judicial deference to legislative determinations and to state and local autonomy rapidly became dominant among the justices and the lower court judges and in the law schools and legal profession. The rules became: (1) that if any set of facts, any social or economic conditions, could exist that would justify the challenged regulation, the Court must presume that they did exist; and (2) that where the Congress or state legislature had struck a balance between individual rights and the gains of regulation, the Court would not substitute its judgment for a rational legislative view.

It is chiefly this extraordinary judicial deference to the legislative process and to state autonomy that leads historians to characterize the late 1930s and 1940s as an era of judicial self-restraint. For many lawyers and judges, that philosophy remains the ideal. The opinions of Justices Rehnquist and O'Connor upholding laws challenged as unconstitutional bear obvious marks of that philosophy, which was dominant while they were law students. The depth of their commitment to that philosophy will be tested when they rule upon new popular legislation with which they disagree.

III

Change set in again in the 1940s and 1950s as civil liberties and civil rights litigation began to crowd the docket. The multiplication and

magnification of government activities increased sensitivity to threats
to civil liberty. Humanitarianism, aided by the prevailing teachings of
the psychological and social sciences, cast doubt upon the sterner
aspects of criminal law. A wave of egalitarianism flowed from the historic impulse of the American people stirred by the war against Hitler's ideas of a "master race" and by the rise of the peoples of Asia and
Africa. A wave of emancipation reflected wide dissatisfaction with social, moral, and legal constraints upon freedom to do one's own thing
provided that others are not visibly affected. In this context a majority
of the justices began to assert with new vigor the Court's responsibility
for protecting individual human liberties, including equality of
opportunity and individual dignity.

In applying the First Amendment's guarantees of freedom of
speech and of the press, the Court flatly rejected appeals for self-
restraint and deference to legislative judgments in applying the First
Amendment, reasoning that those precepts are not applicable to
adjudication under specific guarantees. Under both Chief Justice
Warren and Chief Justice Burger the Court greatly expanded the
constitutional protection for freedom of expression, sweeping aside a
number of traditional legal doctrines such as the rule that false and
defamatory statements of fact are not protected by the First Amendment.

Next, vigorous federal judicial intervention spread to the area of
criminal procedure. The federal Bill of Rights contains many specific
guarantees applicable to the investigation and prosecution of crime,
such as the privilege against self-incrimination, the need for indictment by a grand jury, and broad protection against double jeopardy.
Prior to 1945 few of these restrictions were strictly applicable to the
states. After World War II, however, the Supreme Court ruled that
the Fourteenth Amendment makes the federal restrictions applicable
to state prosecutions, thereby forcing changes in state procedure and
greatly broadening the rights of the accused.

The expansion of the Court's role spread next in decisions under
the Equal Protection Clause. *Brown v. Board of Education* is the most
notable example. Classifications according to race, being "invidious,"
were subjected to the "strictest judicial scrutiny" and could be justified, if ever, only if essential to secure some "compelling public purpose." The category of "invidious" then expanded to invalidate old
and familiar laws treating women differently than men, aliens differently than citizens, illegitimate children differently than legitimate

children, and recently arrived residents differently than old. The expansions were strongly challenged by dissenting justices.

In the "one person, one vote" cases, the Court held that any significant departure from equal per capita representation in apportioning seats in a legislature violates the Equal Protection Clause, reasoning that the vote and political representation are "fundamental rights," and that any inequality of treatment in access to a fundamental right should be subjected to the strictest scrutiny and held unconstitutional unless supported by compelling public purpose. The poll tax was also invalidated upon this ground. For a time it appeared that the Court would subject to the strictest scrutiny any statute differentiating between groups of persons in access to whatever the Court found to be a "fundamental right"; but a majority of the Burger Court rejected the effort to generalize the principle.

Last in the line of progression came *Roe v. Wade* and the companion cases holding that enforcement of state anti-abortion laws during the first six months of pregnancy would unconstitutionally deprive women of liberty without due process of law. The Court applied the strict-scrutiny/compelling-purpose test even though the claim was based upon the generalities of the Fourteenth Amendment. The Court substituted its own judgment for that of the elected legislative representatives of the people not only upon whether freedom of choice is to be identified as a right embraced with the liberty protected by the Fourteenth Amendment but also upon the balance to be struck between a pregnant woman's freedom of choice and the opposing interests in protecting the life or potential life of the unborn child. In terms of judicial method, the Court had arguably completed a circular journey back to *Lochner v. New York.*

Viewed as a body, the decisions of the 1950s, 1960s, and 1970s had five dominant characteristics:

1. They substituted judicially determined values and judicial rules for the detemations of elected legislatures, often old and arguably outmoded determinations but nonetheless determinations of elected representatives of the people. The most dramatic examples are the "one person, one vote" and abortion cases.

2. They substituted national rules for local self-determination. The decisions in the field of criminal procedure may be the best examples.

3. They gave new recognition to theretofore unrecognized constitutional rights and broadened the protection of old rights. Sometimes, once-settled precedents were directly overruled. More often,

the new decisions ran counter to widespread legal practice or assumptions generally accepted although never squarely embedded in Supreme Court precedents.

4. They mandated major institutional changes not only in the administration of justice but in the larger society. Previously the Court's constitutional decisions had done no more than uphold or block legislative or executive initiatives. From 1950 to 1974 the Court was mandating reform. The Desegregation cases reordered society throughout large regions. The Reapportionment cases upset ancient political arrangements. The School Prayer cases banished a practice familiar to generations of students.

5. Effectuation of the reforms mandated by the decisions required the courts to prescribe remedies with many of the characteristics of legislation and executive programs. The school desegregation decrees are the best example. Each decree affects thousands, even millions of people. Each looks to future conduct. Each disappoints some people and benefits others in order to achieve broad social objectives. Each decree may, and many do, require the appropriation of large sums of money.

IV

The expanded and reforming role was bound to stir resistance, controversy, and calls for a return to the past. Under Chief Justice Burger the pace of change slowed almost to a standstill except in the area of freedom of the press, abortion, and women's rights. There were some cutbacks, although none of the great Warren Court reforms was overruled. The critics remained dissatisfied. There are still many people who resent and resist the full implementation of *Brown v. Board of Education* and the civil rights revolution. Others, understandably worried by violence, crime, and unsafe streets, see increasing the guarantees of fair procedure as coddling criminals. Only the innocent are entitled to such safeguards, the attorney general told and untold us; those who are investigated or accused are not the innocent. Still others resent and sometimes resist the elimination of morning prayer from public schools. I scarcely need mention the emotional opposition to the ruling upholding the right to abortion.

There are two ways of judging the work of the Warren and Burger Courts, two levels of criticism and defense; and while they overlap, it is important not to confuse them.

One way is to look exclusively or almost exclusively to the decisions reached, much as one would judge the work of a legislature or other elected policymakers. If I were to accept this test, it would be enough for me that the decisions of the past fifty years have made ours a vastly freer, more equal, more open, and more humane society with greater respect for human dignity. But if I were to accept this test, I should have to acknowledge that those who have a different view of the good society should feel free to pack the Court with men and women who share their view, and that the appointees should feel free to write their political philosophies into the law. The result-oriented approach predicates that all courts, and especially the Supreme Court, are simply engaged in making social policy within ill-defined areas and should therefore decide what is good and just and wise according to the needs of the times.

The second way of judging the past work of the Court puts weight upon the judicial method and compels us to ask, Did the Court too freely read new specific constitutional rights into open-ended phrases like "liberty" and "equal protection of the law"? Did it go too fast in keeping pace with the times? Should it have been as deferential to state legislative restrictions in dealing with claims of human rights as it had been in dealing with claims to economic liberty?

I reject the exclusively or heavily result-oriented approach not only as a description of judicial behavior but as a prescription of future judicial method. Learned Hand, a great federal judge who never reached the Supreme Court, once put part of the objection to me as a young law clerk. "Sonny," he asked, "to whom am I responsible? No one can fire me. No one can dock my pay. Even those nine bozos in Washington, who sometimes reverse me, can't make me decide as they want. Everyone should be responsible to someone. To whom am I responsible?" Then the judge turned and pointed to the shelves of his law library. "To those books about us. That's to whom I'm responsible."

A judge's duty to subordinate his views to the ever-continuing, ever-changing body of law found in "those books about us" is one of the answers to Thomas Jefferson's fear that to give the courts the final word upon constitutional questions would place us under "the despotism of an oligarchy." Oligarchs who feel bound by a professional code of responsibility to seek the answers to the questions before them outside themselves in a body of law are far less dangerous than those who feel unconfined.

There is an even stronger objection to a purely political or result-oriented approach to constitutional interpretation. For the justices unrestrainedly to decide according to their views of policy—and for President Reagan, the attorney general, and other public figures to present constitutional decisions as simply moral or policy choices that are made by one group of justices and can be unmade by handpicking another—would, I fear, threaten the very foundation of our constitutionalism and the rule of law. I can best explain the reasons for my concern by asking another question. Upon what does our constitutionalism ultimately rest?

V

The question confronted me with extraordinary personal intensity during the Watergate crisis. In the summer of 1973 the investigation into the allegations that President Nixon and high White House aides had planned the Watergate break-in and later engaged in a conspiracy to obstruct justice by covering up the responsibility seemed to come down to a question of credibility. Then another former White House aide disclosed that there were tape recordings of all conversations involving President Nixon. Here was a way of ascertaining who was telling the truth, provided that the Watergate Special Prosecution Force could obtain the tapes for the Grand Jury. President Nixon refused to furnish the tapes, even in response to a subpoena, but after extensive legal arguments the U.S. District Court and the Court of Appeals ordered production of the most relevant.

Then came the crunch. Hints of noncompliance began filtering out of the White House. What could I do? What could Judge Sirica or the Court of Appeals do? What good would further court orders be if the president continued to disobey? The stark truth was that the courts had no physical power to enforce their decrees against the executive. Judges control neither the purse nor the sword.

There was a further worry. Suppose that the president's defiance of the courts were successful. The habit of compliance—the notion that a powerful executive official has no choice but to comply with a judicial decree—is a fragile bond. Who could say in an age of presidential aggrandizement that if one president succeeded in his defiance, he and others might follow that example until ours was no longer a government of law? President Nixon seemed to believe that the president was above the law. Later he would argue, "If the President does it, it can't be against the law. The President does it." Was one justified in provoking this kind of constitutional crisis with the outcome so uncertain? Surely it would be irresponsible to play the part of the little child who destroyed the myth of the emperor's marvelous raiment by blurting out that the emperor wore no clothes. On the other hand, what good was the principle that even our highest official is subject to the Constitution and laws if one dared not invoke the principle over executive opposition?

In the end confrontation became unavoidable. On a Friday night President Nixon announced that he would not give the tapes to the courts in accordance with the subpoena. The president also ordered me never again to resort to judicial process in order to obtain White House evidence. When I stated that I must pursue the investigation on the terms on which I began, the president directed Attorney General Richardson to dismiss me. Richardson resigned rather than comply. So did Deputy Ruckelshaus. The third in command carried out the president's wish.

Public support for the rule of law was then put to the test. A firestorm of public outrage overwhelmed the White House. On Tuesday the president's attorney rose in Judge Sirica's courtroom to say:

The President of the United States will comply in all respects with the order of August 29, as modified by the order of the Court of Appeals. . . .

The rule of law prevailed because the people rose up morally and politically. The response doubtless flowed from many sources, but I think that there was present deep and enduring realization, partly conscious and partly intuitive, that all our liberties depend upon compliance with law because the principal bulwark of those liberties against executive or legislative oppression is respect for constitutionalism: the law and the courts.

In some ways Watergate was an easy test. If constitutionalism and the rule of law are to protect our liberties in hard cases, public support for court decrees must be strong enough to compel compliance even from an unwilling president who is carrying on an otherwise popular but unlawful program, such as a military expedition held to violate the War Powers Act or the conduct of unconstitutional intelligence activities in the United States. The all-important question thus becomes, What is it about the Court and the way in which the Court goes about its work that induces the people to give that kind of support? Without such support, the Court could not do the work assigned it.

Some part of the answer is that law, as it binds officials, is seen by the people as a check upon both executive oppression and bureaucratic caprice. "Law" takes its meaning partly from traditional and evocative precepts that symbolize historic struggles for freedom from oppression—for example, "Liberty under Law," and "A government of laws, not of men." Some part of the answer may lie in the belief that the fundamental law is reaching for justice in an area where questions should be resolved not by force, not by the pressures of interest groups, nor even by votes, but by what reason and a sense of justice tell us is right.

Behind such beliefs lies the all-important but fragile faith that "law" has a separate existence—not merely because it applies to all men equally, but because it binds the judges as well as the judged, not just today but yesterday and tomorrow. The judge's authority, Judge Hand once wrote, depends upon his loyalty to a continuing body of law:

His authority and immunity depend upon the assumption that he speaks with the mouth of others: The momentum of his utterances must be greater than any which his personal reputation and character can command, if it is to do the work assigned to it—if it is to stand against the passionate resentments arising out of the interests he must frustrate.

Judge Hand was no slave to precedent. He served a continuing body of law, but he also knew that the law must grow and change to meet the needs of men. New conditions may rob old legal concepts, rules, and even principles of their former meaning, so that the old ideals and even traditional principles call for new applications. Better perception of the true meaning of basic ideals also may call for new developments. In the end, he thought, a judge faces a dilemma:

He must preserve his authority by cloaking himself in the majesty of an overshadowing past; but he must discover some composition with the dominant needs of his times.[1]

Constitutional law faces the same dilemma—it grows and changes yet commands assent by observing both branches of the antinomy. The original Constitution still serves us well despite the tremendous changes in every aspect of American life because the framers had the genius to say enough but not too much. They outlined a unique federal form of government and, shortly later, by amendments to the Constitution, they identified many of the basic individual rights they wished to guarantee against government oppression. In both areas important questions were left open, questions that the framers could not foresee and questions upon which they could not agree. Yet they said enough to provide points of reference. Then, perhaps by chance, perhaps by the wisdom and force of John Marshall, perhaps because it was intended, though not written, in the beginning, the great unanswered questions of federalism and individual right fell to the judiciary and, in the final analysis, to the Supreme Court of the United States, to be decided "according to law." As the plan outlined in the Constitutional Convention succeeded, as the country grew and prospered both materially and in the realization of its ideals, the Constitution gained majesty and authority far greater than that of any individual or body of men. Because enough was written and because decision "according to law" calls for building upon a continuity of principle found in the instrument, its structure and purposes, and in subsequent judicial interpretations, traditional understanding and historic practices, the Court, by always referring back to the sacred document, could bring to its resolution of the new and often divisive constitutional issues of each generation the momentum and authority of an overshadowing past while also serving the dominant needs of the times.

Somehow the Court must live within the horns of this dilemma. To politicize the process of constitutional adjudication by treating all questions as matters of policy would destroy the continuity essential to law. Rigidly to apply the words written in precedent, in "these books about us," despite the changes in societal conditions would fail to accommodate the human needs and aspirations of contemporary times.

VI

The key to resolving the dilemma, I think, lies first in an understanding search for the fundamental ideals or principles underlying the work of the framers, the evolving constitutional tradition, and the practices and body of law built up over two centuries, and then in the application of those underlying principles to contemporary conditions. The search is for "intent," for the "original intent," if discoverable; but here I use these slippery words in a very different sense than do Attorney General Meese and others who belabor the Court for departing from what they call the "original intention." Let me illustrate by a few examples and in the process address the question raised above—whether the Warren and Burger Courts erred on the side of politicizing the course of constitutional decisions.

Suppose that the government, without a search warrant, takes photographs of the papers on my desk through the windows from an airplane high overhead and then seeks to use the photographs to convict me of a crime. Has the government violated the Fourth Amendment's command against unreasonable searches and seizures? We can be virtually certain that a majority of the framers had no conscious, specific intent to bar taking pictures of business papers from an airplane or spy satellite. A holding that the government violated the Fourth Amendment would go beyond the "original intent" in the sense of a particular application consciously intended. Yet the broader, underlying purpose or policy—in that sense, the "intent"—was to secure the privacy of people's homes, offices, papers, and private effects against warrantless governmental intrusions. I do not know how Attorney General Meese would deal with the question. I am sure that the Court would unanimously hold the picture-taking to violate the Fourth Amendment, and that the decision would conform to the original intent in the more meaningful sense of the words. This could fairly be called "bringing the Constitution up to date," and creating a new constitutional right, but surely application of old general principles to unforeseen modern particulars is essential if a 200-year-old document is to continue to serve the country's needs.

The School Desegregation cases provide a more complex example. Some careful students of the history of the Fourteenth Amendment say that the framers of that amendment specifically intended not to forbid school segregation. Others say that history reveals no specific intent one way or the other. Nearly all historians agree that those who supported the amendment revealed no specific, affirmative intent to prohibit segregation in the public schools. Should we say, therefore, that the decision in *Brown v. Board of Education* was a too-activist usurpation of judicial power because it not only went beyond any demonstrable specific intent of the authors of the Fourteenth Amendment but repudiated practices long accepted by the authors of the amendment and their successors and firmly embedded in our law?

Surely the *Brown* decision is an instance of actively accommodating the law to the dominant needs of the times. To have reaffirmed the doctrine of "separate but equal" would have ignored both the revolution sweeping the world and the moral sense of civilization. But equally surely, the decision rendered also had strong, legitimatizing roots in the past and conformed to "the original intent" in the only meaningful sense of the phrase as applied to a Constitution that survives dramatic changes in the human condition—a general purpose or principle whose full meaning unfolds only as applied to future events and to often unseen, particular instances.

The promise of human dignity and equality had been part of the American tradition since before the Declaration of Independence. Racial prejudice and African slavery made a tragic exception for the black individual. The intent—the basic policy or underlying purpose—of the Equal Protection Clause was to ensure—not merely promise—equality by forbidding a state or local government to do anything inconsistent with the ancient ideal. Whatever may have been true in the nineteenth century, by 1954 it was all too obvious that state laws requiring racial segregation provided legal support for a system that denied black people equality of opportunity and equal human dignity with whites, and thus were inconsistent with the underlying intention of the framers of the Equal Protection Clause.

Sometimes the underlying principle is less clear, and the Court must make a creative choice. Discrimination against women had been woven into the fabric of our laws and attitudes from the beginning. The men who wrote the Constitution and their successors who wrote the Equal Protection Clause surely had no conscious purpose to require the government and the law to treat men and women alike. Could an open-minded neutral observer say that, despite the contrary practices, the seek of equality of treatment for women has always been implicit in the historic ideals of human equality and dignity, waiting to flower, much like the seed of equality regardless of race or color? I think so, despite the inconsistent practices, but I find it hard to deny that what I find in the past is influenced by my view of present needs.

The "one person, one vote" cases are very similar. Despite the long history of gross malapportionment, the decisions mandating equal representation *per capita* seem to me to realize an unfolding theme of political egalitarianism that runs through American history. Justice Douglas put it best:

The conception of political equality from the Declaration of Independence, to Lincoln's Gettysburg address, to the Fifteenth, Seventeenth and Nineteenth Amendments, can mean only one thing—one person, one vote.[2]

In the sex discrimination and "one person, one vote" cases there was wide room for judicial choice. Equally conscientious justices could reach quite different conclusions concerning the teaching of history and the scope and import of the principles revealed. The individual justice's experiences, temperament, and vision of the good society would inevitably influence, and in a close case dominate, his choice. Yet surely there is a difference between asking oneself, What do I think the rule should be? and asking, What do I think most consistent with the teachings of our constitutional history and other sources of law, as applied to the present time? The ideal and effort to achieve decision according to law are real even though the reach exceeds the grasp.

Part of the difference lies in a sense of the limits of the judicial role. The "one person, one vote" and sex discrimination cases were great leaps ahead. The Court gave voice to what it judged to be our ideals and condemned our practices. In such cases the roots of the decisions must be already in the nation. The aspirations voiced by the Court must be those the community is willing not only to avow but to live, Even then, too many such leaps endanger the Court's legitimacy by presenting decrees that are the result, not of law, but of the policies favored by oligarchs.

The abortion cases seem to me to present an example of excessive judicial activism. I do not fault the Court solely for substituting a national judicial judgment for the opinions of the legislatures of all fifty states. Surely that should give pause; but if we posit the existence of a constitutional right, then the Court cannot perform its historic function of protecting individual rights against government without judging for itself, at least to some extent, whether the legislature can justify the invasion. The Supreme Court's extraordinary deference to economic regulation after 1937, in effect, rejected all constitutional claims to economic liberty.

Nor do I give much weight to the charge that the Court created a new right not previously known to constitutional text or history. The force of the criticism depends upon what you mean by "a new right." All my previous examples involve the creation of new constitutional rights if the phrase is used with great particularity: the right not to have my private papers photographed from outside the building, the

right to be free from segregated schooling, the right to be free from
sex discrimination. Here, as in the case of "original intent," the question is whether the newly claimed right is truly new and different or
merely a new particular application of an old principle, resulting
from new conditions or perhaps a better understanding of the principle itself.

Perhaps we can fairly say that the right to freedom of choice is
simply a particular application of the emerging constitutional right of
women to equal freedom and equal opportunity with other individuals. But few rights are absolute, and the question becomes
whether the invasion is justified by a sufficiently compelling public
purpose. Respect for the paramount sanctity of human life is the
heart of Western civilization. However narrowly one defines "life" itself, however uncertain we may be about the correct definition, laws
protecting the penumbra, protecting "life-about-to-be" or "near life,"
promote that central public interest. As a legislator, I would agree
that the old laws against abortion should be radically changed. But I
can find no evidence that warrants a court in saying that the basic
values of our society as incorporated into our constitutionalism dictate
that choice. Sustaining the claim overrode the laws of all fifty states—
some over a century old and others quite recently liberalized—and
ran counter to a moral code established for centuries.

Similarly, I would suppose that the Court would be too creative in
the sodomy case that I mentioned above if it were to uphold the claim
of a right to engage without state interference in purely private conduct that has no demonstrable effect on others than the consenting
participants.* Possibly government ought not to impose the moral
views of the majority upon the private conduct of dissenters. But that
belief has no discernible support in law or history; consequently, the
Court would lack justification for writing it into the Constitution. If it
is to prevail, it should prevail by legislative repeal of the old laws, not
by judicial edict under the Constitution.

VII

Martin Shapiro once wrote, "If the myth of the Court is destroyed
in the law schools, the Court loses power. . . ." I agree. I have argued

* Several months after Archibald Cox's lecture, the Supreme Court held that Georgia's sodomy statute did not violate the constitutional rights of homosexuals. Bowers v.
Hardwick, 106 S.Ct. 2841 (1986). EDITOR'S NOTE.

that the foundation of our constitutionalism is the belief in a body of law limiting the power of the justices to make decisions upon political grounds even as they shape the law to the dominant needs of the times. But I would not choose the word "myth." The belief cannot survive, either in the law schools or elsewhere, unless supported by reality, unless judges recognize a duty to be bound by law even as they shape it. The justices can destroy the essential belief by excessively politicizing the course of decisions.

Whether the Court of the 1950s, 1960s, and early 1970s struck the right balance or erred too far in making new law too fast upon policy grounds, without sufficient regard for institutional limitations, is a troublesome question. Each of the great decisions of the past thirty/forty years, with the exception of the abortion cases, seems to me did have roots in what I described as constitutional tradition, in the rule of law, even though it carried the law a step further. Collectively, however, and especially when taken with many decisions of second- and third-rank importance, the use of constitutional adjudication as an instrument of reform seems to me to have strained the ideal of decision according to law.

Whether the strain has been too great, whether the Court by trying to do too much has impaired its own long-range utility, only the future can tell. The answer will depend partly upon how the successors to the five or six older justices view the process of interpretation. Will they see their task as preserving and strengthening the principle of decision according to an existing body of law, including the law built up over the past half-century with much of which they disagree? Or will they see their task as correcting the mistakes of their predecessors, perhaps in the name of returning to an "original intent" confined to the specific expectations of the framers as applied to the world they knew? Possibly, the misuse of the word "intent" would conceal the extraordinary activism, but I fear that the underlying politicization of the process of decision would shine through and further undermine the belief in the independent force of law that sustains our constitutionalism.

Confidence that judges strive to decide according to law and not simply their policy preferences can be destroyed by presidents, attorneys general, and others outside the Court as well as by overly freewheeling justices. For the public's confidence is dependent upon its perception of the process of decisions, and that perception is bound to be influenced by the way in which the process is described by the president, the attorney general, and others who take part in public debate. For the president to attack the decisions of the past few decades simplistically as a foisting of the majority justices' moral or social experiments upon the country contrary to the original intention, and then to cultivate the extreme right by promising to select nominees to vacancies who will sweep those decisions aside, may be shrewd politics, but it presents the task of constitutional interpretation as if it were a purely political function and the meaning of the Constitution could be changed as well. For liberals to join the debate in the same terms is equally destructive.

A president may and often has taken an appointee's political and judicial philosophy into account. Subject to the Senate's like privilege on confirmation, the president has constitutional authority to try to pack the courts with men who will render decisions fitting his own views. In fact, very few presidents have shaped the course of future constitutional decisions according to their desires. Some guessed wrong about how their chosen justices would vote. It is hard to predict how anyone will act when freed from all pressures, ambitions, and commitments. Some could not foresee the new constitutional issues that would take center stage while their appointees were on the bench. Most were influenced by other personal or political considerations.

The president's and the Senate's freedom to try to shape the course of decisions seems to me to be subject to three limitations, two of wisdom and one of propriety:

1. The strength and effectiveness of the judicial system depends upon including men and women who reflect as a group the whole of our diverse society. The narrower the experience or philosophy of the bench as a whole, the poorer the justice it will administer.

2. Choosing only men and women of a particular stamp for the proclaimed purpose of changing the course of decisions presents the whole process of constitutional interpretation as essentially political and thus undermines public confidence in the rule of law.

3. While a senator or the president should not be faulted for looking to a possible appointee's record for his views, it is grossly improper to quiz the appointee upon how he or she would decide a particular question. The wrong is that the question and answer imply some degree of commitment to a future decision. No future judge should give even an implied assurance as to how he or she will decide a particular

question. The essence of justice is impartial judges free from every form of interest, loyalty, obligation, or prior commitment.

What I have said about the processes of presidential appointment and Senate confirmation applies to debate about the Court and its constitutional decisions. Better general understanding of the Court's function is highly important. There is much room for debate over differences of degree—for example, over whether the Court at any given time adheres too closely to established law or veers too far from it in an effort to accommodate the perceived needs of the times. What those needs are is not always apparent. What is said in the political hustings can seldom encompass all the subtleties, nuances, and balances involved in constitutional interpretation. But one function of political leadership is to educate. At the very least, political debate can avoid pretending that the role of the Court is to render policy decisions and that all can be simply settled by asking what was consciously in the minds of the framers in the different and simpler world of 200 years ago.

Arthur J. Goldberg

Equality and Governmental Action

I

The American ideal of equality is an ideal not explicitly articulated in the Bill of Rights but one certainly encompassed in what James Madison called "the great rights of mankind." The storm over the decisions of the Supreme Court of the United States on the constitutional guarantee of equal protection, in cases involving state-sanctioned racial segregation, has tended to obscure the fact that equality and liberty were the "twin themes" of the American Revolution.[1] The united Colonies sought both "to be Free and Independent States . . . Absolved from all Allegiance to the British Crown"[2] and to vindicate the egalitarian principle that no man, including the king, had any natural dominion over another man. Revolutionary thinkers unanimously renounced monarchial titles and trappings.[3] They considered the people, and not the king, to be the sovereign. They advised their sons to "Remember that you are as good as any man—and that you are no better."[4] Jefferson proclaimed the revolutionary creed in the Declaration of Independence: "We hold these truths to be self-evident, that all men are created equal, that they are endowed by their Creator with certain unalienable Rights, that among these are Life, Liberty and the pursuit of Happiness."

Robert J. Harris has pointed out that the American concept of equality has roots deep in the history of Western civilization and "is at least coeval with if not prior to liberty in the history of Western political thought. . . ."[5] To the Hebrew patriarchs and sages the ideal of equality derived from the concept that all persons were created in the image of God; to the Stoics, from the idea that all men are entitled to equal station by the laws of Nature and of Nature's God;[6] to the disci-

Justice Goldberg's lecture was delivered on February 11, 1964, and appeared in 39 N.Y.U.L. Rev. 205 (1964).

ples, from the belief that all are one in Christ. And to the democratic theorists John Locke and Thomas Jefferson—who drew from all these sources—it was self-evident that all men are by nature equal and that rulers "are to govern by promulgated established laws, not to be varied in particular cases, but to have one rule for rich and poor, for the favourite at court and the countryman at plough."[7]

Since the realization of equality was a primary goal of our new nation, it seems strange that the Constitution prior to the adoption of the Fourteenth Amendment did not expressly mention equality. There are in my view several reasons for this omission. Although not expressly mentioned, the idea of equality pervades the document. Section 4 of Article IV guarantees to every state "a Republican Form of Government. . . ." Thus, the ancient inequality of king and subject, of lord and vassal,[8] is rejected and the political equality of all men asserted. More generally, Articles I, II, and III by their terms and necessary effect assume and construct a republican form of government for the nation. Section 2 of Article I mandates that representatives in the national House be chosen "by the People of the several States. . . ." This embodies another Lockean concept—that the legislature should fairly and equally represent the electorate. Benjamin Franklin deemed this necessary since "the *all* of one man is as dear to him as the *all* of another . . . the poor man has an *equal* right but the *more* need to have representatives in the legislature than the rich one."[9]

There is another reason why the framers did not find it necessary to mention equality. They naturally assumed it was encompassed within the concept of liberty[10] whose blessings they heralded in the preamble to the Constitution and later specifically guaranteed in the Due Process Clause of the Fifth Amendment. In treating equality as a component of liberty—and liberty as a synonym for equality—the framers of the Constitution were drawing upon the history and traditions of Western freedom. In the fortieth clause of Magna Carta, King John had promised the barons: "To no one will we sell, to no one will we refuse or delay, right or justice." This became in Anglo-American tradition a guarantee to all of equal justice under law. It was natural, therefore, in 1954 for the Court in *Bolling v. Sharpe*[11] to recognize the merging of the concepts of liberty and equality. In that case, the Court held that federal laws segregating students in the public schools of the District of Columbia violated the Due Process Clause of the Fifth Amendment, just as the Court had concurrently held[12] that state public school segregation laws violated the Equal Protection Clause of the Fourteenth Amendment. The concept of liberty, embodied in the Fifth Amendment, was once again assumed to embrace the American ideal of equality.

A further reason for the omission of equality language was that many of the new states in their constitutions had specifically guaranteed equality before the law.[13] This being so, the framers may have believed it unnecessary to guarantee equality of treatment by the federal government. They may have assumed, as indeed they did in originally omitting a Bill of Rights, that denial would emanate primarily from state action and that the state constitutions were adequate to guard against this risk. The Constitution, it should be recalled, was adopted at a time when the former Colonies still remembered that the Mayflower Compact itself provided, as a social contract, for the framing of "just & equall lawes."[14]

Finally, the omission of "equality" was in part undoubtedly attributable to the political difficulty of achieving union without foundering on the hard reality of slavery. The most the pragmatic framers could achieve was to empower Congress to prohibit the importation of slaves after 1808.[15] It was necessary, however, specifically to guarantee that member states would be obligated to deliver up fugitive slaves.[16] In sum, then, the Constitution of the new nation, while heralding liberty, in effect declared all men to be free and equal—except black men, who were to be neither free nor equal. This inconsistency reflected a fundamental departure from the American creed, a departure which it took a civil war to set right.

With adoption of the Thirteenth, Fourteenth, and Fifteenth Amendments to the Constitution, freedom and equality were expressly guaranteed to all—regardless of "race, color, or previous condition of servitude."[17] These amendments cleared the way for our "new kind of society—fresh, equal, just, open, free, and forever respectful of conscience."[18]

It is in light of the American commitment to equality and the history of that commitment that I read the Equal Protection Clause of the Fourteenth Amendment "as . . . revelation of [one of] the great purposes which were intended to be achieved by the Constitution as a continuing instrument of government."[19] The cases following the decision of the Court in *Plessy v. Ferguson*[20] in 1896 too often tended to negate this great purpose. Since *Brown v. Board of Education*[21] in 1954, however, the Court has firmly and consistently sought to give real meaning to the Equal Protection Clause "as . . . revelation" of a great constitutional purpose. In doing so the Court has unequivocally returned to the Constitution from which it had departed over a half-century before in *Plessy v. Ferguson.* Today, as the framers of the Civil War amendments intended and as Justice Harlan correctly stated in his *Plessy* dissent, "Our Constitution is color-blind, and neither knows nor tolerates classes among citizens."[22]

Brown v. Board of Education has been a much-discussed case. It is significant that the consensus of virtually all commentators, regardless of their otherwise differing analyses, is that the separate-but-equal formula of *Plessy* was not in accord with the precedents before 1896 and that *Brown* and the decisions that followed it "were not an abrupt departure in constitutional law or a novel interpretation of the guarantee of equal protection of the laws. The old doctrine of separate-but-equal, announced in 1896, had been steadily eroded for at least a generation before the school cases, in the way that precedents are whittled down until they finally collapse."[23]

Brown v. Board of Education was decided by a unanimous Court. Four years later in *Cooper v. Aaron* (The Little Rock School Case),[24] the Court, in an unprecedented opinion, signed by all of its members, reaffirmed the *Brown* decision. The Court stated,

The basic decision in *Brown* was unanimously reached by this Court only after the case had been briefed and twice argued and the issues had been given the most serious consideration. Since the first *Brown* opinion three new Justices have come to the Court. They are at one with the Justices still on the Court who participated in that basic decision as to its correctness, and that decision is now unanimously reaffirmed.[25]

Since *Cooper v. Aaron* two new justices—Mr. Justice White and myself—have come to the Court. The subsequent decisions of the Court dealing with state-sanctioned racial discrimination in schools and other public facilities have established that the new justices join in upholding the correctness and logic of the *Brown* decision.[26]

In the cases invalidating state-sanctioned racial discrimination, the Court has found the kind of "state action" which the Fourteenth and Fifteenth Amendments expressly prohibit. The words "state action" do not appear in the amendments but were first used in the early cases interpreting them. The classic statement to which the Court has consistently adhered is that

It is state action of a particular character that is prohibited. . . . [C]ivil rights, such as are guaranteed by the Constitution against State aggression, cannot be impaired by the wrongful acts of individuals, unsupported by State authority in the shape of laws, customs, or judicial or executive proceedings.[27]

In the *Sit-in* cases of last term the Chief Justice, speaking for the Court, said,

It cannot be disputed that under our decisions "private conduct abridging individual rights does no violence to the Equal Protection Clause unless to some significant extent the State in any of its manifestations has been found to have become involved in it." *Burton v. Wilmington Parking Authority,* 365 U.S. 715, 722; *Turner v. City of Memphis,* 369 U.S. 350.[28]

The state-action concept, understandably the subject of much comment and discussion, is of obvious public interest in light of the cases now pending before the Court. Judicial propriety precludes me from discussing these cases. I will only observe—and that by way of comment on past decisions without prejudging future ones—that in my view the Court's decisions finding governmental action in the varying situations which have been presented to it were correct.[29] The rationale has not always been articulated to the satisfaction of the Court's professional audiences,[30] but I have learned even in one term that these, like New York's first-night critics, are hard to satisfy.

II

In the *Slaughterhouse Cases,*[31] following soon after the ratification of the Civil War amendments, Mr. Justice Miller observed: "We doubt very much whether any action of a state not directed by way of discrimination against the Negroes as a class, or on account of their race, will ever be held to come within the purview of [the equal protection] . . . provision."[32] Justice Miller's doubts were soon resolved against him—and with his silent concurrence. Only a few years later, stimulated by the sweep of our Industrial Revolution, cases began coming to the Court involving economic interests and the power of the states to classify businesses for purposes of regulation and taxation. In 1886 the Court unanimously held that the Equal Protection Clause was relevant in cases of this character and applied to corporations as well as individuals. The latter ruling was summarily announced by Chief Justice Waite: "The court does not wish to hear argument on the question whether the provision in the Fourteenth Amendment to the Constitution, which forbids a State to deny to any person within its

jurisdiction the equal protection of the law, applies to these corporations. We are all of the opinion that it does."[33]

As a consequence, from about 1886 until the late 1930s the mainstream of equal protection cases coming before the Court had nothing to do with civil rights, which as Justice Miller had observed, were
the primary subject of the amendments. Instead the cases involved
alleged governmental discrimination against and interference with
economic interests. The history of the Court's treatment of the Equal
Protection Clause in this area has in the main paralleled the application of the Due Process Clause. From their adoption until approximately 1900 the two clauses were seldom actually applied to inhibit
state regulation of economic interests.[34] From about 1900, however,
the Due Process Clause gained ascendancy as a restriction on government regulation of economic activity. The Equal Protection Clause,
though frequently resorted to, was relegated to a secondary role, subsidiary to due process in reviewing government intervention. Thus, in
1927 it was natural for Justice Holmes to characterize the Equal Protection Clause as "the usual last resort of constitutional arguments."[35]
Since the late 1930s, however, the Court has called a halt to the use of
the Due Process Clause as a means of invalidating economic regulatory measures believed by a majority of the Court to be unwise. The
Court's current view as to this was stated by Justice Black last term in
Ferguson v. Skrupa,[36] which involved both the Due Process and Equal
Protection Clauses. Justice Black said,

We refuse to sit as a "superlegislature to weigh the wisdom of legislation," and
we emphatically refuse to go back to the time when courts used the Due Process Clause "to strike down state laws, regulatory of business and industrial
conditions, because they may be unwise, improvident, or out of harmony with
a particular school of thought." Nor are we able or willing to draw lines by
calling a law "prohibitory" or "regulatory." Whether the legislature takes for
its textbook Adam Smith, Herbert Spencer, Lord Keynes, or some other is no
concern of ours. The Kansas . . . statute [in this case] may be wise or unwise.
But relief, if any be needed, lies not with us but with the body constituted to
pass laws for the State of Kansas.[37]

With regard to the Equal Protection Clause, however, the Court's
1957 decision in *Morey v. Doud*[38] demonstrates that the clause still retains vitality in the economic area where a statutory classification is
challenged as not fairly related to the object of the regulation. In that
case the Court invalidated, as a denial of equal protection, an Illinois
statute regulating all money order businesses but specifically ex-

empting the American Express Company.* Perhaps, what appears in such a case to be an attitude more responsive to a complaint based on a denial of equal protection than of due process is to be explained by the analysis of Justice Jackson concurring in *Railway Express Agency v. New York*.[39] He there pointed out that a statute invalidated under the Due Process Clause renders the economic activity beyond the scope of governmental regulatory power. On the other hand, should the same judgment be predicated only on the Equal Protection Clause, all the state need do is revise the statute to insure that, with regard to the purposes of the regulation, those who are similarly situated will be similarly treated.[40]

It has been said that the Court since the late 1930s has unduly expanded the meaning of equal protection in cases involving personal rights and unduly contracted the clause in cases involving economic regulation. This is in effect charging the creation of a "double standard." I do not believe that this charge can be sustained by reference to the intent of the framers. There is every evidence that the Thirty-ninth Congress intended the Civil War amendments to protect the newly freed slaves, and personal rights in general. There is not even a scintilla of evidence in the debates and reports that the Fourteenth Amendment was otherwise to abridge or curtail the police power of the state.[41] In the *Slaughterhouse Cases*, speaking of the Civil War amendments, the Court said,

We repeat, then, in the light of this recapitulation of events, almost too recent to be called history, but which are familiar to us all; and on the most casual examination of the language of these amendments, no one can fail to be impressed with the one pervading purpose found in them all, lying at the foundation of each, and without which none of them would have been even suggested; we mean the freedom of the slave race, the security and firm establishment of that freedom, and the protection of the newly-made freeman and citizen from the oppressions of those who had formerly exercised unlimited dominion over him.[42]

And in *Barbier v. Connolly*, the Court said,

But neither the [fourteenth] amendment—broad and comprehensive as it is—nor any other amendment, was designed to interfere with the power of the State, sometimes termed its police power, to prescribe regulations to promote the health, peace, morals, education, and good order of the people, and to legislate so as to increase the industries of the State, develop its resources, and add to its wealth and prosperity.[43]

* Morey v. Doud was overruled in 1976. New Orleans v. Duke, 427 U.S. 297. EDITOR'S NOTE.

These statements by justices who could rightfully say that the history of these amendments "is fresh within the memory of us all"[44] decisively refute the suggestion—implicit in the "double standard" charge— that the Court has now departed from the Constitution. Rather, it is my conviction, that here the Court has returned to, and is endeavoring to abide by, the single standard of the framers.

III

Throughout its decisions dealing with equality the Court has realistically recognized that "a State may act through different agencies,— either by its legislative, its executive, or its judicial authorities"[45] and that "it can act in no other way."[46] It has also recognized that a state acts and is responsible when its officers, acting under color of law, in fact derogate from that law.[47]

The application of this principle in one of the greatest of equal protection cases, *Yick Wo v. Hopkins*,[48] stands as an important safeguard to all persons of equal justice under law. Yick Wo was a humble Chinese laundryman who invoked the constitutional clause because under a San Francisco ordinance the city authorities denied him a license to operate his laundry. The ordinance was fair and nondiscriminatory on its face, but in applying it the authorities granted licenses only to non-Chinese applicants. The Court held this discrimination unconstitutional and said,

[T]he cases present the ordinances in actual operation, and the facts shown establish an administration directed so exclusively against a particular class of persons as to warrant and require the conclusion, that, whatever may have been the intent of the ordinances as adopted, they are applied by the public authorities charged with their administration, and thus representing the State itself, with a mind so unequal and oppressive as to amount to a practical denial by the State of that equal protection of the laws which is secured to the petitioners, as to all other persons, by the broad and benign provisions of the Fourteenth Amendment to the Constitution of the United States. Though the law itself be fair on its face and impartial in appearance, yet, if it is applied and administered by public authority with an evil eye and an unequal hand, so as practically to make unjust and illegal discriminations between persons in similar circumstances, material to their rights, the denial of equal justice is still within the prohibition of the Constitution.[49]

The authority of the *Yick Wo* decision has never been challenged. And I have no doubt that its principle will be honored so long as the Court sits.

Yick Wo, however, points up a problem which pervades the whole area of equal protection and governmental action. True equality requires governmental protection beyond that which is afforded by litigation in the courts. I am not sure how in the 1880s Yick Wo managed to finance his extended litigation. I surmise that since, as the city of San Francisco conceded, 200 other Chinese laundrymen were similarly mistreated, they may have provided the financial means.[50] But John Smith, applying in 1964 for a license to conduct a small business or to rezone his property or to protest an inequitable tax assessment, may lack the assistance of a "tong," union, or other group interested in protecting his rights. Unless he is willing to expend his resources or mortgage his future in expensive and time-consuming litigation, his constitutional right to equal treatment will exist in theory only. Further, even if his claim is not of constitutional dimensions, his grievance in a democracy devoted to the fair treatment of all deserves a hearing by someone other than a justly or unjustly accused administrator.

In Scandinavia that excellent institution called the Ombudsman assists the ordinary citizen in seeing that the law is not administered with an evil eye or an uneven hand.[51] The Ombudsman—or rather the idea it embodies—could help in the realization of our ideal of equal treatment of all citizens by government officials.

IV

I have spoken of equality in civil rights and equality in economic affairs. I now wish to address myself briefly to equality in political matters. A student of our Constitution, noting the framers' emphasis on representative government and their commitment to political equality, would naturally conclude that the Constitution, whose source is the people, safeguards the right to vote so that the ballot of one citizen would have no more weight or influence than that of another in selecting legislative representatives. He would surely have to agree with what the Court recently said in *Gray v. Sanders:* "The conception of political equality from the Declaration of Independence to the Lincoln's Gettysburg Address to the Fifteenth, Seventeenth, and Nineteenth Amendments can mean only one thing—one person one vote."[52] This concept of political equality basic to a democracy was urged by Madison in the *Federalist Papers* when he said: "Who are to be the electors of the federal representatives? Not the rich, more than the poor; not the learned, more than the ignorant; not the haughty heirs of distinguished names, more than the humble sons of obscure and unpropitious fortune. The electors are to be the great body of the people of the United States. . . ."[53] Yet, until the Court's 1962 decision in *Baker v. Carr*,[54] resort to the courts under the Equal Protection Clause to vindicate this most basic right—the right to political equality—was, with limited exceptions,[55] unavailing. Relief was denied on the ground that deprivations of political equality were not justiciable; rather, they presented "political questions" which courts should refrain from deciding.[56] I was not on the Court when *Baker v. Carr* was decided, but I share the view, reflected by my vote last Term in *Gray v. Sanders*,[57] that *Baker v. Carr* correctly held that a denial of equal voting rights presents a justiciable equal protection claim and this view seems to be shared by an overwhelming majority of my fellow citizens. The storm that broke over the Court following *Baker v. Carr* was, on the whole, one of applause. That decision has unleashed a tremendous amount of legislative activity as well as a host of lawsuits challenging the apportionment of state legislatures and of the national House of Representatives. Whether Justice Brennan, who spoke for the Court in *Baker v. Carr*, is justified in his optimism that judicial standards under the Equal Protection Clause are so "well developed and familiar"[58] as readily to dispose of the numerous cases which have already reached our Court is a matter which is *sub judice*.* Whatever the result in future cases, *Baker v. Carr* will stand as a classic illustration of a situation in which the Court was compelled to act in vindication of constitutional voting rights because of the failure of legislatures to assure equality in this area.[59]

V

I should like to conclude by discussing equality in the administration of criminal justice. One would suppose that the most basic concept protected by the Equal Protection Clause and by the Due Process Clause alike is that equal justice be afforded to the poor and to the rich. In the words of Justice Black,

---

* A few months after Justice Goldberg's lecture, the Supreme Court ruled that states must "make an honest and good faith effort to construct districts, in both houses of its legislature, as nearly of equal population as is practicable." Reynolds v. Sims, 377 U.S. 533, 577 (1964). The standard is, essentially, "one person, one vote." EDITOR'S NOTE.

Providing equal justice for poor and rich, weak and powerful alike is an age-old problem. People have never ceased to hope and strive to move closer to that goal. This hope, at least in part, brought about in 1215 the royal concessions of Magna Charta: "To no one will we sell, to no one will we refuse or delay, right or justice. . . . No free man shall be taken or imprisoned, or disseised, or outlawed, or exiled, or anywise destroyed; nor shall we go upon him nor send upon him, but by the lawful judgment of his peers or by the law of the land." These pledges were unquestionably steps toward a fairer and more nearly equal application of criminal justice. In this tradition, our own constitutional guaranties of due process and equal protection both call for procedures in criminal trials which allow no invidious discriminations between persons and different groups of persons. Both equal protection and due process emphasize the central aim of our entire judicial system—all people charged with crime must, so far as the law is concerned, "stand on an equality before the bar of justice in every American court."[60]

Here as in other aspects of equality we derive our constitutional inspiration from the Bible: "You shall do no injustice in judgment; you shall not be partial to the poor or defer to the great, but in righteousness shall you judge your neighbor."[61] Justices of our Court and many state courts take an oath to "do equal justice to the poor and to the rich."

When the poor are denied equal justice in a criminal trial there can be no question of state action, involvement and responsibility. The state is the "plaintiff"; it elects or appoints the judges; it hires the prosecutors; it retains and compensates expert witnesses and investigators; it arrests and often incarcerates the accused; and it lodges the convicted in its jails.

It is, therefore, rather surprising that while there are hundreds of cases in which the Court has applied the Equal Protection Clause in economic areas and scores dealing with racial discrimination, there are relatively few treating of inequalities in the administration of criminal justice. This paucity of cases, unfortunately, does not accurately reflect the number or extent of the problems in this area. The few decisions, however, stand in the great tradition of judicial recognition that "equal protection to all is the basic principle upon which justice under law rests."[62]

It was not until 1956, in *Griffin v. Illinois*,[63] that the Court made its first broad pronouncement in the area of economic equality in the criminal process. In that case the Illinois law conditioning appeal on the purchase of a transcript applied on its face to rich and poor alike. Its effect, however, was to deny an appeal to potential appellants lacking sufficient funds to purchase a transcript. The Court, laying to rest the notion that equal protection requires only equal laws and that the state is never obliged to equalize economic disparities, held the law unconstitutional. Justice Black's opinion stated that: "There can be no equal justice where the kind of trial a man gets depends on the amount of money he has. Destitute defendants must be afforded as adequate appellate review as defendants who have money enough to buy transcripts."[64]

After *Griffin*, the Court applied these general pronouncements to a number of other state rules which limited the right of the indigent to appeal.[65] And last Term, we invalidated a number of state rules which permitted the trial judge and the public defender to decide, in effect, whether an indigent would be permitted to appeal.[66] We also held that all indigent persons accused of crime must, upon request, be afforded counsel for their defense at trial[67] and on their first automatic appeal.[68]

I cannot, with propriety, predict how much further the Equal Protection Clause will require the Court to go in the elimination of economic inequalities in the administration of criminal justice. But no judge, lawyer or layman is inhibited from emphasizing the moral imperative implicit in the noble concept of equal justice before the law. What the Equal Protection Clause of the Constitution does not command, it may still inspire.

Although the cases which have come before our Court have involved the rights of the indigent at trial and on appeal, it should not be forgotten that problems of equal criminal justice extend to the near-poor and the average wage earner as well as the indigent, and that such problems begin well before trial and continue after the appeal.

When the police conduct a roundup of "suspects," they generally do so in poor neighborhoods, rarely in middle-class communities.[69] As a result, more poor than rich are arrested for crimes they did not commit. We do not know how many of these people lose or fail to obtain jobs because of an "arrest record" resulting from guiltless involvement in such episodes. Nor do we know how many poor people are even aware of their rights in such situations: for example, their right to consult an attorney, to sue for false arrest, or to have their arrest records expunged (in jurisdictions which have procedures permitting this). Moreover, psychologists and sociologists tell us that young people who are close to choosing a criminal identity may have this choice confirmed by their repeated treatment as a criminal type.[70]

After arrest, the accused who is poor must often await the disposition of his case in jail because of his inability to raise bail, while the accused who can afford bail is free to return to his family and his job. Equally important, he is free during the critical period between arrest and trial to help his attorney with the investigation and preparation of his defense.[71] In a recent case a defendant was imprisoned well over two years between the time he was arrested and the time he was ultimately acquitted on appeal, solely because he could not raise the small amount of money necessary for bail.[72]

In preparing for trial the lawyer appointed to represent an accused who is without funds generally has few, if any, of the investigatory resources available to the prosecution[73] or to an accused with means.[74] He may also be limited in his ability to subpoena necessary witnesses to appear at trial. Under the present federal rule,[75] for example, a defendant with means may automatically obtain all necessary subpoenas by simply paying the fee[76] and designating the desired witness. A defendant who cannot afford to pay the fee, however, must submit a detailed affidavit stating why he needs the witness and indicating the substance of the expected testimony.[77] Thus, as a price for obtaining the testimony of a witness, the accused without means must do something not required either of the government or of an accused with means: he must disclose his case in advance.* This result might indeed be desirable if disclosure were required of all parties to a criminal case. But fundamental fairness and equality would seem to dictate that this should not be exacted alone from an indigent as the price of exercising his Sixth Amendment right to obtain the testimony of necessary witnesses.

This and other subtle discriminations against the indigent are frequently justified on the ground that they are necessary to prevent frivolous use of government supplied services by those defendants who are not deterred by the built-in financial brake of paying for the services. But as our Court recently said in related contexts, "Statistics . . . illustrate the undeniable fact that as many meritorious criminal cases [arise] through applications for leave to proceed *in forma pau-*

---

* In 1966, Federal Rule of Criminal Procedure 17 (b) was amended to permit indigent defendants to request subpoenas through an *ex parte* application to the trial judge. The requirement of a motion supported by affidavit was eliminated. EDITOR'S NOTE.

peris as on the paid docket, and that no *a priori* justification can be found for considering them, as a class, to be more frivolous than those in which costs have been paid."[78] "It defies common sense to think that a moneyed defendant faced with long-term imprisonment . . ." will choose not to exercise a valuable right merely to save himself the cost.[79]

After conviction, the defendant's financial conditions may have a significant effect on whether he is placed on probation or sent to the penitentiary, on whether and when he is paroled from the penitentiary, on whether he continues to remain at liberty. Probation and parole frequently depend upon the availability of a job and/or of psychiatric treatment. These conditions can, of course, be met and maintained more easily by one who has means than by one who does not.

The alternative fine-imprisonment penalty still frequently imposed for petty offenses may also be unfair to the defendant without means. The "choice" of paying a $100 fine or spending 30 days in jail is really no choice at all to the person who cannot raise $100.* The resulting imprisonment is no more or no less than imprisonment for being poor, a doctrine which I trust this nation has long since outgrown. Concern has even been expressed that the most serious penalty of all—death—is imposed with disproportionate frequency on the poor. Warden Lawes, who witnessed the execution of many Sing Sing inmates, remarked: "If a wealthy man, or the son of a wealthy man, kills he is insane or deranged and usually either goes scot free or to an insane asylum. If a poor and friendless man kills, he is a sane man who committed wilful murder for which he must die."[80]

Regrettably, there are still on our statute books some substantive laws which in practice tend to operate unequally against the poor. The vagrancy laws are an example in point. Anatole France would surely have said: "The law in its majestic equality forbids the rich as well as the poor" from being able-bodied persons without visible means of support who do not seek employment and who are unable to account for their lawful presence. These laws, as my Brother Douglas has observed,[81] make it a crime to be poor, downtrodden, and unemployed. This is reminiscent of Butler's *Erewhon*, where it was a felony to be afflicted with pulmonary consumption.[82]

---

* The Supreme Court has mitigated this form of discrimination against the poor in the criminal process. Williams v. Illinois, 399 U.S. 235 (1970); Tate v. Short, 401 U.S. 395 (1971). EDITOR'S NOTE.

Courts and other organs of government, both state and federal, have not brought their ingenuity sufficiently to bear on these crucial areas of equal justice. In some states, as in the federal government, the high courts have power to supervise the administration of criminal justice. This is a source of power from which much good can flow, as demonstrated by some recent decisions of our Court,[83] the federal courts of appeals,[84] and some state courts[85] in the area of equal criminal justice. Certainly the legislative and executive branches have ample powers to remedy these injustices.

In some parts of the world—indeed in many parts of this country when men of means are involved—arrests are made whenever possible in a dignified manner. The accused is notified that he is being investigated, and he is called to police headquarters by a summons rather than bodily arrest. I am not suggesting that this can be done in every case, but it certainly can and should be done in many.

Recent studies in the area of bail have indicated that if carefully screened defendants are released pending trial on their own recognizance and treated with dignity, they will appear at trial.[86] Think of the needless waste—to the individual, the family, and the community— every time a responsible person presumed by a law to be innocent is kept in jail awaiting trial solely because he is unable to raise bail money. Careful screening and release without bail should be made the rule rather than the exception throughout the country. Again, I am not suggesting that release without bail should be allowed in every case, but it should be permitted whenever feasible.

The right to counsel at trial and on appeal may prove hollow if appointed counsel is not armed with the tools of advocacy—investigatory resources, expert witnesses, subpoena, trial transcript. If the right to counsel is to be given meaningful content, and if our adversary process is to retain its vitality, the appointed attorney, like the retained attorney, must be permitted to perform as an advocate. Courts are not without resources to achieve this end. In a recent California case, for example, the state supreme court held that "if the attorney is not given a reasonable opportunity to ascertain the facts surrounding the charged crime so he can prepare a proper defense, the accused's basic right to effective representation would be denied."[87] Some courts have held that the right to effective representation includes interpreters, accountants, and other needed medical and scientific aids.[88] If representation is to be as effective for poor as for rich, it follows that services necessary to make this right effective must be supplied at government expense to those unable to afford them.

The government should also assume a certain degree of responsibility for assuring the poor equal access to probation and parole. It could, for example, provide facilities which would enable the parolee without means to obtain outpatient psychiatric treatment without being institutionalized and losing his job—a privilege heretofore reserved exclusively for the wealthy. It could also experiment with the idea of the half-way house, a system under which convicted criminals might be released from prison and still remain under the care and responsibility of the government until they have re-established their roots in the community and have found decent jobs.

Our concern, moreover, should not be limited to the very poor alone. The Council of Economic Advisers in its recent report to the president designated the $3,000 annual family income mark as the boundary of poverty.[89] A family of four earning this amount, if it spent a mere $5 per person a week for food and $800 a year for shelter for the family, would have less than $25 a week for clothing, transportation, school supplies, home furnishings, medical care, insurance and everything else. It is clear that if any member of the almost ten million American families which fit this category were accused of a serious crime, he could not begin to raise the funds necessary for an adequate defense. But, what about the family earning $4,000 or even $5,000. I would doubt whether half of the families in this affluent country could today afford an adequate defense if one of their members were accused of a serious crime. Perhaps they could raise sufficient money for bail or even for a trial lawyer, but what about an investigator, a psychiatrist, or an expert in ballistics or handwriting; and what about a complete transcript to prepare an appeal and the prosecution of the appeal itself? This is a situation that actually does confront many, many of our families each year. It was recently estimated that, "annually, more than a million persons stand before our judges for sentencing after conviction."[90] Few of these people fit the misleading stereotype of the wealthy law breaker well equipped to confront the legal process.

Here, as with the idea of the Ombudsman, we can learn much from the Scandinavian countries.[91] The services provided there are made available to all accused persons. No test of financial capacity is applied in the first instance as a condition to receiving them. Far more than the provision of counsel is encompassed within these systems. For example, in preparing the defense, the appointed lawyer may make use of government laboratories and consult with its experts. If the accused is acquitted, no effort is made to collect the cost of defense regardless of the defendant's means. If he is convicted some of the countries inquire into his means and if found financially able he is charged with some or all of the costs of his defense.[92] In at least one country no effort is made to establish the means of the defendant or to charge him with costs even if he is convicted.[93]

Even if we choose not to go as far as the Scandinavian countries, we should certainly consider adopting procedures whereby persons erroneously charged with crime could be reimbursed for their expenditures in defending against the charge. Without such procedures, acquittal may often be almost as ruinous to the defendant and his family as conviction. At the very least we should extend our provision of free legal services in criminal cases to include many hard-working people who, although not indigent, cannot, without extraordinary sacrifice, raise sufficient funds to defend themselves or a member of their family against a criminal charge.

Whenever the government considers extending a needed service to those accused of crime, the question arises: But what about the victim? We should confront the problem of the victim directly; his burden is not alleviated by denying necessary services to the accused.[94] Many countries throughout the world, recognizing that crime is a community problem, have designed systems for government compensation of victims of crime. Serious consideration of this approach is long overdue here. The victim of a robbery or an assault has been denied the "protection" of the laws in a very real sense, and society should assume some responsibility for making him whole.*

These are but a few—indeed a very few—of the areas in which equal justice is lacking. There are many others. It is said that the government cannot be expected to equalize all economic disparities. Of course it cannot, but this does not meean that it should not try to eliminate disparities in certain critical areas like criminal justice. The real question, as put by the attorney general's Committee on Poverty and

---

* In 1984, Congress established a Criminal Victims Compensation Fund. Criminal fines, penalties, and forfeited bail bonds finance the fund. The attorney general is authorized to provide financial assistance to federal crime victims and to support state crime victim assistance programs with the money from this fund. 42 U.S.C. secs. 10601, 10602, 10603. EDITOR'S NOTE.

the Administration of Federal Criminal Justice is: "has government done all that can be reasonably required of it . . . to render the poverty of the litigant an irrelevancy?"[95] In all candor, we must confess that government in this country—both state and federal—has not done all that can reasonably be required. Equal criminal justice for rich and poor alike is one of the few areas where our country follows rather than leads. If it is true that "the quality of a nation's civilization can be largely measured by the methods it uses in the enforcement of its criminal law,"[96] then this situation cannot long be tolerated. We must lead in equality if we are to continue to lead in liberty. But, while we are making efforts to equalize the treatment of the rich and poor in the criminal process, we must remember that the criminal process is but one tree in a forest of poverty.

A humane and affluent nation such as ours is just now awakening to the stark fact that one-fifth of our families and population live in poverty. President Johnson's recent state of the union message and the Report of the Council of Economic Advisers declared all-out war on poverty in America. "Poverty," the Report said, "is costly not only to the poor but to the whole society. Its ugly by-products include ignorance, disease, *delinquency, crime*, irresponsibility, immorality, indifference. None of these social evils and hazards will, of course, wholly disappear with the elimination of poverty. But their severity will be markedly reduced. Poverty is no purely private or local concern. It is a social and national problem."[97]

Every criminologist will acknowledge the truth of this linkage between poverty and crime. The great bulk of our prison population comes from the ranks of the economically underprivileged. A root cause of crime is economic distress and its by-products—illiteracy and ignorance. If we are to make inroads on crime and delinquency, therefore, we must as a government and people make inroads on poverty in America.

Although the frontiers of these problems are vast, it would be misleading to leave you with a totally dark picture.

The recent report of the attorney general's Committee on Poverty and the Administration of Federal Criminal Justice was a milestone which promises to have continued influence. The Justice Department is carrying through many of the suggestions made in that report, and Congress now has under consideration a major item of legislation emanating from it.

The Manhattan Bail Project also holds great promise. And in the

District of Columbia the entire problem of bail is being re-thought; just a few weeks ago the first experiment was conducted in releasing an accused on his own recognizance pending trial.

In New Haven, Connecticut, a "neighborhood social–legal program" has been put into operation in an effort to confront the basic social, economic, and educational roots of legal problems. A team— consisting of a social worker, a lawyer, and an investigator—is assigned to a poor neighborhood in an effort to uncover and deal with the causes of the legal problems at their sources rather than at the litigation stage. This pioneer program recognizes that problems of poverty cut across the conceptual lines dividing criminal from civil cases, and that the poor person must be made aware of his legal rights and obligations—whether they be in signing a lease, executing a credit agreement, settling a domestic dispute, or paying taxes—before he can be expected to participate in the community as a fully responsible citizen. Programs of this sort hold great promise, especially for our urban population centers.

Our substantive criminal law is also undergoing much needed revamping, prompted in part by the American Law Institute's Model Penal Code. More attention is being paid in our law schools as well to this long neglected area. The practice of criminal law is again becoming as respected as it was at the time of the Constitution and throughout our early history when it was engaged in by men like John Adams, Daniel Webster, and Abraham Lincoln. It is hoped that many more established lawyers will bring their experience, and that many more young law graduates will bring the most recent academic developments, to bear on the problems of criminal justice. The widespread participation of the bar in the criminal process, which will result from our recent decisions holding that all criminal defendants must, upon request, be afforded representation at trial and on appeal, will bring the present inequalities of the criminal process more forcefully to the attention of the bar. This in itself is desirable, for awareness of a problem is the first and most important step toward solution.

VI

Edward S. Corwin has pointed out that we live in "a world whose populations are everywhere fired by the notion of 'equality.'"[98] Our nation's great strength as a leader of such a world lies not only or even primarily in our material resources. It is even more true today than it was over a century ago that "the great advantage of the Americans is that . . . [they are] born equal" and that in the eyes of the law Americans "are all of the same estate."[99] The first chief justice of the United States, John Jay, spoke of the "free air" of American life. We as a people and as a government have not always kept the air "free." We have sometimes forsaken the American ideal for other prejudices. Happily, however, the prejudice most deeply ingrained in Americans is the constitutional prejudice for liberty and equality. If I have merely restated this value, it is because, here as elsewhere, "we need education in the obvious more than investigation of the obscure."[100]

J. Skelly Wright

Public School Desegregation
Legal Remedies for De Facto Segregation

One hundred years ago this country abolished slavery and decreed by solemn constitutional amendment that "all persons born or naturalized in the United States, and subject to the jurisdiction thereof, are citizens of the United States and of the State wherein they reside."[1] Thus, at last, our Negro citizens were included in the truths we hold self-evident, "that all men are created equal, that they are endowed by their Creator with certain unalienable Rights, that among these are Life, Liberty and the pursuit of Happiness."[2]

One hundred years have passed and the promise of equality remains, in large part, unfulfilled. It seems that in these 100 years we have succeeded in changing a system of slavery into a caste system based on race which may, in some respects, be more difficult to uproot than slavery itself.

Before considering the problem of racial discrimination as it confronts this country today, it may be useful briefly to recall how the great hopes and aspirations of 100 years ago were curdled in the aftermath of the Civil War. And it will be particularly interesting to note that the instrument of destruction then—the United States Supreme Court—is now the architect of the new dream of equality and freedom.

I

Immediately following the close of the Civil War, Congress set about the task of insuring, insofar as possible by law, that the rights of the new citizens would be respected. First it considered for enactment a series of civil rights laws. Then, when it became concerned that the

Chief Judge Wright's lecture was delivered on February 17, 1965 and appeared in 40 N.Y.U.L. Rev. 285 (1965).

Supreme Court might declare them unconstitutional, it proceeded to initiate constitutional amendments which embedded Negro rights in our basic law. The implementation of these amendments followed quickly in the form of the Civil Rights Acts.[3]

The congressional concern about the post–Civil War Supreme Court was not unwarranted. Nor did the Thirteenth, Fourteenth and Fifteenth Amendments succeed in protecting the civil rights legislation from the destructive arm of the Court. In a series of decisions, by a restrictive reading of these amendments, particularly the Fourteenth, the Supreme Court made a shambles of the Civil Rights Acts. Statutes protecting the voting rights of Negroes,[4] outlawing the Ku Klux Klan,[5] insuring Negro access to public accommodations,[6] and others, were all declared unconstitutional.

Hardly more than a decade after the close of the Civil War the moral fervor which had supported the recognition of Negro rights was ebbing fast. Discouraged by the action of the Supreme Court, and with this country undergoing an industrial revolution, the great mass of the people turned their attention to more mundane matters. The climate of the times was such that in 1877, after his opponent, Samuel J. Tilden, had won the election for the presidency by over a quarter of a million votes, the followers of Rutherford B. Hayes were able to make a cynical political deal with the Tilden electors in five southern states under which their votes were cast for Hayes, making him president, in return for which the Hayes forces agreed to, and did, end the protection which the federal government, since the Civil War, had afforded the Negro in the South.[7]

Not long after Hayes assumed the presidency, segregation laws cautiously began to make their appearances in the states of the old Confederacy. As a substitute for slavery, the Negro would now be isolated from the mainstream of public life by criminal statutes. Initially, not even the proponents of these laws had confidence in their constitutionality. Enforcement was tentative and usually withdrawn when challenged. Finally, in 1896, a test of the Louisiana statute[8] which made it a crime for a Negro to invade the public accommodation on a train reserved for whites reached the Supreme Court.

Eight justices of the Supreme Court in that case, *Plessy v. Ferguson*,[9] were able to hold that racial segregation, compelled by law, was legal. One lone member of the Court, however, Justice John Marshall Harlan, delivered the most powerful dissent in the annals of jurisprudence. It read in part:

The white race deems itself to be the dominant race in this country. And so it is, in prestige, in achievements, in education, in wealth and in power. So, I doubt not, it will continue to be for all time, if it remains true to its great heritage and holds fast to the principles of constitutional liberty. But in view of the Constitution, in the eye of the law, there is in this country no superior, dominant, ruling class of citizens. There is no caste here. Our Constitution is colorblind, and neither knows nor tolerates classes among citizens. In respect of civil rights, all citizens are equal before the law. The humblest is the peer of the most powerful. The law regards man as man, and takes no account of his surroundings or of his color when his civil rights as guaranteed by the supreme law of the land are involved. It is, therefore, to be regretted that this high tribunal, the final expositor of the fundamental law of the land, has reached the conclusion that it is competent for a State to regulate the enjoyment by citizens of their civil rights solely upon the basis of race.

In my opinion, the judgment this day rendered will, in time, prove to be quite as pernicious as the decision made by this tribunal in the *Dred Scott case.* . . .

If evils will result from the commingling of the two races upon public highways established for the benefit of all, they will be infinitely less than those that will surely come from state legislation regulating the enjoyment of civil rights upon the basis of race. We boast of the freedom enjoyed by our people above all other peoples. But it is difficult to reconcile that boast with a state of the law which, practically, puts the brand of servitude and degradation upon a large class of our fellow-citizens, our equals before the law. The thin disguise of "equal" accommodations for passengers in railroad coaches will not mislead any one, nor atone for the wrong this day done.[10]

Racial segregation, having received the benediction of the Supreme Court, spread like a prairie fire through the Southland. Literally hundreds of statutes were passed requiring segregation from the cradle into the grave[11]—all under pain of imprisonment for violations. The segregation laws were such a success that the legislatures in the southern states soon turned their attention to disenfranchising the Negro. By the use of grandfather clauses and "understanding" tests in registration statutes, the registration rolls in practically all of the states of the Confederacy were purged of Negro voters. In Louisiana, for example, over 99 percent of the Negro voters lost their right to vote. Over 130,000 Negroes in Louisiana alone, one-half of the total registration, were scratched from the voting rolls.[12] Thus, while compelling segregation by law, appropriate steps were taken to insure that the law was not changed.

For almost fifty years from the turn of the century, public apathy toward the plight of the Negro continued. During this time the Negro remained in a state of limbo—half slave and half free. And during this time the politically defenseless and segregated Negro was subjected to 1,780 known lynchings.[13]

After World War II, during which he fought side by side with his white brothers-in-arms, public attention again began to be focused on the plight of the Negro. Guilt feelings were becoming more difficult to suppress. The Supreme Court, now leading the fight for recognition of the Negro's right to full citizenship, began an assault on the wall of segregation. In a series of decisions the Court gradually made it clear that the separate but equal doctrine of *Plessy v. Ferguson* set an unacceptable standard for determining equal protection under the law. And, finally, in the historic *Brown v. Board of Education* opinion, the chief justice, speaking for a unanimous Court, held that "separate educational facilities are inherently unequal."[14]

Once "separate but equal" was outlawed as a constitutional test in the field of educational facilities, the Court had no difficulty in applying the new principle to other areas in which segregation compelled by law had resulted in a caste system adversely affecting the Negro. State statutes requiring racial segregation in transportation facilities,[15] parks,[16] playgrounds,[17] hospitals,[18] and other public places[19] have all been declared unconstitutional, so that now the last vestiges of the iniquitous separate but equal doctrine have been expunged from the law.

But as we have learned from our experience under the post–Civil War constitutional amendments, it is one thing solemnly to declare the legal rights of Negroes; it is quite another to make recognition of those rights a reality. Ten years have passed since the Supreme Court's historic pronouncement in *Brown v. Board of Education*, and while the border states generally have sought to comply, in most of the states of the old Confederacy compliance, if any, has been, at best, grudging. The simple truth is that, in most of these states, integration of the public schools ten years after *Brown* is less than one percent effective.

The 1964 Staff Report on Public Education submitted to the United States Commission on Civil Rights discloses that in seven states of the former Confederacy 499 of every 500 Negro pupils attend 100 percent Negro schools.[20] Less than one Negro pupil in 500 attend desegregated schools, and then only on a token basis. Based on the progress in desegregation made the first ten years after the Supreme

Court handed down its decision in *Brown v. Board of Education*, many more years may be required before the segregated Negro school is eliminated from the Deep South.

Progress in desegregation can be accelerated, however, if courts refuse to countenance gerrymandering as a substitute for segregation compelled by law. It is becoming increasingly clear that as southern school boards change from a dual, that is, separate Negro and white, operation to a single school system, segregation in the schools can remain virtually as before. By careful drawing of neighborhood school boundary lines, the formerly all-white school remains all white, or almost so, and the formerly all-Negro school remains, for all intents and purposes, all Negro. The fact that the segregation is no longer, in terms, compelled by law does not eliminate the discrimination or remedy the inequality. Thus the interdiction of all state statutes compelling racial segregation in public schools is but a short first step on the road to desegregation.

Desegregation in the South may also be accelerated by energetic and effective use of the powers granted the attorney general under the Civil Rights Act of 1964. Under section 407 of that act the attorney general may initiate suits in behalf of individuals and ask the district courts to end racial segregation in the public schools, at least where the segregation results from the deliberate act of state officials pursuant to state statute or discriminatory purpose of their own.[21] It is by no means certain, however, that the attorney general will be any more successful than the NAACP in achieving actual rather than token desegregation. The difficulties inherent in achieving true desegregation are so great, as ten years of experience testify, and the defenses available to school boards resisting every step of the way so many, that only an alert and conscientious continuous effort on the part of both the executive and judicial branches of our government, plus a compelling desire on the part of Negroes generally, can make Section 407 of the 1964 Civil Rights Act an effective instrument in bringing reality to desegregation in the public schools in the Deep South.

II

The obstacles to further integration forecast for the South, once the illegality of de jure segregation is accepted, are already being encountered in other parts of the country. De facto racial segregation infects the public school systems in most urban areas of the North and West. This de facto segregation has its genesis in a combination of conditions, the combination varying from city to city, sometimes from neighborhood to neighborhood in the same city. Historical gerrymandering is a common cause of de facto segregation; restrictive covenants in land titles segregating neighborhoods is another common cause. But more and more it is becoming apparent that perhaps the primary cause of de facto segregation in urban schools is the socioeconomic condition of the Negro. The inability of many Negroes, because of overt and covert job discrimination, to find proper employment drives them and their families into the segregated slums which disgrace many of our metropolitan areas.

To understand the magnitude of the problem of de facto segregation, it may be useful to cite some statistics. Of Chicago's 443 elementary schools, only 40 are integrated; 280 are white schools with student bodies less than 10 percent Negro; and 123 are Negro schools with student bodies less than 10 percent white.[22] Thus, using the 10 percent mixing factor, only 9 percent of Chicago's elementary schools are integrated. If the 10 percent mixing factor were reduced to 1 percent, 77 percent of the elementary schools in Chicago would still be classified as segregated. There is, of course, no compulsory segregation in the Chicago schools. Segregation results from adherence to the neighborhood school assignment policy. But historical gerrymandering has played a significant part in the problem presented by de facto segregation in Chicago today.

Still using the 10 percent mixing factor, only 29.9 percent of the public elementary schools in the nation's capital are integrated.[23] Of Washington's 129 public elementary schools, 87 are Negro, 15 are white, and 27 are integrated. Using the same factor, of New York's 578 public elementary schools 263 (45.5 percent) are integrated, 118 (20.4 percent) are white, and 197 (34.5 percent) are Negro. In Oakland, California, 29 (45.4 percent) of the 64 public elementary schools are integrated, 23 (35.9 percent) are white, and 12 (18.7 percent) are Negro.

These statistics, and more like them from other cities, indicate that racial segregation in public schools in the North and West, except as to cause, is not unlike that in the South. Presumably the effect is the same. As to that effect the Supreme Court said in *Brown*:

We come then to the question presented: Does segregation of children in public schools solely on the basis of race, even though the physical facilities and other "tangible" factors may be equal, deprive the children of the minority group of equal educational opportunities? We believe that it does. . . .

To separate them from others of similar age and qualifications solely because of their race generates a feeling of inferiority as to their status in the community that may affect their hearts and minds in a way unlikely ever to be undone. . . .

We conclude that in the field of public education the doctrine of "separate but equal" has no place. Separate educational facilities are inherently unequal.[24]

Various state officials and agencies in the North and West have affirmed the Supreme Court's finding of the damage suffered by the segregated Negro child. In its Report to the Chicago Board of Education, the Advisory Panel on Integration of the Public Schools, March 31, 1964, stated:

The personality characteristics of the child who has suffered from discrimination, the self-hatred, the deep sense of frustration, the unexpected aggression, and the consequent difficulty in relating to others might be expected to have a major effect on his academic achievement.[25]

The Policy Statement on Integration adopted by the Board of Education of New York City, December 1964, finds segregated schools also damage white children:

The Supreme Court of the United States reminds us that modern psychological knowledge indicates clearly that segregated, racially homogeneous schools damage the personality of minority group children. These schools decrease their motivation and thus impair their ability to learn. White children are also damaged. Public education in a racially homogeneous setting is socially unrealistic and blocks the attainment of the goals of democratic education, whether this segregation occurs by law or by fact.

And Attorney General Stanley Mosk of California, in an opinion dated August 15, 1963, to the president of the California State Board of Education, advised:

The United States Supreme Court in *Brown v. Board of Education* and the Supreme Court of California in *Jackson v. Pasadena City School District* took judicial notice that school segregation results in the emotional crippling of students of minority races. Whether segregation is the result of state policy or merely reflective of neighborhood condition makes little difference to its victims.

Thus it is clear from the Supreme Court in *Brown*, from the various state authorities that have considered the problem, and from the historical background of slavery and the continuing discrimination against the Negro citizen that a segregated Negro school, whether in the North or in the South, is inherently unequal to its white counterpart. In addition to the damage done by segregated education to the minds and hearts and ability to learn of Negro children, to segregate them in public schools, for whatever reason, is to brand them as inferior—in their own minds and in the public mind. The unfortunate fact is that in contemporary America race and color are

associated with status distinctions among groups of human beings. The public schools reflect this larger social fact in that the proportion of Negroes and whites in a given school is often associated with the status of the school. The educational quality and performance to be expected from that school are frequently expressed in terms of the racial complexion and general status assigned to the school. It is well recognized that in most cases a school enrolling a large proportion of Negro students is viewed as a lower status school.[26]

Experience with segregated Negro schools, in the North as well as the South, confirms the public impression that Negro schools, in addition to being per se inferior, are usually demonstrably inferior in fact. Surveys of school systems throughout the country demonstrate time and again that the Negro school, as compared with its white counterpart, is overcrowded and understaffed—usually with inferior teachers. The experienced teachers with a choice of assignment avoid the Negro school. The Negro school buildings themselves are often run down and ill kept. The amount spent to educate the Negro child is, in many cases, substantially less than that spent on the white.

In addition to these overt differences, Negro children in Negro schools suffer from lack of exposure to the middle-class culture found in white but not in Negro schools. Shunted off in the slum school, the Negro child is denied the stimulation of competition and association with children of other races and cultures. In sum, whenever a substantial number of Negro children attend public schools in a given area, it appears that the Negro children usually find themselves in schools populated primarily by other Negro children and that these Negro schools somehow usually seem to receive less attention from the school board in terms of money, teachers, books, and building care.

Thus in most of the school cases arising from the metropolitan areas, it should not be necessary to reach the issue of whether adventitious de facto segregation, without more, is unconstitutional. In the New Rochelle case,[27] for example, an historical gerrymandering pattern resulting in a primarily Negro school was found offensive to the Equal Protection Clause. The school board, of course, defended on the ground that the school in question was a neighborhood school and that there was no intention in fixing the boundaries to limit its attendance to Negroes. The court was unimpressed with the board's professions of innocent intent—with the result that now Negro children in New Rochelle are distributed throughout the school system and a healthy educational situation obtains in that suburban area.

The Negro plaintiffs, however, were not so fortunate in their efforts to desegregate Gary, Indiana, and Kansas City, Kansas. In those cities, in spite of admitted substantial segregation of Negro children and strong proof of historical gerrymandering, inferior Negro school facilities and inferior Negro faculties in the Negro schools, the district courts in those cases[28] were unable to find either inequality or intentional racial segregation. The courts seemed to be satisfied with the neighborhood school concept of school districting, in spite of the fact that the school boards knew when they drew the boundaries for the Negro schools that those schools would be racially segregated. And there is no suggestion in either the Gary or the Kansas City cases that the courts ever heard of the Princeton Plan for eliminating de facto segregation which has worked satisfactorily in that and similar cities for almost a decade, or of selecting school sites on the dividing line between the white and Negro residential areas so that the schools may serve both races, or even of open enrollment, used initially as a corrective in New Rochelle, which would have allowed children in a segregated school district to attend a public school of their choice outside that district.

It seems that the courts in the Gary and Kansas City cases were more than willing to allow this entire matter to be handled by the school boards, relying on the boards' judgment and good faith in spite of a long history of segregated schools in the cities concerned. The courts in these cases seem to have applied the principle that, as long as there was a rational relationship between what the school board did and a legal end to be achieved, the courts' inquiry was concluded. The courts rejected the suggestion that the end intended was racial segregation, and held that the boards' actions perpetuating racial segregation were reasonable under the circumstances.

It is true, of course, that the Supreme Court in the recent past, in the field of private business and economics, has not looked behind an action of a state agency as long as the purpose of the agency in instituting the action was a legal one and the action was rationally related to that purpose.[29] But, as we shall see, the rational-relationship doctrine has no application to cases involving racial discrimination and public education. Even if it did, it would be highly questionable whether permitting segregated Negro schools is rationally related to the education of those children who must attend them.[30]

As I read these de facto segregation cases from the North and West, I must confess to a little amusement. After watching, from close range, some of my judicial brethren in the South twisting and turning and reaching for a result in race cases that will not upset the status quo or the local power structure, it seems that now I may be treated to what appear to be similar performances by my brethren in other parts of the country.

Although the Gary and Kansas City cases both concluded that the federal courts were powerless with respect to relieving de facto segregation, the issue is far from closed. The final word on this subject will, of course, be spoken by the Supreme Court. It is inconceivable that the Supreme Court will long sit idly by watching Negro children crowded into inferior slum schools while the whites flee to the suburbs to place their children in vastly superior predominantly white schools.

Before the Supreme Court acts, some other federal courts[31] no doubt will take a harder look at de facto segregation and will be less inclined to accept the suggestion that the state and its agencies are not, in some degree at least, responsible for it and helpless to correct it. Until now the cases have focused on the responsibility of the school boards administering the segregated schools, and it is clear that these agencies, through historical gerrymandering and other devious means, have contributed to racial imbalance in the schools. But state action contributing to segregated schools is not limited to school boards. And the Fourteenth Amendment speaks to the state itself.[32] As Justice Louis D. Brandeis reminds us, "'It is a question of the power of the State as a whole;' . . . the powers of the several state officials must be treated as if merged in a single officer."[33]

Where state policy expressed by its several agencies lends itself to, and leads toward, segregated schools, the responsibility of the state is plain. For example, where state policy with reference to housing, or state encouragement of private racial covenants in housing, lead to residential segregation and the school board uses the neighborhood plan in making pupil assignments, the school segregation that results is clearly the responsibility of the state. Certainly the state will not be allowed to do in two steps what it may not do in one. By taking a broader look at state policy and all contributing state agencies, federal courts may be more successful in finding state complicity in segregation. Thus, in most cases, where a forthright effort is made by the courts to determine the cause of racial imbalance, it will be unnecessary to reach the question as to what a state may do, or must do, to relieve purely adventitious segregation. In this connection, however, it should be emphasized again that as long as the federal judges hearing segregation cases, in the North or the South, are satisfied with the status quo, it will be more difficult for them to find that racial imbalance in the public schools is not the result of neutral causes.

Where a forthright effort is made to determine the cause of racial imbalance, the probability of finding state action in segregated Negro schools, in some degree at least, is increased immeasurably. Discrimination in job opportunities, housing, and other necessities drives Negroes into the segregated slums, and application of the neighborhood school policy seals their children in the slum school which these children are compelled by law to attend. Theoretically, the state's compulsory attendance laws may be satisfied by admission to an accredited private school. Some white children, of course, do attend private schools. But to the Negro child the compulsory attendance law often means only one thing: he must attend the segregated slum school in his neighborhood. This fact alone, the legal compulsion to attend the segregated school, should be sufficient state action to bring all de facto segregation within the rule of *Brown*.

State action is also obvious in the use of school boundaries which inevitably result in a segregated Negro school. When school authorities consciously use school district lines, knowing the result will be a segregated Negro school, the action and the intention of the state are clear.[34] Again the compulsory attendance law, superimposed on the school boundary, provides segregation compelled by law within the rule of *Brown*.

The argument is made, of course, that, irrespective of the resulting segregation, the action of the school board is rationally related to the purpose of education and, therefore, courts must ignore the segregation. But, as already indicated,[35] rational-relationship is not the test of the legality of state action where that action results in racial segregation. While, "[n]ormally, the widest discretion is allowed the legislative judgment in determining whether to attack some rather than all of the manifestations of the evil aimed at; and normally that judgment is given the benefit of every conceivable circumstance which might suffice to characterize the classification as reasonable rather than arbitrary and invidious,"[36] state action resulting in racial segregation, even though "pursuant to a valid state interest, bears a heavy burden of justification, . . . and will be upheld only if it is necessary, and not merely rationally related to, the accomplishment of a permissible state policy."[37]

In short, where racial segregation results from state action, the officials responsible therefor must show, not that their action was only rationally related to a legitimate state purpose, but that there is no way reasonably to accomplish that purpose absent racial segregation. Otherwise intent to segregate will be inferred. And whatever arguments there may be in favor of a neighborhood school policy, no one would seriously suggest that there is no other rational basis for assigning children to schools.

III

Assuming that in some instances school segregation may be purely adventitious, the question has arisen as to whether a state may voluntarily undertake to relieve the racial imbalance. In my judgment, states may not only take the necessary steps to relieve adventitious segregation, but, in so doing, may consider race. When racial imbalance infects a public school system, there is simply no way to alleviate it without consideration of race. But those who really, but covertly, want to maintain the segregated status quo cry: "The Constitution is color-blind." Securely they wrap themselves in the famous words of Mr. Justice Harlan I, and point to the language in *Brown*[38] indicating that classification on the basis of race violates the Equal Protection Clause.

Like most aphorisms, Mr. Justice Harlan's felicitous phrase cannot be taken literally. Certainly the great justice would be alarmed if he were aware of the use to which it is presently being put. The Constitution not only recognizes Negroes as such, but makes specific provision for their protection in the Thirteenth, Fourteenth and Fifteenth Amendments. And the language in *Brown* relates to invidious recognition of race for purposes of discrimination. There is nothing whatever in *Brown* which suggests that recognition of race to relieve an inequality violates the Fourteenth Amendment. Indeed, as *Brown* fully recognizes, to relieve an inequality with respect to the Negro was, and is, precisely the purpose of the Fourteenth Amendment.

The suggestion that the state must remain neutral with respect to race was rejected in the Japanese relocation cases[39] in which, for national defense purposes, the placing of a burden on a race was approved. It is strange indeed that this suggestion should be advanced again to prevent the state from relieving a racial inequality. Certainly there is no constitutional right to have an inequality perpetuated.

Voluntary action by school authorities seeking to reduce racial imbalance is easily supported once the "the Constitution is color-blind" argument is analyzed and answered. In fact, it is difficult to understand how a court could actually hold that a state may not act to relieve the inequality caused by de facto segregation; yet several courts have done precisely that.[40] There must be something beguiling about the "color-blind" cliché, particularly to those whose sense of social and racial justice leaves something to be desired. "The Constitution is color-blind" is being used by some today the same way the Court in *Plessy v. Ferguson* used the deceptively simple "separate but equal" slogan. Bitter experience has shown, however, that "separate" is never "equal" and that the Constitution, while in some respects color-blind, is not insensitive to inequality.

Several states, principally New York, New Jersey, and California, have undertaken to reduce the racial imbalance in their schools.[41] This effort, of course, has met with stubborn resistance from those enjoying the present inequality. Parents of children attending the pure white, or nearly so, schools have brought law suits in New York to prevent correction of racial imbalance. After some initial success at the trial level, the New York Court of Appeals has upheld the right of the Board of Education to act affirmatively to correct racial imbalance.[42] Thus, as far as New York is concerned, absent arbitrary action, school authorities have a free hand in eliminating the inequality of racial segregation in the public schools.

IV

Whether a state can be, and should be, compelled by law to correct purely adventitious de facto segregation in its public schools admittedly presents serious problems—both legal and practical. This question also involves the emotional area of state's rights. How far should the courts go in requiring the states affirmatively to afford equal opportunity to equal education? Is the enforcement of this right sufficiently important to risk further assaults on the federal courts in general and the Supreme Court in particular? If the Supreme Court does not undertake this burden, at least initially, by recognizing the constitutional right to equal educational opportunity, can we confidently assume that the Congress or the states will protect the Negro in the realization of this right? Perhaps some background on the importance of public education in this country may be helpful in answering these questions.

The importance of generalized education, at least at the elementary and high school level, is no new dogma. It is as old as the theory of popular government. On these shores, it has always been one of the principal articles of the democratic faith. In 1787, in the Northwest Ordinance, the Continental Congress declared: "[S]chools and the means of education shall forever be encouraged."[43] Jefferson termed general education the only "sure foundation . . . for the preservation of freedom,"[44] "without which no republic can maintain itself in strength."[45] Today, all the more, it remains "the very foundation of good citizenship."[46] But, because our society has grown increasingly complex, education is now also an economic necessity. "In these days, it is doubtful that any child may reasonably be expected to succeed in life if he is denied the opportunity of an education."[47] Thus, adequate schooling is no longer a privilege that can be made available to the few; it is the indispensable equipment of all men.

The critical role of education in our contemporary society gives meaning to the associated constitutional rights. But the full importance of the state's obligation to provide equal education cannot be appreciated without noticing the long and consistent history of general education as a governmental function.

Washington,[48] Jefferson,[49] Madison,[50] and John Adams[51] all advocated governmental responsibility in the diffusion of knowledge through common schools. With such leadership, the public school movement soon took root, so that, by 1850, almost every state in the Union had at least made a start toward a comprehensive system of education.[52] There was then no retreat from the view that education is a state function. On the contrary, except for the temporary disruption resulting from the Civil War, the next century is a chronology of progress, studded with important reaffirmations of the doctrine. Very soon most of the states solemnly proclaimed a right to public education in their constitutions. Significantly, the Thirty-ninth Congress, which drafted the Fourteenth Amendment, put down public education as one of the fundamental tenets of republicanism,[53] and their immediate successors imposed it as a precondition to readmission of the states still considered in rebellion and to the admission of new states.[54] The full development came with the adoption of compulsory school attendance laws which necessarily imply free public education.

The courts, also, have long characterized education as a function of the states. As early as 1874, Judge Thomas Cooley, whose *Constitutional Limitations* had appeared in the year of the ratification of the Fourteenth Amendment, expressed "no little surprise" that anyone should question the propriety of the state's furnishing "a liberal education to the youth of the state in schools brought within the reach of all classes."[55] He "supposed it had always been understood . . . that education, not merely in the rudiments, but in an enlarged sense, was regarded as an important practical advantage to be supplied at their option to rich and poor alike, and not as something pertaining merely to the culture and accomplishment . . . of those whose accumulated wealth enabled them to pay for it."[56] In 1907, the Supreme Court, speaking through Mr. Justice Holmes, recognized that education is properly considered "one of the first objects of public care."[57] And in 1947, Mr. Justice Black, also for the Supreme Court, wrote: "It is much too late to argue that legislation intended to facilitate the opportunity of children to get a secular education serves no public purpose."[58] Now even college training has become a public concern. As Justice Felix Frankfurter put it, "The need for higher education and the duty of the state to provide it as part of a public educational system, are part of the democratic faith of most of our states."[59] The full impact of this development was summed up in *Brown v. Board of Education*: "Today, education is perhaps the most important function of state and local governments."[60]

From the fact that public education is the states' most important function, it does not necessarily follow that segregated public education, whatever the cause, is illegal. But the importance of public education in a democratic society imperatively requires affirmative action on the part of the state to assure each child his fair share, and a child in a segregated Negro school does not receive his fair share. Public education, once offered by the state, "must be made available to all on equal terms."[61] And segregated education, being "inherently unequal," is therefore unconstitutional.[62]

A racially segregated Negro school is an inferior school. It is "inherently unequal."[63] No honest person would even suggest, for example, that the segregated slum school provides educational opportunity equal to that provided by the white suburban public school. Thus children compelled by state compulsory attendance laws to attend the segregated Negro school are deprived of equal protection of the law. The fact that the classification to attend the school is based on geography,[64] and not on race, does not necessarily make the school less segregated or less inferior. Nor does it make the classification less illegal unless it can be shown that no reasonable classification will alleviate the inequality.[65]

The touchstone in determining equal protection of the law in public education is equal educational opportunity, not race. If classification by race is used to achieve the invidious discrimination, the constitutional insult is exacerbated. But the focus must remain on the result achieved. If the untoward result derives from racial classification, such classification is per se unconstitutional. Where the result is segregation, and therefore unequal educational opportunity, the classification used, whatever it is, is constitutionally suspect and a heavy burden is placed on the school board and the state to show, not only innocent intent, but also lack of a suitable alternative.[66] In short, since segregation in public schools and unequal educational opportunity are two sides of the same coin, the state, in order to provide equal educational opportunity, has the affirmative constitutional obligation to eliminate segregation, however it arises.

Our experience with the cases involving racial segregation in southern schools has blurred the issue presented by de facto segregation. In the southern school cases the classification was on the basis of race. It was this classification that achieved the segregated, and therefore unequal, schools. What made the classification invidious, and therefore unconstitutional, was the inequality it produced. When the same invidious result is achieved by another classification, that classification likewise must be tested by the Constitution.

Perhaps the clearest statement of the principle involved in adventitious de facto segregation has been made by Chief Judge George C. Sweeney of the United States District Court for the District of Massachusetts in the only case to date, state or federal, squarely holding that a state may be required to relieve racial imbalance in the public schools. In ordering the city of Springfield to file a desegregation plan for its schools by April 3, 1965, Judge Sweeney wrote:

> The defendants argue, nevertheless, that there is no constitutional mandate to remedy racial imbalance.... But that is not the question. The question is whether there is a constitutional duty to provide equal educational opportunities for all children within the system. While *Brown* answered that question affirmatively in the context of coerced segregation, the constitutional fact— the inadequacy of segregated education—is the same in this case, and I so find. It is neither just nor sensible to proscribe segregation having its basis in affirmative state action while at the same time failing to provide a remedy for segregation which grows out of discrimination in housing, or other economic or social factors. Education is tax supported and compulsory, and public school educators, therefore, must deal with inadequacies within the educational system as they arise, and it matters not that the inadequacies are not of their making. This is not to imply that the neighborhood school policy per se is unconstitutional, but that it must be abandoned or modified when it results in segregation in fact.[67]

There can, of course, be no mathematical formula[68] to determine at what point the unequal educational opportunity inherent in racial imbalance and de facto school segregation rises to constitutional dimension. A judgment must be made in each case based on the substantiality of the imbalance under the particular circumstances. Once substantial racial imbalance is shown, however, no further proof of unequal educational opportunity is required. What may be substantial imbalance in Boston, where the Negro school population is relatively small, may not be in Washington, where the Negro school population is approaching 90 percent. Numbers alone do not provide the answer. The relevant population area is an important consideration. Is the relevant area the city alone or the suburbs as well? A variety of other circumstances may also be important in answering this sometimes difficult question.

The judicial process is equipped to develop the necessary evidence and to make the judgment as to substantial racial imbalance. The word "substantial" does not provide a certain or mechanical guide to decision, but judicial judgments based on similar guides are made routinely. The test for negligence in every case is whether the party charged acted "reasonably" or as "the reasonably prudent person would have" under the circumstances. In every jury case, civil and criminal, the judge decides whether the evidence against the defendant is "substantial" before he allows the case to go to the jury. The examples can be multiplied, but the point is already made. The determination as to substantial racial imbalance, and therefore unequal educational opportunity, is clearly within the competence of the judiciary. As in other areas involving due process and equal protection of the law, the guidelines will have to be staked out on a case-by-case basis.[69] Once substantial racial imbalance is shown, however, the case for relief is complete, and the burden of going forward with the evidence falls on the state.[70]

V

Assuming the constitutional question is answered affirmatively in favor of the Negro, the question of appropriate remedy arises. What can a state do—what can a court require a state to do—to relieve racial imbalance? In short, what, if any, remedies are available?

Initially, public school authorities must be cured of the neighborhood school syndrome. The neighborhood school, like the little red school house, has many emotional ties and practical advantages. The neighborhood school serves as the neighborhood center, easily accessible, where children can gather to play on holidays and parents' clubs can meet at any time. But twentieth-century education is not necessarily geared to the neighborhood school. In fact, the trend is definitely in the opposite direction. Educational parks, each consisting of a complex of schools, science buildings, libraries, gymnasiums, auditoriums, and playing fields, are beginning to replace the neighborhood school. Although the development of the educational park idea in education is unrelated to the question of racial segregation, its use in relieving racial imbalance in public schools is obvious. Instead of having neighborhood schools scattered through racially homogeneous residential areas, children of all races may be brought together in the educational parks.

In many areas where the educational park is not feasible, simple changes in the existing school district lines may relieve racial imbalance. For example, the homogeneous character of a school in a segregated neighborhood may be changed by redrawing its district lines along with the district lines of the nearest white school so as to include Negro and white pupils in both schools. Also, under the well-known Princeton Plan, where the district lines of two racially diverse schools are contiguous, the racial imbalance can be relieved by limiting the grades in one school from kindergarten to third and in the other from fourth to sixth. And where new schools are to be built to accommodate the expanding school population, the sites for those schools should be, not in Negro or white residential areas, but near the dividing line so that the children living in both areas may be included in each school district. These plans, alone or in combination, when properly used, may well suffice to eliminate the inequality arising from the segregated school in most areas. But in some sections of our large cities, because of the density of the residential segregation, Negro schools are back to back. Princeton Plans and the like are not geared to this problem, but educational parks do provide the answer to Harlem-type residential situations. And pending the construction of the educational parks, open enrollment may be used as a temporary expedient.

An even more difficult problem is presented by the flight of the white population to the suburbs. The pattern is the same all over the country. The Negro child remains within the political boundaries of the city and attends the segregated slum school in his neighborhood, while the white children attend the vastly superior white public schools in the suburbs. The situation is accurately described in the 1964 Advisory Panel Report to the Board of Education of the City of Chicago:

> Finally, it cannot be too strongly stressed that programs to effect school integration must reckon with the fact that the white elementary school child is already in the minority in the public schools of Chicago and the time is not far off when the same will be true of the white high school student. Unless the exodus of white population from the public schools and from the City is brought to a halt or reversed, the question of school integration may become simply a theoretical matter, as it is already in the nation's capital. For integration, in fact, cannot be achieved without white students.[71]

A court, in proposing or approving a plan of desegregation, may find no great difficulty in ordering the local school authorities to use the Princeton Plan, or one of its variants, or, under the authority of *Griffin v. School Board*[72] in ordering the local taxing authority or the state to levy taxes to raise funds to build an educational park. Relieving the inequality between the suburban public school and the segregated city slum public school presents a greater challenge. Obviously, court orders running to local officials will not reach the suburbs. Nevertheless, when political lines, rather than school district lines, shield the inequality, as shown in the reapportionment cases,[73] courts are not helpless to act. The political thicket, having been pierced to protect the vote,[74] can likewise be pierced to protect the education of children.

Education, as stated in *Brown*, is "the most important function of the state." And, as shown in *Hall v. St. Helena Parish School Board*,[75] and *Griffin v. School Board*,[76] that important function must be administered in all parts of the state with an even hand. The state operates local public schools through its agents, the local school boards; it directly supplies part of the money for that operation; it certifies the teachers; it accredits the schools; and, through its department of education, it maintains constant supervision over the entire operation. The involvement of the state in the operation of its public schools is complete. Indeed, the state is the conduit through which federal money, in increasing amounts, is being funnelled into the public schools. Certainly federal money may not be used to indurate an inequality.[77] Thus no state-created political lines can protect the state against the constitutional command of equal protection for its citizens or relieve the state from the obligation of providing educational opportunities for its Negro slum children equal to those provided for its white children in the affluent suburbs.[78]

When the Supreme Court decided the first reapportionment case, *Baker v. Carr*,[79] just as when it decided *Brown*, it left to the district courts the task of fashioning the remedy. Undoubtedly, if and when the Supreme Court tackles the suburban vis-à-vis the city slum school problem, in the event of a decision in favor of the complainants, it will again remit the remedy to the district courts, with instructions to ignore the state-created political lines separating the school boards and to run its orders directly against state, as well as local, officials.

VI

I am aware, of course, that what I have said will not find favor with the advocates of judicial restraint—many of whom have already expressed the view that de facto segregation is a political and social matter which requires a political, not a judicial, solution, that the Congress and the states are equipped to remedy any inequality which may exist in the public schools, and that any attempted judicial resolution of the problem would adversely affect the balance of our federalism by trenching on states' rights.

These objections to judicial intervention into de facto segregation all have a slightly familiar ring. The Supreme Court's opinion in *Brown* was subjected to just such criticism. Yet because of that decision definite progress has been made toward the recognition of Negro rights. The Court's action unquestionably moved other branches of government to act. Is there anyone who seriously thinks that the Civil

Rights Act of 1964 would be a reality today without *Brown* and other Supreme Court decisions exposing racial injustice? Is it conceivable that the southern states would have abolished segregation compelled by law without prodding from the federal courts?

The reapportionment cases are also in point. Does anyone really believe that the state legislatures would have reformed themselves? Legislators elected via the rotten borough system ordinarily would not be expected to vote for its abolition. Perhaps the reapportionment cases do trench on states' rights, but the people who now have a full vote are not complaining.

The advocates of judicial restraint have also been critical of the Supreme Court's work in the field of criminal justice. It is true that the Court has insisted on civilized procedures in state as well as federal criminal courts. An accused in a serious criminal case must now have a lawyer available to represent him, coerced confessions must be excluded from state and federal criminal trials, and state as well as federal police must now respect the Fourth Amendment. How long should the Supreme Court have waited for the states to civilize their own criminal procedures before it undertook to protect the constitutional rights of persons accused of crime?

The Supreme Court's intervention into these fields of primary state responsibility was not precipitous. The states were given ample opportunity to correct the evils themselves. Before *Brown*, the Supreme Court handed down a series of decisions in the field of education indicating quite clearly that, if the states did not act to eliminate racial segregation compelled by law, it would. The persistence with which reapportionment cases continued to reach the Supreme Court after it had refused to exercise jurisdiction in *Colegrove v. Green*,[80] should have been warning enough to the states that, one way or the other, vote dilution was on the way out. And civilizing of state criminal procedures, under gentle urging from the Supreme Court, has been going on since *Brown v. Mississippi*,[81] in which the Court set aside a death sentence based solely on a confession obtained by hanging the accused from a tree.

There is no indication that the Supreme Court will rush into the de facto segregation arena. Two circuit courts of appeals[82] have already denied relief from de facto segregation and the Supreme Court has stayed its hand. But this is no guarantee that the Court will not act if the problem persists and the states fail to correct the evil. Proper judicial restraint does not include a failure to act where a state has abdicated its responsibility to protect the constitutional rights of its citizens.

Equal educational opportunity is not the only demand of the Negro Revolution of the 1960s, but it is the most important one. Education is the key to social mobility. Without it the Negro will continue to be tied to the segregated slum where the social, intellectual, and educational damage suffered by his children begins the day they are born. Repeated studies have confirmed that the ability of Negro children to learn, given equal conditions, is equal to the white.[83] But, by school age, the segregated slum culture in which they are born and reared has opened an educational gap, as compared with the white child, which not only is never closed, but which actually increases as time goes on.[84]

It is not enough, therefore, simply to provide equal educational opportunity beginning at the age of six. Until society eliminates these segregated slums, cultural and educational enrichment for slum children must begin at birth. To their great credit, some enlightened states, including New York and California, are already planning just such programs. And the president of the United States, in his recent message on education,[85] has asked the Congress for legislation providing financial aid to states undertaking preschool educational programs for slum children.

The American Negro is a totally American responsibility. Three hundred years ago he was brought to this country by our forefathers and sold into slavery. One hundred years ago we fought a war that would set him free. For these last one hundred years we have lived and professed the hypocrisy that he was free. The time has now come when we must face up to that responsibility. Let us erase this blemish—let us remove this injustice—from the face of America. Let us *make* the Negro free.*

* In Swann v. Charlotte-Mecklenburg Board of Education, 402 U.S. 1, 26–28 (1971), the Supreme Court held that the existence of single-race schools within a school district demanded close judicial scrutiny, and it authorized federal courts to alter school attendance zones in order to achieve nondiscriminatory school assignments. The Supreme Court also permitted the use of busing for school desegregation. *Id.* at 30–31. In a companion case, the Court struck down a state antibusing statute. North Carolina v. Swann, 402 U.S. 43 (1971). Subsequently, however, the Supreme Court imposed limits on the federal courts' power to implement sweeping interdistrict school desegregation programs. For example, in Milliken v. Bradley, 418 U.S. 717 (1974), the Court struck down a desegregation plan which would have required school districts in all-white suburbs to exchange students with an all-black inner-city school district to achieve the integration of all schools in the metropolitan Detroit area. EDITOR'S NOTE.

Elbert P. Tuttle

Equality and the Vote

Lowndes County is in the black belt of the state of Alabama. Although the term "black belt" is used to denote the color of its soil, it also very aptly describes a racial characteristic of its people. Eighty percent of the citizens of Lowndes County are Negroes.[1] Just a year ago, not one of the 5,000 Negroes of voting age living in Lowndes County was registered to vote.[2] The newspapers tell us today that Negroes are now a majority of the voters of that county.

The Fifteenth Amendment to the United States Constitution[3] was adopted in 1870. For ninety-five years this part of the Constitution was a dead letter in Lowndes County, Alabama. Now, within a single year, it is the law even there. Many other rural counties of the Old South have witnessed changes almost equally dramatic. Fortunately, in very few of them has the change been so traumatic.[4]

The events of the past ten years, culminating in such revolutionary changes, have taken place very largely within the territorial jurisdiction of the United States Court of Appeals for the Fifth Circuit. Until the passage of the Voting Rights Act of 1965,[5] the action was principally in the courts of our circuit, which, by the midsummer of 1965, had disposed of substantially all of the legal questions that had arisen from the continued reluctance of local officials in some counties to accept the century-old command of the Fifteenth Amendment.

Because of this fact, and also because the Congress has now sought to take the matter largely out of the hands of the local courts,[6] it seems entirely appropriate for me to discuss the subject of equality and the vote. Of course, I do not intend to prejudge any issue, either of fact or law, still remaining for consideration by our court; nor is it my purpose to elaborate or explain any of our decisions. I hope only to dis-

Chief Judge Tuttle's lecture was delivered on March 15, 1966 and appeared in 41 N.Y.U.L. Rev. 245 (1966).

cuss this one specific guarantee of the Constitution and some of the specific enforcement problems, and how they have been solved.

Although I do not intend to discuss primarily the question of universal suffrage, it is, nevertheless, appropriate to consider briefly what James Madison himself thought about the right to vote. In No. 57 of the *Federalist Papers,* discussing his views of the United States House of Representatives, Madison said:

> Who are to be the electors of the federal representatives? Not the rich, more than the poor; not the learned, more than the ignorant; not the haughty heirs of distinguished names, more than the humble sons of obscure and unpropitious fortune. The electors are to be the great body of the people of the United States. They are to be the same who exercise the right in every State of electing the corresponding branch of the legislature of the State.[7]

A study of the voting requirements of the states that were about to become the United States would demonstrate that there is a serious inconsistency between the last two sentences in Madison's statement. This is true because, as we are told by Clinton Rossiter, "Only in leveling Vermont, as portent of things to come, was the traditional property qualification abandoned without reserve."[8] Thus, to the extent that the term "the great body of the people of the United States" comprehended any one other than male, white persons satisfying property qualifications, Madison's description of the voters who would elect the members of the House of Representatives as "the great body of the people of the United States" was something of an overstatement.

According to the chapter written by Irving Brant in *The Great Rights,* Madison, at the time of the Federalist debates, accepted the principle of restricting the suffrage to freeholders, whom he regarded as "the safest depositories of Republican liberty,"[9] but changed his view in later life. "Long afterward," as Brant says,

> he repudiated the restrictive argument entirely, saying he had been too much influenced by Virginia's example. Such a limitation, he wrote, "violates the vital principle of free Government that those who are to be bound by laws, ought to have a voice in making them. And the violations would be more strikingly unjust as the lawmakers become the minority."[10]

In the past 150 years a series of extensions has broadened the electorate from an exclusive propertied class to include successively the landless, members of newly arrived immigrant groups, women, and most recently, members of the nonwhite races. The expansion of the West undermined the rule of the landed gentry of the seaboard and, by the incorporation of new territory, led to the democratizing extension of Jacksonian politics. The white immigrants, by amalgamation, lost their identity and gained the vote. Women's suffrage was a hard battle, won only by an early-day civil rights movement with all the emotion and apparatus of sit-ins, lie-ins, street parades, and mass arrests, aided in some measure by the bedroom techniques of Lysistrata.

Notwithstanding the truth of Mr. Justice Goldberg's statement in his lecture here two years ago, "that equality and liberty were the 'twin themes' of the American Revolution,"[11] it is clear that, under the various colonial and early state constitutions, not even all free men were "equal" when it came to the right to vote.

It is perhaps one of the interesting inconsistencies of the political philosophy of James Madison that he believed the very variety of the *interests* of the mass of the people in any popular government would constitute a curb preventing the ascendency of any one particular interest, or group, and yet he could, with some degree of complacency, accept a government whose legislators were elected solely by the representatives of a *single* well-defined class having a definite special interest, the ownership of property.

It was not until the Emancipation Proclamation created a new, easily identifiable class of citizens, having in common with each other the distinguishing characteristics of race, color, poverty, illiteracy, and lack of attachment to the land, that it became apparent that neither a commonality of interests nor the multiplicity of interests among citizens would be adequate to protect the peculiar interests of the new class. It must be borne in mind that, *politically,* the Negro population of the southern states did not *exist* prior to the adoption of the Thirteenth Amendment to the Constitution.[12]

Then, for the first time, the people of the United States found it necessary to interpose national prohibitions affecting the electorate. This was accomplished, of course, by the adoption of the Fifteenth Amendment.[13]

It was soon discovered that the new amendment, like the First, the Fourth, the Fifth, the Sixth, and the Fourteenth (about all of which the struggle still goes on), was not self-operating. In fact, it had so little practical effect that is was possible for Mr. James J. Kilpatrick, of Richmond, editor of *The Richmond News Leader,* who has been a strong states' rights leader, to say as recently as 1961: "The Negro as a citizen, as a political being possessed of equal rights, never had existed in the white Southerner's past as he begins to exist now."[14] It will probably come as a surprise to most people to learn that the ballot still used by the Democratic party in Alabama for its last primary elections carried a symbol of a crowing rooster under the words "White Supremacy." The newspapers report within the last month that this is to be changed for this year's primary.

The Alabama party emblem of white supremacy was the last visible relic of a political system which, for more than half a century, was the effective means by which the Negro citizens of the states of the Old South, roughly one-third of the total population of the area, were effectively denied the franchise. The system I speak of is the white Democratic primary, which accounted for the much discussed "Solid South." The period I speak of is the last decade of the nineteenth century and the first half of the twentieth. This is a period when broader educational advantages, the wider dissemination of knowledge, participation in two great wars by the United States, the advent of radio and television, together with an awakening perception of the true state of facts by national political leaders, might normally have been expected to end disfranchisement of the Negro. That these circumstances did not do so presents an interesting study in our political history.

It began to appear by the mid-1890s that the Negro might soon hold the balance of power in many southern states. Thereupon, white factions, although bitterly at odds with each other, began to close ranks against him. In addition to requiring payment of a poll tax, nearly every one of these states adopted literacy qualifications from which white applicants for registration were exempted by reason of a "grandfather clause." By the time the grandfather clause was invalidated by the Supreme Court in 1915,[15] it had already had the desired effect—the election rolls in most of the southern states had been effectively purged of most Negro voters, leaving in the hands of the white majority the power to enact almost any kind of restrictive legislation it desired. By this time the white voters of the South had, almost to a man, aligned themselves with the Democratic party.

However, the white majority did not rely solely on these hurdles. They made certain that Negro voters would not infiltrate the Democratic party by providing by law that the parties could control the membership as they saw fit and restrict the right to participate in a primary to party members. Of course, party membership was restricted to white persons. This became so universal that throughout the South the only meaningful election for decades was known as "The White Primary."

Although the device survived its first attack in the Supreme Court of the United States,[16] this decision could not long prevail, and, in 1944, the Court, by a vote of eight to one, decided in *Smith v. Allwright*[17] that the Democratic primary, being conducted by authority of the state law, amounted to state action. Although even Supreme Court decisions are not self-executing, by 1946 or 1947 it had become clear that there was no way around this decision, and in most of the southern states the white primary was, on the surface at least, a thing of the past.

There were 645,000 Negroes registered in 1947 in the twelve southern states. This was from a population of more than five million Negroes of voting age. During the next five years this number was increased to approximately one million nonwhite voters.[18] This increase was far from uniform among the southern states, and it was far from uniform among the counties. As might reasonably be expected, the greatest increases were in the metropolitan areas where the Negroes' pressure to participate in a city government had grown apace and where active intelligent leadership among the members of that race had achieved a substantial weakening of the artificial barriers to registration and voting.

It was not until after the Supreme Court's school desegregation decision in *Brown v. Board of Education*[19] that a true threat to the system of white political domination in the South caused legislators and other officials of many of the southern states to seek new methods to prevent massive registration by the theretofore disfranchised group.

Negro leadership sought immediately to expand the areas in which the *Brown* case was to be applied, and it took little thought to convince all of these leaders that an increase in voting participation was one of the main, if not the most important, roads to political freedom.

The white political leadership was no less alert to this possibility, and it was not slow to raise the old specter of racism in order to make every effort to stem the tide. Moving apace with efforts to enact legislation that would frustrate the effects of the school desegregation decision was new legislation seeking to place new barriers in the way of further Negro registration for voting.

Thus, a collision course was laid out. At the very moment when the Negroes were being imbued with a desire to participate fully in governmental and public affairs and to enjoy all of the fruits of citizenship, state officials, both high and low, were devising new means to deny them these same rights. New requirements were devised for limiting the franchise, which, if objectively administered, would prevent all but the most highly educated members of the community from being registered to vote in the future. This was of no immediate concern to the white citizens, because they were already registered. The new difficult requirements would not apply to them.[20]

An excellent and very readable discussion of the use of the "understanding" clause for the qualification of prospective voters can be found in the scholarly opinion of Judge John Minor Wisdom, of the Court of Appeals for the Fifth Circuit, sitting as a member of a three-judge district court in the case of *United States v. Louisiana*.[21]

Statistics showed that in many counties there was a nonwhite population of between 35 and 50 percent, sometimes more, but that there was either no Negro, or a negligible number of Negroes, registered to vote, whereas from 90 to 140 percent[22] of the number of eligible white persons were shown to be registered. When taken in connection with the subjective tests available to the local registrars, this produced studies which, to the surprise of no one, demonstrated that the registration procedure had become the principal means of disfranchising Negroes.[23] Legal proof of this fact, however, was another matter. Plaintiffs had to rely almost entirely on presumptions. Fortunately, our court had earlier, in the case of *Alabama v. United States*,[24] said: "In the problem of racial discrimination, statistics often tell much, and Courts listen."[25]

Nevertheless, proving a case of racial discrimination in voter registration was difficult because of the many educational, economic, and sociological handicaps that were correlated with race. In short, it was an impossible thing, except in a very circumscribed sense. No individual Negro voter, and hardly any local Negro organization, could afford the long and expensive effort to amass the proof from frequently hostile officials and establish to the satisfaction of a judge, even though he hold a United States commission, that the use of what appeared as objective requirements was in reality part of a scheme and plan to deprive Negro citizens of their right to vote.

That such was frequently the case, however, was so apparent by the middle 1950s that Congress determined to bring an end to what it found to be too long an abstention by the national government from protecting the right that the House Report of April 1, 1957, called "the foundation of our representative form of Government."[26] Thus,

Congress enacted the first voting rights bill in nearly ninety years.[27] While not wholly effective, it made some major changes. It gave official legal status and the power to subpoena records to the Civil Rights Commission. It created an additional position of assistant attorney general for a Civil Rights Division of the Department of Justice. Most important, it broadened the statutory prohibition against the interference with the right to vote by providing that it shall be unlawful for a *private* individual, as well as one acting under color of law, to interfere or attempt to interfere with the right to vote. In addition, the bill provided a new remedy in the form of a civil action to be instituted by the attorney general in the name of the United States to prevent an act that would deprive a person of any right or privilege secured under the law.

The first efforts by the Civil Rights Commission to investigate complaints of voter discrimination on account of race met with a severe rebuff. The Commission scheduled a hearing for July 13, 1959, in response to some 115 sworn voting complaints from Negro citizens from fourteen of Louisiana's parishes. The attorney general of Louisiana filed suit to enjoin the hearing. A temporary restraining order was issued by the District Court for the Western District of Louisiana,[28] and on July 12, this action was sustained by a three-judge court, with Judge John Minor Wisdom dissenting.[29] The ground of the attack was that the registrars were not guaranteed procedural due process in the investigatory proceedings. Although this action was reversed by the Supreme Court on June 20, 1960,[30] a year of compulsory investigation was lost.

Only three suits were filed under the 1957 Civil Rights Act before it was amended to meet the difficulties that still existed. In the first of these suits, involving Terrell County, Georgia, Judge Hoyt Davis held the act unconstitutional because, although there was no doubt that the defendants were acting under color of state law, he found the statute too broad in that the Fifteenth Amendment did not empower Congress to control the actions of private citizens, and this act purported to do so.[31] The United States took a direct appeal to the Supreme Court, which in February 1960, reversed the dismissal of the suit against the registrars, pointing out that they were in no position to claim that the act was too broad, since it clearly covered them.[32]

In the meantime, in a case filed against the registrars of Washington Parish, Louisiana, the then District Judge J. Skelly Wright, now the distinguished judge of the Court of Appeals for the District of

Columbia Circuit, denied the motion to dismiss which had been filed on the same grounds relied upon by Judge Davis in Georgia. Judge Wright said:

The defendants' contention is so obviously without merit that this Court would merely deny the motion to dismiss without more were it not for the fact that a district court has upheld a similar contention and declared Section 1971(c) unconstitutional. In so doing, that Court ignored the most elementary principles of statutory construction, as repeatedly announced by the Supreme Court, and relied on an old case interpreting a criminal statute.[33]

Judge Wright not only enjoined further use of the challenge of registered voters in an improper manner, but also ordered 1,377 Negroes, previously registered to vote, to be reregistered. This judgment was affirmed by the Supreme Court on the same day it reversed the *Raines* case from Georgia.[34]

At about the same time, the United States attorney general filed a suit in the Middle District of Alabama against voter registrars of Macon County, Alabama, the county that is the site of Tuskeegee Institute. The registrars had resigned their office before suit was filed. Thereupon, the United States amended its original complaint, seeking to join the state of Alabama as a defendant. Judge Frank M. Johnson, Jr. who was later to make most effective use of the amended Civil Rights Act to assure Negro voters' rights, found it necessary to dismiss the suit because the individual defendants, having resigned their office, could not be sued as registrars.[35] He also found that there was nothing in the statute that permitted the joining of the state of Alabama as a defendant. This decision was affirmed by the Court of Appeals for the Fifth Circuit.[36] On appeal to the Supreme Court, it was argued on May 2, 1960, four days before the Civil Rights Act of 1960 became law. In view of the provisions of this new law expressly authorizing the attorney general to make the state a defendant, the Supreme Court vacated the judgments of the court of appeals and the district court and remanded the case with instructions to reinstate the state of Alabama as a party defendant.[37]

Partially because of the difficulties involved in the enforcement of the 1957 act, President Eisenhower, in 1959, transmitted to Congress a message of recommendations suggesting improvements in the act touching on assuring the right to vote to Negro citizens. After extensive hearings, the Committee on the Judiciary of the House of Representatives filed House Report No. 956,[38] which stressed the need for access to voting records prior to filing suit.[39]

A bill was passed to become the Civil Rights Act of 1960. It made several important additions to the powers of the federal government in the field of voting rights. These were: first, the requirement that every officer of election shall retain and preserve for a specified period all voting records and related papers; second, the provision that "upon demand in writing by the Attorney General or his representative" containing "a statement of the basis and the purpose therefor," any such record or paper shall "be made available for inspection, reproduction and copying"; third, the United States district court was given "jurisdiction by appropriate process to compel the production of such record or paper"; fourth, the law added a section which provided for joining the state as a party defendant; fifth, there was a provision that made it possible for the court itself, either upon its determination, or upon the appointment of voter referees, to enroll voters found to be qualified if in such litigation the court "finds that any person has been deprived on account of race or color of any right or privilege secured by [the statute]" and after making a finding that "such deprivation was or is pursuant to a pattern or practice."[40]

Thereafter, the battle started afresh. On May 23, 1960, the attorney general served on the Board of Registrars of Montgomery County, Alabama, written demand for voting records within fifteen days.

What followed was a lawyer's field day. It is well described in the Report of the Civil Rights Commission for 1961 on Voting.[41] Before the expiration of the fifteen days, the attorney general of the state of Alabama filed a suit in the state court and obtained an injunction from the Circuit Court of Montgomery County restraining the attorney general of the United States from inspecting or copying the records. The government removed the state court action to the federal district court, in response to which the state of Alabama moved for an order of remand. The government then moved to dismiss the action while in the federal court.

In the meantime, the United States attorney general filed a proceeding in the district court to require the production of the records as provided in the 1960 act. The state of Alabama sought to make a full lawsuit of the government's application to the district court.[42] The trial judge, Judge Johnson, acting with the dispatch that was implicit in the enactment of the 1960 amendments, made short shrift of the issues. He denied the motion for remand and dismissed the state's suit against the United States attorney general. He declined the state's request for a full scale hearing on the suit of the attorney general for access to the records, relying upon the opinion of the Supreme Court in *Hannah v. Larche.*[43]

On August 11, within three months of the time the attorney general had written the first letter demanding access to the records, Judge Johnson entered his order granting the request. No stay was granted. When the case came on for hearing in the court of appeals, the appellate court, in *Dinkens v. Attorney General,* expressly adopted Judge Johnson's opinion and reasoning.[44]

In the meantime, the government did not fare so well in the Southern District of Alabama. There, following a letter request by the attorney general on May 9 of the same year, just a few days before the application was made in Montgomery County, the Board of Registrars of Wilcox County, Alabama, filed an action in the state court on May 20, 1960, against the attorney general of the United States, seeking to enjoin the attempt to enforce the demand for voting records. The state court granted a temporary injunction; on June 3 the attorney general removed the case to the United States district court, and on June 7 moved to dismiss the removed action. This motion was not heard until June 30, 1961, *over a year later,* and on September 28 of that year, nine months after the Court of Appeals for the Fifth Circuit had expressly approved the action taken in the Middle District in the *Dinkens* case on precisely the same facts and pleadings, the trial court *denied* the government's motion to dismiss the state court injunction, and *granted* the state's motion to dismiss the attorney general's application for access to the state records. The government appealed and the court of appeals accelerated the setting of the case by placing it on the next available calendar. It was heard and decided within two months, for, on February 5, 1962, the appellate court reversed the inconsistent holdings of the district court, and in doing so said:

[W]e are unable to find any conceivable justification supporting the trial court's action. Nine months prior to the entry by the trial court of this order denying dismissal, this Court in State of Alabama ex rel. Gallion v. Rogers, Attorney General, supra, expressly adopted the opinion of Judge Johnson, United States District Judge for the Middle District of Alabama, and affirmed his order and the reasons producing it is published in 187 F. Supp. 848. Thus, just as plainly as it could be said, we have decided that the State of Alabama had no power to entertain a suit seeking to review the discretion of or enjoin the acts of the Attorney General of the United States.[45]

Then, commenting on the statistics touching on Wilcox County, Alabama, which showed that there were 2,634 white citizens of voting age, that 112.4 percent of these, or 2,950 white citizens, were registered to vote, and that of the 6,085 Negro citizens of voting age, *not a single one* was registered to vote, the court reaffirmed the proposition that the request of the attorney general was sufficient to require the respondents, members of the board of registrars, to make the records available as requested, and upon their failure to do so to entitle the attorney general to a prompt order of the court requiring such compliance.[46]

We then followed a procedure that had developed in our court to avoid unnecessary delays by the possibility of fruitless efforts to seek reversals in the Supreme Court. We directed that the mandate should issue forthwith. The order actually entered in this case was:

> Because of long delay that has already occurred since the filing of the application that should have been granted as a matter of course, the order of this Court will be transmitted forthwith to the District Court.[47]

The court thus recognized that it was dealing with a summary right to obtain information for investigatory purposes, and it was plain that the whole purpose of the statute would be frustrated unless it was brought to a prompt conclusion.

It will be remembered that this series of lectures, as distinguished from the first four dealing with the general philosophy of constitutional liberty, is devoted to specific guarantees in the Constitution and specific enforcement problems. Here we find that Congress, in 1957 and 1960, sought to provide specific enforcement of the Fifteenth Amendment right to vote without reference to race or color, but that even the enactment of this statute left to the courts difficult enforcement problems. I have discussed the difficulty of obtaining from hostile witnesses proof sufficient to cause a district judge to make the necessary findings of fact. There was also the reluctance of a federal court to interfere unduly with the operation by the states of activities primarily made their responsibility under our dual system. Unusually burdensome here has been the practice of recalcitrant official defendants to treat each case as if no precedent had already been established by the federal courts, thus requiring a county-by-county series of lawsuits to vindicate rights that even the most reluctant defendant must have recognized were regularly being denied American citizens of the Negro race.

Thus it devolved upon the appellate courts, to a greater extent than had theretofore been usual in American jurisprudence, to fashion means to give effect to principles of law, once firmly established, much more rapidly than would be possible if full sway were allowed to the normal procedural maneuvering. Ordering an immediate issuance of the mandate is the first unusual procedural means that our court devised for this purpose.

The case of *United States v. Lynd*[48] demonstrates a second procedural innovation by which the Fifth Circuit has given much prompter effect to rights which the court concludes are clearly overdue. This is the granting of an injunction *pending appeal* by the court of appeals. Such injunctions are authorized by the all writs statute,[49] but it is a procedure that must be sparingly used.[50]

The *Lynd* case was considered by the court to be a proper case in which to utilize this procedural step. On August 11, 1960, the United States formally requested that the defendant Lynd, the registrar of Forest County, Mississippi, make his registration records available for inspection.[51] These efforts proving fruitless, the government, on January 19, 1961, filed an enforcement proceeding in the District Court for the Southern District of Mississippi. Although the court of appeals had, one year earlier, in *Dinkens v. Attorney General,*[52] expressly indicated the summary nature of such a proceeding, the trial judge entered no order with respect to this proceeding until, on July 6, 1961, a full-scale suit for injunction was filed by the United States alleging specific discriminatory conduct by Lynd against Negro citizens seeking to register.[53] Thereupon, following the filing of dilatory pleas by the respondent, the trial court, on February 15, 1962, dismissed the enforcement proceedings as "abandoned."[54] This was a short time after the court of appeals, in *Kennedy v. Bruce,*[55] had stated: "We reaffirm what we previously stated by adopting the opinion of Judge Johnson in the Dinkens case"[56] in which we stated that the relief "should have been granted as a matter of course."[57]

What then happened in the district court dealing with the effort of the United States to obtain a temporary injunction can best be shown by reference to the opinion of the Court of Appeals for the Fifth Circuit in *United States v. Lynd,* where it is said:

Notwithstanding the well-nigh impossible task of showing the true facts, the witnesses produced by the government proved without question that certain serious discriminations had taken place during the term of office of the defendant Lynd. At the conclusion of the presentation by the government of its evidence, the State and the defendant Lynd both reserved the right of cross examination and deferred such cross examination. The defendants then declined to put on any evidence but stated that it would take thirty days to be prepared to file answers to the amended complaint and to prepare for introducing defense witnesses. Thereupon the government moved the Court to issue a temporary injunction. Without doing so, and declining either to grant or refuse a temporary injunction, in terms, the court failed to comply with the motion and granted a recess of thirty days to permit the defendants to file their answer and to prepare for proving their defensive case.[58]

This portrays the situation at the time the court of appeals was requested to enter an extraordinary writ. The government took the position that in such circumstances the failure of the trial court to grant or deny the motion for a temporary injunction amounted to an order of denial, which would be an appealable order under the federal statute.[59] The court held that the "movant . . . was clearly entitled to have a ruling from the trial judge, and since he did not grant the order his action in declining to do so was in all respects a 'refusal' so as to satisfy . . . Section 1292, 28 U.S.C.A."[60]

The court then, after fully discussing the showing that had been made supporting the government's motion, said: "We conclude that the likelihood that the court's refusal to grant the temporary injunction will be reversed as an abuse of discretion is sufficiently great that we are warranted in protecting the rights of the Negro registrants pending a decision of this issue by this Court."[61]

Thereupon our court issued the injunction, effective immediately, that, in effect, required that the defendant Lynd process Negro applications in precisely the same manner as he had theretofore been processing white applications.[62]

This injunction in the *Lynd* case embodied another means of enforcement, which was being tentatively tried by some of the district courts in the Fifth Circuit. In addition to enjoining discriminatory treatment as to the future, the court recognizes that, with permanent registration, something need be done to correct the unequal treatment of the past. With substantially all of the white voters registered, it would be of little help to the Negroes in getting over the new high hurdle of requirements for the court simply to enjoin any further discriminatory treatment. Judge Johnson, in the Middle District of Alabama, had, as early as the fall of 1961, in the case of *United States v. Alabama*,[63] found that the board of registrars had discriminated against Negro applicants in several respects at a time when a very large majority of the qualified white persons of the county had been registered and practically no Negroes were on the rolls. In the meantime the Alabama requirements had been substantially increased.

Stating that the Civil Rights Act of 1960 contemplated that the courts utilize the full equitable powers possessed by them, the court, in its decree, enjoined the defendants from further discriminatory acts and, among other things, from

(3) applying or enforcing different qualification tests or standards to Negro applicants in Bullock County *from those applied and enforced since 1954* to other applicants in Bullock County. . . . (5) using a form of application or questionnaire different from or more stringent that that used *for registering persons in Bullock County prior to March 30, 1961.* (Emphasis added.)

Ordering the registrars to ignore the current state requirements for qualification to the extent that they had not been enforced against white applicants, is what has become known in the Fifth Circuit as "freezing." This principle is fully discussed in *United States v. Duke.*[64] The principle was applied in *United States v. Louisiana,* where it was said:

The cessation of prior discriminatory practices cannot justify the imposition of new and onerous requirements, theoretically applicable to all, but practically affecting primarily those who bore the brunt of previous discrimination. An appropriate remedy therefore should undo the results of past discrimination as well as prevent future inequality of treatment. A court of equity is not powerless to eradicate the effects of former discrimination. If it were, the State could seal into permanent existence the injustices of the past.[65]

When, by the spring of 1965, the Fifth Circuit had repeatedly held that a trial court was required, on a proper showing, to make a finding of pattern and practice and in such circumstances was required to enter an order freezing the standard to that which had been applied to white applicants for a reasonable period to permit Negro registrants to obtain equal treatment,[66] we pursued another new policy in order to cut down the time lag. I have already indicated that many officials determined that unless they were themselves subject to an order of a trial court they would not follow the clear precedent established by litigation arising even in the adjacent county. Just as our court had adopted the policy by the spring of 1965 of entering a summary order requiring a certain uniform plan of school desegregation, where cases came to us on appeal, in order that the schools would be affected by a proper application of the law during the 1965 fall term,[67] so we followed the practice of entering substantially uniform orders in several voters' rights cases in which the trial court had either failed to find a pattern and practice or had failed to enter an order freezing the previous standards.[68] After the passage of the Voting Rights Act of 1965, the orders also required that judgments to be entered by the trial court be subject to modification to the extent that the new law gave further and more explicit rights to Negro applicants.[69]

Again, following a practice developed in our court in the school desegregation cases,[70] the court adopted a procedural step to avoid any misunderstanding on the part of the trial court as to exactly what kind of injunctive order our court had decided was appropriate in the circumstances. More and more we took to framing the precise order to be entered upon remand. In the first place, in *United States v. Duke* we stated that "this Court will not attempt to frame the terms of the order to be issued by the trial court,"[71] but "strongly suggested"[72] what was to be included in that order. The court later, in the last appearance of *United States v. Lynd,* said, "the District Court is *directed* upon remand to enter *forthwith* the following judgment in this matter. . . ."[73] The opinion of this court then explicitly prescribed the order that was to be entered by the trial court.

The criticism by the states of Mississippi, Louisiana, and Alabama of application of the freezing principle was finally answered by the United States Supreme Court in *Louisiana v. United States,*[74] affirming the judgment of the three-judge district court.[75] The Supreme Court said:

> We bear in mind that the court has not merely the power but the duty to render a decree which will so far as possible eliminate the discriminatory effects of the past as well as bar like discrimination in the future.[76]

Although it is impossible to deal adequately with the subject in this lecture, the poll-tax amendment and poll-tax litigation must be mentioned in our discussion. The poll tax as a requirement to the right to vote in *federal elections* was eliminated by adoption of the Twenty-fourth Amendment to the Constitution.[77]

The Voting Rights Act of 1965 contained a finding that "the requirement of the payment of a poll tax as a precondition to voting . . . in some areas has the purpose or effect of denying persons the right to vote because of race or color."[78] It further directed the attorney general to institute "forthwith" actions to test the legality of the poll tax in the remaining four states in which it is still used in *state elections.* An attack was already under way in Virginia, and in late 1964 a three-judge district court there dismissed an attack brought by Negro citizens.[79] The dismissal was appealed, and the case was argued in the Supreme Court on February 1.* In the meantime, the attorney general filed suits in Mississippi, Virginia, Texas, and Alabama.[80]

Three-judge district courts in Texas and Alabama have entered judgments finding that the poll taxes in those states violate the rights of Negro citizens under the Fifteenth Amendment.[81] While there are factual differences in the nature of the legislative history behind the adoption of the poll-tax legislation in the several states, it is expected that the Supreme Court will resolve all of these issues during this term of Court.

Passage of the Voting Rights Act of 1965 appears, on the surface, to have mooted many of the troublesome questions that were continually before the district and appellate courts of the Fifth Circuit during the last five years. It not only abolished literacy tests and other devices as prerequisites to voting in all of the states of the Fifth Circuit in which these cases arose,[82] but it also provided for the designation by the attorney general of voting examiners with authority under the federal statute to place the names of applicants on the registration books without the taking of literacy tests. Throughout the states which were subject to the act, many county registrars immediately followed the terms of the new federal law, even while challenging its validity in the Supreme Court.[83] A very substantial number of registrations of Negro citizens resulted through regular application to the county registrars. In a speech in Atlanta on February 28, the attorney general of the United States stated that some 200,000 names had been added by the state registrars. There was also a substantial number whose names were placed on the books by the federal examiners. In the same speech Mr. Katzenbach said this number exceeded 100,000.[84] The mere pendency of the federal statute brought about an amendment to the Mississippi Constitution that eliminated substantially all of the criticized qualification requirements that had given rise to the many Mississippi voting rights suits referred to in this talk.[85]

On March 7 the Supreme Court sustained the constitutionality of the 1965 act.[86] We may optimistically anticipate that much of the turmoil and conflict over the rights of citizens to participate in this basic governmental function will now be eliminated.

* Ultimately, the Supreme Court held that the Virginia poll tax was unconstitutional. Harper v. Virginia Board of Elections, 383 U.S. 663 (1966). EDITOR'S NOTE.

Thus, the Fifteenth Amendment has now become a real part of the United States Constitution, partly through the intervention of federal courts by application of the Equal Protection Clause of the Fourteenth Amendment and by virtue of the express provisions of the Fifteenth Amendment,[87] and also through the action of Congress in implementing the second paragraph of the Fifteenth Amendment authorizing Congress to enact appropriate legislation to carry it into effect.

Both in legislative halls and in the courtrooms, putting flesh and blood on the bare bones of the Fifteenth Amendment has required a developing legal concept.

In the courts, it was first apparent that more speed was called for than could normally be achieved by the regular processing of trial and appeal. As we all know, laws are not self-executing. However, our whole society depends upon the reasonably ready acquiescence of the people to the rule of law. Either criminal sanctions for violation of the law or the natural respect of lawyers and laymen for the rule of *stare decisis* normally make it unnecessary for each person with a grievance to engage in a lawsuit to vindicate his rights. Lawyers do not ordinarily like to litigate principles of law already decided against them.

In the whole field of civil rights, however, in some of the states of the Fifth Judicial Circuit, the usual rules have not applied. In resisting change, especially in political and sociological areas, time is what counts. Another school year without compliance with the school desegration cases has often been considered by local boards a prize worth fighting for, and thus worth litigating for. In the area of voting rights, every election held without participation of Negro voters meant one more term in office for the beneficiary of the old system. There were no effective sanctions to coerce the reluctant official to take voluntary action to comply with what everyone knew was the law. Thus each school district and each county or parish became a separate unit to be dealt with unless it could be demonstrated that time was no longer on the side of the recalcitrant.

Prompt hearings in the district courts, accelerated settings of appeals in the appellate courts, and temporary relief by way of injunction when the law was clear finally made it plain that the prize of delay could no longer be won. Our court finally entered a number of summary reversals in school cases that pointed the district courts in the way they should go.[88] Also in voter rights cases, the court finally adopted a substantially uniform injunction to be entered on remand. These are the procedural remedies that have been shaped to meet the problem of enforcement.[89]

As stated in the opinion of our court in *United States v. Ward*,[90] the development of the relief finally agreed upon uniformly by the panels of the Court of Appeals for the Fifth Circuit was a normal development of the principles of equity. There we said:

> Like decisions in other fields, this was but new material out of which, with much coming later, and in the best Anglo-American juridical tradition, we synthesize principles and sanctions which experience demonstrates are needed. This experience has been rich, abundant in volume, and instructive.[91]

It is an interesting, but frequently overlooked, fact that no responsible public official has, within the last decade, in even the most race-conscious area of the country, been heard to say that there can be any justification for denying the right of a Negro to vote simply because of race. This is quite different from the stand taken by nearly every public official in the areas of the Old South early in the last decade that denial of equal use of public facilities on account of race was legally permissible and was fully justified. Thus, we have much reason to hope, now that it has been demonstrated beyond peradventure that Negroes *have* been denied the right to vote on account of race, that a quicker public acquiescence to the new order may follow.

Once a man concedes that every qualified person should be entitled to vote, he has little to fall back on in support of his local officials when it is demonstrated beyond doubt that Negro school teachers and school principals, and even college professors with baccalaureate and advanced degrees, have been denied the right to register to vote, while illiterate white persons have been added to the rolls. Once the absolute block to Negro registration falls, then it becomes merely a matter of degree, and it may be hoped that, facing equal application of qualification tests for the future, local sentiment will support the general trend in the rest of the United States toward universal suffrage with minimal qualifications.

Moreover, many people who have been exposed to the troublesome problems occurring in this struggle believe that much has been learned by the members of each race about those of the other race. As a result, a considerable degree of understanding has developed between them. It is not certain that even in those counties in which a large majority of the registered voters are now Negro, the newly enfranchised group will use the power in a punitive manner or that they will immediately elect a complete slate of Negro officials. According to press reports, the Negro citizen with the vote is planning to make a careful and selective use of his newly found power. This is not to suggest that it is either likely or desirable that Negro citizens should not, as do other citizens, vote at the ballot box for those officials and measures that they deem to be for their best interest.

Many observers of the period who have been most involved in the matters which I have discussed have the optimistic feeling that not only the Negro citizens, but the white citizens as well, of the Old South will profit from a recognition at last that the Fifteenth Amendment is just as much a part of the Constitution as is the rest of that great document. Those who share this view agree with a statement made by Ralph McGill, publisher of the *Atlanta Constitution*, that:

> The Civil Rights Act of 1964 with the reapportionment "One Man, One Vote" decision of the Supreme Court, is an Emancipation Act for the South and its politicians. The latter no longer have to truckle to the prejudices of race.[92]

Abe Fortas

Equal Rights—for Whom?

I ask you to proceed with me from analysis to exploration—from consideration of problems that have ripened to those which are in the early stages of liveliness. In a sense, we shall not talk in terms of new doctrines, but of old doctrines and their applicability to new people. We shall consider a process that has been with us since the dawn of man's history—a process which reflects the political and spiritual aspirations of man. This process is the diffusion of liberty, freedom, and opportunity from the few to the many—the democratization of human dignity. Man's organized life has been aimed at this. His progress toward the target has been constant, even if erratic. Now, at last, in some countries of the world, achievement of the goal of a decent life for all people is in sight.

In our own nation the progress toward freedom for all and equality of status has not been in a straight line. It is typical of our nation's people and its institutions that we have progressed in mighty fits and powerful starts, which have been followed by long periods of rest. We made little progress toward the goal, for example, in the period between the adoption of the Bill of Rights amendments to the Constitution and the eve of the Civil War. We made little visible advance during the period from the end of the Civil War and the adoption of the great Civil War amendments and the civil rights statutes, to the time of Franklin Roosevelt and the New Deal. Each of these was a period of relatively little movement toward achievement of the goal of universal democracy. In a sense, however, each was also a period of consolidation of the earlier advance and of preparation for the next.

We are now again involved in a gigantic forward thrust toward this magnificent objective. In the past few years, many mansions in the nation's house have been opened to those who were heretofore ex-

Justice Fortas's lecture was delivered on March 29, 1967 and appeared in 42 N.Y.U.L. Rev. 401 (1967).

cluded. We have declared that the doors to the schoolhouse are open to all; the doors to the voting booth; to libraries and parks, and to jobs and training and opportunity. We have, in effect, issued tickets of admission to participation in our society—in its material and spiritual rewards, and also in its work.

Now we are involved in the formidable, revolutionary task of implementing these declarations—of investing them with reality.

In the law's own house, we have turned a searchlight upon its historic professions of equality to all and justice for all. The disclosures have proved the current poignancy of Anatole France's well-known comment that "the law, in its majestic equality, forbids the rich as well as the poor to sleep under bridges, to beg in the streets, and to steal bread." We have found that the poor as well as the rich are equally entitled to retain Cravath, Swaine & Moore or Arnold & Porter or Edward Bennett Williams; that the poor, equally with the rich, have a right to buy a transcript of the evidence in their trial for purposes of appeal; and that a destitute, friendless Negro is entitled, equally with the pillar of the community, to make clear to the police, in a firm but dignified way, of course, that he will not answer their questions, but will exercise his precious right to remain mute.

But it is the mark of greatness of this age that we have concluded that this is not enough—that it is not enough that these rights exist in theory, like pie in the sky or the smile of the Cheshire cat. It has been our *national* decision that these rights must be made realities, that equality in theory is not enough.

It is fascinating, although disconcerting to some, that the first and fundamental breakthrough in various categories of revolutionary progress has been made by the courts—and specifically the Supreme Court of the United States. It was the great *Brown v. Board of Education* decision in 1954 that began the forward thrust. It was followed by a series of court decisions which opened the polling places and the parks and the libraries to all of our people, and by enactment of a number of laws which constitute a new and greater charter of liberty and democracy for our people, and—perhaps of no less importance— a new sensitivity and awareness of the American people with respect to the rights of their fellow citizens.

In the administration of criminal justice, it has again been the courts which have sparked the move toward equality in fact. Here, too, a number of fundamental decisions have infused with strength and practical meaning the ancient principle that the state owes to the individual the duty to proceed in strict accordance with the law, however humble the individual and regardless of the nature of the accusation against him. These decisions have reiterated the principle that the state must obey the rule books, with full deference to the individual's rights and dignity—that the state as well as the individual is bound by the letter and the spirit of the law. We have given substance and reality to this principle by insisting that counsel be furnished to the poor—because the poor man without counsel is at the mercy of the state! We have insisted that he be supplied with means for appeal; that he be warned of his rights before they are obliterated; and that he be shielded from arbitary arrest and search. In short, we have insisted that the precious rights of the individual, which have been won at the cost of much blood and heroism, must be preserved in fact as well as in theory.

Let me emphasize that in my view these decisions, in their essence and without reference to differences as to detail, are not novelties or inventions. They proceed from the meaning and mandate of the Constitution. They are not judicial grafts upon the constitutional tree. They are not distortions or foreign importations. After all, the Constitution does say that no person shall be deprived of life, liberty, or property without due process of law; that no person shall be compelled in any criminal case to be a witness against himself; that no state shall abridge the privileges or immunities of citizens or deny to any person the equal protection of the laws—these are words of legal mandate, which also set moral and legal and political standards. It is these standards which we, generation by generation, are commanded to realize—to realize to the best of our ability from time to time as our ethical sense and political ideals develop and our conception of their meaning expands. These great admonitions are not codes of conduct. They are not codifications of the practice of the eighteenth and nineteenth centuries. As Learned Hand said, they are "majestic generalities."

As Marshall so clearly recognized, it was a *Constitution* that had been written, a set of principles. In a sense, it was a codification of the greatest moral and ethical principles of the times, gleaned by men of learning and wisdom from the sages of the past, their religious training, and their knowledge of political theory; these were principles stated in response to the needs of the people for protection against the power of the state, and in response to the people's aspirations for equality, dignity, and freedom.

So it is that each generation is required again to take stock. Its task is not to see whether it is replicating, as in a mirror, the habits and customs of our forefathers. Its job is to assure, as fully as possible, that its practices incorporate as fully as its political and ethical understanding permit the basic and total meaning of these magnificent precepts of our Constitution. It is the glory of this generation—its pride and claim to greatness—that we have in fact responded to the constitutional imperative and that we have answered the summons of our Constitution to the never-ending task of fulfillment of its noble commands.

Let me emphasize the obvious fact that the response of our generation to the mandate of the great libertarian principles of our Constitution did not spring, full-blown, from the mind and pen of the Supreme Court. Nor is it confined to the Court. The momentum for the breakthrough has been accumulating for many years. It has been gathering its force in many tributaries until the pressure of their flow produced a response in the nation's mainstream. These pressures for progress have come from the improvement, however modest, in the educational and economic level of the Negroes and others at the bottom of our society; from the growth of expectations due to urban migration; from the expansion of the area of feasible national action as a result of economic growth and affluence; from the participation by Negroes and the poor in labor unions and the participation by Negroes in the armed forces on a nonsegregated basis; and from the emergence, however erratic and limited, of effective Negro leadership. All of these and many other factors induced the restlessness and the ferment which accumulatively led to the current forward thrust.

These revolutionary changes have profoundly affected the realities of American constitutionalism. In a sense, we are witnessing the gradual reduction of the category of constitutional nonpersons. One may look all through the Constitution and yet not find any reference to nonpersons. But if one is honest about our constitutional system, one cannot pretend that the rights guaranteed by the Constitution have been extended to all persons. Accordingly, one is tempted to suggest the existence of a category of nonpersons or its reasonable facsimile. Let me give you a few simple illustrations. In the Constitution itself, the right to habeas corpus was assured, and bills of attainder and ex post facto laws were outlawed. The Bill of Rights was ratified in 1791. It guaranteed "to the people" the right to be secure against unreasonable searches and seizures. It provided that no person should be held to answer for infamous crime except on presentment or indictment; nor be put in double jeopardy; nor be deprived of life, liberty, or property without due process of law. But it was not until after the Civil War that these provisions were generally accepted as applying to slaves, or even to free descendants of slaves.[1] They were nonpersons. Similarly, women occupied the position of nonpersons for many purposes. Not until 1920 were they given a federal constitutional right to vote, and then it required a constitutional amendment. In some states and for some purposes, they are still nonpersons.[2] The American Indian is another—so far as the eye can observe—who for many purposes in many areas is still treated as a nonperson.[3]

At common law, children were treated as persons. Children under the age of seven, it was held, were incapable of criminal intent and therefore could not be prosecuted for offenses. Children above that age were treated as adults. They were given the same legal protections and the same punishments as adults. This system prevailed, with various modifications, in this country until the early part of the twentieth century.[4] The constitutional guarantees were equally applicable to juvenile offenders and to adults. But then, a tidal wave of reform, put in motion by such persons as Judge Julian Mack and the leaders of the Jane Addams School, resulted in a national outcry against the resulting barbarism, as it appeared to them to be, of treating children and juveniles the same as adults. So, in all of the jurisdictions under the American flag, separate systems of courts and separate sets of principles were devised for juveniles, usually including those up to eighteen years of age.

There were many consequences of this reform, one of which was that juveniles became nonpersons in the sense that the constitutional guarantees of jury trial, right to counsel, right to confront accusers, right to bail, privilege against self-incrimination and so forth have not been available to them. In many states, a juvenile accused of "delinquency" as a result of an alleged rape, murder, housebreaking, armed robbery, or similar offense has been substantially at the mercy of police, probation officers, and the juvenile court judge, without the rights which the Constitution guarantees to hardened criminals on trial in adult courts.[5]

This nonperson status of juveniles has provided a pretty good test of the current theory that the application of constitutional principles to those arrested and accused of crime is a prime cause of its incidence—that if the police were only unshackled and the state and trial courts were only freed of the repressive rules of the Constitution as interpreted by the Supreme Court, the rate of crime would sharply drop.

They have had a free hand in respect of juveniles. The Constitution and the Supreme Court have not touched the process.[6] At the time of this writing, the Supreme Court has decided only one case involving the juvenile delinquency process, *Kent v. United States*,[7] and that case involved a relatively narrow point of construction of a District of Columbia statute. The police could arrest and interrogate and search with abandon, and there is evidence that they did so.[8] They could obtain confessions without the *Miranda* warnings,[9] and they did so.[10] The juveniles could be and were tried without the benefit of appointed counsel.[11] Generally, they could not appeal, so that the Supreme Court's decisions in *Griffin v. Illinois*[12] and *Douglas v. California*[13] did not stand in the path of eliminating crime.

But whatever the reason may be, the fact is that nonapplication of the Constitution's principles and the total abstention of the Supreme Court have not eliminated juvenile offenses. On the contrary, the facts show that these offenses—committed by those treated as constitutional nonpersons and outside of the much criticized shelter of constitutional protections—have multiplied at a rate that is proportionately greater than that of adults. Here are some of the figures, as compiled by the President's National Crime Commission:[14]

Between 1960 and 1965, the number of arrests of persons under eighteen for willful homicide, rape, robbery, aggravated assault, larceny, burglary, and motor vehicle theft has jumped 52 percent. Arrests of persons eighteen and over for these offenses rose only 20 percent.

In 1965, one-half of all arrests for serious property offenses were of persons under eighteen.

Juveniles accounted for one-fifth of all arrests for serious crimes. The rate of recidivism continues to increase. For example, in fiscal 1966, about 66 percent of the sixteen- and seventeen-year-old juveniles referred to the Juvenile Court in the District of Columbia had been there before. In 1965, 42 percent had been referred at least twice before.[15]

At this point in our discussion, then, perhaps we may observe with some confidence that there are indeed instances under our Constitution where the term "person" has not meant everybody; where this seemingly universal term has not been given universal application;

that there have been and are nonpersons in our constitutional scheme—nonpersons for all or some purposes; that, as evidenced in the case of women, slaves, and to some extent American Indians, extending the constitutional guarantees to nonpersons does not result in disaster; and that—as evidenced by the case of juveniles—the denial of constitutional guarantees and protections does not necessarily result in improved law observance.*

These modest conclusions, I trust, do not obscure my basic point—that it is our mission, America's commitment to the founders of its Constitution, steadily, relentlessly, and resourcefully to give full scope, and not narrow range, to the coverage of the Constitution's statement of basic rights and principles—to move, wisely but insistently, toward the achievement of real equality, and to the elimination of the category of nonpersons. This is our commitment—our challenge—and, I hope, our destined future.

The battleground has shifted from generation to generation. We are far from having validated the full constitutional Bill of Rights with respect to any of our people except, possibly, white, male, adult Americans who are in reasonably good economic health. For these, our achievements have been spectacular. But others remain, as of this moment of time, in totality or, in particular, constitutional nonpersons.

In the last few years, scholars have called attention to the problems, in this respect, which arise in relation to these persons in our population who are dependent upon government bounty for their livelihood. This category includes the poorest of the poor: those who are entirely dependent upon welfare payments, as well as those who are recipients of public assistance in various categories, such as aid to families with dependent children. It also includes those who are beneficiaries of public housing programs for the lower income groups, and of such forms of public assistance as aid to the disabled or the aged.

There are millions of people in these categories.[16] The problems they present are complicated by the fact that a large percentage of them must bear the burden of being Negro as well as the weight of poverty. If we look, however, merely to the impact of poverty upon their access to constitutional rights, we are forced to agree that the time has come for major reappraisal.

* In In re Gault, 387 U.S. 1 (1967), the Supreme Court held that the Constitution guaranteed due process rights to juveniles accused of delinquency. EDITOR'S NOTE.

Our acceptance of a measure of state responsibility for the poor dates back to the Poor Laws of Tudor England.[17] But from the earliest times to the present, the poor have been indiscriminately classed as vagrants, vagabonds, and rogues. They have been regarded as offending by their "mere existence." They have been considered a "moral pestilence." The Articles of Confederation denied "paupers, vagabonds, and fugitives from justice" the privileges and immunities of citizenship and the right to move from state to state.[18] Until the very recent past it was assumed, with little protest, that the indigent were for many purposes outside of the scope of the Bill of Rights.[19] Under the common law and the laws of the states, they could be seized and jailed because of their status as poverty-stricken.[20] The guarantees of the right to security of the person and of their abode and effects were remote from them. They were, indeed, nonpersons.

In 1837, in *City of New York v. Miln*,[21] the United States Supreme Court had occasion to consider the status of paupers. New York had passed legislation whose purpose was to bar poor persons from entering the state. The Court upheld this legislation as a valid exercise of the state's police power, saying:

We think it as competent and as necessary for a state to provide precautionary measures against the moral pestilence of paupers, vagabonds, and possibly convicts; as it is to guard against the physical pestilence, which may arise from unsound and infectious articles. . . .[22]

It was not until 1941, in *Edwards v. California*,[23] that the Court repudiated this view. In an opinion by Justice James F. Byrnes, the Court held that "poverty and immorality are not synonymous."[24] It decided that California's effort to prevent indigent persons from entering the state was an unconstitutional burden on interstate commerce. In a great concurring opinion, Justice Robert H. Jackson had this to say:

Does "indigence" . . . constitute a basis for restricting the freedom of a citizen, as crime or contagion warrants its restriction? We should say now, and in no uncertain terms, that a man's mere property status, without more, cannot be used by a state to test, qualify, or limit his rights as a citizen of the United States. "Indigence" in itself is neither a source of rights nor a basis for denying them. The mere state of being without funds is a neutral fact—constitutionally an irrelevance, like race, creed, or color.[25]

Since that time, the Court has had occasion to consider Mr. Justice Jackson's challenge only in the context of the criminal process. In this field, the Court has taken unequivocal positions in line with Jackson's views. *Griffin v. Illinois*,[26] in 1956, held that the Equal Protection Clause required the state to provide equal access to its appellate courts by furnishing a trial transcript at its own expense to indigents who had been convicted of crime. In 1963, in *Gideon v. Wainwright*,[27] the Court, harking back to the famous *Scottsboro*[28] case decided in 1932, held that the Constitution requires states to furnish counsel to indigent defendants accused of committing a substantial offense.[29]

The significance of these cases, in terms of our national philosophy, goes beyond the criminal law. Apart from their specific meaning, in terms of vindicating the integrity and morality of criminal justice, they stand for the proposition that the state may be obligated in some situations to bridge the gap which indigency has created between a person and his constitutional rights. They represent a refusal to accept the fact of poverty as relieving the state from an affirmative duty to assure that all persons have access to constitutional rights. They request the state to do whatever is necessary, even if it means spending state funds, to make constitutional rights a living reality for everyone. In *Griffin v. Illinois*, Mr. Justice Harlan, dissenting, bluntly stated the point. He said that "the Court thus holds that, at least in this area of criminal appeals, the Equal Protection Clause imposes on the States an affirmative duty to lift the handicaps flowing from differences in economic circumstances."[30] My Brother Harlan registered his disapproval of this principle in his customary lucid and logical manner.

But these cases certainly do not decide the broader issues which are raised by the substance and administration of welfare laws and other legislation affecting the poor. They are in a somewhat special category. The Constitution contains specific language relating to criminal justice, such as the guarantees of due process of law and the right to counsel; the state is an adversary in these proceedings, and, it may be argued, has a special duty to see that the citizen whose liberty it has placed in jeopardy is provided with the means to defend himself; and, after all, the courts have a special obligation and special mandate to assure that rights of parties in the criminal process are realized in fact.

But what of the situations where, historically, the state's action has been regarded as an exercise of grace—the giving of bounty? Must the state see to it that the constitutional guarantees available to "persons" are safeguarded in this process? And beyond this, is a person entitled by the unwritten social compact, or by the Constitution, to state support if he is indigent? Does he have a right to welfare payments? To subsidized housing? To medical care? These are basic questions which are now receiving fruitful attention at many leading institutions of learning.[31]

There is no room for doubt that the process of welfare administration, as we know it, has been disfigured by practices which, in any other context, by common consent, would not be tolerated. One state's application of the "suitable home" requirement—it found homes containing illegitimate children to be "unsuitable" and cut off all benefits—reached the proportions of a major scandal in 1961 and 1962, inducing the federal government to adopt corrective directions.[32] So-called midnight welfare searches intended to disclose whether a mother receiving aid for her dependent children has a "man in the house," and sometimes conducted as though the Fourth Amendment did not exist, have produced a swelling stream of protest[33]—and tentative movement toward reform.[34] Loyalty oaths have been required of welfare recipients.[35] Residence requirements and laws for the removal of indigents to their state of origin remain on the books.[36] Residents of public housing accommodations are subjected to inquiries and surveillance concerning their morals and private life, on the theory that this is a permissible condition for the receipt of the benefits of public housing.[37] They are kept on a short string, by month-to-month tenure. At least until a regulation was recently adopted by the Department of Housing and Urban Development, it was thought that they could be evicted without any statement of reasons.[38]

Whether or not these practices affront explicit constitutional rights and, if so, whether there is a remedy for the invasion or denial of the guarantees available to the nonindigent, will undoubtedly be the subjects of litigation for some time to come.[39] But these are not the only, or even the basic, issues. The Constitution is more than a set of precepts which can be enforced in the courts. It is more than a chart for litigation—it is a way of life; a national philosophy; a social theory; a political ethic; and a guide to national morality. We must gauge national conduct not merely by the test of whether it can survive court attack in the face of the imperative words of the Constitution; but whether the conduct comports with and advances the achievement of the magnificent purposes and ideals of the Constitution.[40]

For example: It is of course true that the state is entitled to—it must—provide reasonable standards of eligibility and must protect against fraud in the administration of these programs. No sensible person would dispute this. But it does not follow that, because of this necessity, the state is entitled to treat the recipients of its bounty as nonpersons in a constitutional sense; as persons who have, in return for welfare payments, surrendered to the state's social workers their constitutional rights to privacy and personal security. Certainly, as provisions for notice and hearing under the Social Security Act and the rules of some states illustrate,[41] there are available techniques for administering welfare and public housing laws that do not involve destructive assaults upon human values. Certainly, there are reasonable ways reasonably to investigate short of midnight raids.

Indeed, as one reads the accumulating literature on the subject, one may well conclude that much of the surveillance and many of the conditions now attached to the receipt of state bounty serve no rational purpose. Some of them, it seems clear, are nothing more than expressions of disapproval and disdain, sometimes with racial overtones. Some of the practices incident to welfare administration are of more interest to psychiatrists than utility to the objectives of the program. There is little evidence that they serve to encourage morality, thrift, chastity, and industriousness. The search for the "phantom father," for example, for a man—any man—whose presence in the household can justify the termination of welfare payments to the mother and children, suggests a motivation other than concern for the state or federal fisc.[42] It is much more suggestive of the days when the stocks and the pillory and public disgrace were considered suitable for the woman caught in illicit love.

But whatever the broader and more general balance of considerations may be with respect to the policy of attaching various types of conditions to welfare payments and public bounty,[43] it seems to me that there is this clear imperative: There is not—there cannot be—any excuse for a continuation of needless, heedless disregard of constitutional mandates or precepts in the administration of welfare programs. We must not wait upon the outcome of litigation testing constitutionality by the somewhat narrow tests of judicial scrutiny. The value at stake is not constitutionality as determined in the law courts, but constitutionality in the broad sense of the American ideal.

We must, finally and totally, relinquish the notion that recipients of public assistance are constitutional nonpersons. As Mr. Justice Jackson said, "[A] man's mere property status, without more, cannot be used by a state to test, qualify, or limit his rights as a citizen of the

United States."[44] We need not go so far as to embrace the argument that the state has a constitutional duty to provide its indigent citizens with support;[45] but if the state chooses to do so, it must proceed with careful regard to the rights of the recipients, for they, too, are persons within our constitutional scheme. Indeed, it may be that in the final analysis, a nation is measured—perhaps its future is determined—not by the protection which its institutions afford to the rich and strong, but by the meticulous care with which the rights of the weak and humble are safeguarded.*

We owe a great debt to those who have worked in the vineyard of welfare during all these years of its neglect. Fresh appraisal, critical re-examination in light of higher standards, tends, as always, to center upon deficiencies instead of virtues. It would, of course, be a monstrous injustice to those in the front lines of the welfare program—the case workers, psychologists and sociologists, and administrators. We all know that many, perhaps most, of these people are underpaid and overworked, and are frequently themselves prisoners of a system not of their own making.

But I do call upon all of those involved—from lawyers and judges to welfare workers and planners, legislators and taxpayers—to take a fresh look at these problems. The time is long past since the poor were beyond the pale of civilized procedure. In one way or another, our democratic ideals are being applied to more and more areas of real life. On the recipient's part, there is a revolution of hope, of rising expectations, which will not be denied. The poor are banging on the door of the great society. They cannot be excluded.

On the part of scholars, lawyers, and—increasingly—courts, there is a growing determination to open that door and to raise the level of human dignity which obtains in the lowliest sector of our society. In our nation, we as lawyers, legal scholars, and researchers must take the lead in this process.

---

* In Goldberg v. Kelly, 397 U.S. 254, 255 (1970), the Supreme Court held that it was an unconstitutional denial of a welfare recipient's due process rights to stop relief payments "without affording him an opportunity for an evidentiary hearing." The Court noted that "[i]t may be more realistic . . . to regard welfare entitlements more like property rights than a 'gratuity.'" *Id.* at 262 n.8. Thus, the government may not arbitrarily deprive a citizen of welfare benefits, once the state has chosen to confer them, without observing minimum standards of due process. Nevertheless, some constitutional protections are still denied to citizens on public relief. For example, the Supreme Court has held the Fourth Amendment requirements do *not* apply to warrantless inspections of the homes of welfare recipients. Wyman v. James, 400 U.S. 309 (1971). EDITOR'S NOTE.

Thurgood Marshall

Group Action in the Pursuit of Justice

I hope to explain why I believe that organized groups are becoming increasingly necessary in the pursuit of justice. I will also explore the implications that this new development has for the legal profession.

This theme would seem to call, first, for a definition of those rights and liberties which are encompassed by the term "justice." I do not intend to dwell on this point, however. For me at least, justice means more than the traditional concepts embodied in the amendments to our Constitution. True justice requires that the ideals expressed in those amendments be translated into economic and social progress for all of our people.

But we must not let definitional problems detain us here. For there can be no justice—justice in the true sense of the word—until the Bill of Rights and the Civil War amendments, together with the broader ideals they embody, become more than mere abstract expressions. From the perspective of history, we can see that the crucial task is not so much to define our rights and liberties, but to establish institutions which can make the principles embodied in our Constitution meaningful in the lives of ordinary citizens. Only in this way can the solemn declarations embodied in that document be translated into justice. No matter how solemn and profound the declarations of principle contained in our charter of government, no matter how dedicated and independent our judiciary, true justice can only be obtained through the actions of committed individuals, individuals acting both independently and through organized groups.

In the past several decades, committed members of the bar have played a decisive roll in reviving the concepts of justice embodied in the Bill of Rights and in our other constitutional guarantees. We shall have occasion to refer to some of their efforts in a moment. Although

Justice Marshall's lecture was delivered on April 17, 1969 and appeared in 44 N.Y.U.L. Rev. 661 (1969).

their efforts were a significant factor in promoting the cause of justice, my message is that committed action on the part of individual members of the bar will not be enough to consolidate the gains of the past or to accomplish the goals of the future. As we move into the future, the role formerly filled for the most part by individuals will have to be filled to an increasingly large degree by organized group practice. If we are to move from a declaration of rights to their implementation, especially with regard to the politically and economically underprivileged, large numbers of lawyers are needed at the working level. This need for lawyers and supporting personnel cannot be met by individual effort; the task is simply too great. The need can be met only in an organized way.

My message can be aptly illustrated by the history of the Civil War amendments, a history in which I was in recent years fortunate enough to have played a small part. That history demonstrates that mere declarations of rights have not been sufficient to secure justice. It further illustrates that true progress can only be made by organized effort. The rights guaranteed by our Constitution are not self-enforcing; they can be made meaningful only by legislative or judicial action. As we shall see, legislation does not pass itself and the courts cannot act in the absence of a controversy. Organized, committed effort is necessary to promote legislation and institute legal action on any significant scale.

The Fourteenth Amendment, like the Bill of Rights, was a declaration of principle. It enshrined into national law the principles of freedom and equality which an earlier generation had announced in more abstract form in the Declaration of Independence. The framers of the Fourteenth Amendment set their sights high. They spoke during the ratification debates in broad, general terms.[1] The nation was to be given the power to make certain that the fundamental rights of all individuals were respected. It was not a time for defining those rights with any precision; it was a time for creating institutions which would guarantee their maintenance. Without the power to enforce basic human rights, they would become mere paper promises. But the terms of the amendment, however powerful they may seem, could mean little without activism in the pursuit of justice. Each of the two most important sections of the amendment[2] shared the same deceptive positivism; both seemed to solve problems, while they actually only provided tools for the proper solutions.

Section one sets forth the basic ideals of 1868 in positive form. It is self-executing on its face and declaratory in language. Various phrases were used to describe, in their different and overlapping aspects, the fundamental rights which were to be guaranteed to all men—privileges and immunities of citizens of the United States; life, liberty, and property; equal protection of the law, As Senator Howard of Michigan put it during the ratification debates, the language of the amendment "establishes equality before the law, and it gives to the humblest, the poorest, the most despised of the race the same rights and the same protection before the law as it gives to the most power-ful, the most wealthy, or the most haughty."[3]

This self-executing language is, however, deceiving. Its positive form does not guarantee automatic enforcement. The courts, natu-rally enough, exercise the power in cases brought before them to de-cree when the rights guaranteed by the amendment have been infringed. But these rights cannot be enforced unless those who pos-sess them know they exist and are given the legal means to vindicate them. Without the commitment of the bar, those protected by the amendment will ordinarily possess neither the knowledge nor the skills needed to make the promises of the amendment meaningful. Without the commitment of large numbers of lawyers, of "private attorneys-general"[4] if you will, the amendment will mean nothing.

Section 5 of the Fourteenth Amendment is even more dependent for its enforcement upon the active, dedicated work of committed in-dividuals and groups. All it does is grant legislative power. The grant is broad, and the power potentially of great importance.[5] Although the courts were left as the last resort for individuals who felt their in-dividual rights were being infringed, only the legislature could act more generally. The final protection of the basic rights granted by the amendment was, in effect, to be democracy itself; through participa-tion in democracy, those formerly deprived of their rights would help insure their own future equality.

But the hopes of the framers were soon dashed. From the 1870s to the 1950s not a single civil rights measure was placed on the statute books. Without active support for the promises of 1868, the rights granted by the amendment fell from sight and became historical anachronisms. Section 5, its promises and its power for good, was for-gotten.

A quick glance through the history of the century which separates us from 1868 confirms this view. Although three constitutional amendments and four important civil rights bills were passed in the decade following the Civil War, the postwar radical fervor soon died. The judicial decisions of the era only reflected social attitudes as they evidenced the rapid decline of the Fourteenth Amendment as a declaration of justice and equality.

In the *Slaughterhouse Cases*,[6] decided in 1873, the Court echoed the framers and read the amendment as a declaration of "the freedom of the slave race, the security and firm establishment of that freedom, and the protection of the newly-made freeman and citizen from the oppressions of those who had formerly exercised unlimited dominion over him."[7] So sure was the Court of the great purposes for which the amendment was enacted that it explicitly doubted whether the amendment spoke to any problem but racial discrimination.[8] Only the dissents foreshadowed what was too soon to come—the incorporation of *laissez-faire* economics into the Fourteenth Amendment.[9]

For a while, it seemed that the Court meant what it had said in the *Slaughterhouse Cases*. In 1880, a series of state jury laws was found in conflict with the Civil Rights Act of 1875.[10] The language of the Court in these decisions was broad enough to encompas any kind of racial discrimination.[11]

But Reconstruction, already moribund, died with the Compromise of 1877.[12] The attention of both Republicans and Democrats turned to the dominant themes of the day—economic expansion and the nation's surge westward. Negroes could no longer seek help through the political process—all eyes were turned elsewhere. It was thus no surprise in 1883 when the Supreme Court voided the public accommodations sections of the Civil Rights Act of 1875 in an opinion which spelled an end to the great promises of the Fourteenth Amendment.[13] Only the first Justice Harlan foresaw the future, as he warned that "the recent amendments [will become] splendid baubles, thrown out to delude those who deserved fair and generous treatment at the hands of the nation."[14] But the nation was not listening.

While the attention of the nation was directed elsewhere, the South was undergoing a minor revolution of its own. The political structure, thrown into disarray by Reconstruction and its rather abrupt end, was stabilizing in favor of white supremacy. The southern states were seemingly unaware of the Civil War amendments and sought to ensure the perpetuation of that supremacy through legislation—the infamous "Jim Crow laws." The laws seemed blatant violations of the Fourteenth Amendment, and they called out for challenge—a challenge that was not long in coming. But the result of that challenge dealt the basic principles of the Fourteenth Amendment a staggering blow—a blow from which it took sixty years to recover fully.

The state legislature which enacted the segregation statute challenged in 1896 in *Plessy v. Ferguson*[15] ironically included a number of Negroes.[16] In addition, the challenge was at least partially motivated by economic reasons—the railroad found the cost of separate "Jim Crow" cars unduly high. The challenge was in vain. The Court was simply not interested—equal meant equal—it did not mean together. Again, only Justice Harlan called for an application of the spirit of the Fourteenth Amendment.[17]

The states took their cue from *Plessy*. Separation of the races soon became firmly entrenched in the South, and elsewhere for that matter. "Jim Crow" pervaded every aspect of life—even homes for the blind were segregated. Challenges were few and sporadic; and when they succeeded, the states reenacted the same scheme in different forms. Their ingenuity was certainly not taxed. Again, through the first two and a half decades of this century, the minds of the nation and the nation's lawyers and legislators were largely elsewhere, although the next two decades did see a weak but steady legal attack on racial discrimination. The situation was such that in the 1940s one commentator said:

> There is no power in the world—not even in all the mechanized armies of the earth . . . which could now force Southern white people to the abandonment of the principle of social segregation.[18]

And yet, segregation and its incidents, while still with us, are rapidly becoming a thing of the past. What happened? The change was not imposed by mechanized armies. It was not even prompted by the states or by federal legislation. It came from the private citizen, the citizen who believed that equal protection meant just that—the citizen who, with the assistance of those lawyers who still believed in the promise of justice and equality, never gave up the fight against the relics of slavery. The fight has been long, and the targets many. The turning point was of course *Brown v. Board of Education*,[19] whose story is familiar.[20] During the period since 1954, law after law has been struck down, and the tactics of delay are now being met head-on. New life has been breathed into the Civil War amendments and enactments.[21] The fight to reestablish the self-executing sections of the Fourteenth Amendment reawakened the legislatures to their powers, under both the Civil War amendments and other parts of the Constitution as well, to establish racial justice in the land. The acts are familiar, from the Civil Rights Acts of 1957 through the Open-Housing Act of 1968.

The spirit of justice was not limited to racial discrimination. The germ planted was infectious and has spread. It is certainly not an exaggeration to say that the concern for the rights of the criminally accused and for the economically disadvantaged has come in part from the lessons learned in the fight against discrimination. Today, the legislatures, the courts, the bar, and the people of this country are demonstrating a concern for fairness and justice unparalleled in the history of our nation.

The history of the Civil War amendments demonstrates quite clearly, I think, the necessity for committed action. It also demonstrates the second, and most important aspect of my message—that individual effort is not enough to secure justice. Today, even more than in the past, only organized action can hope to insure that the concept of justice remains meaningful to all of our people.

Until only a few decades ago, the efforts to enforce the guarantees of the Fourteenth Amendment and the other post–Civil War enactments were sporadic and largely defensive in nature. It was not until the rudiments of organization were applied to the problem that significant progress was made. Much of that progress was made by the NAACP, an organization I had the honor of being associated with for many years. Its example can be instructive.

During the early period of its existence, the NAACP participated in several cases that resulted in striking down discriminatory legislation. However, it was not until the 1930s that the seeds of significant progress were sown. At that time, the organization developed a conscious program of legal action designed to eliminate discrimination and inequality. The financial and human resources that were funnelled into this program were in large part responsible for recent successes in striking down discriminatory laws and practices. Similar examples could be multiplied. But whichever group you examine, one thing becomes evident: the organized and committed effort of groups of this sort has been of immeasurable importance in making our constitutional guarantees meaningful.

The concept of justice is, however, not a static one. Our tactics must be revised to suit the times. The needs are many and obvious. In traditional terms, there are of course the continuing problems of criminal and racial justice. Perhaps more significant, however, are the problems peculiar to the economically and socially disadvantaged. Lawyers have long spoken for the other segments of our society, both in court and in the legislatures. But now who is to speak for the poor, the disadvantaged, and these days, for the ordinary consumer?

I think the thrust of my argument thus far makes the answer clear. The goals of economic and social justice, like the goal of racial justice, can only be achieved through committed effort. All segments of society are, of course, essential to this effort, but one of the most effective contributions will be that made by lawyers. The brief history I have outlined makes another thing clear. Effective response to the problems facing our society today requires that the contribution of the bar be in terms of organized and focused effort. Individual action was, as we have seen, not sufficient to meet the more simple and identifiable problems of the past. Racial discrimination was effectively attacked only through organized effort. Certainly no less is necessary to meet the complex and pervading problems of today, particularly those problems that do not admit of solutions wholly legal. The role of the individual lawyer remains a necessary ingredient, but he simply cannot do enough to make more than a dent in the complex set of problems facing segments of today's society. The individual lawyer could, and did, secure justice for the criminally accused. But can one man, no matter how dedicated and talented, protect the consumer from the predatory commercial practices so common in many of our cities? Can he secure meaningful compliance with the Supreme Court's desegregation decisions? Clearly, he cannot. Solutions to these problems demand human and financial resources that can be focused on a problem only through organization.

We come then, as always, to the inevitable problem of remedies. If, as I have attempted to show, there are grave inadequacies in the traditional system of individual attorneys protecting particular individual rights, what is to take its place? Of course the traditional system remains perfectly adequate in many traditional contexts. But in the new problem areas, where a new institutional framework is necessary, what approach should we take? What implications will such an approach have for the legal profession?

Although in the final analysis this difficult policy question must be resolved by bar associations and legislative bodies, there are vital constitutional considerations lurking in the background.[22] As a series of recent Supreme Court decisions has made clear,[23] the First and Fourteenth Amendments forbid state interference with certain forms of group legal practice. These decisions rest on a basic assumption about the nature of litigation. As the Court said in *NAACP v. Button,* litigation is often

a form of political expression. Groups which find themselves unable to achieve their objectives through the ballot frequently turn to the courts. . . . And under the conditions of modern government, litigation may well be the sole practicable avenue open to a minority to petition for redress of grievances.[24]

Litigation, the Court has thus held, is a protected mode of group expression. Persons may join together to pursue joint ends through the courts, just as they do through the legislature. And this First Amendment right extends beyond traditional "political" contexts. As we held just last term in the *United Mine Workers* case, "the First Amendment does not protect speech and assembly only to the extent it can be characterized as political."[25] We therefore held that union members have a constitutional right to join together and hire attorneys to represent them in workmen's compensation cases. The union members, although actually seeking only money damages, were engaged in a group activity entitled to First Amendment protection.

These cases make it clear that the states are not free to prohibit all forms of group practice. Of course, as the Court has continually stressed, the states do have vital interests in regulating the practice of law.[26] But the Constitution protects certain kinds of group activities, and to the extent it does, the states must satisfy their legitimate concerns in other ways. The old concept that each lawyer must be an individual practitioner, hired and paid only by individual clients, and associated with other attorneys only through partnership arrangements, must yield to modern realities.

It is obvious, therefore, that the bar must face up to some basic structural questions. Changes must be made, partially because there are severe constitutional problems associated with many of the old rules of champerty and maintenance and the old prohibitions against group practice, but more importantly because the old structure is no longer completely responsive to present needs. The needs of the poor, of minorities, of indigent criminal defendants—these needs can only be met through forms of group practice. If the bar is to live up to its social responsibilities, it cannot let the narrow interests of a few practitioners stand in the way.

We have seen a number of important developments already. The federal government has financed a legal services program for the poor. Some privately financed endeavors have also made important contributions. Legal aid and public defender organizations have grown, often with the support of the large reservoir of talent which can be provided by law schools. The law schools themselves have recognized the changed scope of their responsibilities to society and have instituted programs and curriculum changes more responsive to the needs of today. Thus, we have seen active participation in legal aid and similar programs and more emphasis on courses in criminal law and procedure, social welfare, and the like.

But the basic decisions have not yet been made. The bar has not yet acted definitively to bring its structure into line with current needs. In the process, certain important values must be kept in mind. On one side, we have the clear need for that kind of group practice which brings legal representation to those persons who have previously been left entirely outside the system. On the other, we have the traditional values of professional responsibility which must not be impaired. We have assumed in the past that the fidelity of the lawyer to his client's interest can be strengthened by the financial bond between them. The client pays the bill, and he ultimately will call the tune. The lawyer, while maintaining proper ethical standards, represents only the interests of the person supplying the retainer. In group practice, the old financial tie is broken. The client no longer pays the bill. And yet, the lawyer's ultimate responsibility must still be to his client. The financial link with an intermediary must not be allowed to warp his responsibility.

This is the problem. The solution, however, is not to fall back on the old theory that only the financial tie between lawyer and client can guarantee professional fidelity. Group legal services must be organized in ways which insulate the lawyer–client relationship, which protect it from extraneous influences. Our ingenuity may be challenged in this endeavor. But we must never forget the ultimate goal— making the law a reality for those to whom it is now largely meaningless.

The American Bar Association has taken the first steps toward bringing its Canons of Ethics into line with current day realities. The Special Committee on Evaluation of Ethical Standards has proposed a new Code of Professional Reponsibility. This August, it will be presented to the House of Delegates for action. The preliminary draft recently circulated contains some promising steps forward. It would allow lawyers to be furnished and paid by approved legal aid offices, professional or trade associations, or labor unions. More importantly, similar rights are extended to all bona fide, nonprofit organizations which, as an incident to their primary activities, pay for legal services furnished to members or beneficiaries. Under this provision all sorts of community organizations presumably could be established and provided with counsel; lawyers employed by these groups could then represent their members, or others who would benefit from organization programs. Moreover, the definition of legal aid offices includes programs operated by "bona fide, non-profit community organization[s]."[27]

These provisions of the new code would certainly be a great step forward. Of course other changes would still have to be made; state statutes regulating the practice of law also have to be updated, and even federal procedure—especially administrative procedure— could warrant some reform.[28] But the goal is clear. The structure of the bar must be redesigned to meet the responsibilities faced by a new generation.

I need not dwell here on the mechanical details. What is important is the commitment of men dedicated to the ideals of justice. Change will not be easy. The narrow interests of the few often carry disproportionate weight. But without both structural reform and the commitment of large numbers of men, our grand ideals will speak nothing more than paper promises. The lesson of the past century is clear. The battle will not win itself. If the bar does not move forward decisively, the nation that looks to it for leadership will soon forget the lessons of the past one hundred years. Elihu Root spoke to the point in 1904. His words still hold true:

[The] lawyer's profession demands of him something more than the ordinary public service of citizenship. He has a duty to the law. In the cause of peace and order and human rights against all injustice and wrong, he is the advocate of all men, present and to come.[29]

Irving R. Kaufman

The Medium, the Message, and the First Amendment

I. INTRODUCTION

Once again, as in all critical times in this country, there is considerable speaking about speech. I suppose this recurring phenomenon arises out of the apparent paradox that in times of stress speech is very valuable but talk is always cheap. In any event, I am somewhat hesitant to add my voice to the current clamor. I certainly do not think I can claim to have found a solution to the problems surrounding the freedom-of-speech doctrine. Such problems do not have solutions; at best they have peripherally helpful new formulations that get one from specific point to specific point in the endless anguish of meshing freedom and community. Furthermore, I am not even sure that a slight contribution to that process, even a dim but helpful new light, is wholly desirable, for one should never forget that a flickering candle often obscures more than it illuminates.

Moreover, as a member of the American Bar Association committee redrafting the Judicial Canons of Ethics, I am particularly sensitive to the issues raised in the current debate over whether judges should ever write or lecture on the law. I am, after all, a sitting judge, about to discuss matters that may at some time, in some form, appear in a case before me. Not only am I painfully aware of the close syntactical and other resemblances between the phrases "sitting judge" and "sitting duck," I am also concerned that it will seem to some that I am prejudging issues I may later have to postjudge in earnest. When the question of such "extrajudicial activities" is raised, my general response is that we have more to fear from judicial monasticism than from this kind of quasi-judicial participation. So long as the endeavors

Chief Judge Kaufman's lecture was delivered on March 18, 1970 and appeared in 45 N.Y.U.L. Rev. 761 (1970).

in question are related to a judge's functions, can be thought to advance the law in some manner, and do not detract from the performance of judicial duties, I feel an obligation, rather than a disinclination, to participate in them. But still, why am I going on? Well, the principal purpose of this exercise is a selfish one: a judge, like everyone else, yearns to stretch the particular—in the judge's position, the case—and attempt some tentative broader thinking. There is a grace and joy in powerful generalization that physicists know and the rest of us envy. To accomplish that mental exercise with any rigor, I find that I must write for delivery to a critical and competent audience. To do it without the rigor that comes from public exposure is hardly to do it at all.

In sum then, I think that a judge helps his own intellectual development when he tries to think about broader legal problems than he normally encounters. I think he can carry out that process, even publicly, without fixing his response to particular cases if he recognizes his thinking is necessarily provisional and unavoidably to be modified when it comes up against particular problems in future individual cases. In other words, what follows is my current groping toward some generalized approaches to what seems to be an insoluble set of problems, but woe unto him who seeks to read it like a judicial opinion.

II. A PARADIGM OF SPEECH: THE MEDIUM
AND THE MESSAGE

If anything of value is to come out of this tentative effort, we must begin at the beginning—with our text. The First Amendment to the Constitution provides, among other things, that: "Congress shall make no law . . . abridging the freedom of speech, or of the press."[1] As we all know to our sorrow, there are few equally concise words which, when tested against particulars, have turned out to raise as many difficult problems. I have no intention of talking about all of them. First of all I am not going to be discussing civil disobedience. That does not arise unless the First Amendment does not apply. That does not mean civil disobedience is not an important and challenging topic. It just means that I do not think I can say anything about it that others have not said and said recently. Nor, getting to the text itself, am I going to address myself to whether the word "Congress" now covers any government, state or local, and, if so, what qualifies as a government for such purposes. Those questions are still alive and still interesting, but I am going to slight them. Nor do I intend to talk very much about the difficult questions that cluster around the word "abridging": for instance, whether a tax on newsprint constitutes an "abridgment" of freedom of the press. Again, the issues are deliciously complex and therefore intellectually tempting, but I shall forgo that particular feast.

What I have decided to bite off is enough, in fact more than enough, for analytical chew. What I want to lay out on the table for this meal, lightly garnished at best, are some of the difficulties with that critical word in the text, the word "speech."

The amendment protects speech. What is that? Let us take the easy problems first. "Speech" includes more than spoken words; one would know that even if the extra and specific protection of the press were not also part of the amendment. "Speech" certainly covers methods of propagation like radio and television. Certainly there is also protection for visually perceived messages, photographs, moving pictures, sign language, mime activity, and so on. I suppose that one can "speak" to the nose too, or so at least the perfume ads—not to mention the deodorant ads—tell us day after day, and I can imagine a constitutionally protected smell (though I admit I cannot cite cases). And I suppose one would have to be utterly unaware of what goes on about us to fail to recognize that touch—and all tactile sensations— can be today, and, I suppose, always have been, heavily laden with meaning. In brief, it is easy to find examples of protected "speech"; the difficulty is in saying what "speech" is.

Let us step back from the Constitution for a moment and try to get a nonlegal handle on speech. Speech, in the limited oral sense, is a species of communication. The other processes mentioned above— writing, miming, filming—are other species. Communication, in a broad sense, is the transfer of messages. By messages I mean any patterned output no matter how primitive the patterning, from simple exclamatory directions to highly complex ideational structures.

Is all of that protected by the First Amendment? As you might have expected, the answer is "yes and no." Obviously, some transfers of messages are not protected by the First Amendment, and I will have occasion to mention quite a number of such instances. However, what is most interesting is that the reasons for protecting some kinds of speech and not others seem to me to have much more to do with the word "transmission" than with the word "message." Therefore, my "message" here will mainly concern the medium and its significance to the constitutional law of speech.

Subjective processes are not communication. For any message to move from one man to another, the message must enter the physical world. There can be no communication without a medium. The media are various but not infinite because the messages ultimately must enter through the human senses. They include inpingements on hearing (speech, radio), sight (words on a page), touch (guiding pressure on a blind man's arm), smell (promise her anything but give her . . . whatever it is) and taste (as another route to a man's heart). They also include combinations thereof (television, moving pictures, the theater). But the critical thing to remember, it seems to me, is that there is no medium which does not impinge to some extent upon some senses of the recipient of the message. That statement may be tautological; nevertheless, it is an important facet of the analysis I shall attempt here because from it follows the conclusion that all communication requires physical action and, in the old sense, passion.

What I am trying to convey is that while messages may have an effect upon people, media *must always* have an effect upon people, and the latter effect may be totally unrelated to the message being carried. For instance, even pure noise like static on a radio or traffic on a street can have a material effect upon listeners; anyone who thinks otherwise does not live in New York City.

On the other hand, there are messages that have effects upon people largely unmodified by the medium of transmission. To pick a crude example, the message "hands up, this is a holdup," is equally effective and disturbing whether delivered orally or in a note handed the victim.

What makes things very difficult for us, however, is that the medium and the message are ordinarily highly interdependent. Like Yeats, we confuse the dancer and the dance.[2] A blast on a horn is very different from a spoken "watch out." A mailed threat is very different from a present oral one. A symbolic black armband differs in one way from a screamed protest and in yet another from a letter to the editor. Nevertheless, the "message" in each case may be essentially the same. To refer more precisely to McLuhan's famous formulation,[3] with which I have been so obviously toying up to now, while it may be too much to say that the medium *is* the message, it is certainly true that the medium itself is a *co-message* of any message it carries.[4]

As we shall see, this interpenetration of medium and content is the source of much of the complexity of traditional free speech doctrine and of presently pressing perplexities about new applications. I shall explore how the evolved doctrine has, explicitly or implicitly, dealt with that complexity and point to some still developing trends. Before discussing cases, I would like to make only one more preliminary comment: it is a general (by which I most particularly do not mean universal) rule that messages are regarded for constitutional purposes as noncoercive, that any recipient is a free man able to act or not act on the basis of what is communicated to him. Thus it follows that, again with some exceptions, no man has a right to be free of certain messages because of their content, nor does government have any right to protect citizens from them. In fact, one might say that the purpose of the free speech portions of the First Amendment is to establish a right of Americans both to send and receive any messages. The basic question unsolved by the amendment is this: under what circumstances may government regulate, on behalf of itself or its citizens, the unavoidably assaultive nonmessage aspects of the great protected right of communication?

III. THE CONSTITUTION AND THE MESSAGE

A. *The General Rule of Protection*

As I said, the First Amendment as a rule protects all messages equally. That is, if the speaker is using a medium not in itself objectionable, it cannot become objectionable because of the substance of the message. It is for the people, rather than the government, to weigh the relative merits of ideas and ideologies and to decide which deserve acceptance and which rejection. To use Holmes' metaphor, we rely on the competition in the marketplace of ideas to determine which should prevail.[5]

B. *Unprotected Messages*

Having stated the rule, we must consider those exceptions in which the nature of the message itself has been found relevant to the propriety of its restraint. There seem to exist certain types of messages which the government is thought justified in prohibiting entirely.

1. Clear and Present Danger of Substantive Harm

The broadest and most famous of these categories is speech that gives rise to a clear and present danger of a substantive evil, such as speech exhorting others to immediate and dangerous illegal activity. To justify such a suppression of speech, the evil to be feared must be a serious one, and there must be reason to believe that its occurrence is imminent—"so imminent," as Justice Brandeis put it in *Whitney v. California,*[6] "that it may befall before there is opportunity for full discussion. If there be time to expose through discussion the falsehood and fallacies, to avert the evil by the processes of education, the remedy to be applied is more speech, not enforced silence."[7] Now it should be noted that the justification for this suppression impliedly assumes the potency of communication even to a stipulated free agent. It postulates situations in which a person, otherwise not likely to commit a crime, will become immediately so inclined as the result of communicative exhortation. It would be naïve to doubt that this sometimes does happen: words do have effects (else why protect them?) and among their effects are lynching, riot, and murder.

a. Antagonistic Reactions. There is a secondary application of the clear and present danger rule which has been much harder to deal with. That involves speech giving rise to a clear and present danger of disorder because of the violently hostile reaction it engenders in others. A Jehovah's Witness in a small New Hampshire town called one of his listeners a "damned racketeer" and a "damned fascist." The Supreme Court permitted New Hampshire to convict Mr. Walter Chaplinsky under a statute that forbade addressing another in abusive insulting terms in a public place. The Court there observed that the offensive "fighting" words prohibited by the statute, those which by their very utterance have a direct tendency to cause violence by the individual to whom they are addressed, "are no essential part of the exposition of ideas."[8]*

The problem is far more difficult when the danger of violent public reaction arises not from the audience's fundamental hostility to the message itself. Clearly, speech may not be suppressed merely because the views expressed are unpopular. As Justice William O. Douglas observed in *Terminiello v. Chicago,*[9] "[A] function of free speech under

---

* Subsequent Supreme Court decisions have limited the Chaplinsky holding. For example, in Cohen v. California, 403 U.S. 15 (1971), the Supreme Court declared that the First Amendment protects offensive words, at least when used to express a political viewpoint. In Gooding v. Wilson, 405 U.S. 518 (1972), the Court overturned the conviction of a man who used abusive and offensive language in a confrontation with a police officer; it found the state statute under which the man was convicted to be overbroad because it was not limited to prohibiting words that "have a direct tendency to cause acts of violence by the person to whom, individually, the remark is addressed." EDITOR'S NOTE.

our system of government is to invite dispute. It may indeed best serve its high purpose when it induces a condition of unrest, creates dissatisfaction with conditions as they are, or even stirs people to anger."[10] Nevertheless, the state may under very special circumstances intervene in a particular situation when the hostile reaction of the audience actually threatens to erupt into violence.[11] Obviously, the application of any such policy is fraught with difficulty. Liberally applied, it would allow, and indeed encourage, an intolerant majority to silence the expression of minority views. Nevertheless, in extreme situations there may be no other means to prevent violence. When peaceful protesters are completely surrounded by hostile neighborhood inhabitants, the only way to keep the peace may be to remove the protesters.* We are occasionally met with harsh realities that cannot be resolved simply by reference to the words of the amendment.[12]

b. Elicited Responses. Similar considerations apply when reactions other than speech are not only received from the audience, but are sought by the speaker. For example, speech involving a solicitation of funds or property raises an interest in protecting the public from fraud and deception that may justify some regulation, even if the cause for which solicitation is being made is noncommercial. The rationale is that although the state may not undertake to protect its people against false doctrine, it is permitted to protect them from those who seek to take their money by deception.[13] The permissible scope of such regulation is, nevertheless, very narrow. The Court has indicated that the state may require registration prior to any social or religious solicitation, so that the public may know the identity of one seeking its funds.[14] However, several cases have made it clear that the state cannot delegate total discretion to its officials to determine whether the cause for which the solicitation is undertaken is a beneficial one.[15] Now can the state require the payment of more than a nominal tax for the privilege of soliciting.[16]

2. Libel and Slander

Another variety of message to some extent outside the protection of the First Amendment is libel and slander. That treatment might be

---

* Several years after Judge Kaufman's lecture, a dramatic case study was presented by a small group of American Nazis seeking to march in Skokie, Illinois, a city with many Jewish survivors of Hitler's death camps. After the town attempted to block the demonstrations, the ACLU represented the Nazis in pressing their First Amendment claim and the courts sustained this position. National Socialist Party v. Skokie, 373 N.E.2d 21 (1977); Collin v. Smith, 578 F.2d 1197 (7th Cir.), cert. denied, 439 U.S. 916 (1978). EDITOR'S NOTE.

explained by saying that the injury to the individual defamed is thought to outweigh the lesser interest that might be involved in permitting such speech.[17] But it is illuminating to note that defamation is itself susceptible to analysis as a species of clear and present danger. The "danger" of defamation is that a person's character will be inalterably traduced and that hearers will act differently toward him after hearing the false report. Thus, it is possible to say that the danger is always clear and present once the devastating words are spoken, for the words themselves, their "content," are the harm-producing agent.

3. Commercial Words

In fact, when one thinks about it, perhaps the most anomalously treated words in the constitutional canon are what might be called commercial words. Just to take an example, it is proper for the Securities and Exchange Commission to secure an injunction against offering certain securities for sale.[18] It is proper for the Food and Drug Administration to enjoin the shipment of mislabeled drugs.[19] Cigarette advertising on radio and television will soon be completely forbidden.[20] Note that all of these prohibitions do yield somewhat to a clear and present danger analysis, but the standard of clearness and presentness seems to be relaxed when the subject is "selling speech," as opposed to noncommercial hortatory speech. The distinction is particularly vivid when one looks at the cases delineating the permissible scope of handbilling. Although the state may not constitutionally prohibit the distribution of handbills, circulars, pamphlets, etc. on its public streets when they contain expressions of information or opinion on matters of public interest,[21] it may do so when the message being disseminated is commercial advertising.[22] As the Court has sought to separate religious expression from commercial huckstering,[23] it has also made clear in *NAACP v. Button*[24] that group litigation could be protected from charges of barratry and champerty. These are merely examples of the large gray area in which it is exceedingly difficult to distinguish between so-called commercial activity and speech entitled to full constitutional protection.*

* Since Judge Kaufman's lecture, the Supreme Court has held that commercial speech is covered by the First Amendment, although with a lesser degree of protection than noncommercial speech. See, e.g., Virginia Pharmacy Board v. Virginia Consumer Council, 425 U.S. 748 (1976); Central Hudson Gas & Elec. Corp. v. Public Service Comm'n, 447 U.S. 557 (1980). But see Posadas de Puerto Rico Associates v. Tourism Company of Puerto Rico, 106 S.Ct. 2968 (1986). EDITOR'S NOTE.

4. Obscenity

a. Traditional Outlook. This, of course, brings us to the best known of the message-connected exceptions to the broad sweep of the First Amendment—obscenity. Dealing with this anomaly ought to be easy, for the Supreme Court has repeatedly excluded it from the "speech" protected by the Constitution. We are told in *Roth v. United States*[25] that "obscenity is not within the area of constitutionally protected speech or press."[26] I suppose the idea is that whatever "speech" meant in 1789 when the Constitution was adopted, it did not mean obscenity. But that distinction naturally entails determining one critical factor to make it viable—if obscenity is not speech, then what is it? Unfortunately, efforts to make that determination have not been remarkably successful up to now.

b. New Formulations. I am certainly not attempting to have any fun at the Supreme Court's expense here. I cannot myself offer anything of value toward formulating that inconceivably difficult definition of obscenity, and I am not going to repeat all the tests currently batted around and out. Given the complexity of both communication and people, a definition of obscenity may be beyond the power of discursive language. As anyone who has indulged in that complex dance which used to be called courting will avow, one indeed cannot say everything one knows or feels. Let me just tentatively suggest, without endorsing, two possible new routes toward rationalizing this hopelessly chaotic field, both of which are to some extent suggested by relatively recent Supreme Court opinions.[27] I shall suggest them—repeating my caveat that I am expressing no view on whether these are the paths that should be traversed—and then I shall run off to let others do the actual traveling. (I recognize that this technique is something like Will Rogers' suggestion, during the First World War, that we drive out the U-Boats by heating the oceans to boiling. When asked how he would do the heating he replied that he would leave the details to others.)

1. Clear and present danger test. One route would be to drop the polite fiction that obscenity is not speech for First Amendment purposes and treat it like any other species of speech by subjecting it to the usual clear and present danger test. When Georgia police, searching for gambling apparatus, seized obscene films in Mr. Robert Stanley's private residence, they assumed that obscene material was entitled to no constitutional protection whatsoever. The Court, without explicitly

disavowing *Roth*, declared that "[i]f the First Amendment means anything, it means that a State has no business telling a man, sitting alone
in his own house, what he may read or what films he may watch."[28]
But if it was obscene, how did it receive protection after *Roth*? It is my
view that by distinguishing possession from sale, the Court may have
signaled a move in the direction of requiring the legislature or executive to show that the speech in question presented a clear and present
danger of some substantive evil.[29] Furthermore, such a showing would
be easier with respect to children than adults, thereby squaring with
the approach of *Ginsberg v. New York*.[30]

2. *Regulating the medium*. My second approach, which utilizes the
Eros Magazine case, *Ginzburg v. United States*,[31] as well as *Stanley* and
Ginsberg, would involve removing primary scrutiny from the knotty
and perplexing question of defining obscenity, that is, from the task
of dealing with the *content* of the communication or the message, and
shifting it instead to the *medium*. In effect this would involve regulating the mode of impingement of the arguably offensive message, the
aim being to protect people from unconsented onslaughts of objectionable material.[32] Again, children who cannot consent, as that word
is usually understood at law, would be open for particular statutory
treatment. The constitutional protections surrounding media regulation (into which I am about to go at noxious length) might serve to
strike a balance in the obscenity area too. The result would be that no
one could have obscenity forced upon him. Perhaps these tests would
spare the poor judge who faces the task of projecting the community's
prurient interest over to himself[33] or trying to apply Justice Stewart's
rather simple but appealing test, "I know it when I see it."[34] Even Justice Stewart, by the way, may be having some second thoughts; in
Ginzburg he took some pains to try to define precisely what it was that
he knew when he saw it.[35]*

IV. THE CONSTITUTION AND THE MEDIUM

A. *The Underlying Policies*

Now we come to the Constitution and the medium. We have discussed those few instances in which regulation of the message itself is

---

* In Miller v. California, 413 U.S. 15, 24 (1973), the Supreme Court articulated a
new test for obscenity. A work is obscene if "(a) . . . the 'average person, applying contemporary community standards' . . . find[s] that the work, taken as a whole, appeals to
prurient interest, . . . ; (b) . . . the work, taken as a whole, lacks *serious* literary, artistic,
political, or scientific value" (emphasis added). EDITOR'S NOTE.

deemed permissible. However, apart from words capable of causing a clear and present danger (*e.g.*, slander, commercial speech and obscenity), the bulk of speech regulation falls on the medium. When we turn from the message to the medium the exceptions become the rule; if anything is clear about the First Amendment it is that all message-bearing activity is not equally protected. To clarify the policies involved in media regulation and to suggest the extent to which the regulation may be appropriate, I would like to develop some underlying policies and urge some lines of analysis. The policies I see as important are the right to effective advocacy and the right to treatment that is equal in practice as well as theory. I would also like to pursue these policies by considering the different media available and then by analyzing the situs of the media. As examples of the types of media available, consider a newspaper article versus a red flag; for places, think of a speech in an auditorium as opposed to one in a jailhouse.

B. *The Right to Effective Advocacy*

It is crucial to remember that the right of free speech protected by the First Amendment means considerably more than the right merely to speak or publish one's thoughts. It also means the right to advocate a chosen cause and to advocate it effectively. As the Court has said in *Thomas v. Collins*,[36] " 'Free trade in ideas' means free trade in the opportunity to persuade to action, not merely to describe facts." Thus, a prohibition of the use of a certain medium of propagation may be impermissible because that medium is thought to be a highly valuable means of effective communication. The Court has declared, for example, that "loudspeakers are today indispensable instruments of effective public speech"[37] along with pamphlets[38] and group litigation.[39]

1. *Equal Treatment*

Not only must effective media be available but what regulation of media exists must be applied in a nondiscriminatory manner. Furthermore, equal treatment of media can bring equal effects upon its users only when all upon whom the restraint bears are similarly situated. Some members of our society have plentiful access to radio, television, newspapers, and others means of mass communication to convey their messages; others have almost none. Therefore, if all means of dissemination of ideas in public places were prohibited, the former would be little affected, while the latter would be effectively silenced, giving the views of those with access to the legally favored media over-powering influence.[40] In addition, discrimination may result from the restriction or prohibition of a certain medium because all media cannot convey all messages with equal force. Stated positively, some media are peculiarly effective for the expression of certain specific messages, and the prohibition of those media would greatly impair the ability of speakers effectively to advocate those causes. In a large metropolitan area, a candidate without television time is not a candidate at all.[41]

Because of the difficulty in preventing discrimination—intentional or unintentional—even when the medium has been found to cause sufficient harm to warrant its regulation, the restraint must be as narrow as possible and consistent with its purpose. For instance, if the purpose of a noise restriction is to preserve quiet in the vicinity of a hospital, the quiet zone should encompass an area no greater than necessary to prevent the noise from actually being heard within the hospital. Moreover, the regulation should display a considerable degree of tolerance, that is, we should be sure that the interest to be protected by the regulation is one of real importance to us. Especially since we ordinarily endure a rather high level of noncommunicative noise such as sonic booms by jet aircraft, we should not too readily condemn noisemaking activities when their purpose is communication.

2. Prohibited Media

Some media, nonetheless, are entirely out of bounds. Conduct otherwise illegal cannot be condoned merely because the person engaging in it intends thereby to express an idea. To begin with an easy case, the people who have been converting some New York office buildings into expensive rubble mean to express political dissatisfaction as surely as the political assassin—but their conduct remains punishable. By the same token, those who recently sent 15,000 New Yorkers out on the street through bomb scares—including, I might add, all the judges in the Southern and Eastern Districts and on the Court of Appeals—surely had some message in mind.[42] Were we to protect all such use of media as "symbolic speech," we would soon find ourselves without a society with which to be dissatisfied. Also I should add that such distortions of the right to dissent are particularly galling when they occur at the same time that the courts have been most re-

ceptive to expansive readings of the First Amendment, providing unparalleled opportunities to express dissenting views.

Punishment of draft-card burning, which the Supreme Court has
recently upheld, presented a rather more difficult problem.[43] Flag-
burning statutes raise as yet unresolved questions, though it is clear
from Justice Harlan's opinion in *Street v. New York*[44] that contemp-
tuous words directed toward the flag will not support a conviction. It
is of some interest, however, that the New York Court of Appeals has
recently held that desecrating the flag by using it in a sculpture may
be forbidden.[45] My purpose here is not to express any opinion or critique of these cases. I merely intend to illustrate the general principle
that message-bearing activity, or certain "media" in the broad sense,
may be barred entirely where the harm from the conduct is sufficiently great.

3. Regulated Media

Far more frequently, the problem is not whether use of certain
media should be prohibited, but rather to what extent they may be
regulated. Several general rules govern the propriety of any such regulatory effort.[46] First, the governmental interest furthered by the regulation must be an important one. As the Court has said on several
occasions, the requisite interest must be "compelling,"[47] "substantial,"[48] "subordinating,"[49] "paramount,"[50] "cogent"[51] or "strong."[52] Second, this governmental interest must be unrelated to the suppression
of speech, that is, the restraint must be "incidental" to the speech.[53]
Third, the incidental restriction on free expression must be no
greater than is necessary to achieve its purpose.[54] Fourth, not only
must the regulation on its face not discriminate against the communication of any particular messages, but it must be drawn narrowly
enough to prevent officials from applying it unequally. Indeed, it is
for failure to meet this last requirement that restraints on speech
activity have been most frequently found constitutionally infirm.[55]

It seems clear that the more a medium of propagation involves
activity over and above merely speaking or publishing, the more it is
likely to impinge on other interests deserving government protection,
thus inviting greater restraints. In this regard, it is interesting to note
how often the Court, in assessing the permissible scope of a regulation, has considered the needs of particular groups of speakers and
particular causes in striking a balance. For purposes of analysis, I shall

consider separately the varieties of speech activity and the places in which they are conducted, although in practice the two are really inseparable.

a. Types of Media.

1. Pure speech. The types of conduct engaged in for the purpose of expression may be viewed as forming a continuum of increasing physical activity. At one end of the spectrum lies what the Court has often referred to as "pure speech," that is, speech, not unlawful in itself, unaccompanied by any activity of a type likely to endanger other governmental interests. This conduct is the very prototype of that protected by the First Amendment, and it may not be subjected to restriction of any kind by the state.[56]

2. Leaflets. Proceeding with our illustrations, we reach hand distribution of literature, a means of communication involving slightly more activity than merely speaking and one which has traditionally been afforded a large measure of protection under the First Amendment. Thus, although cities have an interest in preventing littering,[57] a municipality may not forbid the distribution of literature on its streets or in its public places.[58] Nor may the state make the right to distribute literature dependent upon the payment of a tax or the obtaining of a permit to be issued at the unfettered discretion of a public official.[59]

3. Door-to-door distribution. A more activist method of distributing literature is to take it directly to the people in their homes. Just as this means of communication involves a greater degree of activity, so also, it infringes upon more substantial interests which the state may wish to protect, such as the protection of householders from untoward disturbance or from the danger that burglars or undesirables may gain entrance by posing as canvassers. On the other hand, the Court has emphasized that door-to-door canvassing has historically been an important means of communication for groups espousing causes, among them religious organizations, labor groups, and political campaigners. Recognizing this, the Court observed in *Martin v. City of Struthers*[60] that "distribution of circulars is essential to the poorly financed causes of little people."[61] Accordingly, it has held that the state may not prohibit the distribution of literature via doorbell ringing and personal delivery to the householder, unless the individual householder as actually indicated that he does not wish to be disturbed.[62] The state is justified, however, in imposing some restraints upon such activity for the safety and convenience of the people, as, for example, by regulating the time and manner of canvassing or by requiring that anyone seeking to engage in such activity must first register with the state for identification purposes.[63] By means of such minor restrictions, the state is able in large measure to fulfill its purposes without significantly impairing the availability or effectiveness of the door-to-door medium.

4. *Sound amplification.* What has troubled the Court about amplification devices is the manner in which they impose the speaker's message upon unwilling listeners. It has observed that a passerby cannot as easily evade the noise created by a loudspeaker as he can refuse literature offered by one distributing it on a street.[64] Nevertheless, we tolerate such a large volume of noise pollution from other sources, such as jet planes, truck traffic, and construction machinery, that we should not too hastily condemn it when it happens to be employed for the purpose of discussion.[65] On the other hand, totally unfettered sound-trucking would most likely make cities even less bearable than they are now.

5. *Picketing.* Several other media involving group participation are considerably more aggressive and abrasive and pose correspondingly greater problems for the state. One of those widely used is picketing. The Supreme Court has long recognized picketing as a highly effective means of publicizing information and opinion entitled to First Amendment protection unless the particular manner in which it is conducted causes some harm that the state is entitled to guard against.[66] A formulation often used by the Court in this area is that activities such as picketing, parading, or demonstrating involve elements of both "speech" and "conduct." Because of this intermingling of protected and unprotected elements, the activity may be subjected to a greater degree of control than "pure speech" but cannot be prohibited entirely.[67] Actually, as I have indicated, this distinction must break down, for all speech requires the use of some medium and therefore some "conduct." The difference between talking and picketing is—like almost everything else—one of degree, the latter involving the likelihood of more disruption than the former. The Court's formulation, as I view it, is that when speech involves the use of media which may be potentially harmful, explosive, or disruptive, it may constitutionally be subject to a greater degree of regulation for public welfare than when the media carrying the message pose no such threat. Accordingly, we have observed that while picketing may not be

prohibited except when it is directed toward an illegal end, it may be regulated when it obstructs passage to public buildings[68] or disrupts pedestrian or vehicular traffic.[69]

6. *Parades and demonstrations.* Two other closely related examples of expressive conduct are parades and demonstrations. Because of the multitude of people involved, these media may cause serious interference with other legitimate activities. Accordingly, regulation as to the time, place, and conduct of such activities is permissible.[70] Here too, such regulations must be drawn narrowly and be directly related to the danger or harm likely to flow from the activity itself rather than from the message being expressed. Thus, restraints for the purpose of protecting vehicular and pedestrian traffic or reasonably limiting the hours or the places of such activities are constitutionally unobjectionable.[71]

7. *Symbolic protest.* Several other media have quite recently gained—or regained—wide recognition and popularity as important means of expression by protesters. As long ago as 1931, the Court held that the use of a symbol to express a constitutionally protected message is a form of speech protected by the First Amendment. Thus, in *Stromberg v. California*[72] the Court invalidated a statute prohibiting the display of a communist flag for the purpose of expressing, *inter alia*, peaceful opposition to organized government. And in 1969 the Court in *Tinker v. Des Moines Independent Community School District*[73] affirmed the right of high school students to wear black armbands to school to protest the Vietnam War, noting that such conduct is "closely akin to 'pure speech,' which, we have repeatedly held, is entitled to comprehensive protection under the First Amendment."[74] In its opinion the Court cited with approval *Burnside v. Byars*,[75] in which the Fifth Circuit Court of Appeals had similarly upheld the right of children to wear "freedom buttons" to school. Similarly, in *Brown v. Louisiana*[76] the Supreme Court upheld the right of protesters to conduct a silent demonstration in a library. Describing the demonstrators as sitting "quietly, as monuments of protest against the segregation of the [public] library,"[77] the Court reaffirmed that the basic First Amendment rights of speech, assembly, and petition for redress of grievances "are not confined to verbal expression. They embrace appropriate types of action."[78] In both the school and the library cases, it should be noted, the right of silent, symbolic expression recognized by the Court was especially vital because verbal communication would have disrupted

the functioning of the institutions and therefore was not available to the protesters as an alternate means of communication.

8. Litigation. Apart from symbols, another activity which has come to be viewed in certain circumstances as a constitutionally protected mode of expression is litigation. As I have already observed, the Court in *NAACP v. Button*[79] emphasized that "abstract discussion is not the only species of communication which the Constitution protects; it also protects vigorous advocacy." Furthermore, it concluded that "under the conditions of modern government, litigation may well be the sole practicable avenue open to a minority to petition for redress of grievances."[80]

b. Locations for Speech. A second path to understanding media regulation is through examination of the locations in which protected messages are disseminated.[81] Let us shift our focus for a moment from the medium to the place in which it is employed. This is, frankly, an intellectual artifice; situs and medium, like medium and message, are closely intertwined and highly interdependent. Thus, it is impossible to imagine a parade without a street or a park. Yet I think the distinction between situs and medium, albeit artificial, may prove useful, for it is frequently possible to define competing social policies more concretely when we can securely fix the point where they intersect. There *is* a difference between marching down Fifth Avenue and marching up the aisle in a church—as any married man will quickly agree. Also, since the place in which a message is delivered affects both its obtrusiveness and its effectiveness, the development of rules governing the places in which constitutionally protected speech activities may be conducted has closely paralleled the regulation of the activities themselves.

1. Streets and parks. Traditionally, the places most readily available for the communication of ideas and opinions have been public streets and parks. Rejecting the argument that a municipality's ownership of these places entitled it to deny their use for such purposes, the Supreme Court in *Hague v. CIO*[82] long ago set forth the governing principles. They are worth quoting:

The privilege of a citizen of the United States to use the streets and parks for communication of views on national questions may be regulated in the interest of all; it is not absolute, but relative, and must be exercised in subordination to the general comfort and convenience, and in consonance with peace and good order; but it must not, in the guise of regulation, be abridged or denied.[83]

2. *Seat of government.* In addition, when the speech activity is for the purpose of petitioning the government for redress of grievances, the situs of the seat of government (*e.g.,* the state capitol grounds) cannot be closed to those seeking redress.[84] Justice Douglas emphasized this point in *Adderley v. Florida:*[85]

Legislators may turn deaf ears; formal complaints may be routed endlessly through a bureaucratic maze; courts may let the wheels of justice grind very slowly. Those who do not control television and radio, those who cannot afford to advertise in newspapers or circulate elaborate pamphlets may have only a more limited type of access to public officials.[86]

Even peaceful demonstrations, however, may be forbidden at relevant government buildings such as the jailhouse in *Adderley* and the courthouse in *Cox v. Louisiana*[87] because public protest may be overly detrimental to ongoing governmental functions.

3. *Employer's premises.* The legal protection of expression in labor disputes resembles closely the protection of access to the seat of government which I have just discussed. Apparently recognizing the particular effectiveness of proximity to the employer's premises for the communication of labor messages, the Court in *Thornhill v. Alabama*[88] rejected the state's argument that the speakers were free to disseminate their ideas elsewhere.[89] Similarly, comparing a shopping center to the company town in *Marsh v. Alabama*,[90] the Court in *Amalgamated Food Employees Local 590 v. Logan Valley Plaza, Inc.*[91] permitted picketing to publicize a labor dispute with one of the enterprises located in the center. The analogy to *Marsh* is incomplete for the Court specifically raised and refused to answer the question whether the pickets could have been excluded had they been attempting to express some message totally unrelated to the shopping center—for example, if they had been protesting the Vietnam War or distributing religious literature.[92]*

4. *Public schools.* I have reserved for last the area in which First Amendment freedoms are experiencing what I believe to be their greatest expansion—our public schools. In *Tinker v. Des Moines Independent Community School District*[93] the Court, upholding the right of students to wear armbands to school to protest United States involve-

---

* In Lloyd Corp. v. Tanner, 407 U.S. 551 (1972), the Supreme Court permitted the owner of a shopping center to ban distribution of leaflets on the shopping center's publicly accessible premises, because the contents of the leaflets (antiwar messages) were unrelated to the business conducted at the shopping center. Four years later the Supreme Court overruled the Logan Valley case in Hudgens v. NLRB, 424 U.S. 507 (1976). EDITOR'S NOTE.

ment in Vietnam, set forth two very important principles. First, school children are also entitled to the enjoyment of the First Amendment freedoms, and second, schools may not, under the guise of maintaining needed discipline, suppress speech activity by their pupils unless the activity actually disrupts the educational process.[94] Clearly, *Tinker* did not hold that children while in school are entitled to engage in all speech activities permissible in other places; *Tinker* required only that rules formulated by school officials be reasonably related to classroom needs and that these rules should not be promulgated merely for the purpose of suppressing the discussion of controversial ideas.[95] Schools are thus also "market places for ideas." Early involvement in social comment and debate is a good method for future generations of adults to learn intelligent and considered involvement. No doubt the task of judging the actual effects of each demonstration in a public place thought particularly vulnerable to disruption is a delicate and difficult one. Nevertheless, as with other regulations upon speech activities, it is the surest way to preserve the greatest amount of free expression consistent with public order and safety.*

V. CONCLUSION

My "message" has been that the most pressing and difficult problems in the free speech area today generally relate not to what messages may be expressed but to the media that may be employed to communicate them. As I have indicated, with a few well-established and narrowly circumscribed exceptions, the First Amendment protects all ideas and opinions equally. But because different means of propagation impinge to such varying degrees upon other interests the state may wish to protect, the First Amendment guarantees no such neutrality among all media. In general, the regulation of any particular medium is constitutionally permissible only to the extent necessary to protect some legitimate and important interest of the state which the use of the medium jeopardizes—and only as long as the restraint on speech activity is no greater than necessary and is applied even-handedly regardless of the message sought to be communicated.

You may wonder, then, how far we have really come—what new

---

* In Bethel School District No. 403 v. Fraser, 109 S. Ct. 3159 (1986), the Supreme Court held that the administration of a public high school had the power to impose sanctions on a student who used lewd *double entendres* in a speech during a school election campaign. EDITOR'S NOTE.

solutions have I suggested, what problems have I disposed of, what free speech issues are now of only historical interest? The answer, I am afraid, is not very far and not very many. I could take refuge in my position as a sitting judge and claim that I have quite a few answers, and intone, like many public officials, "I am not now free to divulge them." I could say that, and there would be at least an element of truth in it because I do have an obligation, as I suggested at the outset, to avoid prejudging issues that I may find presented some day in an actual case.

The difficulty, however, runs deeper. The reason for the apparent lack of clear-cut solutions lies less in the nature of my position than in the nature of the problem we are addressing. The First Amendment is basically aimed at regulating the *process* of exchanging ideas and forming opinions; in a word, at facilitating the freest possible use of channels of communication consistent with public order and safety. However, because the amendment is not directed at creating a structure but at encouraging an ideal process, it is by its nature incapable of precise definition. Consistency with the purpose and the concomitants of the ideal process implies that there will be a continual task of reevaluating the effectiveness of particular structures and particular solutions, not only from generation to generation, but from day to day. Sharp distinctions—you *may* parade; you may *not* picket; speech *is* protected; conduct is *not*—are far easier to apply and understand, but they do not aid in the process of facilitating exchange of messages; they ignore the almost infinite range not only of the media, but of the locations in which they are employed. Hence, when we deal with implementing a process, the best we can hope for are lines of analysis, specifications of important interests, and perhaps a few—a very few—tentative, groping formulations. Learned Hand with his characteristic boldness put it this way: "Law has always been unintelligible. . . . It ought to be unintelligible because it ought to be in words and words are utterly inadequate to deal with the fantastically multiform occasions which come up in human life."[96] There is an agony, no less severe because it is intellectual rather than physical, in dealing with problems that have no neat resolutions, that defy precision, that mock finality. Yet it is an agony that judges cannot lightly forgo. It is born of a deep concern for expanding the horizons of speech. It reflects an abiding faith in the essential wisdom of reaching accommodation through rational discourse and reasoned persuasion. To quote Learned Hand once again: "[I]f we are to escape, we must not yield a foot upon demanding a fair field and an honest race to all ideas."[97] I believe we have reason to hope that the courts will continue to strive to unshackle the media to the maximum extent consistent with order and safety. In so doing we seek to guarantee that measure of free discourse which makes open minds possible and organized society strong, viable, and free.

David L. Bazelon

New Gods for Old
"Efficient" Courts in a Democratic Society

I. INTRODUCTION

If there is a consensus in America today, it is that our system of criminal justice is in a state of crisis. The more closely we scrutinize any aspect of that process—from the conditions that breed our criminals through the prisons that fail to help them—the more clearly we see how far reality deviates from our ideals. But if we are agreed that there is a problem, we are divided not only over the question of its solution, but even over the question of where the problem lies. Calls for reform arise on all sides, but little agreement has developed about what those reforms should be.

My subject is the role of the courts in the criminal process. This is, I think, a matter of critical importance today. For if there is one area in which a consensus may be developing, it is the matter of court reform. And I fear that the growing consensus is *cruelly wrong*.

Increasing currency today is being given to the notion that we can reduce crime in the street by speeding up the judicial process. I think there is a grave danger that we have been oversold on the benefits of judicial efficiency. In a great burst of wishful thinking, many of us seem to have decided that cutting down on court backlogs will cut down on crime. The theory seems to be that would-be criminals will in large numbers be deterred from unlawful actions by the threat of swift punishment but not by the threat of remote punishment. But in reality, we know next to nothing about the ways in which deterrence may or may not operate. We haven't bothered to find out. I am myself dubious about the proposition that the threat of punishment—whether swift or slow—has much effect at all on the people at the bot-

Chief Judge Bazelon's lecture was delivered on April 21, 1971 and appeared in 46 N.Y.U.L. Rev. 653 (1971).

tom of society's ladder. These people are being punished already; they have nothing to lose from a life of crime and much to gain. And these are the people who commit the violent street crimes that produce the public clamor for swifter justice. There is simply no evidence that speeding up the judicial process is likely to measurably reduce the incidence of crime. Of course, there are needless inefficiencies in the judicial process and many good reasons to reform them. We are courting disaster, however, if we persuade ourselves that speeding up the criminal process will cure crime.

First, if we expect such miracles from judicial reforms, we may put far more important reforms on the back burner. It would be a serious mistake for us, as a nation, to think that it is more important to repair our judicial machinery than to repair the institutions that provide uninhabitable housing, insufficient food, medieval medical care, and inadequate educations to the people who commit the crimes that concern us. Even if we were to dispense with trials altogether and simply lock up everyone not discharged at his preliminary hearing, we would still have a serious crime problem. For every criminal we take off the streets, our institutions will breed a dozen more until we do something about the conditions that mold people into lifelong criminals. As lawyers and judges, we are naturally eager to set our own house in order. But ours is not the only house on the block. And many reforms in the quality of life can do more—far more—than court reforms to reduce the incidence of crime.

Second, in our stampede for faster convictions and fewer appeals, we are in danger of throwing out the baby and serving the bathwater for soup. For courts in the criminal process serve functions far more important than simply clearing people off the streets, no matter how well or accurately they do that job. No matter how much we expand our judicial resources, the courts cannot be the primary agency we rely upon to solve our problems. Other institutions, better adapted to broadscale programs and more institutionally responsive to changing conditions, must handle those jobs. But what the courts *can* do is take the time necessary to see to it that the other institutions are in fact doing what they are supposed to. This, I think, is the most important function of courts in a democratic society. They perform this function in two ways. First, by giving careful, intense attention to the particular situation before them, they can bring to light important problems that would otherwise remain hidden, simply because no one else had the time—or the incentive—to look at the matter closely. Second, courts can see that the other institutions keep their promises. That is, by incessantly asking questions, courts can do a substantial amount to insure that the agencies which are supposed to be dealing with a particular problem are actually looking for answers, instead of simply taking action out of prejudice or ignorance.

These judicial functions, I think, are of critical importance to our society, and if the courts don't perform them, no one will. But these functions take substantial time. Efficiency is nice, but it's really beside the point. The true measure of the quality of a judicial system is how many hidden problems it brings into public view and how well it stimulates the responsible officials and agencies into doing something about these problems.

The critical importance of this feature of the judicial function, in the criminal process and elsewhere, is my central thesis. To develop this thesis, I would first like to explain why it is that I believe this idea of the judicial function best comports with our notions of a democratic society. I will then discuss, in some detail, an example of what I believe to be the proper duty of the courts. Against this background, I will examine some of the currently fashionable proposals for a more "efficient" judicial system. And finally, I will sketch in brief some of the directions that I believe we should take in judicial reform.

II. THE JUDICIAL FUNCTION IN A DEMOCRATIC SOCIETY

Our courts are peculiar institutions in a democratic system. Although a fundamental tenet of our society is that major questions of social policy should be ultimately resolved by the people, we do all we can to insulate our judges from popular pressures so that they will be responsive only to the law and to their own consciences. What this means is that even if judges had the answers to all our problems—and I would be the first to emphasize that judges have very few answers indeed—their proper function would *not* include the promulgation and enforcement of judicial solutions to these problems, unless, of course, we were to substitute rule by platonic guardians for our democratic theory.

This does not mean, however, that the judiciary may become nothing more than a rubber stamp for actions taken by other branches of the government. By constitutional command and through legislative and executive request, courts are inextricably involved in the criminal process. Judges must determine what evidence shall and shall not be admitted; they must charge juries on the law to be applied; and if a defendant has been convicted, a judge must determine what sentence—what deprivation of individual liberty—should be imposed. By their deep involvement in the criminal process, courts lend their prestige and aura of legitimacy to whatever aspects of the process they accept without complaint.

Many of the questions that are routinely presented to the courts for resolution require that an individual's interest in fair treatment be balanced against an alleged social interest in facilitating conviction in order to better "combat crime." The disputes concerning the propriety of forced custodial interrogation, plea bargaining, and the criminal conviction of narcotics addicts for actions taken in consequence of their addiction are all examples of issues that require resolution by the courts. Legislatures (by means of the statutes they have enacted) and executive officials, such as prosecutors, appear regularly in court to argue that the interests of the accused must be neglected because the competing social interest—as evaluated by those officials—outweighs the particular individual interest involved.

These officials are not simply asking the courts to defer to their allegedly superior knowledge. They are asking the courts to accept their answers as true and then to take action upon that basis: to admit into evidence a confession obtained through forced custodial interrogation; to pronounce a defendant guilty on the basis of a bargained plea; to pronounce the moral guilt of a narcotics addict who acted under the compulsion of his illness. But if the courts are to take action on the basis of legislative or executive determinations, I believe that they are constitutionally compelled to scrutinize those determinations and to withhold their approval by refusing action unless they have a confident basis for believing that the determinations are true.

I would emphasize again that courts should not, willy-nilly, improvise their own answers and impose them finally and definitively throughout the criminal justice system. Rather, courts must incessantly ask questions. They must constantly seek to force into high public visibility the actions that are taken by all official and unofficial participants in the criminal process, and the justification for those actions. Nothing breeds more inhumanity than general ignorance of what we are doing to the people we identify as "deviants"; who those "deviants" are; what made them that way; and what caused us to attach this label to them and not to others. If, in response to constant judicial questioning, the official answer is always, "We don't know why we're doing what we're doing," something substantial has been learned. Equally important, there is then simply no reason why courts should accept these official solutions as true and act upon that basis. It is one thing to take judicial action upon the basis of expert knowledge beyond judicial ken. It is quite another to take judicial action on the basis of an expert's conclusion when he himself admits that he doesn't know what he's talking about. But unless the courts ask the necessary questions, they can never be sure which situation is which.

III. THE OLD GODS AND CRIMINAL RESPONSIBILITY

Let me discuss a particular example of this kind of judicial function. In 1954 my court adopted a new test of criminal responsibility in *Durham v. United States*.[1] Since that time we have been engaged in a continuous process of revising and refining that test, and I have every reason to believe that the process will continue. At the moment, the matter is under consideration by the court en banc.[2] But I think I can safely discuss the history of the rule without violating any canons of judicial propriety.

Before 1954, the test of criminal responsibility in the District was the English rule, set forth in the case of Daniel M'Naghten. According to this rule, a defendant would be excused from criminal responsibility only if he were suffering from a mental illness that obliterated his capacity to distinguish right from wrong. Like many American jurisdictions, the District had grafted onto that test another one—the defendant was also excused if his mental illness obliterated his power to control himself, creating an "irresistible impulse." Both these tests sounded like clear legal definitions. There was just one small problem. The psychiatrists who had to testify about the defendant's mental condition insisted that the tests we were using had no basis in reality. They said that mental illness could be disabling in a variety of ways that ought to amount to excusing conditions but that it virtually never destroyed the abstract capacity to distinguish right from wrong—or if it did, the psychiatrist had no way of knowing it. The court was finally persuaded that the existing tests were unsatisfactory, that they didn't correspond either to psychiatric reality or to commonly held notions of responsibility and excuse. But no one had a very clear idea of what to substitute for the old test. It would have been nice to find a new formula, one that more clearly expressed what was wanted as a matter of law, but we didn't quite *know* what was wanted. All we knew was that we needed more information about human behavior. We therefore decided to try a rule that sounded very simple. In *Durham* we said that a defendant would not be responsible if his act had been the product of mental illness. That left it to the psychiatrists to testify in the terms they knew best and to tell the jury as much as they could.

Durham was frankly an experiment—and we embarked on that experiment knowing full well that experience might later lead us to refine or abandon the rule. Putting the merits of the rule aside for the moment, I have always been particularly proud of the court in those days for that willingness to experiment. For it was clear to almost all of us that the old test for responsibility was inadequate. And yet we could not with confidence announce the perfect alternative. In those circumstances, surely it is wrong to continue with a bad rule merely for want of one guaranteed to be better. Too often a court feels obliged to do just that—to preserve its image of infallibility and speak only in the tones of revealed Truth. That approach may help in some small way to maintain the public's respect for the court, but it denies the judicial system its most important opportunity for growth, learning, and improvement. A static system in a changing world is hardly worthy of respect.

The immediate impact of our *Durham* experiment was to open the courtroom door to a wide range of information bearing on the question of criminal responsibility. With a broader legal test, more information became relevant to the question. We soon found, however, that, by casting the test wholly in terms of mental illness, we had unwittingly turned the question of responsibility over to the psychiatric profession; for mental illness is a very loose term with different meanings for different psychiatrists. When the only expert witnesses at trial testified that the defendant was mentally ill, according to their own unstated definitions of that term, the court felt strong pressure to direct a verdict of not guilty by reason of insanity. And when the only witnesses at trial had a narrow notion of mental illness and testified that the defendant was not mentally ill, the court had no basis for rejecting that conclusion either. When the experts disagreed, the jury was left to choose between them without any standard of evaluating their testimony. As the *Durham* years progressed, it became increasingly apparent that the insanity defense was entirely in the hands of the experts involved in a particular case. That state of affairs pleased no one, and we began to attempt to make our test more precise. We made "mental illness" a legal term of art for the purposes of the insanity defense and told juries and judges that they could find mental illness where the psychiatrists found none—we said it is any "abnormal condition . . . which substantially affects mental or emotional processes and substantially impairs behavior controls."[3] Then we instructed psychiatrists to stop worrying about whether the defendant's condition amounted to a mental illness and whether it produced his act. Those questions, we said, are for the jury. The job of the expert is to give the jury the basic information it needs to make that decision—to tell the jury all he can about the defendant's mental and emotional processes, his behavior controls, and about how he came to do his unlawful act.[4] And with that change in emphasis, we turned the entire question back to the jury. We announced that directed verdicts on the issue of insanity would rarely be required because of the complicated nature of the issue and the jury's unique qualifications for resolving it. Criminal responsibility, we said, involves an intricate intertwining of legal, medical, and moral elements—and the jury, representing the voice of the community, is better qualified than either psychiatrists or appellate judges to make that judgment.[5]

In some seventeen years of experimentation with the insanity defense, we've been unable to devise a simple scientific test that can be mechanically applied. Many of us have been forced to conclude that criminal responsibility, like negligence, is at bottom a concept that can only be determined by reference to prevailing community standards. And we are not alone in that view. Almost every modern test of criminal responsibility recognizes that mental disability is a question of degree, and uses some general term like our own requirement of "substantial impairment."[6] And when it comes to determining what is "substantial," we have to depend on the jury—on the full exposition of the public adversary trial—for a just result.

It would be foolish to claim that my court, or any other for that matter, has now finally resolved all of the problems relating to the insanity defense. It may well be that we are more confused now than we were twenty years ago. But if we were sure of ourselves then, it wasn't because the problems that are now evident were not around before *Durham*; it was only because we didn't even see them. But the illustration I have just given exemplifies what I think of as the central function of courts in the criminal process. Before *Durham* psychiatrists were willingly testifying in court in terms that they themselves believed had little or no meaning. When we asked them, they admitted as much. But we had to ask the questions. The psychiatrists didn't simply rear up on the witness stand and say, "Mr. Attorney, that's a meaningless question." Those psychiatrists who might have done that were never called to testify.*

But all of this takes time. The issue of criminal responsibility takes more time to try in 1971 than it did in 1954 and is raised in more cases.† We could return to our old "efficiency" by shoving our problems back under the rug. If we did that, we would not only be turning our backs on whatever we may have learned in the past seventeen years, but would also be abdicating our most important role. For the heart of the judicial process is by its very nature inefficient. The way toward "efficiency" in the courts is not to shortcut judicial procedures in order to dispose of more cases in less time. Such a solution is equivalent to a surgeon's omitting time-consuming diagnostic procedures and simply operating at random on whatever patients are brought before him. He could certainly process more patients this way, but few of us would think his performance had been improved. The way to make medical care more "efficient" is to keep people from getting sick in the first place. And the way to make courts more "efficient" is to deal with the factors that cause people to commit their crimes.

IV. NEW GODS

With these points in mind, I would like to take a look at some of the current proposals for judicial reform. The American Bar Association is returning from its London meetings carrying a host of proposals that we restructure our courts in line with some of the features of the English system. I find it somewhat depressing to note that those aspects of the English criminal justice that I find particularly appealing—virtual elimination of capital punishment, humane treatment of narcotics addicts, allocation of prosecutorial responsibility among the entire bar, shorter sentences, and jury trials for juveniles—seem *not* to

* In 1984, Congress legislated a far stricter test for "insanity" in criminal cases. Now, the defendant must prove by "clear and convincing evidence" that he was "unable to appreciate the nature and quality or the wrongfulness of his acts. Mental disease or defect does not otherwise constitute a defense." 18 U.S.C. sec. 20. This statute seems to amount to a rejection of Durham and a return to a standard similar to the old M'Naghten rule. EDITOR'S NOTE.

† Criminal responsibility issues continue to be litigated more frequently and intensively than in the years prior to the Durham case. EDITOR'S NOTE.

have been included in the package.[7] I also find it interesting to note that, notwithstanding the speed with which the English system operates, crime seems to be on the increase there as well as here. But I would like to say a few words about some of the reforms that have been urged.[8]

First, we are told that we should do all in our power to discourage appeals. "Frivolous" appeals are to be screened out by submitting the papers to a single appellate judge, who will reject them without hearing unless he finds them meritorious. If—heaven forbid!—we should have to hear an appeal, we should whenever possible dispense with transcripts or even briefs and hear and decide the appeal on the basis of the oral argument. So far as we can, we should eschew writing opinions that explain why we did what we did. And what the courts have put together, let no court put asunder. Habeas corpus is to be stripped to its constitutional bones.

I intend no comment whatsoever on the constitutionality *vel non* of any or all of these proposals. but so far as their effect on the judicial process is concerned, I think they are viciously wrongheaded. Devices of this kind will certainly allow cases to be more quickly disposed of. Appeals deemed "frivolous" by a single judge will not be seen by another one. One only has to open the reporters, however, to find a host of situations where dissenting judges have made it entirely clear that they would reject the majority's position as being totally without merit.[9] Whatever gain there may be in speed will be more than counterbalanced by a loss in the quality of decisions. Proposals of this kind are not proposals that we solve our problems; they are nothing more than calls for ignoring them.

I have a similar view of the other proposals. No criminal trial lawyer worth his salt would take an appeal without a full transcript of the case, unless he had no other choice. Legal memories are sufficiently poor that, from the bench I often find that even *with* a transcript the opposing attorneys cannot agree over the question of whether a particular bit of information is or is not in the record. How we are to have any reasonable assurance of what went on at the trial if transcripts are not available for consultation is entirely beyond me. Of course, cutting transcripts out of the process will save time. It will save money. It will also prevent the courts from knowing what went on at the trial, so that they can provide meaningful review. And finally, it will prevent anyone else from being able to judge the performance of the judges themselves, for no one not present at the time will be able to reconstruct with certainty what went on or find out what testimony or other issues the judges chose to ignore. The same applies to the proposal that courts dispense with written opinions. If a case is genuinely frivolous, of course, it can be disposed of by order—or by a one- or two-paragraph opinion. I agree that, in a limited number of cases there is even no bar to affirming the case from the bench except for the effect that such action may have on the feelings of counsel. Once again, however, if this kind of disposition were to become common, I fear it would be only an excuse to duck the hard questions. If this proposal is combined with the previous one, appeal to a higher court would be virtually impossible: there would be no transcript, no briefs, and not even an explanation of why the court below took the action it did. Moreover, the process itself would suffer in a number of ways. Trial courts would know that they had been affirmed or reversed, but would have no idea why. They would be just as much in the dark as anyone else. And, even more importantly, there would be no way an outsider to the process could hope to evaluate its quality. Not only would he be unable to find out *why* a particular action was taken, he would not even be able to determine precisely what was at issue.

Finally, I think that suggestions to cut down on postconviction review have very similar defects. If a case has been properly dealt with the first time—that is, if it has been rightly decided and a proper record of the case and its disposition have been made—postconviction review takes very little time indeed. If any substantial amount of time is to be saved, it will be saved only because judges will no longer have to decide the hard questions or deal with the cases that were wrongly decided to begin with.[10] The savings in time, in short, is directly proportional to the number of problems that can be shoved out of sight or the number of injustices that we can refuse to correct.

Proposals like this, in my view, cannot fairly be called proposals for judicial "reform." They are nothing short of proposals for judicial abdication, proposals that judges stop dealing with trivialities like constitutional legality and get on with the serious business of putting and keeping people in jail. This is a harsh judgment, I know. But we can never forget that problems come to the courts only when every other social institution we possess has failed to solve them. Almost by definition these are hard problems—cruelly hard problems. Speeding up the process of decision doesn't make them any easier to solve. And proposals of the kind I have just discussed will speed up the process only at the sacrifice of the most important functions that courts can serve in a democratic society.

V. NEEDED REFORMS

As I have indicated, I think that many of the current proposals for judicial "reform" are pointed in precisely the wrong direction. In my view, our efforts should be devoted to unearthing our sores and curing them, not to pretending that they don't exist. And along these lines, I see a number of areas of the criminal judicial process that could do with substantial improvement.

To begin with, I think we are relying already far too much on the acceptance of bargained guilty pleas. In hopelessly backlogged courts, most defendants are convicted without any trial at all. Some of our most vital decisions about guilt and sentence are not made out in the open by judges and juries, but behind the scenes by the lawyers for the prosecution and defense. Equal adversaries do not compete in public before an impartial judge and jury. Instead, the two sides meet in secret in a test of nothing more than raw bargaining power.

Today the practice of plea bargaining is widely regarded as indispensable for the operation of our system of criminal justice. We are told that the courts would collapse into chaos if every defendant exercised his right to trial. If so, we are in a sorry state indeed, for the continued functioning of our judicial system is dependent upon the good will of criminal defendants. But if they continue to have our best interests at heart and the practice of plea bargaining is to continue, at the very least we should bring it out into the open and surround it with safeguards. The charade that often accompanies the acceptance of guilty pleas—where the defendant and the prosecutor solemnly aver that no bargains have been struck, no promises of leniency have been made, and the judge with a straight face purports to believe what he know to be an egregious lie—cannot continue. The American Bar Association and other groups have made important proposals in this regard.[11] The courts of the District of Columbia, I am happy to say, are presently experimenting with devices intended to put plea bargains on the public record.[12]

But no safeguards can eliminate the fundamental problems inherent in plea bargaining. When the government actively encourages defendants to forgo the very rights that government is established to secure, it may not offend the Constitution, but it certainly raises some pretty basic problems. With one hand we offer the defendant a public adversary trial, and with the other we rush him out of the courtroom and into the bargain basement, where he can buy a short sentence by pleading guilty. One result of the bargain system is that the resulting sentences are based less on any rational or consistent policy than on the fluctuating demands of the marketplace.

We like to tell ourselves that, in these enlightened times, our sentencing policies are based on the hope of rehabilitating defendants, so that they will return to society less likely to transgress again. I sometimes wonder whether a person who is sent to the prisons we have today comes out more or less able to cope with the problems that led him into crime in the first place—or, indeed, whether rehabilitation on any large scale is possible in any prisons at all. The need for prison reform has recently captured some public attention. With a little luck and a lot of work, we may be able to make our prisons conform to common notions of human decency. Cleaning up our prisons, like cutting down our court backlogs, has much to recommend it. Yet I am not convinced that prison reform can be any more effective than court reforms in reaching and repairing the root causes of crime.

Whatever may be our concept of rational sentencing policy, however, it is hard to square with the concept of plea bargaining. To begin with, a prosecutor negotiating a plea simply doesn't have before him the information necessary to make any sort of informed judgment. He usually knows almost nothing about the defendant. He often has as little as ten or fifteen minutes to reach his decision. And in any event, his options are severely limited by the economics of the marketplace. For in order to buy a guilty plea, he has to offer something in return. What he offers is a sentence significantly shorter than what a defendant would expect to receive if he were found guilty after a trial. If that short sentence is sufficient to serve whatever ends we seek to serve through the sentencing process, then it must be true that sentences handed out to defendants who go to trial are too long. Conversely, if the defendants who go to trial are, by and large, getting sentences of the proper length, then the sentences resulting from the plea bargaining process are too short. If, as I suggested above, the basic aim of our sentencing policy is to rehabilitate defendants, then the result of our commitment to plea bargaining must be either that the prisons are clogged with people who should have been out on the streets a long time ago, or else the streets are clogged with people who should still be receiving rehabilitative treatment. It is a false efficiency indeed that speeds up the criminal process in order to speed up an unrehabilitated defendant's return to the streets. Indeed, it would seem that the process would be more rational if we paid for guilty pleas not by shorter sentences but by simple cash payments. If the idea seems repugnant, I suggest that the fault is not in the form of payment—we don't normally consider money to be inherently evil, and cash payments would at least help alleviate the burden on those who may have depended on the defendant for support. The fault, I suggest, is in the plea bargaining process itself.

In order to speed people through the system, then, we are running a bargain counter that may tempt even innocent people to plead guilty. For any defendant—innocent or guilty—must pay a high price for asserting his right to go to trial. We may be confident that not many innocent defendants are convicted, but we know that imperfections in the factfinding process must mean that some are. And one ironic quirk of the plea bargaining process is that it gives the heaviest sentences to the group most likely to include some innocent people—the group with close cases. For an innocent defendant is most likely to resist the pressure to plead guilty and insist on going to trial. Some of these people will be convicted—after all, no system of justice is perfect—and those innocent people will get the heavy sentences reserved for people who insist on trials.

The problem is even worse in the context of the delays that presently beset the criminal system. For court backlogs increase the pressure on all defendants, innocent or not, to give up and plead guilty. The price of a trial is not only a longer sentence for defendants who are found guilty; for those defendants unable to make bail, insisting on trial may increase the time they spend in jail in another way as well. In many jurisdictions, the usual sentence on a plea of guilty to a misdemeanor is "time served"—the amount of time spent by the defendant in jail before the plea was entered. Since it usually takes a longer time to get a trial than it does to get a plea taken, the price of a trial is several extra months in jail even for an innocent defendant. *Life* magazine told a story that makes the point.[13] One defendant, in jail for ten months, was approached by his lawyer with the suggestion that he enter a guilty plea; he could probably get a one-year sentence which, with credit for time served and good behavior, would put him right out on the street. If he insisted on trial, on the other hand, he would have to spend a few more months in jail before he could get one, and would get a stiff sentence as well if he lost. The poor defendant could hardly believe it: "You mean if I'm guilty I get out, but if I'm innocent I stay in jail?" But that's the way the system works.

That story makes clear, I think, that court backlogs and bargained pleas are both damaging to our system of criminal justice. If we can only reduce backlogs by increasing bargains, it's hard to see what we gain. Criminal trials are too valuable to sacrifice for the sake of efficiency. But there may be other matters that could be removed from the courts at far less cost to society. Automobile negligence cases come immediately to mind. Or Congress—and the state legislatures—could cut down on the judicial burden by providing more efficacious means of challenging criminal prosecutions under statutes that are unconstitutional on their face. At present, it seems that the only way to challenge an unconstitutional statute is often to violate it and wait for trial. Where large-scale political demonstrations are involved, the result may be that literally thousands of people are arrested, processed, and brought to trial before there is ever an authoritative declaration of unconstitutionality. Yet if such statutes could be wiped off the books by a single proceeding before they were ever enforced, the saving in times of crisis could be substantial.

In any event, however, we should bear in mind that even now some jurisdictions manage to try a significant number of their criminal defendants. It has been widely reported that guilty pleas represent 90 percent of all the criminal convictions in this country.[14] But in Philadelphia a few years ago, as the district attorney there proudly pointed out, the figure was closer to 27 percent.[15] In Washington in recent years it's been about 55 percent.[16] If we take steps to clear the courts of unessential matters—and, more importantly, to do something about the causes of crime rather than its results—we may be able to move toward a world in which we mean what we say, a world in which every defendant who wants one can have what the Constitution is supposed to guarantee him—a fair, speedy, and public trial.

While plea bargaining operates to almost entirely deprive the public as well as many defendants of the benefits of our public adversary system of criminal justice, the defendant who goes to trial is often in no better a position. For the adversary system falls on its face when a defendant is not effectively represented by counsel. That we provide most defendants with an attorney tempts us to congratulate ourselves on that and never look to see whether counsel is doing an effective job. The courts in particular have paid far too little attention to the right to *effective* counsel, with devastating results. I think there are two principal reasons for this lack of attention. First, a misplaced concern for the feelings and reputation of counsel often causes us to set the standard too low. We confuse the question whether defendants have received the effective assistance of counsel with the question whether they have received the assistance of effective counsel, and answer the second question rather than the first. In addition, courts often remain blissfully ignorant of an attorney's ineffective performance at trial unless it leaps out of the record because appeals in criminal cases are often handled by the lawyer who represented the defendant in trial. It would be surprising if these lawyers recognized their own errors. It would be even more surprising to find them urging their own mistakes upon an appellate court.

My own court has long followed a policy of appointing new counsel in criminal appeals. There are many reasons for this. Until this year, our local public defender was not authorized to do appellate work. Many of our local trial lawyers are unwilling or unable to handle an appellate case. When private counsel have been appointed to defend a client for no or a limited fee, we have sought to spread the burden by asking someone else to shoulder the load of appeal. And finally, we have found it helpful to have new counsel look with a fresh eye at the proceedings at trial. But now our policy is under severe attack in the name of judicial efficiency. We are urged to appoint trial counsel to prosecute the appeal wherever possible. The argument is that trial counsel will need less time to prepare the case because he will know without studying the transcript what points to raise. It is said in addition that trial counsel, having expended considerable effort on the case will feel less obligation than new counsel to manufacture an appealable claim and that he will therefore not clutter the courts with frivolous claims.

I find these arguments less than convincing. The briefs I have seen where trial attorneys have handled the appeal are ample demonstration that trial attorneys are as able as anyone else to argue endlessly on points devoid of merit. Only a foolish attorney would think that he can serve his client effectively without reviewing the transcript before he takes an appeal. And in any event, since an attorney has the duty to file an appeal if requested by his client and to argue it in any doubtful case, there is little reason to believe that frivolous appeals would be reduced. In my view, there is only one important difference. Trial counsel will almost never explicitly urge that his client was deprived of the effective assistance of counsel. Nor is he likely to raise the issue implicitly by arguing new points that he did not raise at trial. The resulting saving of time is wholly illusory. If the defendant raises either a previously ignored constitutional claim or the issue of inadequate assistance of counsel on habeas corpus, the result is more litigation, not less. And if the issues are never raised at all, what have we gained? One thing, and one thing only. We've swept a few more problems under the rug. The result is that we injure not only the individual defendant, but the whole criminal justice system. For when appellate courts correct errors in past trials, they are preventing similar errors in the future by making trial courts and lawyers more sensitive to the proper handling of difficult issues. And in the long run, the second function may well be far more important.

I would not spend so much time on this subject if my years on the bench had not convinced me how serious a flaw ineffective assistance of counsel may be. In the District of Columbia, some defendants are represented by our exceedingly able Public Defender Service, and others by equally able counsel from the private bar. But too many defendants are represented by appointed—or hired—counsel who lack either the ability or the experience to handle what is in many ways the most difficult and specialized problem in the law—the defense of a criminal charge. Defendants have been represented by patent lawyers and other attorneys who, for all their virtues, have never handled a criminal case. If a paying client walked into their office and asked them to defend him, they would immediately send him down the street. But they know that criminal lawyers are in short supply, and so when asked to take a case for little or nothing, they try to do what they can. The trouble is that it often isn't enough. And yet appellate courts continue to shut their eyes to errors raised for the first time on appeal. Like spectators watching the emperor in his new clothes, they are afraid to see the obvious. My court recently heard a case in which the defendant, a narcotics addict, had sought to defend against charges of possession of narcotics by asserting that the Eighth Amendment prohibited criminal conviction of an addict in possession of drugs solely for his own use.[17] He had been defended at trial by two court-appointed patent attorneys, one of whom began the trial by addressing the court as follows: "Your Honor, at this time I would like to point out that [my partner] and myself are patent lawyers, and we are relatively unfamiliar with criminal procedure. I apologize in advance for any procedural errors we may commit in this courtroom." The trial judge, of course, said he was sure they would do a fine job, and he wouldn't hold any technical mistakes they made against their client. And frankly, I think the trial judge was right. Those two patent lawyers did a pretty good job of presenting the argument that their client was a narcotics addict and that the drugs he had on him were for his use only. And they asked for a jury instruction that if the jury so found, they should acquit him. But the trial judge refused the instruction. When the case came to us on appeal, we refused to decide the question. A majority of the court held that it should have been raised by a motion to dismiss the indictment, and since such a motion hadn't been made, they wouldn't consider the question. I thought that the question had been properly raised below. But even if it hadn't, it is hard to see why the defendant should be blamed because the court-appointed attorneys raised the question the wrong way. I agree that there is value in the doctrine of avoiding difficult constitutional questions when it is unnecessary to decide them. But what has been the result of avoiding this constitutional decision? The defendant in this case can still raise the question on collateral attack. Since this is a federal case, that means that the same question will be presented to the same trial judge who has already decided it. And the case will come up to us again. In the meantime, the trial courts are getting narcotics cases every day, and they don't know what to do. Some of them are deciding the question one way, some of them another. Since the rule we handed down was that the question should be raised on a motion to dismiss and buttressed by a little trial at which the defendant should demonstrate as a matter of fact that he was an addict and that the drugs were for his own use, dozens of little hearings are going on. Under *United States v. Sisson*,[18] I think it is a serious question whether a decision favorable to a defendant in such circumstances is appealable at all. And since the constitutional defense is closely related to the defenses of insanity and duress, on which defendants are entitled to trial by jury, if the trial judge decides against the defendant that same evidence will be repeated a second time before the jury. The point is that, by shutting our eyes to the question of ineffective assistance of counsel, we haven't saved any time at all. We've simply buried our head in the sands—and in so doing we've stirred up a sandstorm.

But aside from the problem of lawyers who, for one reason or another, are unable properly to present the issues in a particular case, there is also the problem of lawyers appointed in criminal cases who view their appointments as part-time commitments. Understandably, many feel that they must devote the major portion of their time to their "real" work—the work that sustains their office. But effective representation in a criminal case is a full-time job. This was pointedly observed by Dr. Benjamin Spock, himself a criminal defendant in a well-publicized case. He was asked by a law student what his experience had taught him about the administration of justice. He said that the most striking thing was how hard and how long lawyers had to work to prepare a case adequately. In his case, six lawyers worked from 8 A.M. until nearly midnight every day during his month-long trial and many days before and after. The lawyers were working only for him, not for the other defendants. They explored every issue in depth from the manner in which the jury was selected to the form of the judge's instructions. He wondered, to this law student, how the normal defendant—who had not written a million-dollar best-seller—could begin to get an adequate defense, if that is what it took. Well, of course, most cases do not take six lawyers working from morning to midnight. But they do take more than—considerably more than—the few hours often allocated by assigned—and sometimes paid—counsel.

Our criminal justice system contemplates that every important issue in a criminal case will be explored and contested by well-matched adversaries, under the searching eye of the public. It is primarily to make that process work that the defendant needs the effective assistance of counsel. If an important issue escapes without exposure to that public adversary process, then it is fair to say that the assistance of counsel has been ineffective, in the sense that it has failed to produce a full-fledged public adversary trial.

The time has come to stop thinking of "ineffective assistance" as a judgment on the motives and abilities of counsel. Counsel may occasionally be ineffective because he is incompetent or uncaring, but it is far more likely that he is ineffective because he simply hasn't had the requisite experience in criminal litigation. We would not ask a pediatrician to perform brain surgery even though he has a medical degree. Modern legal practice is just as complicated and fragmented as medicine. Moreover, trial counsel may be prevented from operating as he should by factors wholly beyond his control. We wouldn't ask a brain surgeon to operate with a hatchet, but we often ask an attorney to try a criminal case without the investigative resources necessary to develop and explore critical issues. And then when his presentation is inadequate, we look at the record and say "Well, it wasn't the attorney's fault." And we think that answers the question.

The point is that whether a defendant has received the effective assistance of counsel does not depend upon whether the attorney did something that should subject him to censure. The question of blame would arise in a tort suit against the attorney or in a disciplinary proceeding against him. But a claim of ineffective assistance should be neither. It should merely be a claim that, for whatever reason, the adversary system has failed to function properly. Maybe we need a new term, one that implicates not the attorney but the system. Maybe instead of "ineffective assistance of counsel," we should speak of "failure of the criminal process." But whether or not we change the label, we cannot afford to let the lawyer's feelings weigh more heavily than the defendant's liberty. My own feelings are as tender as anyone's, but I would certainly have trouble sleeping if I thought the Supreme Court had ever affirmed a judgment denying somebody his liberty or even his life, not because the judgment was correct, but simply because my feelings would be hurt by reversal. The key question, after all, is whether the defendant was deprived of the "essence of a substantial defense,"[19] and not who deprived him. The Constitution gives the defendant the right to a full adversary trial. That right has been denied whether the fault lies with the defense attorney, the prosecutor, the judge—or with no one at all.

Of course we will never achieve the perfect trial in an imperfect world. We can only promise a trial that affords substantial justice. Some people may say that it is neither fair nor efficient—O magic word!—to subject the trial lawyer to the Monday-morning quarterbacking of another lawyer on appeal or (you should forgive the expression) of an "activist" appellate judge. But the doctrine of harmless error makes it unnecessary for appellate courts to concern themselves with errors that could not have affected the result of the trial. That doctrine is highly susceptible to abuse, as Justice Roger Traynor reminded us in his excellent little book.[20] But properly confined, it serves the important function of limiting our attention to the errors that matter. These deserve attention at the appellate level, whatever their source.

Perhaps I can make my point with a few examples. As you may know, I come to my concern for the adversary process at least in part through my longstanding interest in the issue of criminal responsibility—the insanity defense. In case after case I have watched the system deprive the defendant of his right to a full exploration of that fundamental issue, through a public adversary proceeding. At first I blamed the psychiatrists, and then I came to blame the lawyers. Finally I concluded that it matters little who is at fault—the important thing is to find a way to make the public adversary process work.

Consider the case of a defendant with a very low I.Q. charged with the senseless murder of a small child. Surely, there is at least a question about criminal responsibility in this case. But if no one requests a pretrial mental examination, there is no information before the jury on the issue of criminal responsibility. If no one ferrets out the relevant information on such an important issue, surely that reflects a breakdown in the system. I don't care whether we blame counsel for failing to ask for an examination, the court for failing to order one, or nobody at all—the fact remains that the system has failed.

The system often works as badly even when the defendant does get a pretrial examination. In the typical case, the indigent defendant is committed to the public mental hospital for his examination. If the hospital files a report finding no mental illness, there may be a minority of staff members who disagree. What happens if the defendant's lawyer fails to seek out those dissenting doctors and subpoena them to testify at trial? In one case, the lawyer didn't discover until the day of the trial that the dissenting doctor was out of town. The trial judge was exasperated—how could responsible attorneys have a witness in a case and not know he was out of town? Defense counsel had a simple answer: the witness was a government doctor, wasn't he? Well, then, counsel assumed it must be the government's job to get him to trial! Who should pay for this naivete? The defendant?

Finally, the system may fail even if the dissenting doctor appears to testify for the defense at the trial. For the doctors frequently testify in utterly conclusory terms. The lawyer or the judge may ask for the underlying information behind the diagnostic labels, but the doctor is often unwilling or unable to provide or explain it. In that case important information is kept from the jury. I don't know whether the fault lies with the doctor, the lawyer, or the judge—or with no one at all. But it's clear that the defendant is deprived of a fair trial on the issue of responsibility.

Failures like this rob the insanity defense of meaning, no matter how neatly a court states its test of criminal responsibility. You may know that the question concerning how the test should be phrased is presently before my court, so I can hardly talk about substance at this time. The point I can make, however, is that there is another matter far more important than the substantive test. The most important thing is that the trial process must produce for the jury a thorough explanation of the defendant's behavior and its causes. For if it does not, the test can be neither applied nor improved. The words of the test are far less important than the quality of the information presented at trial and the manner in which it is presented.

VI. CONCLUSION

What I think it is important to recognize about the function of courts, then, is this. The judicial process is at its core a fundamentally inefficient process. This must be so, for inevitably problems that are brought before the courts are the problems that no other social institution has solved. The courts themselves, of course, cannot solve these problems. What they can do, however, is take a close look indeed at the situation before them, to bring out factors that have previously remained hidden, and to insure that the responsible agencies are making a genuine effort to deal with the problems instead of simply acting out of ignorance, fear, or prejudice.

It is too easy for all of us to look at the surface of things and ignore the depths below. But as Justice Cardozo once wrote, "[t]he subject the most innocent on the surface may turn out when it is probed to be charged with hidden fire."[21] The judicial process is a social institution designed to guarantee that this probing will be done. We strike at its very reason for being if we seek to eliminate this aspect of the judicial function as a sacrifice on the altar of the Great God Efficiency.

Shirley M. Hufstedler

Comity and the Constitution
The Changing Role of the Federal Judiciary

I. INTRODUCTION

What's in a name? An invitation to attend an address entitled "The Changing Role of the Federal Judiciary" has all of the pulse-throbbing excitement of an invitation to a lecture on Brazilian corn hybridizing to one who is not a South American farmer. If the title were "Should Federal Courts Be Stripped of Power to Order School Busing?," the response would be more electric. Yet, the core of both topics is the same: What should be the functions of the federal courts in contemporary America?

The allocation of power to federal courts has been a thorny political issue since the founding of the Republic. Some of the constitutional draftsmen and many of the members of the First Congress wanted judicial power to be vested only in state courts and one Supreme Court with appellate jurisdiction. Others wanted a national judiciary with broader federal power.[1] Article III is an artful compromise in which vast jurisdiction is granted to the federal courts, but its exercise is restricted to the Supreme Court and "such inferior Courts as Congress may from time to time ordain and establish."[2]

Debates about federal jurisdiction have continued unabated because the federal courts have always been battlegrounds in the struggles over the issues that most seriously divide us. Congressional majorities again and again have used their power over lower federal court jurisdiction to influence the decision of these issues. The Supreme Court has repeatedly used its adjudicatory power to protect minorities from majority overreaching on issues of national impor-

Judge Hufstedler's lecture was delivered on October 23, 1972 and appeared in 47 N.Y.U.L. Rev. 841 (1972).

tance. It has also used its adjudicatory and supervisory powers to regulate the volume of federal litigation and to adjust tensions in federal–state relations.

I shall sketch lightly the history of congressional responses to the federal judiciary and the history of some of the methods used by the federal judiciary to control the work of the federal courts. I shall point out the inadequacy of the existing law and structural framework to meet the contemporary demands on the federal judicial system. And I shall offer some suggestions for jurisdictional, substantive, and structural changes that may enable the federal courts to continue to perform their principal roles.

II. A BRIEF HISTORY OF FEDERAL JURISDICTION

A. Congressional Action

In 1928, Felix Frankfurter examined in detail legislation affecting federal jurisdiction, and he concluded that "[t]he only enduring tradition represented by the voluminous body of congressional enactments governing the federal judiciary is the tradition of questioning and compromise, of contemporary adequacy and timely fitness."[3] A less charitable and equally accurate view is that congressional reaction to issues of federal jurisdiction has always been fitful and that the fits are usually induced by strong pressures imposed by particular events or by powerful constituencies that seek to influence results in particular causes that concern them.[4] Congress has rarely undertaken a comprehensive reexamination of federal jurisdiction. Indeed, it has not made the attempt for almost 100 years.

When Congress created the lower federal courts by enacting the Judiciary Act of 1789, it lavished little acclaim and less jurisdiction on its offspring. Although it gave them exclusive jurisdiction in admiralty,[5] and concurrent jurisdiction in some diversity cases,[6] it withheld federal question jurisdiction and expressly denied habeas power over state prisoners.[7] Four years later Congress deprived the lower federal courts of power to enjoin state judicial proceedings.[8] A flash of jurisdictional largess occurred on the eve of Jefferson's inauguration when the lame duck Federalists granted those courts jurisdiction as broad as Article III allowed.[9] The gift was promptly revoked when Jefferson assumed office.[10]

The Removal Acts of 1815[11] and 1833[12] and the Force Bill of 1833[13] were inspired by New England's resistance to the War of 1812 and by South Carolina's refusal to enforce federal tariffs. The legislation permitted removal to federal courts of state litigation involving federal revenue and customs laws and gave federal courts power to grant habeas relief to state prisoners held for alleged crimes committed under federal laws. This legislation was a milestone in the development of inferior federal courts. Although the statutes were infrequently used,[14] their enactment was the first congressional recognition that the Supreme Court's appellate jurisdiction did not sufficiently protect national interests in federal–state conflicts and that lower federal courts had to be used as additional instruments to promote national policies.

The lessons of the early nineteenth century were not forgotten during the Civil War and Reconstruction.[15] Federal interests in protecting civil rights were reflected by numerous acts extending federal jurisdiction, including the Civil Rights Removal Act of 1866[16] and the Voting Rights Act of 1871.[17] Congressional expansion of federal jurisdiction reached its zenith with the passage of the Judiciary Act of 1875,[18] the last occasion upon which Congress made comprehensive changes in the fare of federal courts.

Since the turn of the century congressional action has been spasmodic. Congress added jurisdiction to accommodate the pressures of interstate railroad development and of burgeoning economic growth[19] and to meet the need for national unification following the Civil War.[20] It diverted jurisdiction when the federal courts thwarted national economic policies designed to meet the crises of the Great Depression.[21] Since the convulsions of the Depression, congressional modifications of the jurisdiction of lower federal courts have been largely stopgap efforts to lighten the workload and some result-oriented tinkering.[22]

B. The Judicial Response

The Supreme Court was never a passive bystander during the jurisdictional struggles. A few historical highlights are illustrative. The eighteenth-century Court made its own forays to capture for its lower brethren some of the state courts' terrain. The early victories were slight and short-lived.[23] The Supreme Court's nineteenth-century role in the slavery cases is well known, but perhaps it is worth a reminder that Chief Justice Roger B. Taney, in the famous fugitive slave case,

Ableman v. Booth,[24] developed the rule that, in order to protect federal court jurisdiction, state courts could not grant habeas relief to federal prisoners.[25]

The impact of the Civil War and Reconstruction was and is of such transcendent importance that it has almost eclipsed other events of the same era—*viz.*, acceleration of industrialization, railroad building, and the emergence of business organizations of national scope. The Supreme Court was soon embroiled in the controversies stemming from those new facts of economic life, and it used them as vehicles for amplifying federal judicial power.[26]

The case with the most lasting impact was *Ex parte Young*,[27] decided in 1908, the high point of judicial self-help in expanding federal jurisdiction. The underlying economic facts arouse no rage and little interest today. (Minnesota had sought to regulate the rates of an interstate railroad by imposing heavy criminal penalties on railroad personnel who did not adhere to Minnesota's rate schedules.) However, the reasoning of the opinion has striking currency. The majority held: (1) state imposition of criminal penalties so severe that the railroad could not afford to risk criminal prosecution to test the validity of the statute denied due process to the railroad; and (2) the anti-injunction statute of 1793, prohibiting federal interference with state judicial proceedings, did not foreclose federal relief because the statute applied only to state judicial proceedings pending at the time federal jurisdiction was invoked.

The dissenting opinion argued that federal courts should abstain from precipitant interference with state policy, especially as expressed in state criminal statutes, to avoid rending the fabric of federalism and to avert unseemly friction between dual sovereigns. The majority answered that state interests must yield to the paramount federal interest in protecting stockholders from confiscation of their property. To the dissent's argument that the railroad had an adequate remedy at law because it could defend a state criminal action by challenging the constitutional validity of the statute, the majority responded, although not in these words, that the "chilling effect"[28] on the exercise of constitutionally protected rights by forcing a person to risk criminal prosecution rendered the legal remedy inadequate. Finally, to the minority's contention that the holding would flood the federal courts with similar litigation, the majority answered that it had confidence that lower courts would issue injunctions sparingly and, to the extent that new burdens were added to the federal court load, they must be borne because vindication of federally secured rights was the principal reason for the existence of federal courts.

The states' indignation quickly surfaced in a flurry of bills to prevent federal courts from enjoining enforcement of state laws.[29] The sorest point was the power *Young* gave to a single district judge to undo in a stroke the actions of multiple state officials. The controversy was compromised in 1910 by legislation creating the three-judge district court and authorizing direct appeal from that court to the Supreme Court.[30]

Even in the heyday of jurisdictional expansion the Supreme Court had some second thoughts. Its swelling dockets led it to develop some reducing principles. In 1872, the Court decided that it would no longer review state decisions that could be sustained on adequate state grounds independent of federal questions.[31] Seven years later, in *Virginia v. Rives*,[32] the Court narrowly restricted the Civil Rights Removal Act to cases in which denial of equal protection was mandated by a state's statutes or constitution. The decision may have been motivated by the Court's concern over its workload more than by an insensitivity to civil rights.[33] By the turn of the century, the Court had begun to sketch the outlines of the doctrines of exhaustion of state remedies and abstention.[34] These modest efforts to curtail its calendar were inadequate to deal with the mounting dockets.

Congress launched a rescue mission in 1891, creating the United States courts of appeals.[35] But it was not until the Judges' Bill of 1925,[36] when Congress reduced obligatory Supreme Court appellate review, that the Court was given any substantial relief from its overburden. The reprieve, as we all know, was temporary.

III. IDENTIFYING THE PROBLEMS OF OUR INADEQUATE JURISDICTIONAL SYSTEM

A few observations can be made from this brief historical recapitulation. A menu of the kinds of cases that lower federal courts should be served cannot be found in the Constitution, in tradition, or in history. The entrees have varied with the demands of the national market, the tastes of congressional chefs, and the Supreme Court's conclusions about the state of federal digestion, especially its own.

Do we now need to rewrite federal jurisdiction? We do not have to do so if we find that federal courts are presently performing the tasks that we think they should and that they can continue to perform them in the foreseeable future.

The principal functions of the Supreme Court are the decisions of federal constitutional issues, the construction and application of federal law of national concern, and the supervision of the federal court system, including maintenance of uniformity of federal law. The Court cannot adequately perform these tasks unless it is again relieved of a tide of litigation that contributes little or nothing toward those functions.

Last year the Supreme Court docketed over 4,500 cases,[37] the great majority of which did not merit any attention by the Court. Yet each justice looked at each case to choose the few cases that should or even could be heard. The chief justice has predicted that, unless something is done, the filings will rise to 7,000 cases by 1980.[38] The inevitable result of this avalanche of cases is obvious; the time used in deciding not to decide will consume almost all of the time that should be devoted to hearing and deciding the cases that fall within the Court's proper sphere.[39]

The lower courts are in better shape, but not much. Circuit after circuit is plagued by intractable backlogs, and all predictions forecast increases.[40] Much of the time of federal trial courts and appellate courts is absorbed by litigation of ordinary disputes and controversies primarily of local concern.[41]

Some state systems also need help, but federal court time is too scarce to be allocated to state systems. The primary institutional tasks of the United States courts of appeals are the resolution of the constitutional issues, the decision of questions of federal law, and the maintenance of a coherent body of federal jurisprudence. Federal district courts should be trying the kinds of cases that raise those issues. Lower federal courts cannot continue to serve as part-time adjuncts of state judicial systems.

The Supreme Court and the lower federal courts cannot fulfill their national duties unless they receive meaningful help. First aid can be given by making some rather simple jurisdictional changes, but long-range assistance cannot be delivered without structural change, reduction of litigation intake, or both. Cosmetic alterations do little to ameliorate the plight of the courts; indeed, they may be counterproductive because they distract us from the larger jobs.

IV. RELIEVING THE STRAIN ON FEDERAL COURTS BY RESTRUCTURING JURISDICTION

A. *Unburdening the Supreme Court—Constructing a New Tier*

Because the Supreme Court is one of the most beleaguered courts in the country and because its vitality is a national imperative, it should receive first attention. Modest but immediate help can be delivered if Congress completes its 1925 reformation by relieving the Court of all remnants of obligatory Supreme Court review. The three-judge district court is an anachronistic luxury, and it should be promptly jettisoned.[42]*

Significant short-term aid could be rendered if all state litigation were channeled through a lower federal court before it could reach the Supreme Court. By using the word "all," I include all state litigation raising constitutional issues and federal questions in both civil and criminal cases, specifically including review of state prisoners' petitions for postconviction relief anteceding federal habeas.

The burden of sifting these state cases is not trivial. Last term almost 22 percent of the cases docketed with the Supreme Court sought review of state criminal convictions.[43] Today, a convicted state defendant potentially has at least three opportunities to receive Supreme Court attention: application for review after his direct appeal has been rejected by his state court of last resort, application for review when he has exhausted his state remedies upon postconviction proceedings, and a third application after he has worked his way through the federal system on federal habeas corpus.

The present routine is procedural nonsense. Some sense could be injected by making a few relatively simple procedural changes:

1. Foreclose all applications to the Supreme Court for direct review of state decisions, both civil and criminal.

2. Route all appeals and applications for review of state decisions in civil cases and all applications for review of criminal convictions after state court direct appeal to a designated federal court below the level of the Supreme Court. Whatever can be said for or against federal habeas corpus—and almost everything has been said several times—there is agreement that the remedy provides an adequate federal

---

* Since Judge Hufstedler spoke, Congress has sharply curtailed the use of three-judge courts. For details, see the 1981 Supplement to Hart and Wechsler's The Federal Courts and the Federal System (2d ed. 1973), pp. 247–250. EDITOR'S NOTE.

forum in which a state defendant can have his federal claims ad-
judicated.[44]

3. Eliminate federal appellate review of state decisions denying a
state defendant postconviction relief. Federal participation in collateral attacks upon a state court conviction should be restricted to
federal habeas corpus. The present opportunity for Supreme Court
review of a defendant's state court collateral attack on his conviction
gives the state defendant an extra shot at the Court that his federal
counterpart does not have. No sound reason exists to continue the
target practice.

These proposals would not change federal habeas corpus. Nor
would they foreclose federal appellate review of state civil cases or of
state criminal convictions after the defendant has exhausted his state
remedies upon direct attack. In both of these instances, however, the
proposals forbid initial Supreme Court review and compel the ap-
pellant or petitioner to seek review from a lower federal court. The
result cannot be reached without conferring appellate jurisdiction to
review state court decisions upon a federal court other than the Supreme Court. Congress has never made such a grant, but there is
nothing to prevent it. Alexander Hamilton, writing in the *Federalist
Papers*, contemplated that lower federal courts would be given appellate power to review state decisions of federal questions.[45]

Which lower federal courts should receive the grant? We can quickly cross out the federal district courts. Although there are other
reasons why these courts should not be used for this purpose, the
overriding reason is that it could not be done. The selection would
offend state sensibilities, and Congress would not be deaf to the cries
of the wounded.

Federal courts of appeals are an obvious choice. They exist. They
should have enough stature to smooth ruffled state feathers. Their
use would add only one rung to the existing state–federal appellate
ladder. They are better able to distribute the burden than is the Supreme Court. However, they are not the best bet. New appellate duty
would increase the burdens of the courts that are now in docket
trouble,[46] and their use would contribute to intercircuit conflicts that
tax the Supreme Court.

The most desirable choice is to give appellate jurisdiction to a new
national court inserted between the existing courts of appeals and the
Supreme Court. Not only could a new court of nationwide jurisdiction relieve the Supreme Court of initial review of state court

proceedings, but it could also assume other burdens, such as the resolution of intercircuit conflicts upon issues that are not of sufficient gravity to receive Supreme Court attention but are of enough importance to require a national answer.[47]

A suggestion to create a new national court is not novel. A number of proposals have been advanced to form a new federal court tier, some of which include suggestions about its composition and jurisdiction.[48] I endorse the concept of the new court and add to its suggested duties appellate review of state court decisions.

A new national court would not materially assist the Supreme Court if the litigants could apply to the Supreme Court for review of the decisions of the national court. Among the methods that could be used to restrict review are to make final all decisions of the new court or to place limitations on review of the new court's decisions. The first method maximizes relief to the Supreme Court, but the price of finality would be foreclosure of Supreme Court consideration of some cases that should receive full attention by the nation's highest Court. Limiting, rather than forbidding, Supreme Court review is preferable. An effective limitation would be to restrict Supreme Court review to those cases certified for review by the national court itself (permitting the Supreme Court to accept or to decline a certified case) and to those cases which the Supreme Court on its own motion orders certified to itself.[49]*

B. Easing the Strain Throughout the Federal Court System

Vertical expansion of a judicial system—that is, the addition of one or more levels of courts—decreases the work of the courts above the new tier, but it provides little or no help to the courts below it. Thus, the creation of a new national court would ease Supreme Court strain by disposing of litigation that would otherwise be presented to that Court, but it will not relieve the lower federal courts of their overburdened workload.

Horizontal expansion of a judicial system—that is, increasing the number of judges on one or more of the tiers—reduces by varying degrees the caseloads of judges serving on the expanded level, but it also

---

* The controversy continues whether a new national court of appeals is needed to alleviate the alleged burden on the Supreme Court. The most extensive study of the issue has been the New York University Supreme Court Project. See nos. 4–6 of vol. 59 of the N.Y.U.L. Rev., particularly Estreicher & Sexton, A Managerial Theory of the Supreme Court's Responsibilities: An Empirical Study, 59 N.Y.U.L. Rev. 681 (1984). EDITOR'S NOTE.

augments the workload of each level above the expanded court. Horizontal expansion of existing federal courts, or circuit-splitting, will swell Supreme Court dockets because more decisions will be produced that can come before that Court.

1. Suggestions for Change Through Legislation

Structural alterations are necessary, but they cannot do the whole job because there are limits to the elasticity of the federal system.[50] The most intractable limitation is the inability to increase significantly the work of the Supreme Court. It is therefore essential to combine intake reduction with structural change to administer long-range relief.

   a. Eliminating or Restricting Diversity Jurisdiction. It is easy to convince any lawyer who practices in the federal courts that cuts should be made in federal jurisdiction as long as none of them affects his own practice. For years and years perceptive students of federal jurisdiction have insisted that diversity jurisdiction must be abolished.[51] Fear of local prejudice, economic or geographic, that originally engendered diversity jurisdiction has largely dissipated.[52] To the extent that the reasons for diversity survive, a shift to the federal courts is not very effective in eliminating them. Since the death of *Swift v. Tyson*,[53] federal courts must apply local substantive law. The hometown folks sit on federal as well as state juries; federal blue-ribbon panels have almost vanished. The backbone of resistance seems to be the tactical attractions of forum-shopping[54] and the widespread and occasionally well-founded belief that some federal courts are better than some state courts.[55] Strategic manipulation of the forum is no justification for preserving diversity jurisdiction. Poor state judicial systems need assistance, but it is not supplied by using federal systems as escape hatches. Relief to federal courts cannot be delayed awaiting the advent of state court utopia.

   One device, short of outright repeal of diversity jurisdiction, that could be used as a palliative would be congressional authorization to the Supreme Court to adopt rules restricting access to the federal courts in diversity cases. Congress could retain a veto power as it does, for example, in court-promulgated rules of procedure.[56]

   b. Revising Federal Criminal Statutes. A different source of relief to the federal courts would be revision of the law of federal crimes. Federal criminal statutes have long been a grab bag into which Congress has thrown grave national offenses, a myriad of offenses primarily or wholly of local concern, and petty violations of federal administrative regulations. The draftsmen of the Federal Criminal Code have taken large steps in the right directions,[57] but, in my view, the residue of crimes triable in the federal courts may still impose greater burdens on the system than it should have to assimilate.

There is indeed a federal interest in the investigation and prosecution of some kinds of local crimes that have reverberations beyond state boundaries, and there are in such cases instances in which state agencies are unable or unwilling to investigate or prosecute them.[58] Federal resources should be used to help state agencies in those cases, but the assistance should stop short of imposing the duty on federal courts to try them. Congress could direct that criminal cases of local concern in which there is such a collateral federal interest shall be tried exclusively in the state courts. In the early days of our Republic, federal statutes regularly provided for state court trials of federal crimes.[59]

A milder approach would be to authorize trial in either the federal or the state courts, committing to the federal district court the selection of the judicial system in which the case would be tried. The grant of discretionary authority to keep the case or to transfer it to a state court would inject flexibility into the federal system and would permit particularly overburdened federal courts to shift a part of the load to those state systems that could better accommodate the work.*

Meanwhile, congressional or prosecutorial rules of deference would materially ease the federal criminal burden. Invariably, federal crimes predominantly of local concern are also state crimes. If federal prosecutors deferred prosecution in favor of state prosecution of such offenses, the federal caseload would be reduced. Deference is especially appropriate when the substantive offense is the same under the laws of both jurisdictions except for the addition of a pinch of federal jurisdiction. Rigorous application of a policy of deference can be very effective.[60] When the Justice Department adopted that policy in automobile theft cases, prosecutions under the Dyer Act fell from 4,092 in 1970 to 2,408 in 1971, or 41 percent.[61]

When states are asked to absorb litigation removed from the federal system, they have reason to expect federal assistance. The federal

---

* Unfortunately, enactment of the Racketeer Influenced and Corrupt Organizations statute (RICO) in 1970 has had the opposite effect: state crimes are becoming federalized. RICO makes it a federal crime to commit two or more state felonies in such a way as to constitute a "pattern." 18 U.S.C. sec. 1961. EDITOR'S NOTE.

government can and should assume that responsibility. Federal law enforcement officers should be more available to aid state officers in detecting and proving crimes. Federal funding, in the form of revenue sharing, impacted-area assistance, or old-fashioned grants, should be authorized to improve state court systems that need help.

c. Eliminating Direct Review of Decisions by Administrative Agencies. Federal courts of appeals should be relieved of direct review of the decisions of administrative agencies, such as the National Labor Relations Board. Some of these cases involve important legal issues; however, the majority concern sufficiency of the evidence to sustain the agency's determinations. District courts are fully equipped to do the initial review. Further review by the courts of appeals should be discretionary, and discretion should be exercised in favor of review only when legal issues extending beyond the periphery of the case require scrutiny.

2. Suggestions for Change Through the Judicial Rulemaking Power

So far, the emphasis has been on congressional actions that would lighten and redistribute the federal caseload. Congress aside, the courts themselves could make some procedural and substantive changes that would affect the kind and quantity of federal litigation. A procedural change that promises relief both to the Supreme Court and to the courts of appeals is the development of omnibus postconviction proceedings following the sentencing of federal offenders, modeled, in part, on existing pretrial omnibus hearings.[62] It is a change that could be imposed by use of the Supreme Court's rulemaking power.

The objectives of the hearing would be to decide all postconviction petitions and motions after a single evidentiary hearing and to permit simultaneous appellate review of the defendant's contentions on both collateral and direct attack upon one appeal with a consolidated record. The proposal does not require any change in the substantive law controlling the grounds upon which direct or collateral relief now can be granted to a federal defendant. It is limited to procedural reformation aimed toward ultimate unification of all posttrial remedies presently available in the form of motions for a new trial, motions to vacate a plea, motions encompassed by section 2255[63], and notice of appeal.[64] Consolidation would not be effective, however, unless a defendant, represented by competent counsel, were foreclosed from all subsequent attacks, except those that could not have been presented at the time of the omnibus evidentiary hearing (such as a claim of newly discovered evidence) or those based on the constitutionality of the statute under which he was convicted, founded on decisions that came down after his hearing.

The present system invites fragmented, repetitious attacks and multiple appellate reviews of different aspects of the same case. At both the trial and appellate levels, successive attacks—often extending over long periods of time—absorb the attention of different trial and appellate judges, each of whom must familiarize himself with the case. Moreover, it produces almost intolerable delays in the finality of convictions, to the detriment of the administration of justice and of the defendant himself.[65]*

V. THE EFFECT OF ABSTENTION ON THE EFFICIENT USE OF THE FEDERAL COURTS

I turn now to the court-created doctrines of comity, abstention, and exhaustion of state remedies, each of which bears upon the kind and quantity of litigation flowing through the federal system. Comity is a label affixed to a patchwork of rules that can be pragmatically summarized as decisions "not to do it now." In the name of comity, federal courts defer to state action, but they do not initially surrender their power to act. If the federal courts do not want to do anything or if Congress does not want them to do anything, comity is transmuted into lack of jurisdiction. Abstention is an incarnation of comity. It is a collection of formalized principles of federal judicial restraint. Exhaustion of state remedies is abstention under an assumed name.

These devices have not been conspicuously successful in preserving the intrinsically fragile concepts of federalism, in maintaining harmonious relationships with states, in adjusting federal jurisdiction to contemporary needs, or in preventing waste of federal and state judicial resources. I will suggest some of the reasons for their shortcomings and, I hope, make a respectable case for thoroughly reexamining them.

* In Stone v. Powell, 428 U.S. 465 (1976), the Supreme Court all but precluded the availability of collateral relief for Fourth Amendment violations. Now, federal courts will decline to review habeas corpus claims if the state had afforded a mere *"opportunity for full and fair consideration"* of Fourth Amendment claims at trial. *Id.* at 482 (emphasis added). EDITOR'S NOTE.

A. Pullman *and the Creation of the Abstention Doctrine—* A Critical Analysis

Our trip through abstention begins with *Railroad Commission v. Pullman Co.*,[66] in which a unanimous Supreme Court required a three-judge district court to withhold decision of federal constitutional issues until Texas decided state questions that might dispose of the litigation. Pullman had obtained an order from the district court enjoining the Commission from enforcing its racially discriminatory order on the ground that it violated the Equal Protection Clause of the Fourteenth Amendment. Pullman had also challenged the validity of the order under Texas law. Mr. Justice Frankfurter gave three reasons for imposing abstention: (1) federal courts should avoid deciding state issues because it is a waste of time, since state courts can ignore the decision; (2) the state courts might resolve the state issues in a way that would avert the need for reaching the constitutional issues; and (3) abstention would avoid federal–state friction. The reasons are plausible, but are they convincing?

First, federal judicial time used to decide state law is largely lost, and that is a good reason not to decide state issues, but it is no explanation for postponing decisions of the federal issues.

The second reason is a restatement of the principles that courts should not prematurely decide constitutional issues and that they should not decide them at all if the case can be disposed of on nonconstitutional grounds. The principles are sound, but they should not be applied unless there is good reason to believe that the constitutional issues will go away during the state litigation or, if they do not, that the issues can be fully litigated in a federal forum.

The only way that the constitutional issues in *Pullman* could vanish was by the state court's overturning the Commission's order on state grounds without reaching the federal issues. How likely was it in 1941 that the Texas courts would hold that the Commission did not have authority under state law to adopt rules discriminating against black porters in favor of white conductors? Mr. Justice Frankfurter seems to have assumed that the Texas court would remand the case to the abstaining court if it upheld the order on state grounds. Is it not more probable that the Texas court would also decide the constitutional issues and thus completely adjudicate the case? Is not that probability increased if Texas were particularly hostile to the federal constitutional policy at issue? If Texas decided both the state and federal issues, the loser's sole recourse would be the Supreme Court because it is the only federal court with appellate jurisdiction to review state decisions. In that event, has abstention accomplished anything other than adding another case to the Supreme Court's crowded docket?

If the Supreme Court refuses review, the door to the abstaining federal court may be shut by res judicata no matter how insensitively the state courts may have treated the federal issues.[67] I say "may" because there is Supreme Court authority that lifts the bar to let some losers of civil cases back into the district court to relitigate their federal claims.[68] If there is an opportunity for a federal rerun, the litigants can pursue the constitutional issues through the whole federal hierarchy, unless they earlier abandon the chase due to penury or fatigue.[69]

Finally, Mr. Justice Frankfurter says that abstention may avoid federal–state conflicts. The assumption is sound only if the constitutional issues are never decided or they are decided in the state's favor. In all other events, the conflict is not averted; it is merely postponed. Is there any reason to believe that Texas would be less miffed if its order were invalidated by the federal courts the second time around instead of the first?

The *Pullman* doctrine rests on some guesses, and they are not very good guesses. The cost of a mistake is either a profligate waste of state and federal judicial resources and of the litigant's as well, or an erosion of constitutionally secured rights, or both. Potential benefits of abstention are limited to nondecision of constitutional issues and the largely ephemeral hope that federal court time may be saved by nondecision.

B. The Pullman *Aftermath*

Despite the frailty of the *Pullman* rationale, the Supreme Court has not overruled it. The Court has continued to apply it without any revealed effort to develop more sensitive criteria or to consider the utility of abstention in any case in which a possibility of avoiding the constitutional issue may exist. Instead, the Court has created some exceptions to *Pullman* to cut it to fit particular cases in which the Court thought that either the constitutional issues were especially compelling or the state statute was especially unconstitutional.

Thus in *Wisconsin v. Constantineau*,[70] the Court refused to apply *Pullman* abstention to compel a three-judge court to await a decision by Wisconsin courts of the constitutionality of a Wisconsin statute prohibiting sale or gift of intoxicating liquors to one whose excessive drinking makes him dangerous to the peace of the community and permitting the names of such community menaces to be posted in all retail liquor outlets. The majority found the statute unconstitutional on its face and refused to require the federal court to await a state decision of invalidity on state grounds. The dissenters thought no more highly of the statute than did the majority, but they thought that Wisconsin should have had the first chance to void it.

The abstention plot thickens when the ingredients of potential or pending state criminal prosecutions are added to the mix. In *Dombrowski v. Pfister*[71] the plaintiffs brought a suit under the Civil Rights Act[72] to enjoin Louisiana officials from interfering with their constitutionally protected activities by harassing them with criminal prosecutions and threats of prosecutions using Louisiana's subversive control laws. The district court abstained on the grounds that Louisiana could and should be permitted to reduce the overreach of its subversive control laws before the federal courts acted and that the plaintiffs had an adequate remedy at law because they could defend any state prosecution by raising the constitutionality issue in the state proceeding. The Supreme Court reversed, using reasoning, with minor embellishments, that echoes the majority in *Ex parte Young*. Except for an oblique reference by Mr. Justice Harlan in dissent, the *Pullman* doctrine was ignored.

Two years later, the Court decided *Zwickler v. Koota*.[73] The plaintiff had been prosecuted for distributing political campaign literature, under a New York statute that facially violated the First Amendment. His conviction was reversed by the New York appellate courts on state grounds. He brought a civil rights action in the federal court seeking declaratory and injunctive relief to invalidate the statute on federal constitutional grounds to thwart future criminal prosecutions. The district court dismissed, ostensibly applying abstention principles. The Supreme Court reversed. Abstention was improper because the statute was irretrievably unconstitutional. *Pullman* was limited to some undefined special circumstances.

In *Younger v. Harris*,[74] a three-judge district court restrained Harris' pending state criminal prosecution on the ground that the statute under which he was being prosecuted was void for vagueness and overbreadth in violation of the First and Fourteenth Amendments. The Supreme Court reversed, holding the facial unconstitutionality of a statute did not justify an injunction against a pending state prosecution absent special circumstances that would warrant equitable relief. Although the Court did not expressly overrule *Constantineau*, *Zwickler*, and *Dombrowski*, it left little of those cases to overrule.

Mr. Justice Black, writing for a plurality, explained that John Harris, Jr. had not fulfilled the equitable requirements for the issuance of an injunction, i.e., irreparable harm and inadequacy of his legal remedy. The fact that Harris would have to defend an ordinary state criminal prosecution and that he would have to present his federal constitutional claim first to the state court fell short of the equitable marks. These reasons appear to be a routine application of principles familiar to any English chancellor. Appearances are deceiving. The equitable terminology masks issues that the chancellor never heard of because he never had to worry about federalism.

Mr. Justice Black's opinion hints at the real issues: "The precise reasons for this longstanding public policy against federal court interference with state court proceedings have never been specifically identified."[75] But a "vital consideration" is

the notion of "comity," . . . a system in which there is sensitivity to the legitimate interests of both State and National Governments, and in which the National Government, anxious though it may be to vindicate and protect federal rights and federal interests, always endeavors to do so in ways that will not unduly interfere with the legitimate activities of the States.[76]

Mr. Justice Potter Stewart's specially concurring opinion in some respects was more revealing. He stated that the *Younger* principles need not be extended to cases that do not involve pending criminal prosecutions. "[W]e do not deal with the considerations that should govern a federal court when it is asked to intervene in state civil proceedings, where, for various reasons, the balance might be struck differently."[77] One reason, he observed, is that "[t]he offense to state interests is likely to be less in a civil proceeding."[78]

There are reasons why federal intervention in civil cases involves considerations different from those in criminal cases, but they are not necessarily the ones to which Mr. Justice Stewart adverted. The degree to which a state is disturbed by federal action depends more on the particular state policy that is challenged than upon the civil or criminal context in which the attack is made. For example, federal entry into a civil school integration dispute may produce impassioned state response, but federal interposition in a state criminal prosecution for littering streets with handbills may be greeted with waves of state apathy.

Significant distinctions between federal deference to states in criminal and civil proceedings rest on procedural and practical considerations. Abstention in a criminal case never forecloses a convicted defendant from litigating his constitutional claims in the federal district court, because he has federal habeas relief. Abstention in a civil case may deprive a litigant of a trial of his federal issues in a federal district court if the court dismisses the action instead of retaining jurisdiction[79] or if the litigant is at all careless in the manner in which he presents his federal questions to the state court to which the federal court has deferred.[80] Moreover, there is no counterpart to federal habeas corpus available to civil litigants. The existence of a possible Supreme Court review of a state court's adjudication of the litigant's federal issues is not a substitute for trial of those issues in the lower federal courts. As Chief Justice Marshall observed, a federal appeal based on factfindings by state courts that are unsympathetic to federal interests is at best an "insecure remedy."[81]

A practical consideration is the volume of litigation that could be injected into the federal system by initial federal entry into ordinary state criminal prosecutions in which a constitutional issue is presented. The constitutionalization of many evidentiary and procedural rules has led to the production of constitutional issues in almost every state criminal prosecution. The federal system cannot permit itself to be engorged by threshold constitutional decisions in all of these cases. In any case, Mr. Justice Stewart's opinion is important because it reveals that the Court is applying some kind of balancing test which it has not yet defined.

The difficulty with *Younger* is not its result, which is acceptable. The problem is that the plurality reasoning is so artificial that it is not much help in deciding future cases that are not Chinese copies of it. The Court itself immediately ran into this difficulty when it tried to apply *Younger* to resolve the question in *Samuels v. Mackell*:[82] Do the restrictions on the issuance of injunctions in pending criminal prosecutions also embrace the issuance of declaratory relief? The Court answered affirmatively, but it had to abandon the effort to use *Younger* to do it. The Court solved the problem by resurrecting an aging civil case that withheld federal declaratory relief.[83]

Equitable doctrines can be sensitive instruments when they are applied to decide personal disputes and to adjudicate the historical conflicts between the law and equity courts. They are clumsy devices, however, when they are used to try to resolve federal–state conflicts that are the byproducts of dual sovereignty, concurrent jurisdiction and federalism.

C. An Alternative—Enlightened Abstention

Young, Pullman, Constantineau, Zwickler, Dombrowski, Younger, and *Samuels* present the same fundamental issues in different factual settings: When should the lower federal courts initially bow to state courts, and when should they immediately seize and decide the constitutional questions presented? The mechanical test of *Pullman* is a failure. The equitable doctrines of *Younger* are not much better.

The place to start is over. If we remove the detritus of undefined notions of comity, of equitable doctrines, and of states-rights rhetoric, we can perceive that abstention is a mechanism for allocating kinds of cases and kinds of issues to state and federal courts. It should be used to retain in the federal system those controversies that raise fundamental constitutional issues and federal questions of national concern. These are the controversies that justify the existence of the lower federal courts. These are the controversies in which unsympathetic adjudication can erode federally secured rights. Cases of lesser federal interest should be routed to state court systems.[84]

Some cases will not easily yield to the broad-gauge test that I have suggested. For them, more sensitive criteria must be drawn. I suggest the following inquiries:

1. How immediate and how substantial is the claimed deprivation of the asserted constitutional right? The purpose of the question is to place the particular issue in perspective. The inquiry encompasses the traditional principles of standing and ripeness and retains the essence of the *Younger* irreparable injury concept. The scope, however, is broader. It includes such subsidiary questions as: Is the complainant immediately affected by the state action he has challenged? How severe is the impact of such action upon him? How many others similarly situated will be affected by the outcome? If the potential injury to the complainant is slight and the probabilities of his exposure are remote, the inquiry need not proceed further. If substantial harm is likely and imminent, we then have considerations to be weighed with others that we will extract from the succeeding questions.[85]

2. Will the claimant have a full, fair, and expeditious hearing of his constitutional issue if he is remitted to state proceedings? If the federal court has reason to believe that the answer is "No," it should not abstain. The risk of dilution of constitutionally secured rights is too

great, and there is no countervailing benefit from postponing federal entry into the controversy. On the other hand, if the probabilities of an effective state hearing are likely, we save that factor for futher consideration.[86]

3. If the state has a real interest in first adjudicating the controversy, is there a compelling federal interest that should override it? A state may be fascinated by a controversy in which it has no legitimate interest. For instance, feelings may run high when state officials have used criminal process as a means of harassing promoters of causes unpopular within the state, but there is no legitimate state interest involved in such a case.

When legitimate state interests are at stake, the decision should turn on an assessment of the benefits and costs that will result from abstention or retention. The potential benefits from abstention include (1) avoidance of unnecessary state antagonism to federal interests, (2) conservation of federal judicial time, (3) avoidance of premature decision of constitutional issues, and (4) enhancement of state court strength and prestige. The costs include (1) delay, (2) potential weakening of federal rights, (3) erosion of the right to a federal forum, and (4) decreased public confidence in the ability of federal courts to execute their primary functions.[87]

When the costs outweigh the benefits, as they did in *Pullman*, the federal courts should decide the case. When the benefits equal or nearly equal the costs, as they did in *Younger*, the federal courts should abstain, dismissing the case if the district court forum is secure for return and retaining jurisdiction if it is not.

VI. CONCLUSION

Federal courts have not yet been added to the list of threatened species. But the Supreme Court is hurtling toward entry, and the federal courts of appeals are following closely. We cannot continue perpetual open season on the federal systems. Essential conservation measures include revocation of some hunting licenses, establishment of new federal preserves, and restriction of the catch to those who have the highest federal priorities.

James L. Oakes

The Proper Role of the Federal Courts in Enforcing the Bill of Rights

While there is no dearth of material on the subject of enforcing the Bill of Rights, the role of the courts today remains shrouded in confusion and controversy.[1] Thus, to draw lines between what are premises and what are hypotheses or conclusions is most difficult. I will first state some of my "givens," the premises which guide my thinking. In doing so, I will eschew code words like "judicial activism" or "restraint."[2] Although some of these premises may seem obvious, I state them to aid communication and because it is worthwhile to build upon good foundations.

I. SOME PREMISES

A. *The Protective Role of the Courts*

My first "given" is that according to the Founding Fathers the diffusion of power was essential to the survival of the government they were to form. As part of an enlightened age, they had learned from Montesquieu that "'[w]hen the legislative and executive powers are united in the same person, or in the same body of magistrates, there can be no liberty,'" and that "'there is no liberty, if the judiciary power be not separated from the legislative and executive.'"[3] What the Fathers were thinking of was not just a separation of powers. It was a dispersion of power. They feared not just the absolute power of monarchy but also the "'brutal power'" that had become "'an irresistable argument of boundless right'" under Cromwell.[4] As Bernard Bailyn has observed, these people believed that "the ultimate explanation of every political controversy was the disposition of power."[5] This conviction was the heart of their great contribution to political

Judge Oakes's lecture was delivered on October 23, 1979 and appeared in 54 N.Y.U.L. Rev. 911 (1979).

thought. Madison's *Federalist No. 10* projected that a large Republic with power delegated to elected officials is a model for government preferable to a pure democracy because it diffuses power both by dispersal and by a clash of interests.[6]

But we must think in terms of "separated institutions *sharing* powers," rather than merely a government of separated powers.[7] This concept—by no means original with me—helps to define the courts' general role in government[8] and points more specifically toward today's principal judicial function: overseeing the relationship between our vast bureaucracies, on the one hand, and groups or individuals on the other.

My second "given" is a corollary to the diffusion of power: the courts are to have a definite protective role, to exercise a checking function. Jefferson writing to Madison from Paris spoke of the "legal check" which a declaration of rights "puts into the hands of the judiciary."[9] "This is a body," he continued, "which if rendered independent & kept strictly to their own department merits great confidence for their learning & integrity."[10] Or as Madison himself was subsequently to say to the First Congress in urging the adoption of the Bill of Rights:

If [the rights] are incorporated into the Constitution, independent tribunals of justice will consider themselves in a peculiar manner the guardians of those rights; they will be an impenetrable bulwark against every assumption of power in the Legislative or Executive; they will be naturally led to resist every encroachment upon rights expressly stipulated for in the Constitution by the declaration of rights.[11]

This checking function of the courts[12] was meant to have two aspects. First, and more obviously, the judiciary was to serve as a check on the executive and legislative branches. Hamilton considered the judiciary "the weakest of the three departments of power,"[13] one by which "the general liberty of the people can never be endangered."[14] He would entrust the judicial branch with the function of preserving express limitations on legislative power by "declar[ing] all acts contrary to the manifest tenor of the Constitution void."[15] Hence the correlative need for independence of the judiciary—tenure for life or during good behavior, coupled with compensation "which shall not be diminished during their Continuance in Office"[16]—and hence the origin of the doctrine of judicial review.[17]

While Hamilton was more concerned about a check on the legislative branch, and Jefferson and Madison about a check on the executive, the Antifederalists, or some of them, feared that the Supreme Court would support Congress in any challenge to federal power by the states.[18] Despite these concerns and other doubts as to the "democratic nature"[19] and propriety of judicial review, the question of its legitimacy has been decided affirmatively, and I accordingly take it as a "given."

But the other aspect of the courts' checking function, of utmost conceptual importance, is the restraint of the majority's power over individuals or groups of individuals who constitute the "minorities." The Founding Fathers were completely aware of this function. Hamilton referred to judges "guard[ing] the Constitution and the rights of individuals," as well as preventing "serious oppressions of the minor party in the community."[20] But—and this is the historical key—the Antifederalists were concerned that there was nothing explicit in the Constitution to give the courts this power. George Madison, for example, the author of the Virginia Bill of Rights, was concerned that Congress, in collecting taxes or legislating for the general welfare, would infringe the right to trial by jury or the freedom of the press.[21] It is significant that "[e]very ratifying convention which considered amendments adopted one or more similar to the present Articles V, VI, and VII."[22] Smilie, Silas Lee, "Cincinnatus," Lincoln of South Carolina, Richard Henry Lee, the Antifederalists generally, wanted to secure the "'Enestimable Provilege'" of a free press.[23] Jefferson and Madison came to believe that a bill of rights was necessary not only to satisfy the minds of their well-meaning opponents, the Antifederalists, but also to provide additional safeguards in defense of liberty.[24] As Madison put it when he made his appeal for the Bill of Rights to the First Congress:

[T]he great object in view is to limit and qualify the powers of Government, by excepting out of the grant of power those cases in which the Government ought not to act, or to act only in a particular mode. They point these exceptions sometimes against the abuse of the Executive power, sometimes against the Legislative, and, in some cases, against the community itself; or, in other words, against the majority in favor of the minority.[25]

And it was in the "community itself" that Madison saw the greatest threat:

[T]he great danger lies rather in the abuse of the community than in the Legislative body. The prescriptions in favor of liberty ought to be levelled against that quarter where the greatest danger lies, namely, that which possesses the highest prerogative of power. But this is not found in either the Executive or

Legislative departments of Government, but in the body of the people, operating by the majority against the minority.[26]

In short, the Bill of Rights itself stands as a barrier, protecting individuals and minorities against "the community," the majority. The bill is thus countermajoritarian and undemocratic, in this limited sense, even though most judicial review *cum* intervention today is directed toward bureaucratic rather than legislative determinations.[27] Moreover, as the bill is more frequently applied on a local or parochial level, who or what constitutes the "majority" is less clearly defined; it is a long way from an Act of Congress to an ordinance of the Village of Belle Terre.[28]

This view of the bill as a restraint on the power of the majority is fundamental to any analysis of the courts' role in enforcing the Bill of Rights and is one, however simple, that is often overlooked. It not only runs counter to any form of totalitarianism; it also puts the courts in a basic posture antithetical to strict utilitarianism, since it serves on occasion to limit the greater good of the many, or what the many think is the greater good. It is the basis for truly "taking rights seriously," as Ronald Dworkin, whose collection of essays bears that title, would be the first to state.[29] As Madison himself made clear in *Federalist No. 10,* while speaking of the inability of a small, pure democracy to cope with the mischiefs of faction: "A common passion or interest will, in almost every case, be felt by a majority of the whole; a communication and concert result from the form of government itself; and there is nothing to check the inducements to sacrifice the weaker party or an obnoxious individual."[30] Thus, the underlying concept is that even "obnoxious individuals" have certain basic entitlements against the majority, secured by the Bill of Rights—rights to personal security, protection of property,[31] and freedom of expression. This leads readily to the proposition that each group in the society may assert those rights vis-à-vis governmental operations. Only in this century has this notion become universally recognized.[32] "Discrete" or "insular" racial groups, women, prison inmates, juveniles, the elderly—minority interest groups have multiplied and gradually society's recognition of their entitlements has broadened.

Democratic government and judicially enforced minority rights are both based on a single conception of respect owed to every individual by the government. To remain faithful to that basic conception, judges must be vigilant—even creative—in their review of the other branches. But they must also maintain a constant awareness of the countervailing value of majoritarian rule and the resulting responsibility of the majority to do what is right. With this qualification, the power of judicial review to limit majoritarian action needs no further justification, since it is a corollary of the diffusion of power.

Important, of course, is the manner in which the power of review is exercised. For the power carries with it heavy responsibilities. It is given to the courts, in Justice Black's phrase, in "sacred trust."[33] It therefore must be exercised only after the deepest consideration and, so to speak, as a last resort, when other avenues have failed. Constitutional meaning, as Madison wrote to Justice Roane, must "be derived from a series of cases actually occurring for adjudication,"[34] that is, be a specific case or controversy as provided in Article III, with overall interpretation to flow from the particular to the general, not the converse.[35] These limitations on the courts include, among other things, the series of seven prudential, procedural rules set forth by Justice Brandeis in his *Ashwander* opinion.[36] We try to ensure that a constitutional question is reached only when reasonable resort to other methods of decision is precluded. Out of respect to our federal system we also defer to state courts and to state institutions; we abstain so as to permit them to clarify their own law.[37] We have a whole system of prudential rules, including the role of precedent itself[38] which I take as givens, though not as ends in themselves.

It is true, as Abram Chayes has pointed out, that we no longer think in simple terms of adjudication based on retrospective, self-contained, party-initiated and controlled biopolar lawsuits seeking to constrain power. We now recognize a form of public law litigation which enforces affirmative values running to groups and which needs prospective judicial enforcement.[39] The limitations I speak of here still apply, but they are no longer the legal straitjackets they were in the past. Expansive concepts of standing[40] and the right to intervene,[41] coupled with the advent of class actions which take into account group interests,[42] the curtailing of the "political question" limitation on what we call justiciability,[43] and other procedural developments, have broadened the originally narrow judicial role.[44] Fortunately these developments have occurred simultaneously with, or perhaps as a result of, a certain universalization of substantive demands for the rights that have always been available in fact to the powerful, or to the well organized.[45]

B. *The Nature of the Bill of Rights*

Another premise underlying my discussion is the interrelationship and interdependence of the various rights. This is not surprising when we view the Bill of Rights as a codification of ethical or moral concepts not unlike the Decalogue, though expressly eschewing any religious commitment. In effect they incorporate a set of principles or standards governing the relationship between the individual and his or her government and they necessarily overlap.

The interrelationship of the specified rights, of course, has a deep historical basis. I will mention only one or two examples. The Puritan minister John Udall,[46] a Hebrew scholar and author of *Demonstration of Discipline*, was apprehended in 1590 in connection with the sensational tracts against church-establishment which were published the year before and denounced by Queen Elizabeth as seditious libel subverting her prerogative. After declining on Magna Carta grounds to answer the questions of a special board, Udall refused to take the oath ex officio, the dreaded weapon of the Court of High Commission, which was an ecclesiastical court with practices reminiscent of the Spanish Inquisition. After six months of solitary confinement he was tried before a jury for seditious libel at common law with one of the members of the commission sitting as one of his judges—shades of the Fifth Amendment Due Process Clause.[47] His request for counsel was denied, and when he asked about challenging jurors he was denied any information—shades of the Sixth Amendment.[48] While defendants were not permitted to testify in common law courts, Udall was asked before the jury to take an oath and answer the question whether he wrote the book; and when he declined to do so, the judges argued his guilt to the jury—shades of the Fifth Amendment self-incrimination clause[49] and of due process generally. Although the statute required proof by two witnesses appearing in person, testimony was solely by depositions—shades of the Sixth Amendment Confrontation Clause[50]—one of which offered hearsay testimony, and none of which Udall was permitted to impeach—and here we think again of due process. The statute punished seditious libel made with a malicious intent to encourage insurrection or rebellion, and we may recall the First Amendment.[51] In holding that Udall's book was, as a matter of law, published maliciously—the jury merely had to find that Udall was the author of the book—the court invaded the province of the jury that the *Zenger* case[52] was to establish as a fundamental tenet of First Amendment law.[53] Ultimately sentenced to hang, though offered expatriation and exile, Udall rotted away in prison and died, a now little-remembered contributor to our First, Fifth, Sixth, and possibly Eighth Amendments, but a contributor nevertheless.

More familiar are the cases of the Whig John Wilkes and his friends. Wilkes's impact on our colonial forebears' thinking is, as Bailyn reminds us,[54] inestimable; he was as familiar to the 1760s to 1790s as were Tom Mooney to the 1920s,[55] the Scottsboro Boys to the 1930s,[56] Robert Oppenheimer to the 1950s[57] and the Chicago Seven to the 1960s.[58] It was in seeking to arrest Wilkes for seditious libel and searching his papers and effects, as well as those of over forty of his associates, including John Entick, that the Crown came to grief: though general warrants had been used for eighty years, in *Entick v. Carrington*[59] they were found illegal and doubly so when issued without probable cause and when no record was made of what was seized. *Entick v. Carrington*, the Supreme Court was later to say, was a "great judgment," "one of the landmarks of English liberty," "one of the permanent monuments of the British Constitution,"[60] and a guide to understanding what the framers meant in writing the Fourth Amendment.[61] I refer to it here, however, for the fact that a First Amendment freedom was also quite directly involved: the Wilkes case was to precipitate the libel defenses of truth and lack of malice, and it was these seditious libel prosecutions that lay at the root of our First Amendment.[62]

The cases of Wilkes and his friends show us the intimate relationship between the First and the Fourth, Fifth, Sixth, Seventh, and Eighth Amendments. There are many other examples.[63] Time and again it was in protecting freedom of thought, of conscience, or of expression that the procedural rights embodied in our Fourth through Eighth Amendments were first asserted, then given substance, and finally enshrined as basic to our institutions.

The interrelationship of the enumerated rights is significant for several reasons. The bill cannot be construed merely taxonomically, as a set of pigeonholes or preconceived rules into which a given factual situation does or does not fit. Rather it must be viewed as a whole; it is an interlocking complex of basic principles of fairness and individual entitlement that carries a continuing meaning applicable to entirely different or changed circumstances. Thus, "penumbral" rights, such as the right to travel[64] or to privacy[65] or to "personhood,"[66] become not only conceptually possible but positively essential, although they are nowhere specifically mentioned.[67] More important, the whole of the Bill of Rights becomes greater than the sum of its parts. It is synergistic, involving a "plus,"[68] which makes the bill not only a charter of our rights, but an inspiration for our daily lives and an ideal unceasingly to be striven for and devoutly to be pursued. I see the Bill of Rights then as a codification of principles of humanism,[69] a document that embodies something as close as we may come to a national religion. It is perhaps not remarkable that this declaration of our ideals also has an international appeal, though it is evident that our national credibility is ineluctably tied to the extent to which we ourselves live by the aspirations that the bill embodies.

The interrelationship of the rights does not necessarily preclude thinking of certain of them as preferred—rights such as freedom of expression and religious belief, which are essential to others that are more procedural in form.[70] But it does tend to raise some of those procedural rights in the scale of importance. For instance, once we recognize that a press may not be free to print if its offices are subject to searches or seizures by the police,[71] what happens to the person suspected of carrying weapons on or off an airplane[72] takes on added importance. Someone who is calumnized for "taking the Fifth" in a political heresy context, it may be pointed out, would be apotheosized if he did so when questioned for religious heresy; that the right against self-incrimination incorporated in our Fifth Amendment was a product of inquisitional processes leading to suppression of freedom of conscience surely gives the right higher standing in our eyes.[73]

But does this "plus" by another name lead to "substantive due process," the ad hoc concept under which the Supreme Court for thirty years or more negated congressional and state legislation looking toward economic and industrial reform? Perhaps, but only in a sense. While the ghost of *Lochner v. New York*[74] probably has been laid to rest,[75] we recognize certain fundamental personal interests with substantive content, which are subject to treatment under the Equal Protection Clause, with its emphasis on the equal citizenship values of respect, participation, and responsibility,[76] as well as under the Due Process Clause, viewed as a provision protecting individual "personhood"[77] and the coordinate interests in being free from governmental intrusion, in "avoiding disclosure of personal matters," and in preserving "independence in making certain kinds of important decisions."[78] There are, in short, both "liberty" and "entitlement" interests that have substantive content and are not subject to governmental deprivation; and to hold this view is not inconsistent with holding a latitudinarian view as to the powers of government with respect to economic matters, at least where there is some rational relationship to a legitimate governmental objective.[79]

Viewed as an interwoven fabric or spirit, with the creative tension this implies, the Bill of Rights also takes on a more fragile aspect. We come to recognize that the illegal police practice,[80] the abuse of a prison inmate,[81] the denial of a termination hearing to a welfare recipient,[82] are all potentially assaults upon our own rights because each of us is protected only as much as others are. This concept is all the more telling as the power of government through technology and sheer size becomes the more awesome and the role of the individual correspondingly less significant.

Suspensions of constitutional rights do occur—have occurred—in other countries. We are aware that on the day following the Reichstag fire, February 28, 1933, Chancellor Hitler forced President Hindenburg to sign a decree " 'for the Protection of the People and the State' " as a " 'defensive measure against Communist acts of violence endangering the state.' "[83] This decree, suspending the seven sections of the Weimar Constitution making up the German bill of rights, stated:

Restrictions on personal liberty, on the right of free expression of opinion, including freedom of the press; on the rights of assembly and association; and violations of the privacy of postal, telegraphic and telephonic communications; and warrants for house searchers, orders for confiscations as well as restrictions on property, are also permissible beyond the legal limits otherwise prescribed.[84]

And then there is the recent proclamation by Nicaragua of a sweeping fifty-two article bill of rights that permits all but five to be suspended for reasons of national security, public order, or an "exceptional situation or emergency that puts the life or the stability of the nation in danger."[85]

One may say these things cannot happen here; our institutions are too secure, we are too stable. I say let us hope so, but meanwhile let us not forget the Mitchell-Palmer raids of 1919 and 1920,[86] the *Korematsu* case upholding the segregation of Japanese–Americans during World War II,[87] our senatorial inquisitions of Joe McCarthy days,[88] and the recent lessons of Watergate.[89] I will not pursue this; I note it. Our institutions fortunately do not hang by a thread, but a deep depression, a serious blow to national pride, extensive internal terrorism, a serious external threat to security, or a combination of these may enlarge the ranks of the elements of society that are ever ready to abandon liberty for order and to abandon freedom for security. In the meantime let us beware lest by default we permit some of these rights to be chipped away.

I agree with Learned Hand that in the final analysis "[l]iberty lies in the hearts of men and women; when it dies there, no constitution, no law, no court can save it."[90] With respect, however, I tend to be less skeptical than he about what can be done to preserve it in the interim. While I surely agree with Justice Douglas's assertion that "the Bill of Rights is not enough,"[91] and thereby fully comprehend that the rights carry with them an equally important duty of good citizenship, I view, as I am sure he did, the day-to-day concrete exposition of those rights not only as a continuing educational process—educative to expositor and expositee alike—but as an activity at the heart of our democratic system. I take for granted the dialogue between the federal judges and the nation,[92] on a substantive level, and insist that our task is to present and to be able to defend reflective, historically aware, and contemporaneously applicable views of what every citizen's rights and correlative duties are, as the questions arise in particular cases. Indeed, there is no other institution in our society that continually carries on a systematic exposition of human rights and their relationship to society. The "dialogue" then serves not only as an inspiration to both judges and nation, but as a bedrock against the encroachment of tyranny, whatever its derivation, and especially when the sources of that tyranny are, as they are sometimes, hidden in the "hearts of men and women."

I readily accept the notion that there is a "risk of error"[93] that goes beyond mere reversal, in the case of lower court judges, by a court above and a risk that is present with the Supreme Court at all times. The proposition advanced must ultimately be persuasive to the people, even against their passions and prejudices, not only because the process of constitutional amendment is always open, but also because "the people" are the ultimate authority in our society. We judges who would be lions must be lions under the throne. We must hope with Cardozo, however, that in the process of dialogue that right decisions ultimately will tend to prevail; as he optimistically put it, "[t]he tide rises and falls but the sands of error crumble."[94]

II. ENFORCEMENT OF INDIVIDUAL RIGHTS

A. *The Function of Constitutional Adjudication*

The courts properly serve as the "pressure cooker" of democracy.[95] By this I do not merely mean to repeat de Tocqueville's over-quoted remark that "[s]carcely any political question arises in the United States that is not resolved, sooner or later, into a judicial question."[96] I mean that as the courts are called upon to resolve some of the most controversial social and political questions, the issues simmer, and the steam they generate escapes in a gradual way. The problems are in the courts usually because they have not been resolved elsewhere, often because the problems are too difficult, too explosive, too charged with passion and prejudice to be solved legislatively or administratively.[97] Thus the courts often decide rights issues by default, because they are there precisely to make such resolutions. Other devices have been unable to resolve them. Three old issues are good examples; whether children of Jehovah's Witnesses have to conform to a school district regulation requiring flag salutes as a daily exercise;[98] whether a federal court may interfere when blacks have been tried for murder under the imminent threat of mob violence;[99] and whether a state may enjoin publication of a radical newspaper that maliciously accuses public officials of corruption.[100] More recent examples include whether the courts may intervene on behalf of retarded children in the custody of the state who are receiving only "custodial" and no other kind of care;[101] whether a citizen must carry around a slogan on his automobile license plate that he finds politically and religiously obnoxious;[102] and whether a local single-family zoning ordinance may prohibit a grandmother from living in one dwelling with her son and two grandsons who are cousins.[103] The constitutional litigation process acts as an "escape valve" in our political system. Happily, the cooking process gives time for the nation to collect its thoughts, for polemics and rhetoric to be displaced by reason, for issues to be clarified. Supercharged issues of grave moment are decided on a case-to-case or particularized factual basis and with a measure of "deliberate speed,"[104] when passions have had a chance to cool.

I come back to Madison's letters on *McCulloch v. Maryland*: how desirable it is that the meaning of a law or of a constitution result "from a course of particular decisions, and not these from a previous and abstract comment on the subject."[105] Consider the whole problem of affirmative action and reverse discrimination—a quite complex series of issues with moral, historical, political, and constitutional overtones, which recently threatened to divide the nation severely. How satisfactory it is that instead of having one remote, abstract proposition advanced as decisive, we have had and are still having a "course of particular decisions": the first, undecided on account of mootness;[106] the second, a voting rights case involving a racially sensitive reapportionment plan;[107] the third, a higher-education case in which purely numerical quotas had rather thoughtlessly been established;[108] the fourth, a privately negotiated labor contract granting preferential treatment to minority hirees in an on-the-job training program;[109] the fifth, a case involving a school system whose numerically disparate assignment of minority teachers rendered the system ineligible for federal grants.[110] During the present Term, the Court will decide a case involving minority hiring quotas affirmatively required in the allotment of construction contracts using certain specified federal funds.[111] One would have been hard put—nay, it would have been an impossible task—to have stated a single overall rule that could have effectively guided the determination of all these cases. I doubt that a legislature conscientiously bent on compromise could have begun to establish an appropriate framework for them. But one can almost see the steam escaping from the valve during the cooking process as each is decided, one by one. Since courts are not omniscient, there is, indeed, a certain amount of trial and error, but even from that there may be profit.[112]

This affirmative pressure-cooker role of the courts has often given this nation time and space to solve problems that otherwise might have been beyond solution.[113] It is a function that the courts may not welcome—some of us might prefer to be deciding securities or antitrust or trademark or admiralty cases—but it is ours as a duty and from it we must not shrink. When the Bill of Rights is properly invoked, we cannot leave all educational matters to the educators, all correctional matters to the correction people, all mental health matters to the psychiatrists.[114] As for those who would have us do so, who present us with the all too attractive alternative of leaving things as they are, of letting our bureaucracies run untrammeled in the thought that any correction must come from the legislature above, I

* Judge Oakes here refers to Fullilove v. Klutznick, 448 U.S. 448 (1980). In Fullilove, the Supreme Court held that a federal statute, requiring that at least 10 percent of federal funds for public works projects go to minority-owned contracting businesses, was constitutional. EDITOR'S NOTE.

can only remind them of the courts' assigned role and point to a real danger to the Republic from within—the danger of too long frustrated expectations.

B. Value Choices in the Decisionmaking Process

True, we must have principles to guide us in our "enforcement." We cannot decide cases merely ad hoc on the basis of our sentiments of the day or how we would *like* things to be. The chancellor's conscience, as John Selden pointed out, varies as much as the length of his foot.[115] Indeed we have taken an oath to the contrary: to "administer justice without respect to persons, and do equal right to the poor and to the rich,"[116] an oath which perforce is inconsistent with this kind of ad hoc decisionmaking.

We must strive toward objectivity, detachment, and fairness; but I expect that we can never follow truly "neutral principles" as Herbert Wechsler would idealistically have us,[117] except in the rather simplistic sense of having a neutral attitude toward the litigants. A principle by definition has reference to a framework; it is a generalization providing a basis for reasoning or a guide for conduct or procedure. The very holding of certain premises with respect to the Bill of Rights, for example, precludes neutrality in any real sense; as I have said, my concept of the Bill of Rights sets it in opposition to strict utilitarianism. Accordingly, I would weigh the rights of the individual a little more heavily in the scales than would a judge who rather favored the parliamentary system.

It is, then, impossible in the process of constitutional adjudication not to apply certain basic principles that involve value choices. And even judges who agree about general principles will disagree in particular cases. I venture, with Samuel F. Miller and Donald F. Howell,[118] to say that all constitutional decisionmaking involves value consequences; and if this is true, then there is a point at which value choices have to be made. The necessity is to acknowledge these value choices when they arise and to reason accordingly. Judges should not overlook or conceal value choices, enshrouding them in some mysterious, semi-Delphic pronouncements from on high.[119] Better to state them explicitly to the end that they will enlighten the national dialogue.

This is obviously not to say that judges, particularly lower court judges, are free to roam at will. Quite to the contrary, when the value choices have been made by the Supreme Court we are bound to follow them, although I see it as our duty to throw light on those choices that have not been fully disclosed to public view and criticism.[120] Judges are also bound to a considerable extent to follow choices made by their own courts so that the law will be uniform, impartial, and nonarbitrary, although here again I see it as our function to identify those choices we think have been made erroneously.[121] But when we decide whether a pretrial detainee or his visitor may be subjected to a strip search,[122] whether a high school teacher has a "liberty" interest in wearing a turtleneck with his jacket rather than a shirt and tie,[123] or whether a state may require its flags to be lowered to half-mast on Good Friday,[124] we are making very real value choices. We may consider that the rights of the individual in the first situation are outweighed by the demands of prison security, that the rights of the teacher in the second case are too trivial to overcome the contrary judgment of the school board, or that the right of the public to freedom from the coercion of state-established preference for the Christian faith must prevail in the third, but each of these cases involves a choice of values. And as we go from enforcing the more specific prohibitions of the Bill of Rights to enforcing the more general directions—to provide "due process" and "equal protection"—our value choices are by no means simplified or our job made easier. To the contrary, in dealing with the more general clauses there is *more* reason to spell out the analysis in greater detail lest, to borrow again Cardozo's felicitous phrases, we "innovate at pleasure" or "yield to spasmodic sentiment."[125]

Recognizing that value choices are a part of the overall process of constitutional adjudication has very specific consequences. The first is that the balancing process in which we all engage depends on what is put into the scales. Chief Justice Warren pointed out that when the nation's security is balanced against the freedom of the individual litigant, the latter usually loses.[126] He would, I suspect, take issue with our present chief justice when the latter occasionally appears to balance the right of the individual criminal defendant against the societal interest in stamping out crime;[127] when any such a balance is struck the individual is likely to lose.

Into the scales—when the Bill of Rights is involved—one must put "survival as a free nation."[128] The issue then becomes not whether the individual wins against society, but how best to accommodate the societal interest in security and order with the need to maintain the spirit of liberty as particularized in the given case. None of us, of course, wants airplanes to be hijacked, but does this mean that any would-be passenger may be physically searched at will and whim? A negative answer given by some courts[129] has led to the relatively nonintrusive accommodation now in effect, subjecting carry-on luggage, briefcases, and pocketbooks to X-ray examination and having the individual walk though a magnetometer.

Recognizing that we are consciously making value choices leads to another, perhaps more startling, thought. In the finding of "facts," the most "elusive elements in human conduct,"[130] on which all judgments necessarily depend in a system of constitutional government, ascertaining the "truth" cannot be the sole aim of either the criminal or the civil process.[131] As Mirjan Damaška has pointed out in his comparison of the continental, inquisitional system to our own accusatorial system of advocacy, the objective of truth discovery must be tempered by the means by which it is sought[132]—the objective must be accomplished in a "'socially acceptable way.'"[133] This concept recognizes at one level that a jury may acquit against the weight of the evidence or contrary to the court's charge.[134] At another level it assumes that there are societal interests—for example, against torture, psychological "brainwashing," or coercion—that are more important than ascertainment of the truth. I put it more bluntly and less elegantly perhaps when I said, in defense of the exclusionary rule after a glimpse of the judicial process in South Africa:

[W]hat is truth? If truth is what the State says it is, is the State always correct? If a state is untrammeled by rules of evidence, its agents can plant evidence; plant the idea of and effectuate the execution of crime; burst down doors of a house in the night and seize anything in or out of sight; obtain admissions from a defendant in the absence of his lawyer; extract confessions by hook, crook or force. Despite the fact that all this evidence would be admissible in the name of "truth," what is to differentiate that state from a police state?[135]

Thus, we must make an accommodation between the values of truth and human rights when they conflict. One such accommodation, for example, may be the exclusionary rule, excluding evidence illegally obtained, restraining the truth-creating tendency of a state's law enforcement apparatus and at the same time permitting the police to gather evidence which is generally adequate to convict the guilty.[136]

The point that I am making here is that our accusatorial system is constructed around a series of concerns about individual rights which set limits on the pursuit of truth and the precision of factfinding. On these concerns we have placed a higher value, having learned that not to do so is to permit and foster an oppressive state, since the people who direct or operate its prosecuting machinery may not be presumed always to act out of the highest motivations or with deepest principle. The ascertainment of "truth," an elusive quest at best, then must sometimes yield to this higher value. It may be, as the chief justice said in dissent in *Brewer v. Williams,* "absurd,"[137] "bizarre,"[138] "remarkable,"[139] "intolerable"[140] that incriminating statements made in violation of the Sixth Amendment may not be admissible in evidence, but would it not be even more "bizarre" and "intolerable" if such evidence were admissible? Why stop with the Fourth and Sixth Amendments? Why not admit confessions extracted involuntarily, as judged by present constitutional standards,[141] at least if they turn out to be "true"? I must leave this argument for another day, but it has numerous other implications. I am distressed, to say the least, by the twelve or so cases decided since 1970 involving the *Miranda* rules, each of which has given lip service to those rules while either denying the claim of a defendant who alleges a violation of the rules or allowing the claim of a prosecutor when the defendant's statements have been excluded.[142] Sometimes the value of truth-finding in our prosecutorial system must yield to the value of those individual freedoms embodied in the Bill of Rights. To acknowledge this choice of values is a positive and a necessary step.

C. *Application of the Bill of Rights to the Courts*

My next point is surely less startling, but equally important. Whether we judges like to think so or not, courts are a part of the government against whom the constraints of the Bill of Rights operate. Article VI includes "judicial Officers" among those required to take an oath "to support th[e] Constitution."[143] To be sure, a technical quibble can be made that the First Amendment applies only to Congress. This argument would be based on that amendment's peculiarly explicit wording that "Congress shall make no law,"[144] language different from the Virginia ratifying convention's recommendation that freedom of the press shall not be abridged "by any authority of the United States"[145] and different from Madison's own original proposal which was not confined to a prohibition on Congress.[146] But Madison himself thought that the First Amendment, as adopted, applied to government generally.[147] So have the courts; if there was any doubt about its application, *New York Times Co. v. Sullivan*[148] and other Supreme Court cases of the last fifteen years have removed it.[149] Certainly all the other amendments apply to government generally, and the courts are a part of the government. The point, while simple, has tremendous significance.

First and most obviously this proposition has direct impact on the Fourth Amendment and the exclusionary rule, which in turns bears on the Fifth and Sixth Amendments. The exclusionary rule is now said by some to be merely a "judicially created remedy designed to safeguard Fourth Amendment rights generally through its deterrent effect, rather than a personal constitutional right."[150] So viewed, the courts are no longer a part of a unitary system of government; as neutral truth-seekers their only job is to assure a fair trial. The rights of the defendant or the marginal increment in deterrence of the police are then balanced against the societal interest in not suppressing relevant evidence; if the latter outweighs the former, the exclusionary rule will be inapplicable.[151]

But the rule excluding illegally obtained evidence was conceived quite otherwise. The unanimous Court in *Weeks v. United States*[152] never mentioned "deterrent effect." Rather, the exclusionary rule represented a personal constitutional right of a defendant to prevent his government, in the form of the judicial branch, from utilizing evidence to convict him when that evidence had been obtained by unconstitutional means.[153] As the Court in *Weeks*—a Court which included Justices Holmes and Hughes—went on to say:

> The effect of the Fourth Amendment is to put the courts of the United States and Federal officials, in the exercise of their power and authority, under limitations and restraints as to the exercise of such power and authority, and to forever secure the people, their persons, houses, papers and effects against all unreasonable searches and seizures under the guise of law. This protection reaches all alike, whether accused of crime or not, and the duty of giving to it force and effect is obligatory upon all entrusted under our Federal system with the enforcement of the laws. The tendency of those who execute the criminal laws of the country to obtain conviction by means of unlawful seizures and enforced confessions, the latter often obtained after subjecting accused persons to unwarranted practices destructive of rights secured by the Federal Constitution, should find no sanction in the judgments of the courts which are charged at all times with the support of the Constitution and to which people of all conditions have a right to appeal for the maintenance of such fundamental rights.[154]

Holmes was to explicate this position further for the Court in *Silverthorne*[155] and Brandeis and Holmes were to echo it in their *Olmstead* dissents:[156] government is unitary; it has a duty in relation to its citizens; that duty does not permit separation of the means—such as the search or seizure by the police—from the ends—such as the use by the courts at trial of the evidence seized. The judiciary cannot, by closing its eyes to the unlawful means used, validate or sanction unconstitutional conduct. This is not, as a recent dissent of Justice Rehnquist would imply,[157] a sort of nostalgic romanticism tracing to the era of bootlegging and rumrunning. It is rather a fundamental precept that holds true, or must be thought to hold true, if we are to uphold the guarantees of the Bill of Rights.

The recognition that the rules apply to the courts as well as to the legislature is equally applicable to the Fifth Amendment in terms of coerced confessions, or to the Sixth in terms of statements obtained from a primary suspect in the absence of counsel. This recognition goes to the heart of the courts' duty to enforce the Bill of Rights.

Under the Sixth Amendment there is a right to counsel in a capital case, as the Court declared in *Powell v. Alabama*.[158] *Gideon v. Wainwright*[159] and *Argersinger v. Hamlin*[160] have extended this right to prosecutions involving felonies and misdemeanors carrying a jail sentence. So far so good. But the Court has yet to reverse a conviction for *inadequacy* of counsel even though the chief justice and others continue to point to numerous, supposed inadequacies.[161]* Some lower courts have done little better.[162]

In any unified theory of government, constitutional rights should be protected in the court processes as out of them. However, one detects, unfortunately, an almost paternalistic attitude that if the matter is in the courts' domain, the rules otherwise applicable do not apply. Pretrial discovery in defamation cases is unlimited regardless of the thought-control potentially involved—indeed, without a mention of it.[163] Here I speak not only of the mass media, the context in which *Herbert v. Lando* arose,[164] but of the "lonely pamphleteer,"[165] the single author, the teacher expressing his views. Newsmen's confidential sources must be revealed at least to grand juries.[166] Pretrial,[167] and,

---

* In Kimmelman v. Morrison, 106 S. Ct. 2574 (1986), the Supreme Court unanimously held that a defendant's attorney was sufficiently incompetent as to warrant remand to the federal district court to determine whether the defendant had been prejudiced. In Kimmelman, counsel had failed to move to suppress illegally seized evidence that was critical to the prosecution's case. Chief Justice Burger, along with Justices Powell and Rehnquist, disagreed with the majority over what constituted prejudice. He proposed a test that would have been extremely difficult for the defendant to meet. EDITOR'S NOTE.

some Supreme Court justices and courts think,[168] trial proceedings may be closed to the public and the press.

Other cases will suggest themselves to the reader. My own court, to my surprise, recently permitted a jury to be drawn anonymously and prevented defense counsel from even inquiring into the backgrounds of prospective jurors.[169] The point I am trying to make is that the federal courts should not forget that the same prohibitions embodied in the Bill of Rights that apply to Congress, the executive, the administrative agencies, the state and local governments, and the state courts, also apply to the federal courts in their judicial domain. We are not somehow by our "guardianship" exempted from the rules prescribing those prohibitions.

D. Remedying Constitutional Deprivations

Most of what I have said relates to the courts' role in defining the substantive values embodied in the Bill of Rights. Here I will refer to the current status of three of the more significant tools used by the courts to give remedial content to substantive rights: structural due process,[170] section 1983[171] and structural injunctions.[172] I will then close with some comments on the legitimacy of the judicial role I am advocating, since I believe it is the far-reaching remedial measures mandated by this stance that most often arouse public and congressional antipathy on the one hand, and concerned, scholarly, and philosophical reservations on the other.

1. Structural Due Process

I have already discussed the importance of some procedural protections to criminal defendants, but their importance to the citizen dealing with government bureaucracy or to the corporation[173] dealing with a regulatory agency is equally great. This does not, of course, mean that every claim to a hearing,[174] to right to counsel, to an explanation of a certain course of action, or to another of the bundle of rights that constitutes "procedural due process" is meritorious. The administrative expenses and time associated with a totally due-processed society would make Aldous Huxley's Brave New World look positively rustic by comparison. I agree in principle with the Supreme Court that, in picking and choosing from among the claims, lines have to be drawn based on the gravity of the private interests affected, the risk of an erroneous deprivation of such interests, the existence of other effective procedural safeguards, and the governmental function involved.[175] The challenge lies in the application of this balancing principle,[176] a problem not readily susceptible of analysis here.

Although procedural due process may impose on governmental agencies a requirement that implementation of policies detrimentally affecting the rights of individuals comport with certain procedural safeguards—most fundamentally the right to be heard[177]—it is limited by the neutral nature of the judicial examination. So I note with favor the developing trend on the part of some legal thinkers and judges toward a new concept of "structural due process,"[178] which expands the scope of the courts' review of the way in which the state imposes limitations on individuals' rights. Structural due process permits a court to examine the fairness of governmental decision-implementing structures. For example, structural due process would prohibit use of a hard-and-fast rule when the government seeks to regulate conduct in an area in which moral views are widely perceived to be in flux.[179] Underlying structural due process is the belief that the courts' role is not properly limited to the protection of clearly defined substantive rights and the neutral enforcement of clearly defined procedures. Rather, by prohibiting the ossification of standards in unsettled areas, the courts play an active role in structuring the expression of social norms in the law.

Thus, the armed forces correctly treat disabilities when suffered by males—*e.g.*, alcoholism—on an individual basis, suspending or terminating a man only after considering his particular situation, ability, and need. They should be required to treat female disabilities—e.g., pregnancy—similarly, as we held in an opinion I wrote for the court in *Crawford v. Cushman*,[180] and I understand that all of the armed services have adjusted happily.[181] Our court recently affirmed the right of a person to individualized consideration by the state in another, perhaps more controversial situation—that of employees of the New York City Transit Authority on methadone maintenance who sought to retain non-safety-related jobs[182]—but a majority of the Supreme Court, perhaps viewing the facts differently from the way the district court and we viewed them, overturned us.[183] Individualized treatment in an increasingly complex, institutional, and bureaucratized society may be hard to come by, even expensive to maintain, but in many cases it is demanded by the notions of due process embodied in the Bill of Rights. Structural due process recognizes the dynamics of change in our governmental structures, specifically the trend away from the legislative and toward the administrative and bureaucratic process. It is a welcome new concept of which we will undoubtedly hear more.

2. *The Narrowing of Section 1983*

Section 1983, the statutory mechanism through which most constitutional rights against state officials are asserted,[184] is under at least four different forms of attack, or, more delicately put, is undergoing four forms of judicial limitation, the seriousness of which is, to me, threatening. Its substantive content is being limited by decisions which hold that certain acts by state officials do not rise to the level of constitutional violations and therefore do not trigger federal remedial relief.[185] According to these decisions, some conduct may give rise only to actions for tort under state common or statutory law and not to section 1983 liability.* This "doctrine" acts as a de minimis rule enabling the courts to avoid the truly trivial. But we must beware lest under this rubric genuine deprivations are permitted to occur. Defining the content of "liberty" or "property" rights by reference solely to state law, as one reading of three recent Supreme Court cases would have us do,[186] can only result in an emasculation of both the Fourteenth Amendment and section 1983.[187]

The substantive content of section 1983 is further limited by the availability to public officials of immunity, good faith, and lack-of-intent defenses, at least when the officials are acting within the scope of their authority.[188] While the Supreme Court in *Monell v. Department of Social Services*[189] finally removed the erroneous reading of section 1983's legislative history in *Monroe v. Pape*[190] so as to permit suits against municipalities, at least if they have a "policy or custom" which results in a constitutional deprivation,[191] the question is open whether municipalities too will have available the defense of good faith.[192]† If they do, as a general proposition, *Monell* may be an empty case, resembling the second civil rights case to hold a state statute unconstitutional on equal protection grounds.[193]

The third limitation on section 1983 recoveries is the damages limitation expressed by the Court in *Carey v. Piphus*.[194] The Court held that recovery may be had only for actual, compensable injuries,[195] to

* This trend, incipient in the cases Judge Oakes discussed in his 1979 lecture, continued in the 1980s. See Justice Blackmun's discussion of Pennhurst State School and Hospital v. Halderman, 465 U.S. 89 (1984); Hudson v. Palmer, 468 U.S. 517 (1984); Parratt v. Taylor, 451 U.S. 527 (1981) at pp. 248–249 infra. EDITOR'S NOTE.

† The Supreme Court did extend "good faith" immunity from section 1983 actions to state and local officials in Davis v. Scherer, 468 U.S. 183 (1984). EDITOR'S NOTE.

be awarded in a manner patterned after, if not exactly paralleling, the common law of torts.[196] It ruled out any recovery other than a nominal one for a deprivation of constitutional rights as such.[197] Thus, a deprivation of procedural due process or of a right to assemble, without proof of actual injury, is actionable only for nominal damages.[198] This is probably as it should be, it may even be as section 1983 was intended, but the danger is that significant distress and personal harm will be treated as noncompensable.

A fourth limitation on section 1983 is what can be called the argument from federalism:[199] the federal courts are, it is argued, interfering with concerns that legitimately are state and local in nature. The force of this argument has resulted in, *inter alia,* Eleventh Amendment immunity of states from damage awards[200] and a series of decisions limiting the availability of federal injunctive relief in ongoing state proceedings.[201] Another result—an application of the expanding doctrines of res judicata and collateral estoppel[202]—may be a sort of judicial cul-de-sac for persons deprived of civil rights. Already, if a person could have asserted his federal civil rights claim in a state action, even one in which he was an involuntary participant, but did not do so, he may be bound by the state court's decision.[203] The "Catch-22" of federal civil rights actions—one fortunately not yet reached[204]—would require that federal courts abstain to permit state adjudication of the federal civil rights claims,[205] and then treat the state court determination as binding.

However much we may respect local autonomy or decentralization of government, or valid the judgments of state court judges,[206] the argument from federalism has disturbing implications. Section 1983 refers only to action taken under color of state law and recognizes a federal interest in the protection of federal civil rights. As my colleague Henry Friendly put it, "[i]t is hard to conceive a task more appropriate for federal courts than to protect civil rights guaranteed by the Constitution against invasion by the states."[207] Why, then, section 1983 should be limited in the interests of comity, federalism, and states' rights is impossible for me to follow. I am concerned lest the combined effect of these four limitations on section 1983 together constitute a throwback to the Court's evisceration of the civil rights statutes during the final quarter of the last century.[208]

3. Structural Injunctive Relief

One area in which the courts' capacity to safeguard constitutional rights remains vital is in the fashioning of injunctive relief, particularly the highly controversial structural injunctions.[209] These have been used by the federal courts not only to carry out the dictates of *Brown v. Board of Education*,[210] as in the recent Boston[211] and Dayton[212] cases, but also in a variety of other institutional situations, involving prisons,[213] mental hospitals,[214] and homes for the retarded,[215] to mention only a few.[216]

In these lawsuits, shaped by the parties and the court, often utilizing class action and intervention procedures,[217] remedial relief is proposed prospectively, perhaps negotiated by the parties to meet overall aims which themselves are often formulated with the defendant's help. The original decree is usually subject to continuous modification, specifying the remedy in even greater detail, and may contain built-in procedures for resolving disputes under, or questions of interpretation of, the decree, with subsequent court intervention only as a measure of last resort.[218] Party-centered administration of the decree is sought, but when that proves inadequate, administrative functions are delegated to a receiver, a master, an advisory committee, or the like.[219]

The efficacy of these devices, to be sure, has varied from case to case, but I join with Owen Fiss,[220] Abram Chayes,[221] and other learned observers in a guarded but overall approval, out of necessity as it were. A simple so-called negative injunction has failed to work or is inadequate to remedy the constitutional evil detected. Rather, affirmative values are implicated when, for example, conditions at a prison are so bad as to warrant a finding that they constitute cruel and unusual punishment,[222] or when retarded children as a group are being denied any treatment.[223] When a "right" to decent treatment or to medical care or to equal educational opportunity is involved, detailed affirmative judicial relief is required. If nothing else, the prior and subsequent history of *Brown v. Board of Education*[224] teaches us that as rights are given the more universal scope which is their due,[225] imaginative and creative methods of remedying their deprivation become essential, lest they be an empty promise. This shoe of judicial activism may pinch many feet, but the other shoe of inaction has already pinched far too many.

Structural injunctions are no panacea for the problems that beset our society; they are only a procedural device. Judicial intervention is a "last resort." The lack of clear standards for such judicial management and the difficulties likely to be encountered when the court seeks to enforce its substantive evaluations—especially when the public fisc must be invaded—signal caution both in the initial decision to intervene and in subsequent efforts to balance competing interests. Sometimes our policy focus may be too narrow: if we require that one prison be closed, we may create overcrowding at another; if we integrate one elementary school we may detract from progress in another; integrating a school system may provoke "white flight."[226] The point, however, is that while courts may need to learn how better to handle this type of case, specifically seeking maximum input from the parties, the groups whose prevailing claims require structural remedies cannot simply be abandoned. We must constantly strive to "manage" in a skillful way when the task is thrust upon us.

E. The Legitimacy of Judicial Intervention

I suspect that much of the opposition to federal courts generally, to their structural injunctions, or to federal court supervision of institutional change, is really based upon an underlying opposition to recognition of the rights in the first instance. Those who would simply enforce legal rights expressly spelled out and historically established— the rights of the status quo—make a remedial argument, that the courts should never intervene, that these matters should be left purely to the politics of "democracy."[227] At least, the argument runs, the courts should defer to the political institutions established, or supposedly established, to handle whatever rights minorities or individual citizens claim.[228] This argument from deference is regularly made,[229] it covers a multitude of cases; it is appealing to the traditionalist in all of us. Courts act only in the last resort after due deference to national and state legislatures, their agencies, local governing bodies, the state courts, and so on, in recognition of this appeal.[230]

Must the final step be taken—must we always refuse to act, out of deference? My concept of the Bill of Rights demands a negative answer, for reasons that are historical, logical, and philosophical. Historical, because failure to act may simply perpetuate an intolerable situation or make it even worse. I used to say that the only thing wrong with *Brown v. Board of Education* was that it was fifteen years too late; I now think it was fifty. Logical, because political relief becomes less and less likely in some cases—for example, where the minorities are more isolated or politically vulnerable and the majorities more firmly entrenched, or where political relief, is as Justice Douglas pointed out,[231] less satisfactory as society becomes more complex and the entrenchment of bureaucracy becomes more complete. And philosophical, because as Ronald Dworkin,[232] Laurence Tribe,[233] and others before them have suggested, there is no underlying reason why all unsettled issues of moral, social, or political principle must be resolved only in or by institutions that are directly accountable to a constituency in a forthcoming election—particularly one that is "single-issue" oriented.

Fairness does not necessarily require that the most troublesome issues of society be settled without court intervention. Decisions about minority rights sometimes will not be fairly determined by the majority, even if one can define what the "majority" is in any given case. Nor is this course necessarily wiser, for proceeding on a case-to-case basis, as courts do, rather than from one overriding principle or policy, is exactly the form taken by most modern legislation seeking to solve the problems, or at least to reconcile the competing demands, of a complicated, pluralistic society. Principles are enunciated by Congress in a preamble, administrative agencies are delegated the task of implementing them, always bearing in mind that totally vague concept of "public interest,"[234] and courts are given the power of judicial review. If case-to-case solution works, as Congress seems to think it does in the fields of, for example, communications,[235] the environment,[236] and employee safety,[237] is there any less reason to supppose that it will work in the case of constitutional adjudication? It should be acknowledged, then, that complaints about judicial intervention regularly involve concerns with the underlying constitutional principles that the courts occasionally enunciate, and with the courts' recognition of the demands from all segments of society for equal treatment under the law, a demand that is so sacred it is engraved on our buildings and in our books if not in the hearts of all of us. Those principles applied may hurt when they disturb the status quo. Judicial "interference" is often simply the scapegoat.

Judges may and do often commit error. They are probably more inclined to do so in the tricky areas of social, political, and economic affairs that intervention in institutional rights cases, for instance, involves. But our mistakes do not go unnoticed, uncorrected, or unchecked. Judicial decisions may be so offensive to public opinion that they are for practical purposes unenforceable, or they may engender a failure of public confidence in the courts and spawn plans to cut the courts' power. But most judges are well aware of these limitations; I know of few, if any, who feel presented with a roving commission to do public good. The responsibility of the judicial oath, the responsibility of office, the responsibility of preserving the reputation of the courts, coupled with the necessity for carrying high the torch given by the Founding Fathers, all weigh heavily on most judicial shoulders.[238]

It is also a bit of a myth to think that lifetime tenure operates to create irresponsibility. Lives are short; reputations are meaningful. There is, I venture to suggest, hardly an institution that operates with so many built-in checks and balances capable of instant criticism; one's fellow judges, higher courts, lower courts, law professors, law reviews, law writers, law clerks, lawyers' associations, families, and, yes, to an ever greater and more professional extent, the press. All or almost all of our actions are matters of public record; most of the reasons for taking them are openly and publicly stated for all to see and to criticize. And there is always the ultimate check on courts that have strayed too far, too irrevocably: the check of constitutional amendment which, fortunately, has had to be used only twice in the history of our Republic to overturn explicit court decisions that were not merely enforcing legislative policy.[239] Thus, the legitimacy of judicial solution to many of the most perplexing problems of the day must be, and is, ultimately supported by the accountability of the judiciary to the people.

CONCLUSION

In the end the role of the courts in enforcing the Bill of Rights is many things: inspirational, dialogue-impelling, operating a societal pressure cooker with an escape valve, and a force that, misused, can interfere unduly with legislative processes or, properly used, may command or, preferably, inspire affirmative conduct—of administrative officials, even of political officers—and public respect. We can, then, as we head into the winds of change and always perilous seas, take two tacks. We can go to starboard and avoid the risk of misuse, and the specter of possible disrespect for the courts, by doing nothing. Or we can go to port and try to minimize that risk by careful management of our business and observation of the prudential rules, considering that total governmental inaction in the recognition of basic human rights may breed a disrespect for our system as a whole. To the strict utilitarian who is interested only in the "bottom line," it is not enough that some of my premises may have been correct; the question is simply what have been the societal benefits. I would address to him the question of where the country would be had the courts taken what I call the starboard tack. As for the rest of us who believe that the qualities of life are not quantifiable and that law and the social sciences are as much art as science, there perforce is no bottom line. There is a challenge, not a statement, a challenge which each of us in the business of judging must face so long as we do judge—a challenge that lies both in our stars and in ourselves for, as Sir James Barrie reminds us, we are underlings.

John Paul Stevens

The Life Span of a Judge-Made Rule

INTRODUCTION

Most of the rules that were taught to law students in my generation were judge-made rules. The rule in Shelley's case, the rule against perpetuities, the hearsay rule, the Rule of Reason, the doctrine of consideration, and the concepts of foreseeability and proximate cause are a few that come readily to mind. Even though it may be one of the oldest of judge-made rules, however, I do not recall receiving any special instruction in the doctrine of *stare decisis et non quieta movere*[1]—the doctrine that teaches judges that it is often wise to let sleeping dogs lie[2]—until after I had graduated, indeed, until after I became a judge.

The doctrine of *stare decisis* is of greater interest to judges than to law students. Justice Stanley F. Reed,[3] Justice Robert H. Jackson,[4] Justice William O. Douglas,[5] Justice Arthur Goldberg,[6] Justice Walter V. Schaefer,[7] and Judge Robert A. Sprecher[8] have all written valuable articles on the subject. Perhaps the doctrine is of special interest to judges because it provides special benefits for judges. It obviously makes their work easier. It was Justice Cardozo who noted that "the labor of judges would be increased almost to the breaking point if every past decision could be reopened in every case, and one could not lay one's own course of bricks on the secure foundation of the courses laid by others who had gone before him."[9]

Adherence to the doctrine of *stare decisis* also enhances the reputation of judges and makes their work product more acceptable to the community at large. For a rule that orders judges to decide like cases in the same way increases the likelihood that judges will in fact administer justice impartially[10] and that they will be perceived to be

Justice Steven's lecture was delivered on October 27, 1982 and appeared in 58 N.Y.U.L. Rev. 1 (1983).

doing so.[11] This perception, which obviously enhances the institutional strength of the judiciary, is of greatest importance because of its stabilizing effect on the private ordering of economic relationships[12] and on the entire system of government.

My purpose, however, is not to extol the well-known virtues of *stare decisis*, but rather to explore certain aspects of the rule's impact on the work of the Supreme Court of the United States. A general rule of decision that requires judges to follow earlier precedents obviously tends to prolong the life of particular judge-made rules. The question I shall ultimately address is the extent to which the rule of *stare decisis*, and the considerations that underlie that rule, justify or require the preservation of a quite different judge-made rule—the so-called Rule of Four that is followed by the Supreme Court in processing its certiorari docket.

My point of beginning will be a brief inquiry into the present state of health of the rule of *stare decisis* itself.[13] That inquiry will be illuminated by the reaction of some of our greatest justices to another judge-made rule known as the *Jensen* rule.[14] I shall then comment on the history of the Rule of Four, and finally raise the question whether anything in its past makes the rule impervious to future change.[15]

I

In 1944, the Supreme Court overruled five of its earlier precedents.[16] In that year Justice Roberts[17] and Justice Jackson[18] both expressed concern about the viability of the doctrine of *stare decisis*. During the last ten years of the tenure of Chief Justice Warren, the Court overruled twenty-three cases; in the first ten years of the tenure of Chief Justice Burger, the Court overruled twenty-four cases.[19] The cumulative effect of these overrulings prompted a student of the doctrine of *stare decisis* to write an epitaph in the 1980 volume of the Wisconsin Law Review entitled "Some Thoughts on the Death of *Stare Decisis* in Constitutional Law."[20] The suggestion that the life of such a well-respected rule of law has come to an end raises serious questions about the legitimacy of the Court's exercise of its powers. Let me therefore explain why I am convinced that the report of the death of the doctrine is exaggerated.

My conviction is based on my participation in the routine work of the Court. The decisional process invariably involves a study and analysis of relevant precedents. In conference deliberation precedents regularly provide the basis for analysis and discussion. The framework for most Court opinions is created by previously decided cases. Admittedly, relevant precedents are sometimes ignored or treated with disrespect. But again quoting Justice Cardozo: "We shall have a false view of the landscape if we look at the waste spaces only, and refuse to see the acres already sown and fruitful."[21]

Numbers can be misleading. Two or three overrulings each Term are, indeed, significant. But it must be remembered that the Court disposes of literally thousands of cases each year; over and over again the Court's action involves nothing more than the application of old precedent to new controversy. Moreover, as the body of precedent continues to grow year after year, the likelihood that doctrinal inconsistency may force the Court to reject one precedent in favor of another must likewise increase.[22] As the nation itself grows older—surviving and adjusting itself to changes in the economy and changes in the temper of its people—it is inevitable that judge-made rules that were fashioned in different periods of our dynamic history will be subjected to increasingly frequent reexamination.[23] Quite clearly the mere number of overruling decisions is not sufficient to warrant the conclusion that the rule of *stare decisis* has passed away.

Nor can the mere fact that the Court has refused to follow a precedent be fairly criticized as illegitimate. The rule of *stare decisis* has never required adherence to a former determination that is most evidently contrary to reason, or that is "plainly unreasonable and inconvenient."[24] Even if an earlier decision is not founded on plain error, the court that made the decision still retains the power to disavow it. Arguably every such disavowal might appear illegitimate simply because it demonstrates that judges do in fact participate in the process of lawmaking and do not merely interpret and apply law that is entirely made by others.[25] For a literal interpretation of the precept that ours is "a government of laws and not of men" would condemn all such judicial activity. But every practicing lawyer knows that the judgment of human beings—the judgment of juries, the judgment of administrators, and the judgment of judges—determines the precise meaning of our law as it is applied in countless situations. Rules of law constrain and guide the exercise of judgment in our legal system,[26] even when that judgment focuses on the question whether an old rule should be preserved or discarded.

In 1917 the Court decided a case that gave its name to what became known as the "*Jensen* rule."[27] That case, and others that followed it, shed light on the legitimacy of properly constrained judicial lawmaking and the doctrine of *stare decisis*. In *Jensen,* the Court held that the constitutional grant of admiralty and maritime jurisdiction to the federal courts prevented the state of New York from applying its workmen's compensation statute to a longshoreman who was fatally injured on a gang plank about ten feet seaward of Pier 49 in New York City. The case raised profound questions concerning the source of the substantive rules of law that are applied on the high seas. The discussion of these questions in Justice Holmes's dissenting opinion is famous both for its candid acknowledgment of judicial lawmaking power and for its biting condemnation of the abuse of that power.[28]

A few months after the *Jensen* case was decided, Congress tried to overrule it by passing a special statute authorizing the states to apply their workmen's compensation laws in accidents subject to federal admiralty and maritime jurisdiction.[29] The Court promptly held the federal statute unconstitutional,[30] and again Justice Holmes, joined by Justices Pitney, Brandeis, and Clarke, dissented. In that dissent, Justice Holmes again rejected the majority's reasoning in *Jensen,* arguing that the claimants before the Court had an even stronger case than Jensen's widow: "I thought that claimants had those rights before. I think that they do now, both for the old reasons and for the new ones."[31] Note that he considered it entirely proper to continue to rely on the reasons that had been rejected by the majority in *Jensen*; the repetition of his dissenting views was not foreclosed by the doctrine of *stare decisis.*

In 1922 Congress made a second attempt to overrule the *Jensen* case by revising the language and reenacting the substance of the law invalidated in the *Knickerbocker Ice* case.[32] In *Washington v. W. C. Dawson & Co.,*[33] the Court held that the new act could not be reconciled with the doctrine of the *Jensen* case. The vigor of the *Jensen* rule—which arguably was either the brainchild of five judges or the offspring of a "brooding omnipresence in the sky"—is demonstrated by the three simple majestic sentences with which the Court concluded its opinion: "The subject is national. Local interests must yield to the common welfare. The Constitution is supreme."[34]

Justice Brandeis's dissenting opinion was devastating. The organization of his dissenting argument is of special interest. First, he convincingly demonstrated that the majority's analysis of the applicable legal principles was unsound.[35] Second, he argued that the correct result could be reached by placing a limit on the *Jensen* rule and merely rejecting dicta in the Court's prior opinions.[36] Third, assuming a necessary conflict with recent decisions, he set forth the reasons why those cases should be frankly overruled.[37] Finally, he addressed the doctrine of *stare decisis* in these words:

> The doctrine of *stare decisis* should not deter us from overruling that case and those which follow it. The decisions are recent ones. They have not been acquiesced in. They have not created a rule of property around which vested interests have clustered. They affect solely matters of a transitory nature. On the other hand, they affect seriously the lives of men, women and children, and the general welfare. *Stare decisis* is ordinarily a wise rule of action. But it is not a universal, inexorable command. The instances in which the court has disregarded its admonition are many.[38]

That passage, written in 1924 by one of our greatest judges, is entirely consistent with each of the appraisals of the doctrine of *stare decisis* which I have already cited.[39] *Stare decisis* is ordinarily a wise rule of decision. The doctrine creates a presumption that generally should be followed. The conclusion that there are persuasive reasons for rejecting a prior decision is a predicate to the entirely separate consideration of the question whether the doctrine of *stare decisis* should deter the Court from overruling an earlier case.

The separate character of these two inquiries is illustrated by still another chapter in the history of the *Jensen* case. In 1942 the Court was asked to decide whether the state of Washington could make an award under its compensation law to the widow of a workman drowned in a navigable river.[40] The Court upheld the award by creating a "twilight zone" in which employees might receive compensation under either federal or state law.[41] In his dissent from that holding, Chief Justice Stone suggested that he would have joined the Court's judgment if it were prepared to overrule the *Jensen* case,[42] but without that predicate he found the Court's holding totally illogical. Justice Frankfurter, in a concurring opinion, acknowledged both the illogical character of the Court's disposition and the desirability of repudiating the *Jensen* doctrine,[43] but nevertheless concluded that intervening events during a twenty-five-year period precluded a simple judicial repudiation of the *Jensen* rule.[44] An admittedly erroneous judge-made rule had taken on a life of its own and even today continues to survive despite its questionable origins.[45]

Thus, the question whether a case should be overruled is not simply answered by demonstrating that the case was erroneously decided and that the Court has the power to correct its past mistakes.[46] The doctrine of *stare decisis* requires a separate examination. Among the questions to be considered are the possible significance of intervening events, the possible impact on settled expectations, and the risk of undermining public confidence in the stability of our basic rules of law.[47] Such a separate inquiry is appropriate not only when an old rule is of doubtful legitimacy—as was true of the *Jensen* rule—but also when an old rule that was admittedly valid when conceived is questioned because of a change in the circumstances that originally justified it. Let me turn to a discussion of such a rule.

II

Whenever four justices of the United States Supreme Court vote to grant a petition for a writ of certiorari, the petition is granted even though a majority of the Court votes to deny. Although the origins of this so-called Rule of Four are somewhat obscure,[48] the rule is probably a contemporary of the *Jensen* rule. It was first publicly described by the justices who testified in support of the Judges' Bill[49] that became the Judiciary Act of 1925.[50] That act enabled the Supreme Court to cope with the "utterly impossible" task of deciding the merits of every case on its crowded docket.[51] The act alleviated the Court's problem by giving it the power to refuse to hear most of the cases on its docket.[52] Since 1925, most of the cases brought to the Supreme Court have been by way of a petition for a writ of certiorari—a petition which requests the Court to exercise its discretion to hear the case on the merits—rather than by a writ of error or an appeal requiring the Court to decide the merits.

In their testimony in support of the Judges' Bill, members of the Court explained that they had exercised discretionary jurisdiction in a limited number of federal cases since 1891 when the Circuit Courts of Appeals were created,[53] and also in a limited number of cases arising in the state courts since 1914.[54] They described in some detail the procedures they had followed in processing their discretionary docket and made it clear that they intended to continue to follow those practices in managing the enlarged certiorari jurisdiction that would be created by the enactment of the Judges' Bill.

Several features of the Court's practice were emphasized in order to demonstrate that the discretionary docket was being processed in a responsible, nonarbitrary way.[55] These four are particularly worthy of note: (1) copies of the printed record, as well as the briefs, were distributed to every justice;[56] (2) every justice personally examined the papers and prepared a memorandum or note indicating his view of what should be done;[57] (3) each petition was discussed by each justice at conference;[58] and (4) a vote was taken, and if four, or sometimes just three, justices thought the case should be heard on its merits, the petition was granted.[59] In his testimony, Justice Van Devanter pointed out that in the 1922 and 1923 Terms the Court had acted on 398 and 370 petitions respectively.[60] Since these figures indicate that the Court was processing only a handful of certiorari petitions each week, it is fair to infer that the practice of making an individual review and having a full conference discussion of every petition was not particularly burdensome. Indeed, at that time the number was so small that the Court was then contemplating the possibility of granting an oral hearing on every petition for certiorari.[61] Times have changed[62] and so have the Court's practices.

In the 1947 Term, when I served as a law clerk to Justice Rutledge, the practice of discussing every certiorari petition at conference had been discontinued. It was then the practice for the chief justice to circulate a so-called dead list identifying the cases deemed unworthy of conference discussion. Any member of the Court could remove a case from the dead list, but unless such action was taken, the petition would be denied without even being mentioned at conference.

In the 1975 Term, when I joined the Court, I found that other significant procedural changes had occurred. The "dead list" had been replaced by a "discuss list"; now the chief justice circulates a list of cases that he deems worthy of discussion and each of the other members of the Court may add cases to that list. In a sense, the discuss list practice is the functional equivalent of the dead list practice, but there is a symbolic difference. In 1925, every case was discussed; in 1947 every case was discussed unless it was on the dead list; today, no case is discussed unless it is placed on a special list.

Other changes have also occurred. It is no longer true that the record in the court below is routinely filed with the certiorari petition. It is no longer true that every justice personally examines the original papers in every case. Published dissents from denials of certiorari were unknown in 1925 but are now a regular occurrence.[63] Today law clerks prepare so-called pool memos that are used by several justices in evaluating certiorari petitions. The pool memo practice may be an entirely proper response to an increase in the volume of certiorari petitions from 7 or 8 per week when the Judges' Bill was passed in

1925 to approximately 100 per week at the present time. It is nevertheless noteworthy that it is a significant departure from the practice that was explained to the Congress in 1924.

The rule that four affirmative votes are sufficient to grant certiorari has, however, survived without change. Indeed, its wisdom has seldom, if ever, been questioned. Perhaps it is time to do so.

III

The doctrine of *stare decisis* teaches us to respect well-settled rules. A proponent of change confronts a strong presumption against stirring up sleeping animals, for the consequences of change are never completely predictable. I am neither persuaded myself nor prepared to shoulder the burden of persuading my colleagues, that the Rule of Four should be abandoned—either temporarily or permanently. I am, however, prepared to demonstrate that it would be entirely legitimate to reexamine the rule, that some of the arguments for preserving the rule are unsound, and that there are valid reasons for making a careful study before more drastic solutions to the Court's workload problems are adopted.

First, I would put to one side any suggestion that the representations made to Congress when the 1925 Judges' Bill was enacted created some sort of estoppel that would make it dishonorable for the Court to change the Rule of Four. The justices' testimony in 1924 contained a complete and candid explanation of the practices then being followed and a plain expression of an intent to continue to follow essentially the same practices in the future. The purposes of the testimony were to demonstrate that the selection of cases for review would be based on neutral and relevant considerations, rather than the arbitrary choice of particular justices, and that the Court would continue to hear an adequate number of cases. The testimony, however, contained no representation or even suggestion that the Court might not make various procedural changes in response to changes in the condition of its docket. I have found nothing in the legislative history of the 1925 act that limits the Court's power to modify its internal rules governing the processing of its certiorari docket.[64]

But even if I have misread that history, ample precedent—and therefore the doctrine of *stare decisis*—supports the proposition that the Court has the authority to modify the certiorari procedures that were being followed in the 1920s. The Court has already eliminated the record filing requirement; it has abandoned the practice of individual discussion of every petition at conference; there have been substantial changes in the way each individual justice evaluates each certiorari petition. In my judgment, each of those procedural modifications was an entirely legitimate response to a dramatic change in the character of the docket. They are precedents that establish the legitimacy of making such other internal procedural changes—specifically including a possible modification of the Rule of Four—as may be appropriate to cope with a problem whose present dimensions were not foreseen in 1925.[65]

During most of the period in which the Rule of Four was developed, the Court had more capacity than it needed to dispose of its argument docket. The existence of the rule in 1924 provided a persuasive response to the concern—expressed before the Judges' Bill was enacted—that the Court might not accept enough cases for review if its discretionary docket were enlarged. In my judgment, it is the opposite concern that is now dominant. For I think it is clear that the Court now takes far too many cases. Indeed, I am persuaded that since the enactment of the Judges' Bill in 1925, any mismanagement of the Court's docket has been in the direction of taking too many, rather than too few, cases.

In his talk on *stare decisis* in 1944, Justice Jackson noted that the substitution of discretionary for mandatory jurisdiction had failed to cure the problem of overloading because judges found it so difficult to resist the temptation to correct perceived error or to take on an interesting question despite its lack of general importance.[66] In a letter written to Senator Wheeler in 1937 describing the workload of the Supreme Court, Chief Justice Hughes, after noting that less than 20 percent of the certiorari petitions raised substantial questions, stated: "I think that it is the view of the members of the Court that if any error is made in dealing with these applications it is on the side of liberality."[67] In a recent letter Paul Freund, who served as Justice Brandeis's law clerk in 1932, advised me that the justice "believed the Court was granting review in too many cases—not only because of their relative unimportance for the development or clarification of the law but because they deprived the Court of time to pursue the really significant cases with adequate reflection and in sufficient depth."[68]

It can be demonstrated that the Rule of Four has had a significant impact on the number of cases that the Court has reviewed on their merits. A study of Justice Burton's docket book for the 1946 and 1947 Terms reveals that, in each of those Terms, the decision to grant certiorari was supported by no more than four votes in over twenty-five percent of the granted cases.[69] It is, of course, possible that in some of those cases a justice who voted to deny might have voted otherwise under a Rule of Five, but it does seem fair to infer that the Rule of Four had a significant impact on the aggregate number of cases granted.

A review of my own docket sheets for the 1979, 1980, and 1981 Terms confirms this conclusion. No more than four affirmative votes resulted in granting over 23 percent of the petitions granted in the 1979 Term, over 30 of those granted in the 1980 Term, and about 29 percent of those granted in the 1981 Term.[70] In my judgment, these are significant percentages. If all—or even most—of those petitions had been denied, the number of cases scheduled for argument on the merits this Term would be well within the range that all justices consider acceptable.

Mere numbers, however, provide an inadequate measure of the significance of the cases that were heard because of the rule. For I am sure that some Court opinions in cases that were granted by only four votes have made a valuable contribution to the development of our jurisprudence. My experience has persuaded me, however, that such cases are exceptionally rare. I am convinced that a careful study of all of the cases that have been granted on the basis of only four votes would indicate that in a surprisingly large number the law would have fared just as well if the decision of the court of appeals or the state court had been allowed to stand.[71] To enable interested scholars to consider the validity of this judgment, I have prepared footnotes listing twenty-five cases granted certiorari by a mere four votes in the 1946 Term[72] and thirty-six such cases granted certiorari in the 1979 Term.[73]

The Rule of Four is sometimes justified by the suggestion that if four justices of the Supreme Court consider a case important enough to warrant full briefing and argument on the merits, that should be sufficient evidence of the significance of the question presented.[74] But a countervailing argument has at least equal force. Every case that is granted on the basis of four votes is a case that five members of the Court thought should not be granted.[75] For the most significant work of the Court, it is assumed that the collective judgment of its majority is more reliable than the views of the minority.[76] Arguably, therefore, deference to the minority's desire to add additional cases to the argument docket may rest on an assumption that whether the Court hears a few more or a few less cases in any term is not a matter of first importance.[77]

History and logic both support the conclusion that the Rule of Four must inevitably enlarge the size of the Court's argument docket and cause it to hear a substantial number of cases that a majority of the Court deems unworthy of review. What light does this conclusion shed on the current debate over possible solutions to the problems created by the Court's crowded docket? I shall mention just two points. First, this conclusion refutes one of the arguments that is made to support the creation of a new national court of appeals to enlarge the federal judiciary's lawmaking powers by deciding cases referred to it by the Supreme Court.[78] It has been argued that because the Court now grants a smaller percentage of certiorari petitions than it did in the past, it is not granting enough.[79] But that argument rests on the untenable assumption that the correct standard was set at some unspecified time in the past—an assumption that simply ignores the impact of the Rule of Four.[80]*

Second, reflection about the impact of the Rule of Four on the size of the docket demonstrates that the Court has a greater capacity to solve its own problems than is often assumed. We might, for example, simply abandon the Rule of Four, or perhaps refuse to follow it whenever our backlog reaches a predetermined point. But there are reasons to beware of such a procedural change. For even if the Rule of Four had nothing more than a distinguished parentage, an unblemished reputation, and a venerable age to commend itself to posterity, it would be entitled to the presumptive protection provided by the rule of *stare decisis*. Moreover, the Rule of Four has additional redeeming virtues. It gives each member of the Court a stronger voice in determing the makeup of the Court's docket. It increases the likelihood that an unpopular litigant, or an unpopular issue, will be heard in the country's court of last resort: Like the danger of awakening a sleeping dog, the costs of change are not entirely predictable. Surely those costs should not be incurred if less drastic solutions to the Court's problems are available.

* With regard to the proposal of a new national court of appeals, see the editor's note on page 157 supra. EDITOR'S NOTE.

At least two such solutions are quite obvious. If Congress were concerned about our plight, it could provide us with significant help by promptly removing the remainder of our mandatory jurisdiction.[81] Second, as I suggested last summer, in the processing of our certiorari docket we are often guilty of ignoring the teachings of the doctrine of judicial restraint;[82] if we simply acted with greater restraint during the case selection process, we might be able to manage the docket effectively under the Rule of Four. But if neither of these remedies materializes or is effective, we may find it necessary to acknowledge that the Rule of Four is a luxury we can no longer afford.[83] I hope we can retain the rule, but I would much prefer temporary, or possibly even permanent, abandonment of the Rule of Four to certain kinds of major surgery that have been suggested.[84]

In conclusion, I will merely note that my primary objective has been neither to praise nor to bury the Rule of Four, but rather to suggest that one may legitimately ask questions about its future life span.

Wilfred Feinberg

Constraining "The Least Dangerous Branch"
The Tradition of Attacks on Judicial Power

I intend to discuss attempts, both current and past, by those who are upset by federal court decisions to make fundamental changes in the structure and jurisdiction of the federal judiciary. That structure, of course, owes much to James Madison. At the Constitutional Convention, many argued that the federal judiciary should consist only of a Supreme Court. Lower federal courts would not be necessary, they felt; the needs of the national government would be satisfied by the Supreme Court's exercise of appellate jurisdiction over state supreme court decisions. Madison and his allies disagreed, and the result was the compromise language that continues to fuel academic, and not so academic, debate about how much control Congress can exert over the jurisdiction of the federal courts.[1]

Article III, section 1 of the Constitution provides: "The judicial Power of the United States, shall be vested in one supreme Court, and in such inferior Courts as the Congress may from time to time ordain and establish." As the chief judge of one of those "inferior courts," I have more than a passing interest in the meaning and effect of that one not-so-simple declaratory sentence. The debate over whether the lower federal courts serve any function that could not be handled as well or better by state courts continues to this day. The framers built further ambiguity into the Constitution by providing in Article III, section 2 that the Supreme Court's appellate jurisdiction be subject to "such Exceptions, and . . . such Regulations as the Congress shall make."

There is controversy over the extent to which the language of section 1 authorizes Congress to exert substantial control over the lower federal courts by altering their jurisdiction. The exceptions clause of

Chief Judge Feinberg's lecture was delivered on October 26, 1983 and appeared in 59 N.Y.U.L. Rev. 252 (1984).

section 2 has given rise to similar dispute regarding Congress's power over the Supreme Court. These sections, particularly the first, are the backdrop to attempts by members of Congress and others in the body politic to change significantly and to limit the jurisdiction of the federal courts.[2]

As I will discuss in greater detail in a moment, it is not unusual for legislators to regard an independent federal judiciary as a political inconvenience or even as an outrage. And today, as always, the courts are making decisions that are unpopular with some segments of the political spectrum, and their representatives in Congress are seeking to undo those decisions, directly or indirectly. Some of the current proposals are benign in intent, but others are overtly hostile to an independent judiciary. As David R. Brink said when he was president of the American Bar Association, these measures "threaten the rights of all of us."[3] As a whole, the proposals are particularly dangerous because they come at a time when the federal courts are facing a critical overload that must be dealt with soon, or the system will collapse. This crisis can be used to justify attempts to alter and restrict the courts' jurisdiction.

After a brief survey of the history of attacks on the federal courts, I will examine in detail a bill introduced in the last session of Congress.[4] My message is that such attacks are not new and that by and large they have not been successful. But given the current crisis in the workload of the federal courts and the resentment over their decisions on highly charged constitutional issues, all those who treasure the independence of the federal judiciary must be alert to attempts to override interpretations of the Constitution by drastic jurisdictional overhauls.[5] Of course, I shall not comment on the constitutionality of the proposals. That question might well come before the courts; until it does, I leave it to law professors and other commentators. And now for a little history, the better with which to understand the present.

I. HISTORICAL BACKGROUND

Article III, section 1 of the Constitution, in the language I already have quoted, provides for the creation of federal courts. But another part of Article III—section 2—defines the kinds of cases the Supreme Court and the "inferior courts" may hear. Section 2 states, among other things, that "the judicial Power shall extend . . . to Controversies . . . between a State and Citizens of another State." This provision gave rise to the first instance in which Congress attempted to overrule a judicial decision by restricting the federal courts' jurisdiction—in this case by successfully setting in motion the mechanism that led to a constitutional amendment.

Very early in our history, several suits were brought in federal court by individuals against states: Eleazer Oswald filed against New York in 1791,[6] and in 1792 William Grayson sued Virginia and Alexander Chisholm sued Georgia.[7] The defendant states refused to acknowledge effective service of process, and the attorneys for the state of Georgia even refused to argue in the Supreme Court on the question whether the federal courts had jurisdiction of the case.[8] The Supreme Court held that there was jurisdiction, and *Chisholm v. Georgia*[9] and the other two cases proceeded amidst angry protests and calls for a constitutional amendment from the legislatures of Georgia, Massachusetts, Virginia, and New York.[10] The temper of the time was revealed by an act of the Georgia House of Representatives, which provided that any federal marshal attempting to execute any process of the Supreme Court in a suit against the state of Georgia should be "deemed guilty of felony, and shall suffer death without the benefit of clergy, by being hanged."[11] On the day after the Supreme Court entered judgment for Chisholm in February 1793, the text of what became the Eleventh Amendment was introduced in the Senate.[12] When it was finally ratified in January 1798, suits by individual plaintiffs against states, which had continued in the interim, were no longer regarded as cognizable in the federal courts.[13]

A few years later, the federal courts became a focus of the battle between the Federalists and the Jeffersonians. The system of circuit courts established by the Judiciary Act of 1798 had developed a number of problems.[14] In particular, circuit riding by the Supreme Court justices was intolerably difficult, dangerous, and time consuming, given travel conditions of the day.[15] Moreover, circuit riding placed the justices in the unseemly position of passing judgment on appeals in cases they had decided below.[16] The Judiciary Act of 1801, enacted in the last days of the defeated Adams administration, addressed these problems,[17] including the demands on the justices' time caused by the "itinerant dispensation of justice."[18] The Judiciary Act eliminated circuit riding and created new circuit courts with sixteen new circuit judges and a full force of federal marshals, clerks, and United States attorneys.[19]

The Jeffersonians, however, perceived the Judiciary Act as a last-

ditch effort by a lame-duck president to control the country by appointing Federalist judges.[20] The Jeffersonians also were angered by
what they considered the misuse of the judicial power by Federalist
judges in the following English common law precedents,[21] in enforcing the Sedition Act,[22] and in using grand jury charges to instruct the
public in federalism.[23] Jefferson told his attorney general that what
was needed was a "removal of excrescences from the judiciary."[24] In
1802, the Jeffersonians repealed the Judiciary Act of 1801 and abolished the new judgeships,[25] legislatively recessed the Supreme Court
for over one year,[26] and embarked on a program of impeaching
Federalist judges with the ultimate aim, it seems, of bringing charges
against the chief justice, John Marshall.[27]

For those of you who are puzzled that a dispute as intense as that
between Jefferson and Marshall could stem merely from different
views on the proper role of the judiciary, let me quote a little-known
fact from Richard Morris's superb book, *Seven Who Shaped Our
Destiny*.[28] Morris explains that, as a youngster, Jefferson had courted
Rebecca Burwell, then a sixteen-year-old orphan. Rebecca apparently
was not responsive to Jefferson's overtures; while he was studying
abroad, she married another man. Her daughter, in turn, married
John Marshall. Richard Morris points out that "Jefferson's intense dis-
like for the jurist may well have, unconsciously, sprung from this relationship. After all, but for the vagaries of female passion, Marshall
might have been [Jefferson's] own son-in-law!"[29]

It is interesting to note that the Jeffersonians regarded a program
of impeachment as a proper means of popular control over judicial
decisionmaking. James Monroe suggested that use of English common law precedent was a ground for impeachment;[30] Senator Giles
added that impeachment was proper if a judge was "disagreeable in
office" or "opposed to the administration & wrong headed."[31] To be
sure, not all of the targets of impeachment were model judges. Judge
Pickering of the District of New Hampshire, who was impeached and
convicted, was mentally ill and alcoholic.[32] The impeachment of Justice Chase was triggered in part by his delivery of a charge to a grand
jury in Baltimore criticizing the repeal of the Judiciary Act of 1801,
universal suffrage in Maryland, and the Jeffersonian ideal of equal
liberty and rights for all men.[33] Apparently, though, this kind of com-
mentary was less shocking then than it would be now—judges were
more outspoken politically, and politics was not yet considered incompatible with the judicial role.[34] After Justice Chase was narrowly ac-

quitted, impeachment was abandoned as a common political method of attack, but at least one of the desired ends was achieved: grand jury charges became more cautious.[35]

In the meantime, the passage of the Eleventh Amendment had not ended the struggles between state governments and the national judiciary. Throughout the early nineteenth century, indeed throughout the Civil War era, states and states' rightists railed against the power of the Supreme Court to review certain decisions of the state courts, and the power of the federal courts to declare state laws unconstitutional.[36] In some instances, states simply refused to comply with Supreme Court orders;[37] some state legislatures passed laws forbidding compliance.[38] In 1832, the South Carolina legislature passed a statute forbidding any appeals to the United States Supreme Court, but the state supreme court declared the law unconstitutional.[39]

Occasionally, violence threatened to break out, as in the so-called Olmstead affair.[40] Two rival groups of claimants to the sloop *Active*, the first headed by a Connecticut sailor named Olmstead and the second connected with another armed sloop fitted out by the Commonwealth of Pennsylvania, made claims to the vessel in an action in the Pennsylvania Court of Admiralty in 1778. A jury awarded 25 percent of the net proceeds of the sale of the vessel to Olmstead and 75 percent of the proceeds to the Pennsylvania group.[41] In 1779, the Continental Congress's Standing Committee on Appeals, which had jurisdiction of appeals from state admiralty courts at the time, reversed the decision and gave the entire judgment to Olmstead. The Pennsylvania authorities, however, refused to execute the revised decree, arguing that pursuant to a Pennsylvania statute the jury's findings of fact were conclusive.[42] Eventually, the Pennsylvania Supreme Court so held.[43] In the meantime, Pennsylvania's share of the prize had been paid over to the treasurer of that Commonwealth.[44] Olmstead's efforts to enforce the revised decree in his favor eventually led to a United States Supreme Court order that it be enforced.[45] The Pennsylvania legislature promptly enacted resolutions against the decision and called for the creation of an impartial tribunal to resolve federal–state disputes. The governor sent out the state militia to resist enforcement of the judgment, but a posse turned out to support the federal marshal. Eventually, the governor backed down, and the legislature provided the losers with funds for satisfaction of the judgment. The state militia officers were convicted of treason and sentenced, but President Madison later pardoned them.[46]

In another typical but dramatic instance, Pennsylvania again came into conflict with the Supreme Court when the Court was asked to decide several questions regarding Pennsylvania's obligations to persons receiving land under a Pennsylvania statute enacted in 1792.[47] The Court treated the statute as a contractual obligation and determined that it could be enforced against the state.[48] The Pennsylvania legislature reacted by approving a resolution passed by the Kentucky legislature calling for a constitutional amendment depriving the federal courts of diversity jurisdiction and land-grant jurisdiction.[49] Another Pennsylvania resolution denied the authority of the federal courts to take jurisdiction over suits brought under the 1792 statute involving the interest and sovereignty of the state.[50] The governor of Pennsylvania, although an anti-Federalist, vetoed the resolution as an intrusion into the federal judicial process,[51] a principled act of statesmanship of the kind that would recur in the years that followed.

Congress did not remain aloof from these struggles. Many proposals to change the federal judiciary were introduced, although none was enacted. Section 25 of the Judiciary Act of 1789 provided for appeals from state court decisions to the United States Supreme Court. Attempts to repeal this section were frequent, as were proposals to require a supermajority of the members of the Court to hold state statutes unconstitutional.[52] It was also proposed that, in cases where a state was a party or where the constitution or laws of a state were questioned, appeal be had to the United States Senate rather than to the Supreme Court.[53]

Despite the strong sentiment in many states for curbing the federal courts, these and other measures for change failed to pass Congress. In some cases, this failure was a result of the efforts of influential lawmakers who opposed the measures. For instance, an 1830 bill to repeal section 25 was defeated largely because of the persuasive opposition of Representative James Buchanan, then chairman of the House Judiciary Committee.[54] In other cases, changes in the Court itself forestalled more radical measures from the legislative branch. For example, a wave of proposals in the 1820s was deflected by the appointment to the Court of Smith Thompson, an advocate of states' rights.[55] Congress's attack on the Court of the early 1830s was deterred by the Court's announcement that it would thenceforth not render judgment in constitutional law cases unless four justices concurred in an opinion, even though one or more of the seven justices (as the Court was then constituted) could not sit in a particular case.[56] All in all, then, despite the dissatisfaction with, and occasional outright defiance of, the federal courts in this period, those who sought to curb the federal judiciary achieved no permanent results.

The climactic struggle between the national government and the advocates of states' rights was, of course, the Civil War. We tend to think of the federal government as allied with antislavery forces against the southern states that asserted the right to maintain the institution of slavery. But before the war, many northerners feared that the federal government would force slavery on them.[57] Lincoln himself expressed this concern in his famous "House Divided" speech in the Senate in 1858.[58] The Supreme Court was a major cause of that fear, with its decision in *Dred Scott v. Sandford*.[59] The *Dred Scott* decision held that national citizenship could not extend to a freed slave[60] and went on to state that the Constitution prevented Congress from barring slavery from the territories.[61] Northern states attacked the decision. The Maine Supreme Judicial Court gave an advisory opinion to the legislature that blacks could vote in state and federal elections in Maine.[62] The Ohio Supreme Court held that any slave coming into Ohio with the consent of his master was permanently freed, even if he later returned to a slave state.[63] The New York Court of Appeals rendered a similar decision.[64] Other northern legislatures adopted anti-slavery and anti-*Dred Scott* resolutions and laws.[65] The issue was not destined to be resolved by legislation or by judicial decision, but by civil war. The Supreme Court as an institution survived that war, but *Dred Scott* did not; it was overruled by the Fourteenth Amendment.

In the midst of Reconstruction, William McCardle of Mississippi published a series of inflammatory editorials attacking military rule in the South. His editorials set in motion a series of events that were to ensure his future prominence in constitutional law casebooks. Arrested by order of General Ord, the Commander of the Fourth Military District, McCardle was held in military custody pending trial by a military commission.[66] On November 25, 1867, the United States Circuit Court for the District of Mississippi denied McCardle's application for habeas corpus.[67] McCardle then appealed to the Supreme Court, pursuant to the recently passed Habeas Corpus Act of 1867, which, for the first time, provided for direct appeal from a circuit court decision denying habeas relief.[68] It is ironic that this new act, which was intended to protect the wives and children of former slaves against obstinate former masters,[69] was invoked by an ex-Confederate who called the Reconstruction leaders "infamous, cowardly, and abandoned villains, who, instead of wearing shoulder straps and ruling millions of people, should have their heads shaved, their ears cropped, their foreheads branded, and their precious persons lodged in a penitentiary."[70]

The Republican majority in Congress moved quickly, concerned that, in response to McCardle's challenge to military trials for nonmilitary offenses, the Supreme Court might declare part of the Reconstruction Acts unconstitutional.[71] Two weeks after the oral argument in *Ex parte McCardle*, Congress repealed the portion of the Habeas Corpus Act of 1867 that permitted direct appeals from decisions of the circuit courts.[72] The Court then dismissed McCardle's suit in a terse opinion, ruling that as a result of the repeal it lacked jurisdiction to give the case further consideration.[73]

Despite its anticlimactic ending, the *McCardle* case has spurred a long-lasting debate over the extent to which Congress can invoke the Exceptions Clause to restrict the appellate jurisdiction of the Supreme Court. For reasons already indicated, I will not give you my own reading of *Ex parte McCardle*. Instead, I will set out the competing positions, since they define the controversy that still exists today. Before doing that, a few observations are pertinent. First, before the passage of the Habeas Corpus Act of 1867, the Court reviewed habeas cases under its certiorari jurisdiction, pursuant to section 14 of the Judiciary Act of 1789.[74] Second, the Court acknowledged this power at the time it decided *Ex parte McCardle*. It stated in dictum that Congress's repealer act in 1868 did not remove any cases from the Supreme Court's appellate jurisdiction except appeals from circuit courts under the Act of 1867. The Court stated that the 1868 act did not "affect the jurisdiction which was previously exercised."[75] In addition, while *McCardle* was still under advisement, the Court suggested to a lawyer representing a group of prisoners charged with the murder of a black man that he invoke the jurisdictional provisions of the Judiciary Act of 1789.[76] And, in *Ex parte Yerger*, decided only a few months after *McCardle*, the Court explicitly rejected the government's contention that Congress's repeal of part of the Habeas Corpus Act of 1867 limited the appellate jurisdiction the Court had enjoyed over habeas cases prior to 1867.[77]

Based on these considerations, some commentators believe that *Ex parte McCardle* did not decide the question whether categories of constitutional law cases can be insulated from Supreme Court review by means of the Exceptions Clause. What *McCardle* decided, under this view, is that Congress can choose the mechanism by which the Supreme Court exercises its appellate jurisdiction over a given class of cases. Congress may eliminate certain avenues for review only when others remain open.[78]

Other commentators dispute this assessment. Instead of focusing on the facts surrounding the *McCardle* decision, they dwell on the Court's dictum linking the repeal of the Habeas Corpus Act with the Exceptions Clause. They argue that nothing in the opinion suggests that the power to "except" is limited to "inessential" exceptions, and thus urge us to read broadly the Exceptions Clause and congressional power over the Supreme Court's appellate jurisdiction.[79]

One year after *McCardle*, in *Hepburn v. Griswold*,[80] the Court declared that the Legal Tender Act of 1862, which made paper money legal tender for all debts, was unconstitutional as to debts contracted before the passage of the act. Had the Court's position remained law, there would have been a drastic gold shortage, and debtor classes would have suffered.[81] Only one year later, however, the Court upheld the constitutionality of the Legal Tender Acts in *Knox v. Lee*.[82] In the interim, President Grant had named William Strong and Joseph P. Bradley to the Court. Questions were raised at the time as to whether Grant chose these justices with the knowledge that they would uphold the Legal Tender Acts. At least one historian has concluded from the available evidence that Grant did indeed "pack" the Supreme Court to obtain a politically desirable turnaround, an incident in which that historian saw obvious parallels to the Court-packing plans that were in the air as he wrote in 1935.[83]

A generation after *Hepburn*, in 1895, we come to *Pollock v. Farmers' Loan and Trust Co.*,[84] which was the third Supreme Court decision to be overruled by a constitutional amendment.[85] In *Pollock*, the Supreme Court held the income tax unconstitutional. The issue was a highly political one. In a separate opinion, Justice Field referred to "[t]he present assault upon capital" that, if unchecked, would bring about "the sure decadence of our present government."[86] One notes with wistful longing for a bygone day that the actual tax imposed was 2 percent of ordinary income over $4,000, and 2 percent of corporate profits! The burden of paying this outrageous sum would have fallen on less than 2 percent of the population.[87] The Sixteenth Amendment, effective in 1913, reversed the result in *Pollock* by granting Congress the power to tax income "without apportionment among the several States, and without regard to any census or enumeration."

If we move ahead another four decades, we come to a classic political dispute with the federal courts at its center. The onset of the Depression and the election of Franklin D. Roosevelt in 1932 precipitated a dramatic clash between the Supreme Court and the other two branches of government. Even before the Supreme Court held much of the New Deal legislation unconstitutional, lower federal courts had intensified a trend toward enjoining enforcement of federal legislation. By late 1933, federal judges had granted some 1,600 injunctions restraining the federal government from enforcing acts of Congress.[88] After the Supreme Court held the Agricultural Adjustment Act of 1933 unconstitutional, irate farmers hanged the six majority justices in effigy.[89] Between 1934 and 1936, the Supreme Court invalidated more federal statutes than in any comparable period in the nation's history.[90] Between May 1935 and August 1937, over thirty different constitutional amendments aimed at changing the Court's membership or limiting its power to declare legislation unconstitutional were introduced in Congress.[91]

After his landslide victory in the 1936 election, Roosevelt considered several approaches to the problem, including a constitutional amendment and legislation curbing the Court's jurisdiction.[92] He ultimately proposed to Congress on February 5, 1937, that the president be empowered to appoint a new justice for each justice over seventy years old who failed to retire, with the proviso that the total membership of the Court not exceed fifteen. This measure would have assured Roosevelt the opportunity to appoint six new members of the Court.[93] Opposition to the proposal by the American Bar Association, Republicans, and dissident Democrats was fierce.[94]

In the midst of the fight, Justice Roberts joined the pro-New Deal faction on the Court, voting to uphold the Wagner Act and the state of Washington's minimum-wage law.[95] This gave Roosevelt a five to four majority. Two months later, Justice Van Devanter announced his retirement, making possible a six to three division.[96] Even though the New Deal legislation now seemed relatively out of danger, Roosevelt continued to fight for the Court-packing bill. In the end, the bill was abandoned only after Senate majority leader Joe Robinson, who was shepherding the bill through the Senate, died of a heart attack.[97]

Within two-and-a-half years after rejection of the measure, Roosevelt had made five appointments to the Court.[98] It is often said that Roosevelt lost the battle but won the war because the new Court greatly expanded the scope of permissible economic regulation. But a prominent historian of the New Deal, William Leuchtenburg, concludes that Roosevelt in fact lost the war, because, by pushing so hard for the Court plan, he destroyed the unity of the Democratic majority in Congress. Thus, Leuchtenburg notes, while the new Court "might be willing to uphold new laws . . . an angry and divided Congress would pass few of them for the justices to consider."[99]

Some twenty years later, the pendulum swung the other way with the federal courts again the center of contention. The Supreme Court's reaction to McCarthy-era legislation and to activities of congressional committees was mixed. Under Chief Justice Vinson, the Court upheld the legislative anti-Communist campaign.[100] After the appointment of Earl Warren in 1953, the Court's stance began to change. By the 1955 Term, the Court was using statutory interpretation to limit state antisedition legislation,[101] administrative inquiries,[102] and dismissals of government employees under the Internal Security Act of 1950.[103] The Court also ruled that the Due Process Clause prevented the dismissal of a Brooklyn College professor solely on the ground that he had invoked the Fifth Amendment before a congressional committee.[104] In the next Term, the Court held that it was a violation of due process for state bar associations to deny admission to qualified applicants with a Communist background.[105] On so-called Red Monday, June 17, 1957,[106] the Court announced decisions curbing prosecutions under the Smith Act[107] and dismissals of State Department employees under the McCarran rider,[108] and limiting congressional and state investigations of political activities.[109]

Congress responded with a flurry of bills designed to thwart these rulings.[110] Shelden Elliott classified the various approaches as "selective scattergun" curbs on the Supreme Court's jurisdiction; "single-shot" curbs on the federal courts' jurisdiction; measures that would correct "mistaken" statutory interpretations; and bills to change the terms of office, qualifications, or selection processes for federal judges.[111] The most notable "scattergun" bill was introduced by Senator Jenner during the debates on the Civil Rights Act of 1957.[112] Paul Murphy characterized it as "an omnibus anti-Court bill."[113] Elliott summarized its provisions:

[T]hey would deny the Supreme Court jurisdiction to review any case involving the validity of (1) the practices or jurisdiction of congressional committees, (2) the national government's enforcement of federal employee security regulations, (3) state control of intrastate subversive activities, (4) school board regulation of subversive activities of teachers, and (5) state action or regulation pertaining to admission to practice law in the state.[114]

The Senate Judiciary Committee generally reported the anti-Court bills favorably, but none was passed.[115]

At about the same time as the sedition and the red-hunt cases, the problem of pervasive racial discrimination came to a dramatic head in *Brown v. Board of Education*.[116] That watershed case and its implementation by the lower federal courts created a furor that inspired a number of bills designed to prevent school desegregation or busing.[117] A 1957 bill would have withdrawn federal court jurisdiction to hear suits challenging state laws on public schools.[118] Another bill would have withdrawn appellate jurisdiction from the Supreme Court in cases attacking a public school system "on grounds other than substantial inequality of physical facilities and other tangible factors."[119] A number of statutes and constitutional amendments were proposed to forbid courts to order busing.[120] None passed both Houses, although the House of Representatives passed a bill forbidding courts to order busing beyond the two schools closest to a student's home.[121]

A similar response was triggered by the legislative apportionment decisions.[122] After *Reynolds v. Sims*,[123] announcing the "one man, one vote" rule for state legislatures, Senator Everett Dirksen proposed a constitutional amendment to override the decisions,[124] and a bill to withhold federal court jurisdiction over cases seeking reapportionment of state legislatures was introduced in the House.[125] Neither proposal received the necessary approval of Congress.[126]

II. THE CURRENT ASSAULT

And so we come to the present day. This survey has, of course, been sketchy, but it is sufficient, I believe, to prompt a few observations.

First, it is clear that since its inception the federal judiciary has been at the center of turbulent controversy. Sometimes the outrage in the body politic has come from the right, sometimes from the left. But regardless of the source of the passion, over the course of our history particular decisions have upset segments of the citizenry enough to invite attempts to change the results by one means or another.

Second, the assaults on the federal courts have generally not been successful. In four instances, when the Supreme Court's interpretation of the Constitution was unpopular enough, decisions have been

overturned by constitutional amendments—the Eleventh, the Fourteenth, the Sixteenth, and the Twenty-sixth. In other instances, the
Court has changed an unpopular course because of new appointments or simply because of the pressure of public opposition; in the
words of Mr. Dooley, the Court has displayed a capacity to follow the
election returns.[127] These methods of change are built into our system,
and that is as it should be: by and large, they do not damage the
courts, but protect them by giving them a needed flexibility. For the
most part, legislative attempts to nullify decisions of the federal courts
indirectly by tinkering with their structure and jurisdiction for substantive, political ends have failed. It is true that, in the anti-court
campaign of the early 1800s, the Jeffersonians stopped the Supreme
Court dead in its tracks for over a year and were able to repeal the
Judiciary Act of 1801, abolishing many new judgeships. But the plan
to control the judiciary with politically motivated impeachments did
not succeed in its ultimate aim.

No other similar legislative attack on the federal courts since then
has met with true success. For example, the result in *Ex parte McCardle*
turned out to be a limited victory, perhaps good for one performance
only. In particular, Congress has in no other instance enacted any of
the myriad bills to strip the federal courts of jurisdiction to hear certain classes of constitutional cases.[128] The attempts of states' rightists to
curb federal review of state statutes and court decisions, the McCarthy-era Congress's efforts to prevent the courts from protecting individual liberties, and the battery of bills aimed at undercutting the
school desegregation decisions have all failed. I am not sure why this
is so. One can attribute the failure to the difficulty of changing fundamental institutions, to inertia, to a residual consensus regarding the
courts, or, in some instances, to just plain chance. There is no doubt
that, from time to time, acts of principled statesmanship by individual
legislators or lawyers have helped to prevent the passage of ill-
considered measures.

Third, despite this lack of success, the attacks have continued over
most of our history. This is not surprising when one considers the
depth of feeling stirred by the basic issues in the cases just discussed.
Indeed, the surprise may be that such attempts have not occurred
more often. The failures of the past rarely discourage outraged
citizens of the present. It is true that we have come a long way since
the turbulent days of the early 1800s. I doubt that any member of
Congress would propose today, for example, that the Supreme Court

be required to stay in recess for one year. But history has a way of repeating itself. When then-Congressman Gerald Ford led the attempt
to impeach Justice Douglas in 1970, the Congressman stated that an
impeachable offense is "whatever a majority of the House of Representatives considers [it] to be at a given moment in history."[129] This
statement did not differ much from Senator Giles's definition in 1802
that impeachment was warranted if a judge was "opposed to the
administration & wrong headed."[130]

Decisions in the last decade or two involving prayer in the schools,
abortion, capital punishment, and school desegregation raise issues
about which people feel strongly, even passionately. With this background in mind, perhaps you will not be too surprised to learn that in
the last Congress there were more than thirty bills introduced that,
according to former American Bar Association president Brink,
"would deprive the federal courts of their historic and vital jurisdiction or power to grant remedies in what all agree are constitutional
cases."[131] Almost all of these bills single out narrow categories of constitutional claims for jurisdictional oblivion. It is worthwhile, I believe,
to examine more closely what may be the most comprehensive and in
some ways the most sophisticated of these bills, the "Judicial Reform
Act of 1982."[132] No action was taken last year on that bill, S. 3018, but
Senator Joseph R. Biden, Jr., of Delaware, the ranking minority
member of the Senate Judiciary Committee, expects it to be reintroduced in one form or another.[133]

S. 3018 proposes to limit the jurisdiction of the federal courts and
to alter their decisions on important issues. One provision would repeal the general federal question jurisdiction of 28 U.S.C. section
1331,[134] thus depriving the federal courts of jurisdiction to hear cases
arising under the Constitution, treaties, or federal law, unless Congress has specifically provided for jurisdiction in another provision of
Title 28 or in the substantive statute creating the alleged federal right.

The bill would also reverse several judicial rules designed to protect
civil and statutory rights. It would render the incorporation doctrine,
which applies many of the provisions of the Bill of Rights to the states,
unenforceable in the federal courts by depriving the Supreme Court
and the district courts of jurisdiction to hear cases claiming that a state
or any state agency or subdivision has deprived a party of any right secured by the first eight amendments to the Constitution.[135] In addition, the exclusionary rule would be overturned, and in its place the
courts would be given the power to punish violations of the Fourth

Amendment connected with cases pending before them as contempt of court.[136] The bill would also provide that no cause of action may be implied from any federal statute; only those causes of action explicitly provided for by Congress would be cognizable.[137]

The bill would also curtail the courts' jurisdiction in several other areas. Federal habeas corpus relief for prisoners in custody under a state court judgment would be limited to cases involving a substantial constitutional claim, rather than *any* claim under the Constitution, laws, or treaties of the United States. Moreover, the federal courts could not entertain a habeas petition raising an issue that had been, could have been, or still could be raised and determined in a state court proceeding subject to Supreme Court review by certiorari.[138] Thus, state prisoners would apparently face an almost inescapable Catch-22. The exhaustion doctrine would require resort to the state courts, but a determination on the merits there would bar a suit in the federal courts. In any event, I find it difficult to imagine that many petitioners could come up with substantial claims that would survive the emasculation of the incorporation doctrine. So it appears that habeas petitions from state prisoners would virtually disappear from the federal courts if this provision became law.

An analysis of the bill by the staff of the Senate Subcommittee on Separation of Powers, excerpts of which have been published—and I quote only from those—stated: "'These provisions should provide both a practical solution to the habeas deluge and an opportunity to explore the jurisprudence which made that deluge inevitable. It would return to the states the power to establish rules of criminal law and thus restore the principle of federalism in this important area.'"[139]

The bill would also severely limit civil rights litigation in the federal courts. It would amend 42 U.S.C. section 1983 in four ways: (1) claims of deprivation of rights secured by federal statutes would be limited to those under statutes "providing for equal rights;" (2) courts would be unable to enjoin state court proceedings; (3) no action could be maintained against a local government, municipal corporation, or other local body; and, finally, (4) even those claims remaining within section 1983 could not be heard in the federal courts unless "[s]tate law provides no adequate remedy or the remedy is not as a practical matter available."[140] Those few hardy civil rights plaintiffs whose claims could still be brought in the federal courts would be further deterred by the repeal of the provision for award of attorneys' fees to successful plaintiffs.[141]

Another provision of Title I of the bill would require that injunctions against a state or a subdivision, agency, or officer of a state be entered by a three-judge district court.[142] Title I also provides for the elimination of two of the three categories of class actions: those under Federal Rule of Civil Procedure 23(b)(2), which is often used for civil rights suits seeking injunctive relief, and those under Federal Rule of Civil Procedure 23(b)(3), where the court, in its discretion, determines that a class action is the fairest and most efficient way to settle the controversy, and that common questions of law or fact predominate.[143] The Subcommittee staff's analysis makes clear what motivates this provision: "'[M]embers of a particular race or sex now easily constitute classes given the sociological bent of modern federal jurisprudence. Abstract rights provide the bases for classes which render modern federal litigation more like legislation than like traditional adjudication of rights among concerned litigants.'"[144]

Before I describe Title II, we should step back for a moment to examine the effect of Title I. Of course, there have been abuses in prisoner suits under section 1983 and in habeas corpus proceedings. My focus is not, however, on specific provisions of the bill but on the effect of the bill as a whole. The message is clear enough: The federal courts are welcome to decide diversity cases under state law and routine federal law questions involving economic regulation or copyright infringement, but they had better not get the idea that one of their main functions is to guard the rights of individuals under the Constitution and laws of the United States. That function is left primarily to the states—and if the states choose to ignore the Bill of Rights, so be it.

The hostility toward the federal judiciary that permeates Title I of the bill is even more evident in Title II, called "Judgeships." Most revealing is Part A, "Oversight of Judiciary,"[145] which would repeal the recent statute providing for discipline of judges through the chief judges and judicial councils of the circuits,[146] and would set up a "Joint Committee on Judicial Conduct."[147] This committee would be composed of five senators and five representatives, appointed by the president pro tem of the Senate and the Speaker of the House,[148] respectively. The committee would review the conduct of each federal judge—including Justices of the Supreme Court[149]—at least once every ten years,[150] and would recommend impeachment if the judge's conduct "fail[s] to meet the standard of good behavior."[151] Judicial "conduct" is defined to include a judge's decisions. "Good behavior" is said to have the same meaning as in the Constitution.[152] Conduct "failing to meet the standard of good behavior" is further defined, however, as including "usurpation of the authority of the Congress, the President or the States"[153] and the "exercise of will instead of judgment by substituting the pleasure of the judge for that of the legislature—either Congress or the ratifiers of the Constitution of the United States, as the case may be—rather than declaring the sense of the law."[154]

I think it is obvious that the bill as a whole is an attempt to overrule a judicial philosophy that is unpopular with the bill's proponents. The standard established in Title II seems dangerously vague. The very threat of review by these overseers would have a profound effect on federal judges—indeed, it would destroy their independence. It would lead to the precise dangers that Alexander Hamilton feared: that "representatives of the people" might attempt to act in ways incompatible with the provisions of the existing Constitution. According to Hamilton, to guard against "legislative invasions" of the Constitution requires an "uncommon portion of fortitude in the judges." Thus, he viewed the independence of the judiciary as an essential characteristic of our constitutional system of government.[155]

We have seen that in the 200-year history of our Constitution there have been many attempts to subjugate the courts to the will of the political majority. These attempts have by and large been responses to particular decisions or trends of decision in the courts. But if this bill became law, it would end the need to proceed piecemeal. Congress would assume effective control of the judiciary. I wonder if the proponents have considered that the Supreme Court has often been attacked, as it was in the Roosevelt era, for defending conservative values against liberal legislation passed by Congress with the support of most voters. Similarly, in the 1970s, liberal dissatisfaction with Supreme Court decisions on standing led to introduction of a bill in Congress to remove the jurisdiction of the federal courts, under Article III of the Constitution, to determine whether plaintiffs have standing to bring a suit in federal court.[156] Majority control of the courts is a two-edged sword.

You may wonder why, given the failure rate of similar anti-court proposals in the past, this speech is devoted to the current assault. There are several reasons. First, these attacks have failed in the past usually because opposing political forces have combined with those who value the independence of the judiciary for its own sake to blunt or thwart the attack. Senator Biden, in a passionate speech before the Association of the Bar of the City of New York, reported that the sponsors of the bill intend to present it to Congress piecemeal if, as is quite likely, it fails to pass in its present form.[157] Senator Biden expressed great concern that this second effort might succeed, since the issues involved "are difficult for the public at large to understand" and the method of attack is largely procedural. Thus, the measures are not likely to arouse widespread interest and opposition. Senator Biden called upon the organized bar to recognize this bill and others like it as a threat to the Constitution and to oppose them actively.[158]

The second principal reason for my concern is that the forces that resent federal decisions are today reinforced in their calls for change by the judges' complaints, including my own, about the excessive caseload in the federal courts. If there are aspects of S. 3018 with which you disagree, mere opposition to this bill and to others like it is not sufficient; you must put forth and support alternative proposals to strengthen the federal courts while relieving them of some of the current burden of work.

Those of us who work in the system are acutely aware that something must give soon. Filings on all three levels of the federal judiciary have increased spectacularly in the past twenty years. In the district courts, the number of civil cases filed has increased three-and-a-third times.[159] The Supreme Court's docket has multiplied by a factor of two-and-a-half.[160] And the most staggering increases have been in the courts of appeals, where filings are almost six times what they were twenty years ago.[161] The addition of judgeships to the district and circuit courts has not kept pace with this increase in work, and of course the Supreme Court has not been enlarged at all.

S. 3018 would indubitably reduce the federal courts' workload considerably. But in the process it would substantially strip the courts of what I believe to be their special role in the federal system. While there may be room for constructive debate over some of the provisions of S. 3018, that debate should not be skewed by efficiency considerations because there are other, far more desirable, ways of reducing judicial workload. For example, the federal courts should not be deciding purely state law cases; if diversity jurisdiction were eliminated, 25 percent of the civil caseload of the district courts[162] and 17 percent of civil appeals in fiscal 1982[163] would have been removed, leaving the federal courts to do what we need them to do: enforce the Constitution's scheme of separation of powers; carry out the policies of the Constitution and of federal statutes; assure their supremacy in relation to the states; and guarantee federal constitutional rights against the encroachment of government, both federal and state. These functions are, of course, precisely what S. 3018 would in great part remove from the federal courts while leaving diversity jurisdiction intact.

While we ponder these questions, it might be instructive to recall a debate on overworked judges that took place over a century ago. Then, while Congress was deciding what to do about the appellate jurisdiction of the Supreme Court in habeas corpus cases, one senator argued that a statute that forces the Court to hear "long arguments upon a matter of trifling importance" when it is "two or three or four years behind in its business and the vast interests of the country are delayed" should be repealed. But when pressed, the senator admitted that he knew of no habeas appeal that had "overburdened" the Court other than McCardle's.[164] Recalling this episode should make us wary when efficiency arguments are used to justify removing constitutional law questions from the federal courts.

Those of us who believe that James Madison was right—that the Supreme Court needs the help of a system of lower federal courts and that the country needs an independent federal judiciary—must be alert to the fact that even after almost 200 years, there are those who disagree. Now, when the federal judiciary faces a workload crisis of unprecedented proportions, the federal courts are particularly vulnerable to the attacks of those who do not like their decisions. As we seek to make the federal judicial system work better, let us remember the job we want it to do.

Harry A. Blackmun

Section 1983 and Federal Protection of Individual Rights—Will the Statute Remain Alive or Fade Away?

Section 1983 of Title 42 of the United States Code provides:

Every person who, under color of any statute, ordinance, regulation, custom, or usage, of any State or Territory or the District of Columbia, subjects, or causes to be subjected, any citizen of the United States or other person within the jurisdiction thereof to the deprivation of any rights, privileges, or immunities secured by the Constitution and laws, shall be liable to the party injured in an action at law, suit in equity, or other proper proceeding for redress.

I

I suspect that even for those of us who are not lawyers the statute is not an unfamiliar one. It has become increasingly well known as the vehicle or, to put it less sympathetically, the "device" by which a citizen is able to challenge conduct by a state official that he claims has deprived or will deprive him of federal constitutional or statutory rights. Many of the Supreme Court's most significant constitutional decisions of the past generation, such as *Brown v. Board of Education*[1] and the legislative reapportionment cases, were the product of suits brought under section 1983.

At the same time, the statute increasingly has become a source of controversy, a battleground on which is fought much of the continuing debate over the proper role of the federal courts in protecting individual rights. One brand of criticism has focused on the extent to which section 1983 cases are claimed to be overburdening the federal courts. Critics rehearse statistics as to the number of section 1983 ac-

Justice Blackmun's lecture was delivered on November 14, 1984 and appeared in 60 N.Y.U.L. Rev. 1 (1985).

tions filed each year, with emphasis on those filed by state prisoners challenging the terms or conditions of their confinement.[2] There appears to be a growing belief that section 1983 actions are likely to be frivolous complaints by litigants who seek to use the statute to convert or bootstrap garden-variety state-law tort claims into federal cases.[3]

A more far-reaching set of complaints concerns the perceived tension between section 1983 and traditional values of American federalism. With increasing frequency, section 1983 actions are condemned as being inconsistent with the thesis that federal courts not interfere with state affairs unless absolutely necessary. Particularly when the statute is used to challenge an action by an official not pursuant to a state policy, critics tend to view 1983 as a misguided aberration, a left-over of the Supreme Court's allegedly activist period of two decades ago, when, in the view of some, responsible federalism concerns were thrown to the wind.

These perceptions have resulted in demands that section 1983 actions be restricted, both in their number and in their reach. Various proposals for "reform," short of repealing the statute, have been urged. These range from the imposition of an exhaustion requirement to the preclusion of damages awards, thus discouraging the initiation of section 1983 suits.[4] Although many reform proposals have been directed at congressional action, others have been addressed to a judicial audience, with commentators arguing for more restrictive interpretations of section 1983 and its developed doctrinal basis. Perhaps not surprisingly, the latter criticisms have begun to find an echo in the judicial response to section 1983 actions. In particular, recent opinions of the Supreme Court appear to reflect a growing uneasiness with the heretofore pronounced breadth of the statute and, in my view, a tendency to strain otherwise sound doctrines in order to ease the perceived federalism tensions generated by section 1983 actions.

Controversy over the role of section 1983 has been going on for over a century, and it shows no sign of coming to an end. Because I believe it to be an important controversy, not only for lawyers and the courts but also for individual citizens, I think it is worth taking time to try to understand the role section 1983 plays in the protection of individual rights in this country and how this controversial statute came to play that role. I therefore shall pass on to you my thoughts on the current debates, particularly my concern that any restriction of what has become a major symbol of federal protection of basic rights not be made in irresponsible haste.

II

One must begin by going to the origins of the statute, for where section 1983 came from casts important light on how far it has come and on what it has become. Most of what I have to say in this recall of history is not at all new, but perhaps it is time to review and consider it seriously—and not unsympathetically—once again.

To appreciate fully the profound revolution in federalism of which section 1983 was a part, it is useful to remember just how limited a role federal law played in protecting individual rights against state governments before the War Between the States. For present purposes, three features of this "prehistory" of section 1983 are important. First, the federal Constitution provides few substantive protections against oppressive state laws. Apart from section 10 of Article I, which forbids states from, among other things, passing any *ex post facto* law, bill of attainder, or law impairing the obligation of contracts, and apart from the developed application of the Bill of Rights to the states, the Constitution does not directly impose any barrier between the citizen and coercive state power. And even the protections guaranteed by the Bill of Rights, in their literal language, run against only the federal government.[5] Second, federal law provided no affirmative remedy for the vindication of those constitutional rights that were specifically expressed and as to which state action was limited. To borrow a well-worn metaphor, the Constitution, as amended by the Bill of Rights, provided a shield rather than a sword. It is because of this that, in the first seventy years of the Republic, many of the Supreme Court's important constitutional decisions came in suits in which defendants sought, on constitutional grounds, to avoid liability, rather than in suits in which plaintiffs sought to obtain damages or injunctive relief for alleged constitutional violations.[6] Third, federal courts had no general jurisdiction over federal claims, constitutional or otherwise. As a result, a litigant who wanted to challenge the constitutionality of state action was remitted to the state courts, unless the happenstance of diversity of citizenship allowed him to place his suit on the federal side.[7] Almost without exception, the Supreme Court's most significant constitutional holdings in the years before the Civil

War were reached in cases that came up through the state-court systems.[8]

The War and Reconstruction transformed the legal relations between the federal government and the states in each of these three respects. The most obvious change is that which is visible on the face of the Constitution itself—the Thirteenth, Fourteenth, and Fifteenth Amendments, adopted in 1865, 1868, and 1870, respectively. The Thirteenth Amendment abolished slavery; the Fourteenth defined state and national citizenship and granted all persons constitutional rights enforceable against the states; and the Fifteenth prohibited states from denying citizens, on racial grounds, the right to vote. The specific goal of these amendments was to dismantle the legal framework of slavery and to guarantee freed slaves the same political rights enjoyed by their former masters. The draftsmen of the Fourteenth Amendment, however, chose to speak in general terms that went far beyond the racial concerns of the moment—a decision whose significance, in retrospect, cannot be overstated.

This constitutional assault on the Old South was complemented by a series of statutes, the most significant of which were the several Civil Rights Acts passed between 1866 and 1875. The 1866 act,[9] which followed on the heels of the Thirteenth Amendment, was the statutory precursor to the Fourteenth Amendment. Section 1 of that act granted citizenship to all persons born in the United States and provided that all citizens, without regard to color, were entitled to the equal benefit of the laws, including the rights to make and enforce contracts, sue, give evidence, and purchase and own property. Section 2 imposed criminal sanctions on any person who, "under color of any law," deprived any inhabitant of any state or territory of rights recognized in section 1. Section 3 conferred jurisdiction on federal courts to hear all causes, civil and criminal, affecting persons who were denied or who could not enforce in state courts the rights secured by section 1.

Following the adoption of the Fourteenth Amendment in 1868, Congress reenacted the 1866 Act in the Enforcement Act of 1870, adding additional criminal penalties and specifically providing for jurisdiction in the federal courts over suits alleging racially inspired interference with the right to vote.[10] In the following year came the 1871 Civil Rights Act,[11] aimed specifically at the activities of the Ku Klux Klan. Section 1 of that act, now section 1983, added civil remedies. It provided a civil remedy for deprivations, under color of state law, of any of the rights, privileges, and immunities secured by the Constitution.[12] Sections 2 and 3 of the act imposed civil and criminal penalties for conspiracies to deprive persons of constitutional rights. The act was meant to reach the activity of a person who did not necessarily have the formal authorization of the state government involved, but for which the state either was unwilling or unable to provide a remedy. Finally, the 1875 Civil Rights Act[13] outlawed racial discrimination in places of public accommodation and provided civil and criminal penalties for violation of its provisions.

During the same period, Congress in three significant ways enlarged federal-court jurisdiction. Between 1863 and 1866, Congress expanded removal jurisdiction by allowing removal of cases alleging state interference with civil rights, as well as all criminal and civil suits brought against federal officers for acts committed during the war under the authority of Congress or the president.[14] In 1867, Congress passed a Habeas Corpus Act[15] that for the first time gave federal courts authority to consider the judgments of jurisdictionally competent state courts. Finally, in 1875, Congress created general federal-question jurisdiction in civil actions.[16]

Taken collectively, the Reconstruction amendments, the Civil Rights Acts, and these new jurisdictional statutes, all emerging from the caldron of the War Between the States, marked a revolutionary shift in the relationship among individuals, the states, and the federal government.[17] The Reconstruction Congresses vested individuals with three distinct kinds of protection against state governments, protections that were absent in the prewar structure: federal rights, federal remedies, and federal forums. It bears noting that section 1983 was only one arrow in this large federal quiver. The Supreme Court described the magnitude of the overall change in *Mitchum v. Foster:*[18]

This legislative history makes evident that Congress clearly conceived that it was altering the relationship between the States and the Nation with respect to the protection of federally created rights; it was concerned that state instrumentalities could not protect those rights; it realized that state officers might, in fact, be antipathetic to the vindication of those rights; and it believed that these failings extended to the state courts.

* * *

Section 1983 was thus a product of a vast tranformation from the concepts of federalism that had prevailed in the late 18th century. . . . The very purpose of section 1983 was to interpose the federal courts between the States and the people, as guardians of the people's federal rights—to protect the people from unconstitutional action under color of state law, "whether that action be executive, legislative, or judicial."[19]

The significance of the reach of the Civil Rights Acts and their encroachment of state prerogatives was lost on no one. In debates over the 1866 act, opponents of the bill described it as "one of the most dangerous that was ever introduced into the Senate of the United States,"[20] as proposing to "reform the whole civil and criminal code of every State government,"[21] as interfering with the duties of state officials, and as promising to result in a flood of petty cases removed to federal courts.[22] Proponents, in their turn, conceded that its reach was substantial, but insisted that the unwillingness of the states to protect the freedmen or citizens of other states made the bill necessary.[23]

The 1871 act provoked similar outcries. Describing the bill as a whole, Representative Holman complained that "the jurisdiction of the Federal courts, hitherto confined to questions of national concern, is to invade the provinces of the State courts with new laws and systems of administration."[24] Representative Eldredge found no apparent limit in the bill "beyond which the Federal Government may not go to the exclusion of the heretofore conceded jurisdiction of the States in the redress of the violation of the rights of person and property."[25] Discussing section 1 of the act, Representative Arthur described it in this way:

It overrides the reserved powers of the States. It reaches out and draws within the despotic circle of central power all the domestic, internal, and local institutions and offices of the States, and then asserts over them an arbitrary and paramount control as of the rights, privileges, and immunities secured and protected, in a peculiar sense, by the United States in the citizens thereof. Having done this, having swallowed up the States and their institutions, tribunals, and functions, it leaves them the shadow of what they once were.[26]

Section 2 of the act, authorizing civil and criminal penalties for private conspiracies to deprive individuals of civil rights, was even more controversial. The Democrats saw the bill as an extension of federal authority over common crimes.[27] In the words of Representative Arthur, the act "absorbs the entire jurisdiction of the States over their local and domestic affairs; the first section as to civil rights and remedies, and the second as to wrongs and punishments."[28]

Reconstruction thus established a new legal order that contemplated direct federal intervention in what had been considered to be state affairs, a system in which federal courts were to enforce newly created federal constitutional rights against state officials through civil remedies and criminal sanctions. The story of how this edifice crumbled during the succeeding half-century might be characterized by some as a somber one in American legal history. Even before the Civil Rights Acts found their places on the statute books, critics sharply questioned not only the acts' expediency but their constitutionality. The crucial issue in this debate was the scope of the authority granted Congress by the Reconstruction amendments, particularly the Fourteenth. The Radical Republicans, as they were called, defended the bills on the ground that the Fourteenth Amendment had altered the balance between the states and the national government so that Congress for the first time had the authority to protect life, liberty, and property by legislating directly against offending activity.[29] Moderate Republicans agreed that Congress had the authority, under the Fourteenth Amendment, to reach private action, although they disagreed with the Radicals over the actual scope of the bills.[30] In the Democrats' view, however, the Fourteenth Amendment was simply a remedial measure—it stepped in to protect citizens directly only when the state government itself violated their civil rights.

Although the Radicals won the day in Congress and the Civil Rights Acts went into effect, the Supreme Court arrived at different conclusions about the scope of the authority granted Congress by the Fourteenth Amendment. In short order, the Court acted to declare numerous provisions of the acts unconstitutional and to render others ineffectual by narrow construction. In 1873, in the *Slaughterhouse Cases*,[31] the Court construed the Privileges and Immunities Clause of the Fourteenth Amendment and concluded that the amendment did not federalize any substantive rights that were not already incidents of national citizenship. The Court then reviewed a series of actions brought under the Civil Rights Acts and held in each that Congress's power under the amendment was limited to addressing direct encroachment of civil rights by states. *United States v. Cruikshank*[32] invalidated an indictment under the conspiracy section of the 1870 act. A private conspiracy to violate constitutional rights, in the Court's view, lacked the state action required of legislation passed under the Fourteenth Amendment. Similarly, in *United States v. Harris*,[33] the Court found no constitutional basis for the criminal conspiracy section of the 1871 act, because the section was aimed at private action. In the *Civil Rights Cases*,[34] the Court invalidated the 1875 act's prohibition of private racial discrimination in accommodations and public conveyances. The legislation could not be upheld under the Fourteenth Amendment, the Court ruled, because it was not aimed at state action. Nor could it be upheld under the Thirteenth, because even though that amendment reached private action, denial of admission to a public place was not a badge or incident of slavery. Only the first Justice Harlan dissented. He would have found the statute supportable under the Thirteenth Amendment. More relevant to our purposes, his view of the necessary state action was less strict. The fact that most of the public accommodations at issue in the *Civil Rights Cases* were licensed by the states satisfied the requirement. He added the following prophetic conclusion:

I may be permitted to say that if the recent amendments are so construed that Congress may not, in its own discretion, and independently of the action or non-action of the States, provide, by legislation of a direct character, for the security of rights created by the national Constitution; if it be adjudged that the obligation to protect the fundamental privileges and immunities granted by the Fourteenth Amendment to citizens residing in the several States, rests primarily, not on the nation, but on the States; if it be further adjudged that individuals and corporations, exercising public functions, or wielding power under public authority, may, without liability to direct primary legislation on the part of Congress, make the race of citizens the ground for denying them that equality of civil rights which the Constitution ordains as a principle of republican citizenship; then, not only the foundations upon which the national supremacy has always securely rested will be materially disturbed, but we shall enter upon an era of constitutional law, when the rights of freedom and American citizenship cannot receive from the nation that efficient protection which heretofore was unhesitatingly accorded to slavery and the rights of the master.[35]

There is some debate about the extent to which the Supreme Court's nineteenth-century interpretations of the Fourteenth Amendment and the Civil Rights Acts really were inconsistent with then-prevailing notions of the proper relationship between the states and the federal government.[36] The fact remains, nevertheless, that with a few quick thrusts, the Court cut the heart out of the Civil Rights Acts. Fundamental rights of citizenship were placed beyond the protection of the Fourteenth Amendment by the Court's narrow reading of that amendment's Privileges and Immunities Clause. And the uncontrolled private abuses that had so concerned the majority in Congress apparently could not constitutionally be reached by the federal courts, since those private abuses did not constitute "state action." By the Court's decisions, major provisions of the acts either were declared unconstitutional or were emasculated. Although the Court did not address section 1 of the 1871 act and thus never held that the "color of state law" requirement of that section and of section 2 of the 1866 act was limited to official state action, the tribunal's thinking and direction were clear. Those sections that were not struck down were largely forgotten.

There is another reason why the Civil Rights Acts slipped out of sight. The political climate changed and the harsh grip of the Radicals over the southern states loosened. The Democrats made gradual gains in Congress. In 1875, in the last half of the second Grant administration, control of the House passed to them. By 1879 they controlled both the House and the Senate. In 1871, Congress repealed the requirement that former Confederate soldiers take an oath of allegiance to the Union and disavow their disloyal acts. In 1872, it restored full political rights to most of the former Confederates.[37] Senator Lucius Q. C. Lamar of Mississippi, later an associate justice of the Supreme Court and the subject of a chapter in John F. Kennedy's 1956 book, *Profiles in Courage*, expressed the growing sentiment toward reconciliation. After the death of Republican Senator Charles Sumner of Massachusetts, Lamar in 1874 delivered in the House of Representatives a eulogy for Sumner that marked a significant change in attitude in both the North and the South toward the task at hand. According to Lamar, Sumner,

in life believed that all occasion for strife and distrust between the North and South had passed away. . . . Is not that the common sentiment, or if it is not ought it not to be, of the great mass of our people, North and South? . . . Shall we not, over the honored remains of . . . this earnest pleader for the exercise of human tenderness and charity, lay aside the concealments which serve only to perpetuate misunderstandings and distrust, and frankly confess that on both sides we most earnestly desire to be one . . . in feeling and in heart? . . .

* * *

Would that the spirit of the illustrious dead whom we lament today could speak from the grave to both parties to this deplorable discord in tones which should reach each and every heart throughout this broad territory, "My countrymen, *know* one another, and you will *love* one another."[38]

It indeed was time to rebuild and put old wounds behind. With the move toward reconciliation, however, the nation lost the urgency of its zeal to protect the individual rights and freedoms for which the war in part had been fought. In the Revised Statutes of 1873, the Civil Rights Acts were divided and scattered.[39] Federal prosecutions under the acts declined precipitously. In 1873, 1,304 prosecutions were brought, 1,271 of which were in the South. By 1878, that figure dropped to 25.[40] In 1877, Congress would have repealed much of the 1870 Enforcement Act, but President Hayes vetoed the measure. In 1894 and 1909, Congress repealed a number of the provisions of the Civil Rights Acts, including, in the former year, thirty-nine sections of the Revised Statutes dealing with the right to vote.[41]

Reconciliation grew into a nationwide amnesia about the events of the Civil War and Reconstruction. In 1876, President Hayes agreed to withdraw federal troops from the South. Almost immediately, Negroes were disenfranchised. In 1890, Mississippi passed a new suffrage law, imposing a $2 poll tax and exhaustive literacy requirements. In 1895, South Carolina did the same, adding to the list an imposing property requirement. Louisiana passed a similar statute, with a grandfather clause and prohibitive education and property requirements. By 1910, every southern state had followed suit. The statutes served their purpose well. In 1896, 130,344 Negroes were registered in Louisiana. By 1900, only 5,320 remained on the books.[42]

The first segregation laws were passed in 1892, requiring railroads to assign Negro passengers to separate cars. Jim Crow spread from passenger trains to streetcars, restaurants, washrooms, and residential communities. Lynch mobs reared their ugly heads. One author reports records of 3,000 lynchings from 1883 to 1903, with few if any reprisals against the participants.[43]

Thus, as the twentieth century dawned, the nation's commitment to civil rights lay in remnants. It was our Dark Age of Civil Rights. For the first forty years of this century, the only judicial relief available was in suits involving official action denying Negroes the right to vote. Whatever doubts there may have been about the intent of the Reconstruction Congresses, there was no denying Congress's purpose to ensure Negroes the right to vote. Even if there were any doubts about the reach of the Fourteenth Amendment, the Fifteenth stood as a certain basis for federal action to protect voting rights. In addition, the challenges almost always addressed only official state policy.

The significant cases are few and can be quickly recounted. In 1915, the Court relied on the Fifteenth Amendment to strike down "grandfather clauses" in the suffrage laws of Maryland and Oklahoma.[44] In 1917, the Court struck down, as an infringement of property rights without due process of law, a racially restrictive city ordinance.[45] In 1927, the Court granted injunctive relief under section 1983 and the Fourteenth Amendment against enforcement of a Texas statute which prevented Negroes from voting in Democratic primaries.[46] Five years later, the Court granted a damages award against state officials who effectuated the same white primary, even though the state had shifted responsibility to an executive committee.[47] Finally, in 1939, the Court granted damages under section 1983 and the Fifteenth Amendment against officials who had sought to avoid the earlier ruling against Oklahoma's grandfather clause by repealing the clause but giving Negroes only twelve days to register to vote after the repeal.[48]

As one can see, from the 1890s to the 1940s, the Civil Rights Acts lay virtually dormant. Although they were called on occasionally to remedy the most blatant affronts to the Reconstruction amendments, little thought was given to utilizing them to address other incidents of slavery.

Outside the courts, however, the nation was not quiescent. Gradually and increasingly, public sentiment was growing against the continuing second-class status of Negroes. In the summer of 1905, a small group of Negroes met at Niagara Falls committed, as was stated a year later, to obtaining "every single right that belongs to a freeborn American, political, civil, and social," and vowing that "until we get these rights we will never cease to protest and assail the ears of America."[49] Shortly after that meeting, race riots in Springfield, Illinois served as the catalyst for a group of concerned white leaders who organized the first meeting of the National Association for the Advancement of Colored People.

The organization's first efforts were political. It fought for anti-lynching legislation. A bill was finally proposed in 1935, but did not pass. The NAACP sought President F. D. Roosevelt's help, but it is said the president could not afford to alienate the South and lose support for his New Deal legislation.[50] By threatening a massive protest march on Washington, the organization did persuade Roosevelt to establish in 1941 a temporary Committee on Fair Employment Practices and to order that employers and unions "provide for the full and equitable participation of all workers in defense industries, without discrimination because of race, creed, color, or national origin."[51] It also worked from World War I on to end segregation in the Armed Forces. President Truman finally agreed to this.

The NAACP also participated in and won some legal battles, even in the early years. It took part in *Guinn v. United States*, where the challenge to Oklahoma's "grandfather clause" amendment denying Negroes the right to vote was successful.[52] It also participated in *Buchanan v. Warley,* where Louisville's racial zoning ordinance was struck down,[53] and it persuaded the Court to overturn the death sentences of twelve Negroes convicted in a mob-dominated court.[54]

Prior to 1939, the association's legal work was done on an ad hoc basis by individual members of the organization and by volunteers. But a national legal committee was formed to advise the association. Members included Clarence Darrow, Felix Frankfurter, Frank Murphy, Arthur Garfield Hays, and Morris L. Ernst.[55] By 1939, however, the association had determined to make a concerted legal effort to attack racial segregation in education, transportation, and housing. It established the NAACP Legal Defense and Education Fund, with Thurgood Marshall at its head.

The success of the fund's subsequent efforts is well known. In 1948, it won its battle to have racially restrictive housing covenants declared unconstitutional.[56] And in 1954, the Supreme Court, in *Brown,* finally rejected the "separate but equal" doctrine, and declared that racially segregated public schools deny the equal protection of the laws guaranteed by the Fourteenth Amendment. Beginning in 1939, however, the fund was not alone in its efforts. In that year, the president appointed Frank Murphy attorney general. Murphy set up the first Civil Rights Division in the Department of Justice. A year later, he succeeded Pierce Butler as an associate justice of the Supreme Court.

The work of the Civil Rights Division went on. In the early years, it focused primarily on police brutality and, despite the absence of federal antilynching legislation, on the prosecution of lynch mobs. In 1946, a series of lynchings prompted renewed efforts for an antilynching bill. William White, secretary of the NAACP, sought the aid of President Truman. No bill was forthcoming, but Mr. Truman created the Presidential Committee on Civil Rights to study the growing racial problems. The Committee issued a report, entitled *To Secure These Rights,* on October 29, 1947. Among the recommendations of the committee was a request that the Justice Department enter the fight against racially restrictive covenants. The week after the publication of the committee's report, the department decided to intervene as *amicus curiae* in *Shelley v. Kraemer.*[57]

The report also assessed the weaknesses in the federal civil rights enforcement machinery. Prime among these was the lack of available tools with which to address the deprivations of which the nation was becoming increasingly aware. That criticism soon became a familiar refrain. One author surveyed the statutory tools available and concluded:

It is doubtful if much can be done by way of existing federal statutes to implement effectively the civil rights of individuals. There are some encouraging signs in the application of some of those statutes to the broad rights which have come to be protected against state action under the due process clause. But the greatest source of violations, the actions of private individuals, are beyond the power of present statutes to reach in any substantial degree.[58]

The obstacles to the use of the Civil Rights Acts, in the view of the commentators, were two. First, the criminal provisions had limited value in view of the narrow construction the Court had given them during Reconstruction. And it was private action, uncontrolled by the states, that was the greatest source of violations. The civil provisions were subject to a similar narrow construction. In addition, a civil remedy was thought to be of limited value as a means of enforcing civil liberties. In a 1947 book about the Civil Rights Division, the author applauded its work, but insisted that existing statutory tools were inadequate for the division to be effective. The criminal sanctions were too narrow and the civil sanctions, while they had been employed on a few occasions, could never be effective on a large scale. "The victim in a civil liberty case virtually is left to his own resources in invoking this sanction, and since the victim in such a case is usually a poor person, without standing or prestige in his own community, he often lacks the courage and financial ability to go to court in defense of his rights. Society cannot depend on this device to assure a thorough and continuing enforcement of legal controls."[59]

Despite dire prophecies, the Civil Rights Division went to work with the tools it had and it is those efforts that paved the way for the rebirth of section 1983. Through the division's efforts, the first crack in the armor the Court had built against effective use of the Civil Rights Acts was made. Again, it appears that the weakest spot in that armor was in the area of voting rights. *United States v. Classic*[60] was a 1941 case pursued by the division to test whether the criminal provisions, now 18 U.S.C. sections 241 and 242, authorized the federal government to prosecute state election officials accused of stealing and miscounting ballots in a state primary election. Section 51, originally section 6 of the 1870 act, made it a crime for two or more persons to conspire to injure or intimidate any citizen in the free exercise or enjoyment of any right or privilege secured to him by the Constitution or laws of the United States. Section 52 made it a crime for anyone, under color of any law, willfully to subject any inhabitant of any state to the deprivation of any rights secured or protected by the Constitution or laws of the United States. The Court concluded that the right of the elector to have his ballot counted at the primary is protected by the Constitution. It also held that both section 51 and section 52 reached the challenged conduct. The aspect of that ruling that has had the most profound impact on the course of civil rights litigation is the Court's decision that the "under color of state law" requirement was satisfied even though the state officers were accused of committing acts clearly not authorized by state law.

The interpretation of "under color of state law" adopted in *Classic* was expanded beyond the protection of voting rights in the now well-known 1945 case of *Screws v. United States*.[61] The background to the *Screws* case is worth recounting. Here is the first paragraph of the plurality opinion:

> This case involves a shocking and revolting episode in law enforcement. Petitioner Screws was sheriff of Baker County, Georgia. He enlisted the assistance of petitioner Jones, a policeman, and petitioner Kelley, a special deputy, in arresting Robert Hall, a citizen of the United States and of Georgia. The arrest was made late at night at Hall's home on a warrant charging Hall with theft of a tire. Hall, a young negro about thirty years of age, was handcuffed and taken by car to the court house. As Hall alighted from the car at the court-house square, the three petitioners began beating him with their fists and with a solid-bar blackjack about eight inches long and weighing two pounds. They claimed Hall had reached for a gun and had used insulting language as he alighted from the car. But after Hall, still handcuffed, had been knocked to the ground they continued to beat him from fifteen to thirty minutes until he was unconscious. Hall was then dragged feet first through the court-house yard into the jail and thrown upon the floor dying. An ambulance was called and Hall was removed to a hospital where he died within the hour and without regaining consciousness. There was evidence that Screws held a grudge against Hall and had threatened to "get" him.[62]

The petitioners were convicted of violating section 52 of the Criminal Code. Before the Supreme Court they urged that whatever offense they had committed was one only against the state and that their action was not authorized by state law and therefore was not action "under color of state law." Justice Roberts, joined by Justices Frankfurter and Jackson, agreed. In their view, to construe section 52 to reach the conduct of the petitioners would be to attribute to Congress an intent it did not have, to make "overnight . . . a revolutionary change in the balance of the political relations between the National Government and the States."[63] On the contrary, Congress intended "to leave undisturbed the power and the duty of the States to enforce their criminal law by restricting federal authority to the punishment only of those persons who violate federal rights under claim of State authority and not by exerting federal authority against offenders of State authority."[64]

Relying on the Court's holding in *Classic* that "[m]isuse of power, possessed by virtue of state law and made possible only because the wrongdoer is clothed with the authority of state law, is action taken 'under color of' state law," the plurality of the Court disagreed.[65] Justice Rutledge, in a separate opinion, noted that it did not appear that the state had taken any steps toward prosecution for violation of its law.[66] One writer has pursued that point further. He examined the Justice Department's files in the case and found evidence that:

the federal government made every effort to persuade the state of Georgia to prosecute the offenders. Georgia failed to take any action. The reason for Georgia's failure to prosecute the perpetrators of such an extremely brutal crime is not clear. Apparently, the state authorities were willing to see action taken, but the initiative in such an affair lay with local officers. The district solicitor general, whose duty it was to start criminal proceedings, is reported by the United States Attorney to have felt "helpless in the matter." "He has no investigative facilities and has to rely upon the sheriff and policemen of the various counties of his circuit for investigation." Such assistance in this case would have had to come from the accused persons themselves![67]

Classic and *Screws* signalled a general relaxation of the strict "state action" requirement that had shackled the Fourteenth Amendment and its enforcing Civil Rights Acts since Reconstruction. Shortly after *Classic*, the NAACP, in *Smith v. Allwright*,[68] was successful in a section 1983 challenge to the Texas white primary. Relying on *Classic*, the Supreme Court held that although the state had delegated to a political party the responsibility for fixing qualifications for voting in a primary, the state endorsed and enforced the discrimination practiced by the party to decide who may vote. The action of the party therefore was taken under color of state law. Then, in *Shelley v. Kraemer*, the Court found sufficient state action in the willingness of the state courts to enforce private racially restrictive covenants.

Against this background, *Monroe v. Pape*,[69] decided in 1961, should have come as no surprise. The issue in *Monroe* was whether thirteen

Chicago police officers charged with conducting an unconstitutional search and arrest could be liable under section 1983 even though their actions were not specifically authorized by state law. The complaint, as paraphrased by Justice Frankfurter in his opinion dissenting in part, alleged:

that . . . thirteen Chicago police officers, led by Deputy Chief of Detectives Pape, broke through two doors of the Monroe apartment, woke the Monroe couple with flashlights, and forced them at gunpoint to leave their bed and stand naked in the center of the living room; that the officers roused the six Monroe children and herded them into the living room; that Detective Pape struck Mr. Monroe several times with his flashlight, calling him "nigger" and "black boy"; that another officer pushed Mrs. Monroe; that other officers hit and kicked several of the children and pushed them to the floor; that the police ransacked every room, throwing clothing from closets to the floor, dumping drawers, ripping mattress covers; that Mr. Monroe was then taken to the police station and detained on "open" charges for ten hours, during which time he was interrogated about a murder and exhibited in lineups; that he was not brought before a magistrate, although numerous magistrate's courts were accessible; that he was not advised of his procedural rights; that he was not permitted to call his family or an attorney; that he was subsequently released without criminal charges having been filed against him.[70]

One commentator has noted the similarity between the complaint in *Monroe* and a story told by a South Carolina Negro, Joshua Wardlaw, and read into the record of the Forty-second Congress in 1871 while the Congress was debating the Ku Klux Klan Act. Wardlaw recounted:

Pres. Blackwell kicked one of my little children that was in the bed. They took my brother-in-law's gun and broke it against a tree in the yard. They laid me down on the ground, after stripping me as naked as when I came into the world, and struck me five times with a strap before I got away from them. After escaping they fired four shots at me, but did not hit me. I was so frightened I laid out in the woods all night, naked as I was, and suffered from the exposure. Mr. Richardson afterward told me he was very sorry that I had escaped from them. My brother-in-law died from the beating he got that same night.[71]

As in *Screws*, there was a strong voice in *Monroe* urging that the "color of state law" requirement should operate to confine the reach of the federal courts to official state conduct. Justice Frankfurter surveyed the legislative history and concluded that section 1 of the 1871 act, unlike section 2, was not intended to extend beyond official state action. He then expressed sentiments remarkably similar to those of the opponents of the 1871 bill. In the justice's view, to have section 1983 reach unauthorized acts of state officials would be to make "the extreme limits of federal constitutional power a law to regulate the quotidian business of every traffic policeman, every registrar of elections, every city inspector or investigator, every clerk in every municipal licensing bureau in this country."[72]

Once again, however, a majority of the Court disagreed. The majority also surveyed the legislative history of the act and concluded, as was done in *Classic* and in *Screws,* that the Reconstruction Congresses had intended to reach the kind of conduct complained of in *Monroe.* It found it "abundantly clear that one reason the legislation was passed was to afford a federal right in federal courts because, by reason of prejudice, passion, neglect, intolerance or otherwise, state laws might not be enforced and the claims of citizens to the enjoyment of rights, privileges, and immunities guaranteed by the Fourteenth Amendment might be denied by the state agencies."[73] It emphasized that it was the activities of the Ku Klux Klan and the inability or unwillingness of the state governments to cope with those activities that prompted the act. It noted that speaker after speaker had emphasized that the problem was not with state laws as written, but with the failure of the states to enforce those laws to protect Negroes and Union sympathizers. And opponents of the bill objected to the act's "transfer [of] all criminal jurisdiction from the courts of the States to the courts of the United States . . . upon the assumption that the courts of the southern States fail and refuse to do their duty in the punishment of offenders against the law."[74]

Monroe, although later overruled in part,[75] is correctly credited as being a watershed in the development of section 1983. Between 1939 and 1961, the significant section 1983 cases, like those prior to 1939, were few. It is difficult to compile an accurate list. Often, there is no mention in the Court's opinions of the statutory basis for jurisdiction and remedial authority. An opinion might simply note that certain conduct is challenged as violative of the Constitution. I have not attempted to survey the significant section 1983 cases that did not reach the Supreme Court. I have looked back, however, into the complaints and records in a number of Supreme Court cases during this twenty-two-year period before *Monroe.* The cases can almost be counted on one hand. They include a challenge to official state actions preventing the plaintiffs from assembling to discuss the National

Labor Relations Act and to organize a union,[76] the NAACP's successful challenge to the Texas white primary,[77] and a First Amendment
challenge to a state requirement that teachers file affidavits listing all
the organizations to which they belong.[78]

Probably the most significant pre-*Monroe* case was *Brown v. Board of
Education*. Interestingly, in the Court's opinion there is no citation of
either section 1983 or of the jurisdictional statute. Two of the *per
curiam* opinions following *Brown,* with which the Court expanded
Brown to beaches, buses, and other public accommodations, also were
section 1983 cases.[79]

After *Monroe*, however, the list expands. One now could claim surprise at the significance of the role that section 1983 played in civil
liberties litigation in the last twenty years. It is also interesting to note
that many of these cases probably could have been brought successfully before *Monroe; Monroe* simply focused attention on the availability of the section 1983 remedy.

In the context of racial equality, many of the major school desegregation cases were filed as section 1983 actions. In the First Amendment area, section 1983 was relied on for a challenge to state laws that
required loyalty oaths,[80] or prevented the wearing of armbands in
protest of our policy in Vietnam.[81] It was also used to restrain prosecutions under Louisiana's Subversive Activities and Communist Control
Law.[82] It was utilized by the NAACP to establish that organization's
authority to advise Negroes of their legal rights.[83] It was used to challenge bans on lawyer advertising and spending limitations on the public education activities of charities.[84] Section 1983 has been the vehicle
for establishing significant due process rights. The case establishing
that a welfare recipient has a right to notice and a hearing before his
benefits are terminated was a section 1983 case.[85] Along the same line,
section 1983 cases have confirmed the due process rights of recipients
of utility service,[86] of public employees,[87] of employees entitled under
state law to seek redress for unlawful discharge,[88] and of debtors
whose property is about to be seized by individuals or by the state.[89]
Section 1983 has been used to challenge mandatory maternity leave
policies[90] and state restrictions on social security benefits.[91] This list includes challenges to state restrictions on the right to vote, from poll
taxes on white primaries to unequal apportionment schemes.[92] It includes a challenge of unequal age limitations for males and females
on the sale of beer,[93] and on limitations on the right to marry the person of one's choice.[94] And it includes successful efforts by mental

patients and by prisoners to achieve First Amendment freedoms, basic medical care, and due process rights while within institutional walls.[95]

III

The current criticisms of section 1983 are a by-product, of course, of the revival of the statute as a vehicle for vindicating constitutional rights against state officials. The least persuasive criticisms for me, or at any rate the least complete, are those that claim that section 1983 actions are burdening the federal courts. Since any such "burden" presumably is worth bearing when an action is meritorious, the criticisms must assume that the suits generally are without merit. But I am aware of no statistics demonstrating what percentage of section 1983 actions are bound to be meritless. Prisoners, especially those who proceed *pro se*, are popular candidates for the group likely to present consistently frivolous claims. But ever since *Jackson v. Bishop*,[96] a case in which I take pride in having participated on the Court of Appeals, despite improvements in state prison systems, I am not prepared to exclude the possibility that a particular prisoner will be subject to a serious deprivation that warrants the attention of a federal court. In fact, I suspect that improvements in prison conditions of recent years are traceable in large part, and perhaps primarily, to actions under section 1983 challenging those conditions.[97] In any event, it is not clear to me why screening out frivolous suits should be considered a problem peculiar to section 1983, rather than a part of a more general problem of federal litigation that must be addressed on its own terms. If critics are concerned by the sheer burden placed on the federal judiciary by section 1983 actions, they might do well to turn their attention, too, to other sources of federal litigaton. My point is simply that if we want to nominate a particular group of cases for exclusion from the federal courthouse, we should look first at groups in which federal law is not sensitively at issue rather than at one in which fundamental constitutional rights are at stake.

The related concern that a section 1983 action may be used to bootstrap a state-law tort claim into a federal forum has been greatly undercut, in my view, by the combined effects of the Court's recent decisions in *Parratt v. Taylor*,[98] *Hudson v. Palmer*,[99] and *Pennhurst State School and Hospital v. Halderman*.[100] Whatever else may be said about these decisions, they have made it difficult, if not impossible, for a plaintiff who has only a state-law tort claim against a state official to hale the official into federal court under the guise of a section 1983 action. The Supreme Court gives ample evidence of being able to devise protective measures for itself and other federal courts.

The criticisms on which I would like to focus particularly are those concerning the impact of section 1983 on federalism and federal–state comity. My first response is that the so-called federalism problem created by section 1983 is largely an illusory one. We tend to forget that section 1983 does not stand alone in the legal universe, but is part of a much broader set of legal protections for individual rights. Section 1983 is only a vehicle for substantive claims that have their base elsewhere. It is not an independent source of constitutional or statutory rights. Indeed, given the presence of *Bivens v. Six Unknown Fed. Narcotics Agents*,[101] in which the Court implied a private right of action for damages against federal officials who violate the Constitution, it might well be that federal courts would feel obliged to assume the authority to remedy constitutional violations by state officials even without an imposed statutory remedy. Many complaints about section 1983's ostensible impact on federalism really are complaints about the breadth of the underlying constitutional rights—a separate issue that surely deserves to be debated on its own terms.

More important is the fact that the one-sided model of federal supervision of state officials that was put in place after the Civil War has given way, not especially by design, to a more balanced system of judicial protection of individual rights. The new balance of which I speak involves all three aspects of the post–Civil War revolution in federal power and individual liberty—that is, rights, remedies, and forums. As for rights, when the Supreme Court in 1954 brought about the "reverse incorporation" of the Equal Protection Clause into the Fifth Amendment in *Bolling v. Sharpe*,[102] it ensured that all the fundamental constitutional rights of the Fourteenth Amendment bind the federal government as well as the states. Seventeen years later, in *Bivens*, the Court put together a working equivalent of section 1983 for constitutional claims against federal officials. Lastly, while the question has not been settled finally by the Supreme Court, the current weight of authority elsewhere is that state courts may assume jurisdiction over constitutional claims for injunctive relief or damages against federal officials.[103] When these developments are looked at together, a surprising degree of symmetry emerges: individuals enjoy common constitutional rights against the federal government and the states; they may obtain injunctive relief and damages against both federal and state officials; and both state and federal courts may entertain constitutional suits and award constitutional remedies against any official, federal as well as state, who deprives or threatens to deprive an individual of his constitutional rights. Any perceived slight to state autonomy by reason of section 1983 actions looks much less compelling when viewed from this perspective than it does when section 1983 is viewed in isolation.[104]

My second response to the criticisms concerning the impact of section 1983 on federalism is that to the extent the statute does create problems, those problems are political rather than judicial. It is not improper, of course, to take issue with the balance struck by the Reconstruction Congresses, nor is it improper to call for greater deference toward the states. We must recognize, however, that such arguments are better addressed to Congress than to the courts. It is not enough to argue before a court that a particular construction of section 1983 is inconsistent with "principles of federalism" or "federal–state comity." To do so is to put the cart before the horse, for the only principles of federalism and comity that justify restricting the scope of section 1983 are those found in the Constitution or section 1983 itself. We must avoid the temptation to let "federalism" become the Natural Law of the 1980s, a brooding omnipresence to which duly enacted statutes are made to pay homage. Indeed, there is more than a little irony in litigants' and commentators' asking the Supreme Court to restrict the scope of section 1983 in order to prevent unwarranted intrusions on the democratic processes of state governments. If section 1983 as presently construed does shift political authority from elected officials to unelected judges—and I do not concede that it does—the remedy, it seems to me, lies with the elected members of the Senate and House of Representatives and not with the unelected members of the Supreme Court.

It is in part for this reason that one might be troubled by the overtones of some of the Court's recent decisions in this area. The tenor of the times perhaps has changed, and the judicial pendulum, which swung from retrenchment in the years after Reconstruction to a renewal of federal responsibiliy for constitutional rights during the last two generations, may have begun to swing once more toward retrenchment. In certain instances, the Court appears inclined to cut back on section 1983 in any way it can, short of ignoring the language of the statute or existing rulings. The common theme of some of the recent decisions seems to me to be that section 1983 should be construed to minimize federal judicial intervention in state affairs whenever possible, regardless of the impact on the ability of federal courts to protect constitutional rights.

For example, the Court has limited damages awards available under section 1983 by expanding doctrines of immunity—an absolute Eleventh Amendment immunity for states,[105] an absolute immunity from damages for judges and legislators,[106] and a good-faith immunity for state and local officials that appears to require the plaintiff to demonstrate that the exact requirements of the constitutional right at issue had been spelled out by a federal court prior to the alleged violation.[107] The Court's Eleventh Amendment ruling in *Pennhurst*, while not directly limiting relief available on a section 1983 claim, also whittles away at the section 1983 remedy, since a plaintiff with both state and federal claims against a state official no longer is able to seek relief for those claims in federal court.

Actions for damages have been limited in other ways as well. Although the Court thus far has declined to impose a requirement that section 1983 plaintiffs exhaust state remedies, the Court's holding in *Parratt v. Taylor* has the potential for doing just that. I joined the Court's opinion in *Parratt* and in the extension of *Parratt* last term in *Hudson v. Palmer*, but I am sensitive to the need to confine the *Parratt* rule lest it swallow the remedy it was designed only to limit. The Court in *Parratt* concluded that, where the claim was that a state prison official had negligently deprived the plaintiff of property, the availability of a state tort-claim procedure through which the plaintiff could be reimbursed for his loss satisfied the requirements of due process. As the six separate opinions in that case illustrate, there was little consensus as to why the plaintiff had not been denied due process. Justice Powell, for instance, concurred in the result because he saw no deprivation of life, liberty, or property in the negligent action of a state prison official.[108] He expressed concern, however, over the implications of the Court's reliance on the availability of compensation under state law as sufficient due process for the deprivation of a substantive constitutional guarantee. I concurred on the understanding that the Court's opinion reached only negligent deprivations of property and that it would not apply to a case concerning deprivations of life or liberty.[109]

Last term, in *Hudson*, the Court extended the rule of *Parratt* to intentional deprivations of property. The holdings of *Parratt* and *Hud-*

son have been confined to unauthorized deprivations of property, and I would hope that they would continue to be so confined. In *Logan v. Zimmerman Brush Co.*, the Court did decline to rely on *Parratt* or to accept the availability of a state tort-claim procedure as sufficient to satisfy the constitutional demands of due process when a plaintiff had been deprived by the state of his interest in pursuing a state-created employment discrimination claim. Nevertheless, the reasoning of *Parratt* and *Hudson* could be used to deny a section 1983 action to anyone claiming a constitutional violation by an official unauthorized to act as he did, as long as the state provides a damages remedy after-the-fact.[110]

Closely related to the issues surrounding *Parratt* and its progeny is a third way in which the Court has limited the damages remedy available under section 1983. Although *Parratt* and *Hudson* were careful not to say so, they suggest a reluctance on the part of the Court to find a constitutional violation in a state official's conduct if it is neither pursuant to an official state policy nor authorized by the state, unless and until the state declines to act to redress the injury.[111] As I have indicated, the question of how far beyond official state action the acts reach is a dispute at the heart of the federalism tensions inherent in the Civil Rights Acts. Thus, it is interesting to note that in two recent cases the Court has addressed directly aspects of this fundamental issue. In both cases, the Court has given a narrow construction to the "color of state law" and "state action" requirements, reminiscent of the interpretations of similar issues in the last decades of the nineteenth century. In *Polk County v. Dodson*,[112] the Court concluded that the official activities of a public defender, a fulltime state employee, were not "under color of state law." And, in *Carpenters and Joiners v. Scott*,[113] the Court determined, despite the fact that section 2 of the Ku Klux Klan Act clearly reaches private conspiracies, that when the claimed deprivaton was of First Amendment rights, state action was required in order for the plaintiffs to state a claim for relief under that section.

A similar litany can be recited of cases limiting the availability of injunctive relief. Although suits for injunctive relief are not so numerous and therefore in one respect not so troublesome as suits for damages, injunctive relief generally presents even greater federalism tensions than do suits for damages. Damages awards operate retrospectively, and often only against individual actors. Injunctive relief introduces an ongoing federal presence in the conduct of the affairs of a state or local government. To preserve the delicate balance, the Court had made clear that federal courts are not authorized to intervene in ongoing state judicial proceedings.[114] But until recently, the Court has not extended the inviolate state realm beyond ongoing judicial proceedings.[115]

In several cases, however, the Court now has expanded the prohibition against federal intrusion and refused to allow federal relief against alleged patterns of unconstitutional conduct. In *O'Shea v. Littleton*[116] and *Rizzo v. Goode*,[117] the Court concluded that plaintiffs could not obtain injunctive relief under section 1983 against alleged patterns of judicial and police mistreatment of minority citizens, because the threat of injury was not sufficiently real and immediate and because injunctive relief would constitute an unwarranted intrusion into an area that should be left to the discretion of state and local officials. Two Terms ago, relying on those cases, the Court, by a 5–4 vote, in *City of Los Angeles v. Lyons*,[118] concluded that the petitioner lacked a sufficient stake in the outcome to bring a claim for injunctive relief against a police practice of using a chokehold where the arrested person presented no reasonable appearance of immediate use of deadly force. The basis for the Court's decision was that even though the petitioner had been subjected to the chokehold in the past when arrested for a traffic violation, there was no evidence that he would be arrested for such a violation in the future or that the officer who arrested him would use a chokehold. The Court went on to indicate that even if Article III were satisfied, the desired equitable relief would be unavailable, since "the need for a proper balance between state and federal authority counsels restraint in the issuance of injunctions against state officers engaged in the administration of the States' criminal laws."[119] The dissenters, whom I joined, decried both aspects of the decision and asserted: "The Court's decision removes an entire class of constitutional violations from the equitable powers of a federal court. . . . The federal judicial power is now limited to levying a toll for such a systematic constitutional violation."[120]

I do not mean to present a picture of uninterrupted retreat by the Court. In some contexts, the Court has held a firm line against procedural and substantive doctrines that would limit the role of section 1983. The Court has declined to read into the statute a requirement that a section 1983 litigant exhaust his state administrative remedies,[121] or to accord immunity to a judicial officer against a section 1983 suit for injunctive relief, where there was no basis in the common law for such immunity.[122] The Court also has been careful in addressing the question of what statute of limitations should be applied to a section 1983 action, deciding last Term that a six-month state statute for an administrative proceeding was not the analogous statute for section 1983 because the purposes and policies behind the state administrative proceeding were inconsistent with section 1983's provision of an independent judicial remedy for a civil rights violation.[123] Finally, the Court has been careful to maintain the independence of the remedy provided in section 1983 and the other Civil Rights Acts against implied repeal by other federal statutes, requiring that congressional intent to do so be clear.[124]

Any desire for wholesale judicial retrenchment would be met by an additional obstacle—namely, the fact that the major questions of interpretation of section 1983 already have been settled. There is now little doubt that Congress was within its authority in authorizing remedies that reach private as well as state action.[125] And the dispute over legislative intent has been resolved and the results accepted. For better or for worse, the Court agrees that Congress intended, in certain sections of the Civil Rights Acts, to reach private actions and, in section 1983, to reach unauthorized conduct of state officials. One of the sounder canons of judicial restraint is that once a court has spoken conclusively on a question of statutory interpretation, it should reconsider the question only when faced with compelling evidence that its initial answer was incorrect.[126] Unless critics of the section 1983 precedents can produce the same kind of evidence that led the Court to reconsider the scope of municipal liability in *Monell*, the underlying principles of section 1983 liability should be secure.

IV

Despite these restraints on the impulse to restrict section 1983 through judicial revision, that impulse remains alive. In fact, both the impulse and the federalism concerns behind it will increase as state courts prove more willing to protect individual rights and less deserving of the mistrust that was the genesis of section 1983. For that reason, while it is not my purpose to review the various reform proposals that have been addressed to the Congress and the courts, I close by explaining why I am generally skeptical about proposals to limit the reach of section 1983.

In my view, any plan to restrict the scope of section 1983 comes with a heavy burden of justification—a burden that is both constitutional and historical. The constitutional burden is the need to demonstrate that the interests of federalism, comity, or judicial efficiency can be advanced without sacrificing protection for our constitutional rights. If increased state autonomy and reduced federal caseloads can be purchased only with the coin of more constitutional violations and fewer constitutional remedies, the price is high and is one I am not prepared to pay. Nor is it one, by the way, the critics of section 1983 usually attempt to justify.

The historical burden is the need to show, in light of the systematic disregard of civil rights by state governments and state courts that led to the original Civil Rights Acts, that constitutional claims can safely be committed to state courts, not only for the present but for the future. It is no reflection on the current good faith of state governments and state courts to observe that history is not a one-way street. While we all can work to prevent a return to the judicial indifference and paralysis of the past, none of us can guarantee that the day will not return when a litigant who cannot vindicate his constitutional rights in federal court will not be able to vindicate them at all. If that day should come, it will be far harder to reconstruct a statutory remedy that has been judicially interred or legislatively undone in the meantime than it would be to resort to a remedy that has been intact and working in the intervening years. In short, once we restrict the role of federal courts in protecting constitutional rights, we may find ourselves hard pressed to recover what has been given up.

In making this argument, I suppose that I am relying in part on the symbolic importance of section 1983. The symbolism that I have in mind, and the symbolism that section 1983 has come to possess for those whose rights depend on it, is not the symbolism the statute bore when it was enacted in 1871. Then section 1983 was part and parcel of the Radical Republican assault on the ashes of the Old South. Today, section 1983 properly stands for something different—for the commitment of our society to be governed by law and to protect the rights of those without power against oppression at the hands of the powerful. When the Fourteenth Amendment became part of the Constitution, it committed this nation to an order in which all governments, state as well as federal, were bound to respect the fundamental rights of individuals. That commitment, too, is a part of "Our Federalism," no less than the values of state autonomy that the critics of section 1983 so passionately invoke. One might well ask, rhetorically, whether section 1983 could be enacted in today's political climate, or, indeed, whether we dare repeal it. What a vibrant and exciting old statute it is. As Edmond Cahn so aptly observed, "[F]reedom is not free."[127] Whatever is the fate of section 1983 in the future, I do hope that it survives both as a symbol and as a working mechanism for all of us to protect the constitutional liberties we treasure.

William J. Brennan, Jr.

The Bill of Rights and the States

The Revival of State Constitutions as Guardians of Individual Rights

Twenty-five years ago I had the honor to deliver one of the first James Madison lectures.[1] It is uniquely appropriate that a lecture series born out of a concern for the enhancement and appreciation of our civil liberties should bear the name of James Madison. Our constitutional structure of separate powers and limited government is known as the Madisonian system, for it was Madison who laid down its basic design in the Virginia Plan and Madison who led the congressional battle for the adoption of our national Bill of Rights.

When I spoke here in 1961, our nation stood on the threshold of great changes, in which the Supreme Court would play a major role. The Court was preparing to hand down the first in a series of decisions that were the most important of the Warren era. I reserve this characterization not for *Brown v. Board of Education*[2] or for *Baker v. Carr*,[3] though surely the banning of racial segregation and the recognition of the principle of one person—one vote were great triumphs for our nation and our Constitution. Instead, I believe that even more significant for the preservation and furtherance of the ideals we have fashioned for our society were the decisions binding the states to almost all of the restraints in the Bill of Rights.

The vehicle for this dramatic development was the Fourteenth Amendment. "[I]t is the amendment that has served as the legal instrument of the equalitarian revolution which has so transformed the contemporary American society,"[4] protecting each of us from the employment of governmental authority in a manner contravening our national conceptions of human dignity and liberty. This country has been transformed by the standard, promises, and power of the Four-

Justice Brennan's lecture was delivered on November 18, 1986 and appeared in 64 N.Y.U.L. Rev. 401 (1986).

teenth Amendment—"that the citizens of all our states are also and no less citizens of our United States, that this birthright guarantees our federal constitutional liberties against encroachment by governmental action at any level of our federal system, and that each of us is entitled to due process of law and equal protection of the laws from our state governments no less than from our national one."[5]

The passage of the Fourteenth Amendment fulfilled James Madison's vision of the structure of American federalism. During the debates over the Bill of Rights, Madison expressed serious reservations over the bills of rights then present in various state constitutions. He stated, "[S]ome states have no bills of rights, there are others provided with very defective ones, and there are others whose bills of rights are not only defective, but absolutely improper; instead of securing [rights] in the full extent which republican principles would require, they limit them too much to agree with common ideas of liberty."[6]

Madison crafted a solution to this problem and proposed it as one of the seventeen amendments to the Constitution that he originally submitted to the House. Coincidentally numbered 14, the amendment read: "No State shall infringe the right of trial by Jury in criminal cases, nor the rights of conscience, nor the freedom of speech, or of the press."[7] Because Madison thought there was "more danger of . . . powers being abused by the State Governments than by the Government of the United States,"[8] he labeled this "the most valuable amendment in the whole list."[9] After passage in the House, however, his amendment was defeated in the Senate by the forces Madison feared most, those who wanted the states to retain their systems of established churches.[10]

Madison's fears of excessive and arbitrary state power were not widely shared at the time the Bill of Rights was adopted. Instead it was believed that personal freedom could be secured more accurately by decentralization than by express command. In other words, the states were perceived as protectors of, rather than threats to, the civil and political rights of individuals. The enactment of the Fourteenth Amendment seventy-nine years later signaled the adoption of Madison's view and banished the spectre of arbitrary state power, his lone fear for our constitutional system.

Prior to the passage of this Civil War amendment, the Supreme Court had made it plain that the Bill of Rights was applicable only to the federal government. In 1833, in *Barron v. Baltimore*,[11] Chief Justice Marshall held that the Bill of Rights operated only against the power of the federal government and not against that of the states. The federal Constitution, he stated, "was ordained and established by the people of the United States for themselves, for their own government, and not for the government of the individual states."[12]

Only after the Civil War did the demand arise for the national protection of individual rights against abuses of state power. The war exposed a serious flaw in the notion that states could be trusted to nurture individual rights: the assumption of "an identity of interests between the states, as the level of government closest to the people, and the primary corpus of civil rights and liberties of the people themselves—an identity incomplete from the start and . . . impossible to maintain after the great battle over slavery had been fought."[13] In fact, the primary impetus to the adoption of the Fourteenth Amendment was the fear that the former Confederate states would deny newly freed persons the protection of life, liberty, and property formally provided by the state constitutions. But the majestic goals of the Fourteenth Amendment were framed in terms of more general application: "No state shall make or enforce any law which shall abridge the privileges or immunities of citizens of the United States; nor shall any state deprive any person of life, liberty or property without due process of law; nor deny to any person within its jurisdiction the equal protection of the laws."[14]

Section 5 of the new amendment further authorized Congress to enforce its requirements through appropriate legislation. Thereafter, in March 1875, Congress granted the federal courts jurisdiction "of all suits of a civil nature at common law or in equity . . . arising under the Constitution or laws of the United States. . . ."[15] This legislation, in my view, revealed Congress's intention to leave the definition and enforcement of the protections and prohibitions of the Fourteenth Amendment to the federal judiciary. The authors of the Fourteenth Amendment, like the authors of the original Bill of Rights and the Constitution, realized that the written guarantees of liberty are "mere paper protections without an [independent] judiciary to define and enforce them."[16]

In my 1961 lecture, I detailed the historical development of the relationship between this modern Magna Carta and the protection of civil rights in the states. Initially, the Fourteenth Amendment served to protect the excesses of expanding capital and industry from even limited control by the government. The Court firmly rejected the suggestion that any of the guarantees of the federal Bill of Rights were among the "privileges or immunities of citizens of the United States."[17] But I also observed that the Court had not "closed every door in the Fourteenth Amendment against the application of the Federal Bill of Rights to the states."[18] The Court utilized the Due Process Clause to apply certain safeguards in the first eight amendments to the states. Unfortunately, the Court expressly rejected any notion that the Fourteenth Amendment mandated the wholesale application of any of the first eight amendments to the states; instead the Court held that certain of the protections in the bill were "of such a nature that they are included in the conception of due process of law."[19] The Court felt that it could give the Due Process Clause of the Fourteenth Amendment a meaning or content independent of the liberties secured by the Bill of Rights by picking and choosing those rights it considered "of the very essence of a scheme of ordered liberty."[20]

Pursuant to this analysis, the Court, at the time of my lecture, had held that all the protections of the First Amendment extended to restrain the unlawful exercise of state power.[21] Aside from the First Amendment, however, only three specific rights from the federal bill had been deemed to apply to the states when I stood before you in 1961: the Fifth Amendment's requirement that just compensation should be paid for private property taken for public use,[22] the Sixth Amendment's requirement that counsel be appointed for an accused in a capital case,[23] and the Fourth Amendment's prohibition of unreasonable searches and seizures, absent its corollary, the exclusionary rule.[24]

I left the audience with a prediction and a question. My prediction was that, having applied the guarantee against unreasonable searches and seizures to the states, the Court would soon determine that states must also exclude from their proceedings any evidence obtained by such illegal means.[25] In other words, the Court would have to impose adherence to the exclusionary rule on the states. This prediction came to pass four months after the delivery of the lecture.[26] Needless to say, I decline to spoil my perfect record by making any further predictions at this time.

The question I asked in 1961 has now been answered by the actions of the Court. I asked what James Madision would have thought of the Court's refusal to apply many of the protections and prohibitions of the federal bill to the states, protections such as the right of a person not to be twice put in jeopardy of life or limb for the same offense; not to be compelled in any criminal case to be a witness against one's self; as an accused, to enjoy the right in criminal prosecutions to a speedy and public trial by an impartial jury of twelve, to be informed of the nature and cause of the accusation, to be confronted with the witnesses against him, to have compulsory process for obtaining witnesses in his favor, and to have the assistance of counsel for his defense.[27]

I asked whether Madison would have conceded that any of these rights were unnecessary to " 'the very essence of a scheme of ordered liberty,' " or that any were not among " 'those fundamental principles of liberty and justice which lie at the base of all our civil and political institutions,' " or not among those personal immunities which are " 'so rooted in the traditions and conscience of our people as to be ranked fundamental?' "[28]

It is with deep satisfaction that I answer the rhetorical question I posed twenty-five years ago. Of course, the historical record demonstrates clearly what Madison's answer would be: he felt that it was vital to secure certain fundamental rights against state and federal governments alike. Recent history reveals that the Supreme Court finally agreed with him. In the years between 1961 and 1969, the Supreme Court interpreted the Fourteenth Amendment to nationalize civil rights, making the great guarantees of life, liberty, and property binding on all governments throughout the nation. In so doing, the Court fundamentally reshaped the law of this land.

Two questions recurred throughout this period of change. The first was whether the Bill of Rights should be selectively or fully incorporated. Although the full incorporation of the Bill of Rights into the Fourteenth Amendment has never commanded a majority of the Court, we have "looked increasingly to the Bill of Rights for guidance [so that] many of the rights guaranteed by the first eight Amendments"[29] have been deemed selectively absorbed into the Fourteenth. Second, assuming that a particular guarantee in the federal bill should be applied to the states, there remained the question of the scope or extent of its application. For example, for a great many years after the Fourth Amendment had been applied to the states, the Court refused to extend application of the exclusionary rule, labeling it a mere rule of evidence and not a constitutional requirement. The reversal of this decision was the forerunner of the trend toward the broad and complete nationalization of the bill which occurred in the 1960s.

The first signal that change was in the air came in 1961 with the Court's decision in *Mapp v. Ohio*,[30] reversing *Wolf v. Colorado*[31] and applying the Fourth Amendment *and* the exclusionary rule to the states. Evidence obtained through an unconstitutional search was excluded from consideration in state court cases, as it had been for some years in federal cases. This decision was, in its time, "the Supreme Court's most ambitious effort to affect and determine the quality of state criminal justice . . . subject[ing] the state officer to a constitutional standard of performance no lower or different from that governing federal law enforcement."[32] Anthony Lewis, who covered the Court for the *New York Times*, perceptively noted that a significant corner had been turned in the relationship between the Bill of Rights and the states and speculated that other rights in the bill, too, might be fully applied to the states.[33]

Although, in retrospect, it is plain that *Mapp* was a turning point, at the time the future of the incorporation doctrine did not appear settled. The case was decided by the narrowest of margins—five to four. Opponents of the decision violently denounced it, arguing that it offended principles of federalism and symbolized the Court's determination to impose a national system of individual rights at the expense of traditional state controls.

The opinion of the Court itself firmly and properly rejected this argument. A *healthy* federalism is not promoted by allowing state officers to seize evidence illegally or by permitting state courts to utilize such evidence. The Court has long recognized the paramount importance of procedural safeguards in the administration of a system of criminal laws. In our modern world, "the criminal procedure sanctioned by any of our states is a procedure sanctioned by the United States,"[34] The mere invocation of the slogan "states' rights" does not authorize the judiciary to "administer a watered-down, subjective version of the individual guarantees of the Bill of Rights when state cases come before [the Court]."[35]

Between 1962 and 1969, in a flurry of activity, the Court extended nine of the specific provisions of the federal bill to the states; these decisions have had a profound impact on American life, deeply involving state courts in the application of rights and protections formerly perceived as creatures solely of federal courts. The Eighth Amendment's prohibition against cruel and unusual punishment was applied against the states in 1962 in the case of *Robinson v. California*.[36] Walter Robinson was arrested in Los Angeles for the "crime" of addiction to narcotics. Almost as an afterthought, Robinson's attorney argued that the narcotics addiction statute inflicted cruel and unusual punishment, first because it punished an involuntary status, and second because it required an offender to undergo a "cold turkey" withdrawal from his or her addiction. In June 1962, the Court accepted these arguments and determined that the Cruel and Unusual Punishment Clause of the Eighth Amendment applied to the states. We held that drug addiction was akin to mental illness, leprosy, or affliction with venereal disease and that, "in the light of contemporary human knowledge, a law which made a criminal offense of such a disease would doubtless be universally thought to be an infliction of cruel and unusual punishment in violation of the Eighth and Fourteenth Amendments."[37]

The opinion of the Court did not make plain whether the Court was holding that the Cruel and Unusual Punishment Clause applied to the state in exactly the same way it applied to the federal government or whether it was holding only that the Due Process Clause, as the embodiment of a more generalized notion of fairness, prohibited the punishment inflicted upon Robinson. In other words, the Court did not state clearly that the Fourteenth Amendment applied the full scope of protections embodied in the Cruel and Unusual Punishment Clause of the Eighth Amendment to the states. Subsequently, it was made clear that the clause was indeed incorporated to its full extent. The importance of this decision cannot be overestimated, for it was pursuant to this clause that the death penalty as then administered was struck down in 1972.[38]

In *Gideon v. Wainwright*,[39] the Court once again avoided a direct holding on the question of incorporation but did deal a devastating blow to an ad hoc, fundamental fairness approach to the application of the federal bill. The case came to the Court by way of a handwritten petition for certiorari in which Clarence Gideon stated the question quite plainly: "It makes no difference how old I am or what color I am or what church I belong to if any. . . . The question is very simple. I requested the court to appoint me [an] attorney and the court refused."[40] Abe Fortas, who was appointed to represent Gideon before the Court, did not primarily argue that the Assistance of Counsel Clause of the Sixth Amendment applied in state criminal trials through incorporation in the Fourteenth Amendment; instead, he forcefully maintained that indigent defendants simply could not possibly receive a fair trial in serious state criminal cases unless represented by counsel. It was evident at oral argument that Fortas was willing to accept the application of the right of counsel to the states whether or not the Court accomplished this through specific incorporation of the Sixth Amendment.[41]

When the decision was handed down, the Court held that the Due Process Clause required the appointment of counsel for indigent defendants charged with serious state criminal offenses. We stated that any provision of the federal bill which is " 'fundamental and essential to a fair trial' "[42] is made obligatory on the states by the Fourteenth Amendment, and that representation by counsel is one such fundamental right. Justice Harlan, however, insisted in his concurrence that *Gideon* did not mean that the right to counsel that applied to the states was identical to that guaranteed in the Sixth Amendment.[43] He rejected the idea that the Fourteenth Amendment incorporated the Sixth and found instead that the right to counsel was embraced within the Due Process Clause's conception of "fundamental fairness."[44]

Ironically, it was in *Gideon* that the opponents of incorporation were hoisted by the petard of their own traditional argument that a proper consideration of the principles of federalism would block the full application of the guarantees of the federal bill to the states. When asked by the attorney general of Florida to submit briefs in support of his state's position in *Gideon*, the attorneys general of twenty-three states instead urged the Court to require appointed counsel in all cases involving indigent defendants. The states argued that the existing rule—that counsel would only be appointed when necessary due to "special circumstances"—led to friction between state and federal courts because it required a posttrial assessment of the fairness of the adversary proceeding conducted absent counsel, necessitating a "most obnoxious" federal supervision[45] of the state court's actions. Essentially, twenty-three states had requested incorporation of the right to counsel, hoping to avoid unpredictable and arbitrary intrusions of federal judicial power in state proceedings and expressing a desire for clear standards of conduct. The position of the states in *Gideon* illustrated that federalism is better served by incorporation of the guarantees of the federal bill than by a case-by-case assessment of the degree of protection afforded to particular rights.

The momentous consequence of this decision is that "counsel must now be provided in every courtroom of every state of this land to secure the rights of those accused of crime."[46] By this decision, the Court removed one of the most egregious examples of differential treatment for poor and rich; effective advocacy is no longer exclusively enjoyed by the wealthy criminal defendant.

In *Malloy v. Hogan*,[47] the Court finally decided a case by speaking in explicitly incorporationist terms. *Twining v. New Jersey*[48] was reversed, and the Self-Incrimination Clause of the Fifth Amendment was applied to the states. The state had insisted that only the core of the Self-Incrimination Clause, that is, the prohibition against use of physically coerced confessions, applied to the states, not the full clause or all of the procedural refinements applicable in federal proceedings.

Writing for the majority, however, I stated that the Court must refuse to accord "the Fourteenth Amendment a less central role in the preservation of basic liberties than that which was contemplated by the framers when they added the amendment to our constitutional scheme"[49] and rejected the suggestion that a "watered-down" version of the Fifth Amendment applied in state court. In *Mapp, Robinson,* and *Gideon*, the Court had not proceeded explicitly on the basis of incorporation, but the Court's opinion in *Malloy* made clear that the rights and prohibitions nationalized in the past were now considered to apply to the states with full federal regalia intact.

It has been said that "the nationalization process took on an inexorable quality after the decision in *Malloy v. Hogan*."[50] The explicit articulation of the incorporation theory clarified the reasoning of the Court's earlier decisions and advanced significantly the progress toward full nationalization. Moreover, the decision to extend this particular guarantee held profound significance for the future. Eventually, "after decades of police coercion, by means ranging from torture to trickery, the privilege against self-incrimination became the basis of *Miranda v. Arizona*, requiring police in every state to give warnings to a suspect before custodial interrogation."[51]

Between 1965 and 1967, in rapid-fire succession, the Court extended to the states four of the Sixth Amendment's guarantees—the right of an accused to be confronted by the witnesses against him,[52] the right to a speedy trial,[53] the right to a trial by an impartial jury,[54] and the right to have compulsory process in order to obtain witnesses.[55] In the course of these decisions, however, it became clear that a majority of the Court was unwilling to embrace incorporation of all the amendments in the Bill of Rights. In 1968, in *Duncan v. Louisiana*,[56] the Court attempted to explain the theoretical basis for its decisions requiring the states to adhere to certain provisions of the bill

while excluding others. Applying the right to trial by jury for all serious offenses to the states, the Court reasoned that "state criminal
processes are not imaginary and theoretical schemes but actual systems bearing virtually every characteristic of the common-law system
that has been developing contemporaneously in England and this
country."[57] As a consequence, the Court explained that each decision
to incorporate was founded on a determination of whether "a procedure is necessary to an Anglo-American regime of ordered liberty."[58]

Justice Black concurred in this decision, stating that he was willing
to accept the majority's selective incorporation of rights because it limited the discretion of the Court to application of specific protections,
and because it had "already worked to make most of the Bill of Rights'
protections applicable to the States."[59]

Finally, on June 23, 1969, in *Benton v. Maryland*,[60] the Double
Jeopardy Clause of the Fifth Amendment was applied to the states
and the modern revolution was virtually complete. Only the Second
and Third Amendments, the Grand Jury Clause of the Fifth Amendment, the Seventh Amendment, and the Excessive Fines and Bail
Clause of the Eighth Amendment remained unincorporated, and the
latter was subsequently absorbed. Although the Court had rejected
Hugo Black's theory of total incorporation, it had accepted one vital
element of his analysis—that once a provision of the federal bill was
deemed incorporated, it applied identically in state and federal proceedings. To this day that remains the position of the Court.

The nationalization process stretched over the 100 years after the
passage of the Fourteenth Amendment. Most fittingly, the date upon
which *Benton*, the capstone of the revolution, was handed down was
also the final day of Earl Warren's service on the Court. The tenure of
this great chief justice saw the conversion of the Fourteenth Amendment into a guarantee of individual liberties equal to or more important than the original Bill of Rights.

This series of decisions transformed the basic structure of constitutional safeguards for individual political and civil liberties in the nation and profoundly altered the character of our federal system. The
agenda of the national Court was radically altered by the nationalization of the first eight amendments. Only rarely in the nineteenth century did individuals challenge the exercise of federal authority. Now
modern constitutional law revolved around questions of civil and political liberty. The Court's reinvigorated construction of the Four-

teenth Amendment, and particularly the nationalization of the Bill of Rights through the Due Process Clause, are the primary reasons for that development.

I do not believe, however, that these revolutionary changes are due solely to the triumph of the doctrine of selective incorporation. Even those justices who resisted the sway of this theory interpreted the Due Process Clause of the Fourteenth Amendment to require progressively more stringent standards in a state criminal trial. This truth is revealed most clearly in the Court's judgment in *Gideon* which, despite the lack of consensus as to rationale, was a unanimous decision. Every member of the *Gideon* Court concurred in the holding that the Constitution required that indigent defendants receive the benefit of counsel when charged with a serious criminal offense. Some felt that the Fourteenth Amendment incorporated the Sixth Amendment's requirements and applied them to state criminal proceedings, but others simply concluded that principles of fundamental fairness mandated equal representation for rich and poor alike. By different paths, each member of the Court arrived at the same constitutional endpoint. Modern critics of incorporation who insist that the doctrine has dealt the principle of federalism a "politically violent and constitutionally suspect blow"[61] ignore this significant fact.

Most Americans have come to think of the Bill of Rights as the source of their liberties. Even in casual parlance, people speak of "taking the Fifth" or of their "First Amendment rights." In most relevant instances, Americans receive the protections they take for granted only due to their application to the states through the Due Process Clause of the Fourteenth Amendment, which has most appropriately been called "our second Bill of Rights."[62]

I would prefer to end my tale here with the legal fulfillment of the original promise of the Fourteenth Amendment. Although we have not yet achieved equal justice for all members of our society, Congress and the judiciary did much in the decade of the 1960s to close the gap between the promise and the social and political reality envisioned by the framers of the Fourteenth Amendment. But today, though unmistakable inequities should disrupt any observer's complacency, the Court is involved in a new curtailment of the Fourteenth Amendment's scope. Although this nation so reveres the civil and political rights of the individual that they are sheltered from the power of the majority, these rights are treated as inferior to the ever-increasing demands of governmental authority. Although both economic and po-

litical power are more intensely concentrated in today's urban indus-
trialized society than ever before, threatening individual privacy and
autonomy, we see an increasing tendency to insure control rather
than to nurture individuality.

The issue of application of the Bill of Rights to the states involves
two separate questions: whether the guarantee in question should
apply to the states, and what its content should be when applied. For
several years now, there has been an unmistakable trend in the Court
to read the guarantees of individual liberty restrictively, which means
that the content of the rights applied to the states is likewise diminished.

The Fourth Amendment has been most clearly targeted for attack.
For many years, the rule was that a valid search warrant had to be
supported by probable cause; if it was not, the fruits of the search
could not be used in evidence. In 1984, in *United States v. Leon*,[63] the
Court revoked this rule and determined that the products of a search
based on a police officer's "reasonable" reliance on a warrant not supported by probable cause would not necessarily be suppressed.[64] I
joined the dissent, in which three justices stated that this holding—"that it is presumptively reasonable to rely on a defective warrant"[65]—is the product of "constitutional amnesia"[66] and suggested
that the Court was converting the Bill of Rights "into an unenforced
honor code that the police may follow at their discretion."[67]

The Court has further determined that we do not have a legitimate
expectation of privacy in our bank records,[68] permitting their seizure
without our consent or knowledge; that private diaries may be seized
and utilized to convict a person of a crime;[69] that police searches are
lawful when grounded on consent even if that consent is not a knowing or intelligent one;[70] that states may convict persons of crimes by
nonunanimous juries;[71] that private shopping centers may prohibit
free speech on their premises;[72] and that it is neither cruel nor unusual punishment to sentence a repeated writer of bad checks to a
lifetime in prison.[73] These decisions reveal most plainly that retrenchment is following the Warren era, a time in which the Court played
"the role of keeper of the nation's conscience."[74]

This trend is not visible solely in the enfeebled protection of individual rights under the federal bill and the Fourteenth Amendment. The venerable remedy of habeas corpus has been sharply limited in the name of federalism, the Equal Protection Clause has been
denied its full reach, and a series of decisions shaping the doctrines of

justiciability, jurisdiction, and remedy "increasingly bar the federal courthouse door in the absence of showings probably impossible to make."[75]

For a decade now, I have felt certain that the Court's contraction of federal rights and remedies on grounds of federalism should be interpreted as a plain invitation to state courts to step into the breach. In the 1960s, the "understandable enthusiasm that championed the application of the Bill of Rights to the states . . . [contributed] to the disparagement of other rights retained by the people, namely state constitutional rights."[76] Busy interpreting the onslaught of federal constitutional rulings in state criminal cases, the state courts fell silent on the subject of their own constitutions. Now, the diminution of federal scrutiny and protection out of purported deference to the states mandates the assumption of a more responsible state court role. And state courts have taken seriously their obligation as coequal guardians of civil rights and liberties.

As is well known, federal preservation of civil liberties is a minimum, which the states may surpass so long as there is no clash with federal law. Between 1970 and 1984, state courts, increasingly reluctant to follow the federal lead, have handed down over 250 published opinions holding that the constitutional minimums set by the United States Supreme Court were insufficient to satisfy the more stringent requirements of state constitutional law.[77] When the United States Supreme Court cut back the reach of First Amendment protections, the California Supreme Court responded by interpreting its state constitution to protect freedom of speech in shopping centers and malls.[78] The Massachusetts, Pennsylvania, and Washington courts responded in kind when confronted with similar questions involving freedom of expression.[79] Under the federal Constitution, a motorist stopped by a police officer for a simple traffic violation may be subject to a full body search and a search of this vehicle.[80] Such police conduct offends state constitutional provisions in California and Hawaii, unless the officer has articulable reasons to suspect other illegal conduct.[81] South Dakota has rejected the inventory search rule announced in *South Dakota v. Opperman.*[82] Other examples abound.[83] Truly, the state courts have responded with marvelous enthusiasm to many not-so-subtle invitations to fill the constitutional gaps left by the decisions of the Supreme Court majority.[84]

As Lawrence Sager has so convincingly argued,[85] the institutional position of the national Supreme Court may cause it to "underenforce" constitutional rules.[86] The national Court must remain highly sensitive to concerns of state and local autonomy, obviously less of a problem for state courts, which *are* local, accountable decisionmakers. It must further be remembered that the federal bill was enacted to place limits on the federal government while state bills are widely perceived as granting affirmative rights to citizens.

In addition, the Supreme Court formulates a national standard which, some suggest, must represent the common denominator to allow for diversity and local experimentation. In the Warren era, federalism was unsuccessfully invoked to support the view of the anti-incorporationists—that the rights granted in federal courts need not apply with the same breadth or scope in state courts. Dissenting justices "extolled the virtues of allowing the States to serve as 'laboratories'" and objected to incorporation as "press[ing] the States into a procrustean federal mold."[87] Justice Harlan and others felt that the phenomenon of incorporation complicated the federal situation, creating a kind of "constitutional schizophrenia" as the Court attempted both to recognize diversity and faithfully to enforce the Bill of Rights.[88] In order to make room for such diversity, Justice Harlan felt that the bill should not apply to the states exactly as it applied to the federal government.

As is well known, however, I believe that the Fourteenth Amendment fully applied the provisions of the federal Bill of Rights to the states, thereby creating a federal floor of protection and that the Constitution and the Fourteenth Amendment allow diversity only *above and beyond* this federal constitutional floor. Experimentation which endangers the continued existence of our national rights and liberties cannot be permitted; a call for that brand of diversity is, in my view, antithetical to the requirements of the Fourteenth Amendment. While state experimentation may flourish, we have made a national commitment to this minimum level of protection through enactment of the Fourteenth Amendment. This reconciliation of local autonomy and guaranteed individual rights is the only one consistent with our constitutional structure. And the growing dialogue between the Supreme Court and the state courts on the topic of fundamental rights enables all courts to discern more rapidly the "evolving standards of decency that mark the progress of a maturing society."[89]

This rebirth of interest in state constitutional law should be greeted with equal enthusiasm by all those who support our federal system, liberals and conservatives alike. The development and protection of individual rights pursuant to state constitutions presents no threat to enforcement of national standards; state courts may not provide a level of protection less than that offered by the federal Constitution. Nor should these developments be greeted with dismay by conservatives; the state laboratories are once again open for business.

As state courts assume a leadership role in the protection of individual rights and liberties, the true colors of purported federalists will be revealed. Recently, commentators have highlighted a substantial irony; it is observed that "the same Court that has made federalism the centerpiece of its constitutional philosophy now regularly upsets state court decisions protecting individual rights."[90] When state courts have acted to expand individual rights, the Court has shown little propensity to leap to the defense of diversity. In fact, in several cases, the Court has demonstrated a new solicitude for uniformity. The Court has reminded the residents of Florida that when their state court's decisions rest only on state constitutional grounds, citizens have the power "to amend state law to insure rational law enforcement."[91] Some state courts and commentators have taken umbrage at the suggestion that proceeding in lockstep with the Supreme Court is the only way to avoid irrational law enforcement. As one state court judge reminded us recently, the United States Supreme Court is not "the sole repository of judicial wisdom and rationality."[92] One wonders if ringing endorsement of state independence will be transformed into assertions of the importance of federal uniformity in law enforcement.

State experimentation cannot be excoriated simply because the experiments provide more rather than less protection for civil liberties and individual rights. While the Fourteenth Amendment does not permit a state to fall below a common national standard, above this level, our federalism permits diversity. As tempting as it may be to harmonize results under state and national constitutions, our federalism permits state courts to provide greater protection to individual civil rights and liberties if they wish to do so. The Supreme Court has no conceivable justification for interfering in a case plainly decided on independent and adequate state grounds.

Finally, those who regard judicial review as inconsistent with our democratic system—a view I do not share—should find constitutional interpretation by the state judiciary far less objectionable than activist intervention by their federal counterparts. It cannot be denied that state court judges are often more immediately "subject to majoritarian pressures than federal courts, and are correspondingly less independent than their federal counterparts."[93] Federal judges are guaranteed a salary and lifetime tenure; in contrast, state judges often are elected, or, at the least, must succeed in retention elections. The relatively greater degree of political accountability of state courts militates in favor of continued absolute deference to their interpretations of their own constitutions. Moreover, state constitutions are often relatively easy to amend; in many states the process is open to citizen initiative. Prudential considerations requiring a cautious use of the power of judicial review, though not insignificant, should weigh less heavily upon elected state judges than on tenured federal judges."[94]

Some critics fear that the Supreme Court will become increasingly hostile to state courts' protection of individual rights and will meddle in those cases, refusing to find that a decision is based on independent and adequate state grounds.[95] I am not so pessimistic. Despite the recent tendency of the Court to give gratuitous advice to state citizens to amend their constitutions,[96] I believe that the Court has set appropriate "ground rules"[97] for federalism with its recent decision in *Michigan v. Long*.[98] If a state court plainly states that its judgment rests on its analysis of state law, the United States Supreme Court will honor that statement and will not review the state court decision. So long as the Court adheres strictly to this rule, state courts may shield state constitutional law from federal interference and insure that its growth is not stunted by national decisionmakers. I join Justice Mosk of the California Supreme Court in his most apt observation: "I detect a phoenix-like resurrection of federalism, or, if you prefer, states' rights, evidenced by state courts' reliance upon provisions of state constitutions."[99]

This said, I must conclude on a warning note. Federal courts remain an indispensable safeguard of individual rights against governmental abuse. The revitalization of state constitutional law is no excuse for the weakening of federal protections and prohibitions. Slashing away at federal rights and remedies undermines our federal system. The strength of our system is that it "provides a double source of protection for the rights of our citizens. Federalism is not served when the federal half of that protection is crippled."[100]

Federalism does not require that one level of government take a back seat to the other when the question involved is one of individual civil and political rights; federalism is not an excuse for one court system to abdicate responsibility to another. Indeed, federal courts have been delegated a special responsibility for the definition and enforcement of the guarantees of the Bill of Rights and the Fourteenth Amendment. Our founders and framers, and here I include the framers of the Fourteenth Amendment, took it as an article of faith that this nation prized the independence of its judiciary and that an independent judiciary could be counted upon to enforce the individual rights and liberties of our citizens against infringement by governmental power. As James Madison said, "the independent tribunals of justice will consider themselves in a peculiar manner the guardian of those rights."[101]

Twenty-five years ago, when the Supreme Court finally began to seek achievement of the noble purpose of the Fourteenth Amendment, it took giant steps in the direction of equality under the law for all races and all citizens. While the full breadth and depth of the promise of the Fourteenth Amendment have not been fulfilled, the promise itself remains—a vibrant symbol of the hopes and possibilities of this nation and a forceful challenge to those who have become complacent. As a nation, we must renew our commitment to its ideal: "[J]ustice, equal and practical, for the poor, for the members of minority groups, for the criminally accused, . . . for all, in short, who do not partake of the abundance of American life."[102]

Notes

Archibald Cox

1. Hand, Mr. Justice Cardozo, 52 Harv. L. Rev. 361 (1939).
2. Gray v. Sanders, 372 U.S. 368 (1963).

Arthur J. Goldberg

1. See Harris, The Quest for Equality 14 (1960).
2. The Declaration of Independence (1776).
3. U.S. Const. art. I, § 9 ("No Title of Nobility shall be granted by the United States. . . ."); § 10 ("No State shall . . . grant any Title of Nobility.").
4. Hartz, The Liberal Tradition in America 56 (1955), quoting Roots of American Civilization 315 (Nettels ed. 1938).
5. Harris, supra note 1, at 4.
6. Ibid.
7. Locke, The Second Treatise of Civil Government 71 (Gough ed. 1946).
8. Hartz, supra note 5, presents the thesis that American institutions were shaped by the fact that feudalism never took root in the New World. He takes his text from Alexis de Tocqueville: "The great advantage of the Americans is that they have arrived at a state of democracy without having to endure a democratic revolution, and that they are born equal instead of becoming so." 2 Democracy in America 108 (Bradley ed. 1945).
9. Harris, supra note 2, at 14, quoting 10 The Writings of Benjamin Franklin 59–60, 130–31 (Smyth ed. 1910). The inequality implicit in the constitutional provisions for the selection of senators were, from the egalitarian point of view, a compromise necessary to attain a national government. Other restrictions on equal suffrage—such as conditions based on economic means, race, religion or sex—have been eroded by time and the logic of equality. See, e.g., U.S. Const. amends. XV, XVII, XIX, XXIV.
10. Cf. Hartz, supra note 4, at 57.
11. 347 U.S. 497 (1954).
12. Brown v. Board of Educ., 347 U.S. 483 (1954).
13. See 1 Chafee, Documents on Fundamental Human Rights 181–237 (1951) (state constitutions before 1791).
14. Id. at 60.
15. U.S. Const. art. I, § 9: "The Migration or Importation of such Persons as any of the States now existing shall think proper to admit, shall not be prohibited by the Congress prior to the Year one thousand eight hundred and eight, but a Tax or duty may be imposed on such Importation, not exceeding ten dollars for each Person."

16. U.S. Const. art. IV, § 2: "No Person held to Service or Labour in one State, under the Laws thereof, escaping into another, shall, in Consequence of any Law or Regulation therein, be discharged from such Service or Labour, but shall be delivered up on Claim of the Party to whom such Service or Labour may be due."
17. United States v. Reese, 92 U.S. 214, 218 (1875).
18. Cahn, A New Kind of Society, in The Great Rights 3 (Cahn ed. 1963).
19. United States v. Classic, 313 U.S. 299, 316 (1941) (Stone, J.).
20. 163 U.S. 537 (1896).
21. 347 U.S. 483 (1954). A process of erosion had set in long before the Brown decision. See, e.g., Missouri ex rel. Gaines v. Canada, 305 U.S. 337 (1938); Freund, The Supreme Court of the United States 173 (1949).
22. 163 U.S. at 559.
23. Black, The Lawfulness of the Segregation Decisions, 69 Yale L.J. 421 (1960); Freund, supra note 21, at 173.
24. 358 U.S. 1 (1958).
25. Id. at 19.
26. See Goss v. Board of Educ., 373 U.S. 683 (1963); Watson v. City of Memphis, 373 U.S. 526 (1963).
27. Civil Rights Cases, 109 U.S. 3, 11, 17 (1883).
28. Peterson v. City of Greenville, 373 U.S. 244, 247 (1963).
29. See, e.g., Peterson v. City of Greenville, supra note 28; Burton v. Wilmington Parking Authority, 365 U.S. 715 (1961); Barrows v. Jackson, 346 U.S. 249 (1958); Terry v. Adams, 345 U.S. 461 (1953); Shelley v. Kraemer, 334 U.S. 1 (1948); Marsh v. Alabama, 326 U.S. 501 (1946); Steele v. Louisville & N. Ry., 323 U.S. 192 (1944); Smith v. Allwright, 321 U.S. 649 (1944); United States v. Classic, 313 U.S. 299 (1941); Yick Wo v. Hopkins, 118 U.S. 356 (1886); Ex parte Virginia, 100 U.S. 339 (1880); Strauder v. West Virginia, 100 U.S. 303 (1880).
30. See, e.g., Henkin, Shelley v. Kraemer: Notes for a Revised Opinion, 110 U. Pa. L. Rev. 473 (1962); Lewis, The Meaning of State Action, 60 Colum. L. Rev. 1083 (1960); Lewis, The Sit-In Cases: Great Expectations, 1963 Sup. Ct. Rev. 101; Pollak, Racial Discrimination and Judicial Integrity: A Reply to Professor Wechsler, 108 U. Pa. L. Rev. 1(1959); St. Antoine, Color Blindness But Not Myopia: A New Look at State Action, Equal Protection, and "Private" Racial Discrimination, 59 Mich. L. Rev. 993 (1961); Wechsler, Toward Neutral Principles of Constitutional Law, 73 Harv. L. Rev. 1 (1959).
31. 83 U.S. (16 Wall.) 36 (1873).
32. Id. at 81.
33. Santa Clara County v. Southern Pac. Ry., 118 U.S. 394, 396 (1886).
34. See McCloskey, The American Supreme Court 115–35 (1960).
35. Buck v. Bell, 274 U.S. 200, 208 (1927).
36. 372 U.S. 726 (1963).
37. Id. at 731–32. But cf. Schware v. Board of Bar Examiners, 353 U.S. 232 (1957); McCloskey, Economic Due Process and the Supreme Court: An Exhumation and Reburial, 1962 Sup. Ct. Rev. 34.
38. 354 U.S. 457 (1957).
39. 336 U.S. 106, 111 (1949). But see Bickel, The Least Dangerous Branch 221–28 (1962).

40. See generally Tussman & tenBroek, The Equal Protection of the Laws, 37 Calif. L. Rev. 341, 343–53 (1949); Note, 70 Yale L.J. 1192 (1961).
41. See Flack, The Adoption of the Fourteenth Amendment (1908). Compare the dissent of Justice Black in Adamson v. California, 332 U.S. 46, 68 (1947).
42. 83 U.S. (16 Wall.) 36, 71 (1873). See Strauder v. West Virginia, 100 U.S. 303, 306–07 (1880).
43. 113 U.S. 27, 31 (1885).
44. Slaughterhouse Cases, 83 U.S. (16 Wall.) 36, 68 (1873).
45. Virginia v. Rives, 100 U.S. 313, 318 (1880).
46. Ex parte Virginia, 100 U.S. 339, 347 (1880).
47. See, e.g., Screws v. United States, 325 U.S. 91 (1945).
48. 118 U.S. 356 (1886).
49. Id. at 373–74.
50. The State of California, in its brief in the Supreme Court of California, asserted: "That the *Tung Hing Tong* represents 300 laundries employing 3,000 persons and controlling nearly a quarter of a million of capital. . . . That the concentrated power wielded by the *Tung Hing Tong*, springing from the united contributions of its numerous constituents, renders it a formidable opponent to the municipal government of San Francisco, and that in the matters which affect its interests it employs very acute lawyers, who by their subtlety and superior management, obstruct the enforcement of the law in the lower courts."
51. See, e.g., Christensen, The Danish Ombudsman, 109 U. Pa. L. Rev. 1100 (1961); Davis, Ombudsmen in America: Officers to Criticize Administrative Action, 109 U. Pa. L. Rev. 1057 (1961); Jägerskiöld, The Swedish Ombudsman, 109 U. Pa. L. Rev. 1077 (1961); British Section of the International Commission of Jurists, A report by Justice on the Citizen and the Administration: The Redress of Grievance (1961). For current proposals see S. 593, 88th Cong., 1st Sess. (1963) ("To establish an Office of Federal Administrative Practice and to provide for the appointment and administration of a corps of hearing commissioners and for other purposes."); H.R. 3560, 88th Cong., 1st Sess. (1963).
52. 372 U.S. 368, 381 (1963).
53. The Federalist No. 57, at 384 (Wright ed. 1961).
54. 369 U.S. 186 (1962).
55. In Baker v. Carr, supra note 54, at 208, the Court noted that "A citizen's right to a vote free of arbitrary impairment by state action has been judicially recognized as a right secured by the Constitution, when such impairment resulted from dilution by a false tally, cf. United States v. Classic, 313 U.S. 299; or by a refusal to count votes from arbitrarily selected precincts, cf. United States v. Mosley, 238 U.S. 383, or by a stuffing of the ballot box, cf. Ex parte Siebold, 100 U.S. 371; United States v. Saylor, 322 U.S. 385." See also the "white primary" cases, e.g., Terry v. Adams, 345 U.S. 461 (1953); Smith v. Allwright, 321 U.S. 649 (1944).
56. Colegrove v. Green, 328 U.S. 549 (1946).
57. 372 U.S. 368 (1963).
58. 369 U.S. at 226.
59. See Lamb, Pierce & White, Apportionment and Representative Institutions: The Michigan Experience (1963).
60. Griffin v. Illinois, 351 U.S. 12, 16–17 (1956).

61. Leviticus 19:15.
62. Pierre v. Louisiana, 306 U.S. 354, 358 (1939).
63. 351 U.S. 12 (1956).
64. Id. at 19.
65. Burns v. Ohio, 360 U.S. 252 (1959); Eskridge v. Washington, 357 U.S. 214 (1958).
66. Draper v. Washington, 372 U.S. 487 (1963); Lane v. Brown, 372 U.S. 477 (1963).
67. Gideon v. Wainwright, 372 U.S. 335 (1963).
68. Douglas v. California, 372 U.S. 353 (1963).
69. An example of this practice, now happily abandoned in the Capital City, occurred a few years ago. A waitress had been robbed by someone whom she described in very general terms. The police immediately conducted a dragnet roundup in the second precinct, which is populated primarily by poor people. Within a few hours 90 young men, including 25 juveniles were arrested for questioning. Sixty-three of them were held overnight and released only after the victim did not identify any of them as her assailant. Many of those held overnight were forced to miss work the following day. Another man, not among those picked up in the dragnet, was ultimately charged with the crime. See Wash. Daily News, Jan. 21, 1958, p. 5; Wash. Evening Star, Mar. 3, 1958, p. B1.
70. See e.g., Erikson & Erikson, The Confirmation of the Delinquent, in Psychoanalysis and Social Science 153 (Ruitenbeek ed.).
71. See generally Rep. Att'y Gen. Comm. on Poverty and the Administration of Federal Criminal Justice C. III (1963) [hereinafter cited as Att'y Gen. Rep.]. See also Pannell v. United States, 320 F.2d 698 (D.C. Cir. 1963).
72. Att'y Gen. Rep. 103–04.
73. For an excellent discussion of the imbalance between the accused and the prosecution, see Goldstein, The State and the Accused: Balance of Advantage in Criminal Procedure, 69 Yale L.J. 1149 (1960).
74. See e.g., Simpson v. United States, 320 F.2d 803, 804 (D.C. Cir. 1963) (Bazelon, C.J., concurring in part and dissenting in part).
75. Fed. R. Crim. P. 17.
76. The fee in the District of Columbia, for example, is six dollars plus eight cents a mile for transportation.
77. See Greenwell v. United States, 317 F.2d 108 (D.C. Cir. 1963).
78. Coppedge v. United States, 369 U.S. 438, 449 (1962).
79. Draper v. Washington, 372 U.S. 487, 495 n.4 (1963).
80. Lawes, Life and Death in Sing Sing 248 (1928).
81. Douglas, Vagrancy and Arrest on Suspicion, 70 Yale L.J. 1 (1960).
82. Cf. Robinson v. California, 370 U.S. 660 (1962).
83. See, e.g., Hardy v. United States, 84 Sup. Ct. 424 (1964); Coppedge v. United States, 369 U.S. 438 (1962).
84. See, e.g., Greenwell v. United States, 317 F.2d 108 (D.C. Cir. 1963).
85. See, e.g., People v. Paiva, 31 Cal. 2d 503, 190, P.2d 604 (1948); Zamora v. State, 309 S.W.2d 447 (Tex. Crim. App. 1957).
86. See, e.g., Ares, Rankin & Sturz, The Manhattan Bail Project: An Interim Report on the Use of Pre-Trial Parole, 38 N.Y.U.L. Rev. 67 (1963).
87. Cornell v. Superior Court, 52 Cal. 2d 99, 102–03, 338 P.2d 447, 449 (1959).

88. See id., 52 Cal. 2d at 103, 338 P.2d at 449.
89. Report of the Council of Economic Advisers 58 (1964).
90. Botein & Gordon, The Trial of the Future 51 (1963).
91. See generally, Orfield, The Growth of Scandinavian Law (1953).
92. See Att'y Gen. Rep. 32.
93. Ibid.
94. One effect of requiring the accused to employ his available funds to pay the costs of his defense may be to exhaust or limit the funds from which the victim may recover in a civil suit for damages against the accused. This is among the problems worthy of consideration.
95. Att'y Gen. Rep. 96.
96. Schaefer, Federalism and State Criminal Procedure, 70 Harv. L. Rev. 1, 26 (1956). Sir Winston Churchill, on July 20, 1910, speaking in the House of Commons as Home Secretary, said,

> The mood and temper of the public in regard to the treatment of crime and criminals is one of the most unfailing tests of any country. A calm, dispassionate recognition of the rights of the accused, and even of the convicted criminal, against the State—a constant heart-searching by all charged with the duty of punishment—a desire and eagerness to rehabilitate in the world of industry those who have paid their due in the hard coinage of punishment: tireless efforts towards the discovery of curative and regenerative processes: unfailing faith that there is a treasure, if you can only find it, in the heart of every man. These are the symbols, which, in the treatment of crime and criminal, mark and measure the stored up strength of a nation, and are sign and proof of the living virtue within it.

97. Report of the Council of Economic Advisers 55 (1964). (Emphasis added.)
98. The Constitution and What It Means Today vii (12th ed. 1958).
99. Tocqueville, 2 Democracy in America 108 (Bradley ed. 1945).
100. Holmes, Law and the Court, in The Occasional Speeches of Justice Oliver Wendell Holmes 169 (Howe ed. 1962).

J. Skelly Wright

1. U.S. Const., amend. XIV, § 1.
2. U.S. Declaration of Independence.
3. See generally Fairman, Does the Fourteenth Amendment Incorporate the Bill of Rights?, 2 Stan. L. Rev. 5 (1949); Gressman, The Unhappy History of Civil Rights Legislation, 50 Mich. L. Rev. 1323–26 (1952).
4. United States v. Cruikshank, 92 U.S. 542 (1875); United States v. Reese, 92 U.S. 214 (1875).
5. United States v. Harris, 106 U.S. 629 (1882).
6. Civil Rights Cases, 109 U.S. 3 (1883).
7. Woodward, Reunion and Reaction (2d ed. 1956).
8. La. Acts 1890, No. 111.
9. 163 U.S. 537 (1896).
10. Id. at 559, 562.
11. For the citations of many of these statutes, see Supplemental Brief for the United States as Amicus Curiae, pp. 50–63, Bouie v. Columbia, 378 U.S. 347 (1964); Bell v. Maryland, 378 U.S. 226 (1964); Robinson v. Florida, 378 U.S. 153 (1964); Barr v. Columbia, 378 U.S. 146 (1964); Griffin v. Maryland, 378 U.S. 130 (1964).

12. Woodward, The Strange Career of Jim Crow 68 (1955).
13. Hearings on H.R. 41, H.R. 57, H.R. 77, H.R. 223, H.R. 228, H.R. 278, and H.R. 800 Before Subcommittee No. 4 of the House Committee on the Judiciary, 80th Cong., 2d Sess. 39 (1948).
14. 347 U.S. 483, 495 (1954).
15. Gayle v. Browder, 352 U.S. 903 (per curiam), affirming 142 F. Supp. 707 (M.D. Ala. 1956).
16. New Orleans City Park Improvement Ass'n v. Detiege, 358 U.S. 54, affirming 252 F.2d 122 (5th Cir. 1958).
17. Watson v. Memphis, 373 U.S. 526 (1963).
18. Simkins v. Moses H. Cone Memorial Hosp., 323 F.2d 959 (4th Cir. 1963), cert. denied, 376 U.S. 938 (1964).
19. See Holmes v. City of Atlanta, 350 U.S. 879 (1955) (per curiam); Mayor and City Council v. Dawson, 350 U.S. 877 (1955) (per curiam).
20. United States Commission on Civil Rights, 1964 Staff Report on Public Education 290–91.
21. 78 Stat. 248, 42 U.S.C.A. § 2000(c)–6 (1964).
22. Advisory Panel on Integration of the Public Schools, Report to the Board of Education of the City of Chicago 56 (1964).
23. The statistics on the Washington, New York, and Oakland public schools are from United States Commission on Civil Rights, 1963 Staff Report on Public Education 144–45.
24. Brown v. Board of Educ., 347 U.S. 483, 493–95 (1954).
25. Advisory Panel on Integration of the Public Schools, supra note 22, at 46.
26. Statement Proposed by the New York State Education Commissioner's Advisory Committee on Human Relations and Community Tensions, June 17, 1963.
27. Taylor v. Board of Educ., 294 F.2d 36 (2d Cir.), cert. denied, 368 U.S. 940 (1961).
28. See Downs v. Board of Educ., 336 F.2d 988 (10th Cir. 1964) (affirming unreported opinion of district court), cert. denied, 380 U.S. 914 (1965); Bell v. School City, 213 F. Supp. 819 (N.D. Ind.), aff'd, 324 F.2d 209 (7th Cir. 1963).
29. See Ferguson v. Skrupa, 372 U.S. 726, 731–32 (1963); Williamson v. Lee Optical Co., 348 U.S. 483, 491 (1955).
30. "Segregation in public education is not reasonably related to any proper governmental objective. . . ." Bolling v. Sharpe, 347 U.S. 497, 500 (1954).
31. Barksdale v. Springfield School Comm., 237 F. Supp. 543 (D. Mass. 1965); Blocker v. Board of Educ., 226 F. Supp. 208 (E.D.N.Y. 1964); Branche v. Board of Educ., 204 F. Supp. 150 (E.D.N.Y. 1962), indicate that the rationale of the Gary and Kansas City cases is not acceptable in the Eastern District of New York or in the District of Massachusetts. See also Jackson v. Pasadena City School Dist., 59 Cal. 2d 876, 382 P.2d 878, 31 Cal. Rptr. 606 (1963).
32. Griffin v. School Bd., 377 U.S. 218 (1964); Hall v. St. Helena Parish School Bd., 197 F. Supp. 649 (E.D. La. 1961 (per curiam), aff'd, 287 F.2d 376 (5th Cir.), aff'd, 368 U.S. 515 (1962) (per curiam).
33. Iowa-Des Moines Bank v. Bennett, 284 U.S. 239, 244–45 (1931).
34. Taylor v. Board of Educ., 294 F.2d 36 (2d Cir.), cert. denied, 368 U.S. 940 (1961). Compare Gomillion v. Lightfoot, 364 U.S. 339 (1960).

35. See note 30 supra and accompanying text.
36. McLaughlin v. Florida, 379 U.S. 184, 191 (1964).
37. Id. at 196.
38. Brown v. Board of Educ., 347 U.S. 483, 495 (1954).
39. Korematsu v. United States, 323 U.S. 214 (1944); Hirabayashi v. United States, 320 U.S. 81 (1943).
40. See, e.g., Strippoli v. Bickal, 42 Misc. 2d 475, 248 N.Y.S.2d 588 (Sup. Ct.), reversed, 21 App. Div. 2d 365, 250 N.Y.S.2d 365 (4th Dep't 1964); Application of Vetere, 41 Misc. 2d 200, 245 N.Y.S.2d 682 (Sup. Ct. 1963), modified, 21 App. Div. 2d 561, 251 N.Y.S.2d 480 (3d Dep't 1964); Balaban v. Rubin, 40 Misc. 2d 249, 242 N.Y.S.2d 973 (Sup. Ct. 1963), rev'd, 20 App. Div. 2d 438, 248 N.Y.S.2d 574 (2d Dept.), aff'd, 14 N.Y.2d 193, 199 N.E.2d 375, 250 N.Y.S.2d, cert. denied, 379 U.S. 881 (1964).
41. The New York and California State Boards of Education require local school authorities to establish attendance areas for schools which, insofar as practicable, will avoid racial segregation. The Commissioner of Education of the state of New Jersey has taken a similar position.
42. Balaban v. Rubin, 14 N.Y.2d 193, 199 N.E.2d 375, 250 N.Y.S.2d 281, cert. denied, 379 U.S. 881 (1964).
43. Ordinance of 1787, § 14, art. 3.
44. Letter from Thomas Jefferson to Whyte, Aug. 13, 1786, in 5 Writings of Thomas Jefferson 396 (Berg ed. 1907).
45. Letter from Thomas Jefferson to John Tyler, May 26, 1810, in 12 Writings of Thomas Jefferson 393 (Berg ed. 1907).
46. Brown v. Board of Educ. 347 U.S. 483, 493 (1954).
47. Ibid.
48. See, e.g., Letter from George Washington to Samuel Chase, Jan. 5, 1785, in 28 Writings of George Washington 27 (Bicentennial ed. 1938).
49. For Jefferson's own summary of his proposed "Bill for the More General Diffusion of Knowledge," see his Notes on the State of Virginia 146–49 (Peden ed. 1955).
50. Letter from James Madison to Thomas W. Gilmer, Sept. 6, 1830, in The Complete Madison 314–15 (Padover ed. 1953).
51. See Adams, Dissertation on the Canon and the Feudal Law (1765), in 3 Works of John Adams 455–56 (Charles Francis Adams ed. 1851).
52. See Brown v. Board of Educ., 347 U.S. 483, 489 n.4 (1954) and authorities cited therein.
53. See, e.g., Act of July 16, 1866, ch. 200, 14 Stat. 173, 176 (1866); Act of March 2, 1867, ch. 157, 14 Stat. 434 (1867).
54. McCollum v. Board of Educ., 333 U.S. 203, 220–21 & n.9 (1948) (opinion of Mr. Justice Frankfurter).
55. Stuart v. School Dist. No. 1, 30 Mich. 69, 75 (1874).
56. Ibid.
57. Interstate Consol. St. Ry. v. Massachusetts, 207 U.S. 79, 87 (1907).
58. Everson v. Board of Educ., 330 U.S. 1, 7 (1947).
59. Board of Educ. v. Barnette, 319 U.S. 624, 656 (1943) (dissenting opinion).
60. 347 U.S. 483, 493 (1954).
61. Ibid.
62. Id. at 495.
63. Brown v. Board of Educ., 347 U.S. 483 (1954).

64. Compare the reapportionment cases: Reynolds v. Sims, 377 U.S. 533 (1964); Wesberry v. Sanders, 376 U.S. 1 (1964); Gray v. Sanders, 372 U.S. 368 (1963). See also Barksdale v. Springfield School Comm., 237 F. Supp. 543 (D. Mass. 1965).
65. McLaughlin v. Florida, 379 U.S. 184 (1964). Compare Sherbert v. Verner, 374 U.S. 398, 406–09 (1963).
66. McLaughlin v. Florida, supra note 65.
67. Barksdale v. Springfield School Comm., 237 F. Supp. 543, 546 (D. Mass. 1965).
68. For example, a school, though mathematically racially imbalanced as compared with other schools in the area, ordinarily would not be racially segregated in the constitutional sense unless the Negro population of the school outnumbered the white.
69. Davidson v. New Orleans, 96 U.S. 97, 104 (1877).
70. See note 65 supra.
71. Advisory Panel on Integration in the Public Schools, Report to the Board of Education of the City of Chicago 12 (1964).
72. 377 U.S. 218 (1964).
73. See note 64 supra.
74. Baker v. Carr, 369 U.S. 186 (1962).
75. 197 F. Supp. 649 (E.D. La. 1961) (per curiam), aff'd, 287 F.2d 376 (5th Cir.), aff'd, 368 U.S. 515 (1962) (per curiam).
76. 377 U.S. 218 (1964).
77. Simkins v. Moses H. Cone Memorial Hosp., 323 F.2d 959 (4th Cir. 1963), cert. denied, 376 U.S. 938 (1964); see Bolling v. Sharpe, 347 U.S. 497 (1954).
78. See note 64 supra.
79. 369 U.S. 186 (1962).
80. 328 U.S. 549 (1946).
81. 297 U.S. 278 (1936).
82. Downs v. Board of Educ., 336 F.2d 988 (10th Cir. 1964), cert. denied, 380 U.S. 914 (1965); Bell v. School City, 324 F.2d 209 (7th Cir. 1963).
83. See The Effects of Segregation and the Consequences of Desegregation: A Social Science Statement, 37 Minn. L. Rev. 427 (1953) (Appendix to Appellants' Briefs in the School Segregation Cases).
84. Ibid.
85. 111 Cong. Rec. 499–500 (daily ed. Jan. 12, 1965).

Elbert P. Tuttle

1. U.S. Bureau of the Census, Dep't of Commerce, County and City Data Book 12 (1962).
2. White v. Cook, Civil No. 2263-N, M.D. Ala., Feb. 7, 1966. The 1960 Census shows that there were 5,322 Negro and 1,900 white residents of the county twenty-one years of age or older.
3. Section 1. The right of citizens of the United States to vote shall not be denied or abridged by the United States or by any State on account of race, color, or previous condition of servitude.
   Section 2. The Congress shall have power to enforce this article by appropriate legislation.
   U.S. Const. amend. XV.

4. Lowndes is the county in which Mrs. Viola Liuzzo and the young semi-narian, Jonathan Daniels, were killed while participating in voter activity among the Negro citizens.
5. 79 Stat. 437, 42 U.S.C.A. § 1973 (Supp. 1965).
6. See Voting Rights Act of 1965, § 14(b), 79 Stat. 445, 42 U.S.C.A. § 1973*l*(b) (Supp. 1965).
7. The Federalist No. 57, at 384 (Wright ed. 1961).
8. Rossiter, Seedtime of the Republic 425 (1953).
9. Brant, The Madison Heritage, in The Great Rights 13, 26, (1963).
10. Id. at 26–27.
11. Goldberg, Equality and Governmental Action, 39 N.Y.U.L. Rev. 205 (1964).
12. While, of course, the Thirteenth Amendment abolished slavery, it took § 1 of the Fourteenth Amendment to give the former slaves citizenship within the state of their residence and of the United States:

    All persons born or naturalized in the United States, and subject to the jurisdiction thereof, are citizens of the United States and of the State wherein they reside. No State shall make or enforce any law which shall abridge the privileges or immunities of citizens of the United States; nor shall any State deprive any person of life, liberty or property without due process of law; nor deny to any person within its jurisdiction the equal protection of the laws.

    U.S. Const. amend. XIV, § 1.
13. U.S. Const. amend. XV.
14. Kilpatrick, The South Sees Through New Glasses, 10 National Rev. 141 (1961).
15. Guinn v. United States, 238 U.S. 347 (1915). Typical of these grand-father clauses is that of the state of Oklahoma, which was held unconstitutional by Guinn as in violation of the Fifteenth Amendment:

    [N]o person who was, on January 1, 1866, or at any time prior thereto entitled to vote under any form of government, or who at that time resided in some foreign nation, and no lineal descendant of such person, shall be denied the right to register and vote because of his inability to so read and write sections of such constitution.

    Id. at 357.
16. Grovey v. Townsend, 295 U.S. 45 (1935).
17. 321 U.S. 649 (1944).
18. U.S. Comm'n on Civil Rights, Report on Voting 22 (1961).
19. 347 U.S. 483 (1954).
20. See United States v. Duke, 332 F.2d 759, 770 n.12 (5th Cir. 1964).
21. 225 F. Supp. 353 (E.D. La. 1963), aff'd, 380 U.S. 145 (1965).
22. Of course, the percentage in excess of 100 is attributable to the failure to purge dead and departed white persons' names from the rolls, a further threat to an honest election.
23. See U.S. Comm'n on Civil Rights, Report on Voting 133–38 (1961).
24. 304 F.2d 583, 586 (5th Cir.), aff'd, 371 U.S. 37 (1962).
25. Id. See also United States ex rel. Goldsby v. Harpole, 263 F.2d 71, 78 (5th Cir.), cert. denied, 361 U.S. 838 (1959), where the court said:

    We cannot assume that Negroes, the majority class in Carroll County [Mississippi], had en masse, or in an substantial numbers, voluntarily abstained from registering as electors and, by such action, had rendered themselves ineligible for jury duty. If the registration officials freely and fairly registered qualified Negroes as electors, that fact rested more in the knowledge of the State. The burden was on appellee, as the State's representative, to refute the strong prima facie case developed by the appellant. The only Negroes ever proved registered as electors in Carroll County were two who had died before 1954.

26. H.R. Rep. No. 291, 85th Cong., 1st Sess. 12 (1957).
27. Civil Rights Act of 1957, § 131, 71 Stat. 637, as amended, 42 U.S.C. § 1971 (1964).
28. Larche v. Hannah, 176 F. Supp. 791 (W.D. La. 1959).
29. Larche v. Hannah, 177 F. Supp. 816 (W.D. La. 1959).
30. Hannah v. Larche, 363 U.S. 420 (1960).
31. United States v. Raines, 172 F. Supp. 552 (M.D. Ga. 1959).
32. United States v. Raines, 362 U.S. 17, 26 (1960).
33. United States v. McElveen, 177 F. Supp. 355, 357 (E.D. La. 1959).
34. United States v. Thomas, 362 U.S. 58 (1960).
35. United States v. Alabama, 171 F. Supp. 720 (M.D. Ala. 1959).
36. United States v. Alabama, 267 F.2d 808 (5th Cir. 1959).
37. United States v. Alabama, 362 U.S. 602 (1960).
38. H.R. Rep. No. 956, 86th Cong., 1st Sess. (1959).
39. Id. at 6–7.
40. Civil Rights Act of 1960, § 601(a), 74 Stat. 90, 42 U.S.C. § 1971(e) (1964).
41. U.S. Comm'n on Civil Rights, Report on Voting 234 n.88 (1961).
42. In re Dinkens, 187 F. Supp. 848 (M.D. Ala. 1960), aff'd sub nom. Dinkens v. Attorney General, 285 F.2d 430 (5th Cir.), cert. denied, 366 U.S. 913 (1961); Alabama ex rel. Gallion v. Rogers, 187 F. Supp. 848 (M.D. Ala. 1960), aff'd, 285 F.2d 430 (5th Cir.), cert. denied, 366 U.S. 913 (1961).
43. 363 U.S. 420 (1960).
44. 285 F. 2d 430 (5th Cir.), cert. denied, 366 U.S. 913 (1961).
45. Kennedy v. Bruce, 298 F.2d 860, 862 (5th Cir. 1962).
46. Id. at 863.
47. Id. at 864.
48. 301 F.2d 818 (5th Cir.), cert. denied, 371 U.S. 893 (1962). The Fifth Circuit affirmed on the merits, but reversed the district court on procedural points. United States v. Lynd, 321 F.2d 26 (5th Cir. 1963) (per curiam). In a companion case, the court of appeals reversed the action taken by the trial court in dismissing the original action filed to obtain copies of the records, Kennedy v. Lynd. 306 F.2d 222 (5th Cir. 1962), cert. denied, 371 U.S. 952 (1963). See also United States v. Lynd, 349 F.2d 785 (5th Cir. 1965); United States v. Lynd, 349 F.2d 790 (5th Cir. 1965) (judgment of contempt).
49. 28 U.S.C. § 1651 (1964).
50. See United States v. Lynd, 321 F.2d 26, 28 (5th Cir. 1963) (Bell, J., concurring specially).
51. See Kennedy v. Lynd, 306 F.2d 222, 227 (5th Cir. 1962), cert. denied, 371 U.S. 952 (1963). Such demands are made under Title III of the act, 74 Stat. 88 (1960), 42 U.S.C. § 1974(b) (1964).
52. 285 F.2d 430 (5th Cir.), cert. denied, 366 U.S. 913 (1961).
53. See United States v. Lynd, 301 F.2d 818, 819–20 (5th Cir.), cert. denied, 371 U.S. 893 (1962).

54. See id. at 820.
55. 298 F.2d 860 (5th Cir. 1962).
56. Id. at 863.
57. Id. at 864. This order of the trial court dismissing the enforcement proceedings was also appealed to our court and it was reversed sub nom. Kennedy v. Lynd, 306 F.2d 222 (5th Cir. 1962), cert. denied, 371 U.S. 952 (1963).
58. 301 F.2d 818, 821 (5th Cir.), cert. denied, 371 U.S. 893 (1962).
59. § 1292. Interlocutory decisions. (a) The courts of appeals shall have jurisdiction of appeals from:
   (1) Interlocutory orders of the district courts of the United States, . . . or of the judges thereof, granting, continuing, modifying, refusing or dissolving injunctions, or refusing to dissolve or modify injunctions, except where a direct review may be had in the Supreme Court. . . .
   28 U.S.C. § 1292 (1964).
60. 301 F.2d at 822.
61. Id. at 823.
62. See ibid.
63. 7 Race Rel. L. Rep. 1146 (M.D. Ala. Sept. 13, 1961).
64. 332 F.2d 759, 768–69 (5th Cir. 1964).
65. 225 F. Supp. 353, 393 (E.D. La. 1963) (three-judge court), aff'd, 380 U.S. 145 (1965).
66. See, e.g., United States v. Lynd, 349 F.2d 785, 787 (5th Cir. 1965); United States v. Ward, 345 F.2d 857, 860 (5th Cir. 1965) (Mississippi); United States v. Mississippi, 339 F.2d 679, 683 (5th Cir. 1964); United States v. Mayton, 335 F.2d 153, 158–59 (5th Cir. 1964). See also discussion in United States v. Ward, 349 F.2d 795, 801 (5th Cir. 1965) (Louisiana).
67. See Carter v. School Bd., 349 F.2d 1020 (5th Cir. 1965) (per curiam), and six similar per curiam opinions at 349 F.2d 1020–22.
68. See United States v. Lynd, 349 F.2d 785, 787 (5th Cir. 1965); United States v. Ward, 349 F.2d 795, 805 (5th Cir. 1965).
69. See, e.g., United States v. Ward, 349 F.2d 329 (5th Cir. 1965) (modified on rehearing). See generally United States v. Ramsey, 353 F.2d 650 (5th Cir. 1965).
70. See, e.g., Stell v. Savannah-Chatham County Bd. of Educ., 318 F.2d 425 (5th Cir. 1963).
71. 332 F.2d 759, 770 (5th Cir. 1964).
72. Id. at 771.
73. 349 F.2d 785, 787 (5th Cir. 1965). (Emphasis added.)
74. 380 U.S. 145 (1965).
75. 225 F. Supp. 353 (E.D. La. 1963).
76. 380 U.S. at 154.
77. This amendment was proposed by the 87th Congress, in the Senate on March 27, 1962, 108 Cong. Rec. 5072 (1962), and in the House of Representatives on August 27, 1962, 108 Cong. Rec. 17654 (1962). It had been ratified by the requisite number of states by January 23, 1964.
78. Voting Rights Act of 1965, § 10(a), 79 Stat. 442, 42 U.S.C.A. § 1973h (Supp. 1965).
79. Harper v. Virginia State Bd. of Educ., 240 F. Supp. 270 (E.D. Va. 1964) (per curiam).

80. United States v. Mississippi, Civil No. 3791, S.D. Miss., filed Aug. 7, 1965; United States v. Virginia, Civil No. 4423, E.D. Va., filed Aug. 10, 1965; United States v. Texas, Civil No. 1570, W.D. Tex., filed Aug. 10, 1965; United States v. Alabama, Civil No. 2255-N, M.D. Ala., filed Aug. 10, 1965.

81. United States v. Texas, Civil No. 1570, W.D. Tex., Feb. 9, 1966; United States v. Alabama, Civil No. 2255-N, M.D. Ala., March 3, 1966.

82. It applied to states where it was determined by the Director of the Bureau of the Census that less than 50 percent of the voting-age residents were registered or voted in the 1964 election. Voting Rights Act of 1965, § 4(b), 79 Stat. 438, 42 U.S.C.A. § 1973b (Supp. 1965).

83. See South Carolina v. Katzenbach, 86 Sup. Ct. 803 (1966).

84. N.Y. Times, March 1, 1966, p. 43, col. 1.

85. See United States v. Ramsey, 353 F.2d 650, 653 nn.7 & 8 (5th Cir. 1965).

86. South Carolina v. Katzenbach, 86 Sup. Ct. 803 (1966).

87. Cf. Louisiana v. United States, 380 U.S. 145, 151–53 (1965).

88. See cases cited in note 68 supra.

89. See Note, Federal Protection of Negro Voting Rights, 51 Va. L. Rev. 1053 (1965), comprehensively dealing with the efforts to complete fruition of the Fifteenth Amendment and dealing with the basic material here discussed but in much greater detail and with more freedom in its discussion of the performance of the officials and the courts.

90. United States v. Ward, 349 F.2d 795 (5th Cir. 1965).

91. Id. at 802.

92. The Atlanta Constitution, July 26, 1965, p. 1, col. 1.

Abe Fortas

1. In Dred Scott v. Sandford, 60 U.S. (19 How.) 393 (1856), the Supreme Court returned a negative answer to the question:

   Can a negro, whose ancestors were imported into this country, and sold as slaves, become a member of the political community formed and brought into existence by the Constitution of the United States, and as such become entitled to all the rights, and privileges, and immunities, guarantied by that instrument to the citizen? One of which rights is the privilege of suing in a court of the United States in the cases specified in the Constitution.

   Id. at 403.

2. Some states, for example, exclude women from jury service. Ala. Code tit. 30, § 21 (1958); Miss. Code Ann. § 1762 (1962); S.C. Code Ann. §§ 38–401 to 38–405 (1962). The Mississippi statute has been sustained against constitutional challenges. State v. Hall, 187 So. 2d 861 (Miss. 1966) (Etheridge, C.J., dissenting). The Alabama statute has been declared invalid by a three-judge federal court. White v. Crook, 251 F. Supp. 401 (M.D. Ala. 1966). Married women, particularly, suffer a variety of disabilities, including restrictions on their right to contract and to convey realty. See United States v. Yazell, 382 U.S. 341, 351–52 (1966). In a few states they may not sue for loss of consortium when their husbands are injured, although the husband does have such a cause of action in the event his wife is hurt. See, e.g., Krohn v. Richardson-Merrell, Inc., 406 S.W.2d 166 (Tenn. 1966), cert. denied, 386 U.S. 970 (1967).

3. See Konvitz, Expanding Liberties: Freedom's Gains in Postwar America 343–49 (1966).
4. Mack, The Chancery Procedure in the Juvenile Court, in The Child, the Clinic, and the Court 310 (1925).
5. Pee v. United States, 274 F.2d 556, 561–63 (D.C. Cir. 1959); Paulsen, Kent v. United States: The Constitutional Context of Juvenile Cases, 1966 Sup. Ct. Rev. 167.
6. See generally Note, Juvenile Delinquents: The Police, State Courts, and Individualized Justice, 79 Harv. L. Rev. 775 (1966).
7. 383 U.S. 541 (1966).
8. Note, 79 Harv. L. Rev. 775 (1966). A few jurisdictions have adopted rules for juvenile proceedings which come much closer to the standards required with respect to adults. See, e.g., N.Y. Family Ct. Act §§ 721, 741, 744; Matters of Gregory W. and Gerald S., 19 N.Y.2d 55, 224 N.E.2d 102 (1966); Interests of Carlo and Stasilowicz, 48 N.J. 224, 225 A.2d 110 (1966); Two Brothers and a Case of Liquor, Nos. 66–2652-J, 66–2653-J (D.C. Juv. Ct. Dec. 28, 1966); Children's Bureau Publication, Standards for Juvenile and Family Courts, No. 437–1966 (1966).
9. See Miranda v. Arizona, 384 U.S. 436 (1966); Escobedo v. Illinois, 378 U.S. 478 (1964).
10. See Kent v. United States, 383 U.S. 541, 544 (1966).
11. A few states, however, have recently provided for appointment of counsel in juvenile proceedings. See Minn. Stat. Ann. § 260.155(2) (Supp. 1966); N.Y. Family Ct. Act §§ 241, 249; Ore. Rev. Stat. § 419.498(2) (1965). California does so where the offense would be a felony if committed by an adult. Cal. Welfare & Inst'ns Code § 634. Still others permit the judge to appoint counsel if he concludes it is necessary. E.g., Ala. Code tit. 13, § 359 (1958).
12. 351 U.S. 12 (1956).
13. 372 U.S. 353 (1963).
14. President's Comm'n on Law Enforcement and Admin. of Justice, The Challenge of Crime in a Free Society 55–56 (1967).
15. President's Comm'n on Crime in the District of Columbia 773 (1966).
16. The Office of Economic Opportunity estimates that over 34 million people in this country are "poor," meaning that they are living on cash incomes insufficient to purchase goods and services vital to health. OEO, Dimensions of Poverty in 1964 (1965). In 1965, over two million persons received old-age assistance, over one million families received aid to dependent children, and there were at least 300,000 cases of general assistance. See Statistical Abstract of the United States 302 (1966).
17. In a series of statutes beginning in 1536 and culminating in the Elizabethan Poor Law of 1601, 43 Eliz. 1, c. 2 (1601), Tudor England evolved an arrangement whereby the state, in the person of the parish as supervised by the justice of the peace, would assume the obligation of dealing with the poor. This was earlier discharged principally by the Church (which, after Henry VII's plundering, was no longer in a position to do so). At the heart of the Poor Law was the notion that the able-bodied or "sturdy vagrant" was a criminal, whose third offense at times was punishable by death. See Coll, Perspectives in Public Welfare: The English Heritage, in Welfare in Review, March 1966, p. 1; Rosenheim, Vagrancy Concepts in Welfare Law, 54 Calif. L. Rev. 511 (1966).

18. Articles of Confederation, Art. IV, ¶ 1.
19. See Bendich, Privacy, Poverty and the Constitution, 54 Calif. L. Rev. 407, 435 n. 78 (1966); Douglas, Vagrancy and Arrest on Suspicion, 70 Yale L.J. 1 (1960).
20. See City of New York v. Miln, 36 U.S. (11 Pet.) 102 (1837).
21. Ibid.
22. Id. at 142.
23. 314 U.S. 160 (1941).
24. Id. at 177.
25. Id. at 184–85.
26. 351 U.S. 12 (1956).
27. 372 U.S. 335 (1963).
28. Powell v. Alabama, 287 U.S. 45 (1932).
29. For developments since Griffin and Gideon, see, e.g., Solomon, "This New Fetish for Indigency": Justice and Poverty in an Affluent Society, 66 Colum. L. Rev. 248 (1966).
30. 351 U.S. at 34.
31. I refer in part to New York University's Project on Social Welfare, whose purposes and scope are set out in its publication, Welfare Law Bulletin, No. 1, December 1965. I might also observe that an outstanding compilation of the early fruits of these efforts appears in a symposium, Law of the Poor, 54 Calif. L. Rev. 319 (1966).
32. See Bell, Aid to Dependent Children 137–38 (1965). At its height, the crisis saw aid terminated to 6,200 families, involving over 23,000 children. The Department of Health, Education, and Welfare responded with a ruling requiring states wishing to cut off aid to "unsuitable homes" to provide otherwise for the children affected. See 76 Stat. 189 (1962), amending 75 Stat. 77 (1961), 42 U.S.C. § 604(b) (1964).
33. See Reich, Midnight Welfare Searches and the Social Security Act, 72 Yale L.J. 1347 (1963).
34. See HEW, Handbook of Public Assistance Admin. pt. IV, § 2230 (Handbook Transmittal No. 77, March 18, 1966).
35. E.g., Economic Opportunity Act of 1964, § 616, 78 Stat. 533. This provision is no longer in effect. See 79 Stat. 978 (1965), 42 U.S.C. § 2966 (Supp. 1966). See Willcox, Invasions of the First Amendment Through Conditioned Public Spending, 41 Cornell L.Q. 12, 48–52 (1955). See Speiser v. Randall, 357 U.S. 513 (1958), and Sherbert v. Verner, 374 U.S. 398 (1963), on the relationship between conditioned benefits and the First Amendment.
36. See generally Harvith, The Constitutionality of Residence Tests for General and Categorical Assistance Programs, 54 Calif. L. Rev. 567 (1966).
37. See Friedman, Public Housing and the Poor: An Overview, 54 Calif. L. Rev. 642, 656–61 (1966).
38. Dep't of Housing and Urban Development, Circular to Local Housing Authorities (February 7, 1967). See Housing Authority v. Thorpe, 267 N.C. 431, 148 S.E.2D 290 (1966), reversed, 393 U.S. 268 (1968).
39. See Housing Authority v. Thorpe, supra note 38; Note, Federal Judicial Review of State Welfare Practices, 67 Colum. L. Rev. 84 (1967). The cases in state and federal courts are kept track of in the Welfare Law

Bulletin, published by the Project on Social Welfare of New York University School of Law.

40. See Board of Educ. v. Barnette, 319 U.S. 624, 670 (1943) (dissenting opinion).
41. See Note, 67 Colum. L. Rev. 84, 117–29 (1967).
42. See Bell, supra note 32, at 184–86. A Mississippi study, conducted before and after discontinuance of welfare payments to mothers with dependent children, showed the percentage of "illegitimate" children rising from 41.5% to 91.4% *after* benefits were cut off, suggesting to Bell that such a cut-off "only increases their vulnerability to out-of-wedlock pregnancies." Id. at 182–83.
43. Compare Reich, The New Property, 73 Yale L.J. 733 (1964), and Reich, Individual Rights and Social Welfare: The Emerging Legal Issues, 74 Yale L.J. 1245 (1965), with O'Neil, Unconstitutional Conditions: Welfare Benefits with Strings Attached, 54 Calif. L. Rev. 443 (1966).
44. Edwards v. California, 314 U.S. 160, 184 (1941) (concurring opinion).
45. Cf. Universal Declaration of Human Rights, art. 22, Res. 217 (III) A, U.N. Gen. Ass. Off. Rec. 3d Sess., 1st pt., p. 71 (1948), which provides in part that "everyone, as a member of society has the right to social security and is entitled to realization . . . of the economic, social and cultural rights indispensable for his dignity and the free development of his personality."

Thurgood Marshall

1. See generally H. Flack, The Adoption of the Fourteenth Amendment 55–139 (1908); J. James, The Framing of the Fourteenth Amendment 182–202 (1956); J. ten Broek, Equal Under Law 201–33 (1956).
2. U.S. Const. amend. XIV, §§ 1, 5.
3. Cong. Globe, 39th Cong., 1st Sess. 2766 (1866).
4. See Note, Private Attorneys-General: Group Action in the Fight for Civil Liberties, 58 Yale L.J. 574 (1949).
5. United States v. Guest, 383 U.S. 745, 784 (1966) (Brennan, J., concurring and dissenting in part).
6. 83 U.S. (16 Wall.) 36 (1873).
7. Id. at 71.
8. Id. at 81.
9. See id. at 83 (Field, J., dissenting); at 111 (Bradley, J., dissenting); at 124 (Swayne, J., dissenting).
10. Ex parte Virginia, 100 U.S. 339 (1880); Virginia v. Rives, 100 U.S. 313 (1880); Strauder v. West Virginia, 100 U.S. 303 (1880).
11. See, e.g., Strauder v. West Virginia, 100 U.S. 303, 307–08 (1880).
12. See J. Franklin, Reconstruction: After the Civil War 212–17 (1961).
13. Civil Rights Cases, 109 U.S. 3 (1883).
14. Id. at 48 (dissenting opinion).
15. 163 U.S. 537 (1896).
16. See 2 The Constitution and the Supreme Court 247–57 (L. Pollak ed. 1966).
17. 163 U.S. at 552 (dissenting opinion).
18. Mark Ethridge, quoted in C. Woodward, The Strange Career of Jim Crow 120 (2d ed. 1966).

19. 347 U.S. 483 (1954).
20. See A. Blaustein & C. Ferguson, Desegregation and the Law 95–113 (2d ed. 1962).
21. See, e.g., Jones v. Alfred H. Mayer Co., 392 U.S. 409 (1968).
22. See Zimroth, Group Legal Services and the Constitution, 76 Yale L.J. 966 (1967); Note, Group Legal Services, 79 Harv. L. Rev. 416 (1965).
23. United Mine Workers, Dist. 12 v. Illinois State Bar Ass'n, 389 U.S. 217 (1967); Brotherhood of R.R. Trainmen v. Virginia ex rel. Virginia State Bar, 377 U.S. 1 (1964); NAACP v. Button, 371 U.S. 415 (1963).
24. 371 U.S. at 429–30.
25. 389 U.S. at 223.
26. See, e.g., Sperry v. Florida ex rel. Florida Bar, 373 U.S. 379, 383 (1963).
27. Three months after Justice Marshall's address, the ABA House of Delegates unanimously adopted the new Code of Professional Responsibility, to become effective January 1, 1970. The American Bar News observed (14 American Bar News 9 (1969)):

> The issue of group legal services brought the only controversy over the code on the House floor. The Special Committee on Availability of Legal Services proposed an amendment that would have approved and regulated extension of group service arrangements such as those provided by a union for its individual members. This proposal was defeated by a voice vote. The code as adopted limits group services to nonprofit organizations whose group plans have been upheld as constitutional by court decisions.*

28. See Bonfield, Representation for the Poor in Federal Rulemaking, 67 Mich. L. Rev. 511 (1969).
29. W. Seymour, The Obligations of the Lawyer to His Profession 12 (1968).

Irving R. Kaufman

1. U.S. Const. amend. I.
2. "O body swayed to music, O brightening glance/How can we know the dancer from the dance?"—W. Yeats, "Among School Children," in Collected Poems 212, 214 (Macmillan Co. ed. 1956).
3. See, e.g., M. McLuhan, Understanding Media (1964); M. McLuhan & Q. Fiore, The Medium Is the Message (1967).
4. It is claimed that President Nixon, who makes considerable use of televised speeches in preference to the traditional news conferences with the daily press, has taken this course because he believes that without the medium of television the message would not have the desired impact. N.Y. Times, Feb. 1, 1970, § 4, at 1, col. 1.
5. "[T]he best test of truth is the power of the thought to get itself accepted in the competition of the market. . . ." Abrams v. United States, 250 U.S. 616, 630 (1919) (Holmes, J., dissenting).
6. 274 U.S. 357 (1927), overruled, Brandenburg v. Ohio, 395 U.S. 444 (1969).

---

* Since 1970 there have been significant further changes that are conducive to group legal services by nonprofit and for-profit organizations. These are reflected mainly in Rules 5.4 and 7.3 of the Model Rules of Professional Conduct adopted by the ABA on August 2, 1983. As of August 1987, twenty-four states have adopted these rules in various forms. EDITOR'S NOTE.

7. Id. at 377 (Brandeis, J., concurring).
8. Chaplinsky v. New Hampshire, 315 U.S. 568, 572 (1942).
9. 337 U.S. 1 (1949).
10. Id. at 4.
11. See Feiner v. New York, 340 U.S. 315 (1951).
12. But see Bachellar v. Maryland, 397 U.S. 564 (1970) (overturning conviction of antiwar protesters because the charge might have permitted a guilty verdict based on crowd reaction to demonstrators); Gregory v. City of Chicago, 394 U.S. 111, 117 (1969) (Black, J., concurring); Wright v. Georgia, 373 U.S. 284 (1963). One interesting question is whether the protesters must be arrested before they can be removed.
13. Thomas v. Collins, 323 U.S. 516, 544 (1945) (Jackson, J., concurring).
14. Id.; Cantwell v. Connecticut, 310 U.S. 296, 305 (1940). But cf. Zwickler v. Koota, 389 U.S. 241, 250 (1967).
15. E.g., Staub v. City of Baxley, 355 U.S. 313 (1958); Largent v. Texas, 318 U.S. 418 (1943); Cantwell v. Connecticut, 310 U.S. 296 (1940).
16. E.g., Murdock v. Pennsylvania, 319 U.S. 105 (1943); Jones v. Opelika, 319 U.S. 103 (1943), vacating 316 U.S. 584 (1942).
17. See, e.g., Beauharnais v. Illinois, 343 U.S. 250, 257 (1952) (group libel).
18. 15 U.S.C. § 77t(b) (1964).
19. 21 U.S.C. §§ 331(b), 332 (1964).
20. Public Health Cigarette Smoking Act of 1969, Pub. L. No. 91–222, § 6, 84 Stat. 87.
21. E.g., Schneider v. State, 308 U.S. 147 (1939).
22. Valentine v. Chrestensen, 316 U.S. 52 (1942).
23. Murdock v. Pennsylvania, 319 U.S. 105 (1943).
24. 371 U.S. 415 (1963).   25. 354 U.S. 476 (1957).
26. Id. at 485.   27. See notes 28–31 infra.
28. Stanley v. Georgia, 394 U.S. 557, 565 (1969).
29. See Karalexis v. Byrne, 306 F. Supp. 1363, 1366 (D. Mass. 1969) (*Stanley* applies the clear and present danger test and therefore Massachusetts could not regulate movies shown for willing adults).*
30. 390 U.S. 629 (1968).
31. 383 U.S. 463 (1966).
32. See Redrup v. New York, 386 U.S. 767, 769 (1967) (per curiam); The Supreme Court, 1968 Term, 83 Harv. L. Rev. 62, 153–54 (1969). If the only danger from obscene displays is thought to be their effect on unconsenting members of the public, then this approach may be seen as a variant of the clear and present danger test.
33. See Roth v. United States, 354 U.S. 476, 489 (1957).
34. Jacobellis v. Ohio, 378 U.S. 184, 197 (1964) (concurring opinion).
35. Ginzburg v. United States, 383 U.S. 463, 499 n.3 (1966) (Stewart, J., dissenting). The Supreme Court recently upheld the constitutionality of a statute permitting addressees to have their names removed from mailing lists of advertisers whom the addressees deem to be distributors of obscene mail. Rowan v. United States Post Office Dep't, 397 U.S. 728 (1970).
36. 323 U.S. 516, 537 (1945). At this point, connoisseurs of that particular message would probably call attention to Louis Armstrong's views when

* The Supreme Court vacated this judgment on other grounds, 401 U.S. 216 (1971). EDITOR'S NOTE.

asked to define jazz: "If you have to have it defined, you ain't never going to understand it."

37. Saia v. New York, 334 U.S. 558, 561 (1948). But see Kovacs v. Cooper, 336 U.S. 77 (1949).

38. Schneider v. State, 308 U.S. 147 (1939) (pamphlets as effective instrument in dissemination of opinion).

39. NAACP v. Button, 371 U.S. 415 (1963) (group litigation as a means of redress of grievances).

40. See, e.g., Adderley v. Florida, 385 U.S. 39, 50–51 (1966) (Douglas, J., dissenting); Kovacs v. Cooper, 336 U.S. 77, 102 (1949) (Black, J., dissenting); Martin v. City of Struthers, 319 U.S. 141, 146 (1943).

41. See note 4 supra.

42. It seems that bomb threats have become the modern-day equivalent of the cry of "fire" in a crowded theater.

43. United States v. O'Brien, 391 U.S. 367 (1968).

44. 394 U.S. 576 (1969).

45. People v. Radich, 26 N.Y.2d 114, 257 N.E.2d 30, 308 N.Y.S.2d 846, affirmed, 401 U.S. 531 (1971) (per curiam). But see Commonwealth v. Sgorbati, 38 U.S.L.W. 2617 (Phila. C.P. May 15, 1970) (wearing flag over boxer shorts when reporting for draft induction held not to "cast contempt upon the flag").

46. See United States v. O'Brien, 391 U.S. 367, 376–77 (1968).

47. NAACP v. Button, 371 U.S. 415, 438 (1963). See also Sherbert v. Verner, 374 U.S. 398, 403 (1963).

48. NAACP v. Button, 371 U.S. 415, 444 (1963); NAACP v. Alabama ex rel. Patterson, 357 U.S. 449, 464 (1958).

49. Bates v. City of Little Rock, 361 U.S. 516, 524 (1960).

50. Thomas v. Collins, 323 U.S. 516, 530 (1945). See also Sherbert v. Verner, 374 U.S. 398, 406 (1963).

51. Bates v. City of Little Rock, 361 U.S. 516, 524 (1960).

52. Sherbert v. Verner, 374 U.S. 398, 408 (1963).

53. See United States v. O'Brien, 391 U.S. 367, 377 (1968).

54. Id.

55. E.g., Shuttlesworth v. City of Birmingham, 394 U.S. 147 (1969); Staub v. City of Baxley, 355 U.S. 313 (1958); Kunz v. New York, 340 U.S. 290 (1951); Niemotko v. Maryland, 340 U.S. 268 (1951); Saia v. New York, 334 U.S. 558 (1948); Largent v. Texas, 318 U.S. 418 (1943); Hague v. CIO, 307 U.S. 496 (1939). See also Cantwell v. Connecticut, 310 U.S. 296 (1940).

56. Thomas v. Collins, 323 U.S. 516, 540 (1945).

57. See Schneider v. State, 308 U.S. 147 (1939).

58. Tucker v. Texas, 326 U.S. 517 (1946); Marsh v. Alabama, 326 U.S. 501 (1946); Jamison v. Texas, 318 U.S. 413 (1943); Schneider v. State, 308 U.S. 147 (1939); Hague v. CIO, 307 U.S. 496 (1939); Lovell v. City of Griffin, 303 U.S. 444, 451 (1938).

59. Murdock v. Pennsylvania, 319 U.S. 105 (1943).

60. 319 U.S. 141 (1943).

61. Id. at 146.

62. Id. at 148; Schneider v. State, 308 U.S. 147 (1939).

63. Martin v. City of Struthers, 319 U.S. 141, 143 (1943).

64. Kovacs v. Cooper, 336 U.S. 77, 86–87 (1949) (ordinance prohibiting "loud and raucous noises" upheld).
65. "Loud-speakers are today indispensable instruments of effective public speech. . . . It is the way people are reached." Saia v. New York, 334 U.S. 558, 561 (1948).
66. See, e.g., Amalgamated Food Employees Local 590 v. Logan Valley Plaza, Inc., 391 U.S. 308 (1968); AFL v. Swing, 312 U.S. 321 (1941); Thornhill v. Alabama, 310 U.S. 88 (1940).
67. E.g., Amalgamated Food Employees Local 590 v. Logan Valley Plaza, Inc., 391 U.S. 308 (1968); Cameron v. Johnson, 390 U.S. 611 (1968); Cox v. Louisiana, 379 U.S. 536 (1965).
68. Cameron v. Johnson, 390 U.S. 611 (1968).
69. Cox v. Louisiana, 379 U.S. 536, 554 (1965).
70. E.g., Cox v. New Hampshire, 312 U.S. 569 (1941).
71. Id.
72. 283 U.S. 359 (1931).
73. 393 U.S. 503 (1969).
74. Id. at 505–06.
75. 363 F.2d 744 (5th Cir. 1966). I will resist the temptation to discuss the "long hair" case law development. See, e.g., Breen v. Kahl, 296 F. Supp. 702 (W.D. Wis), aff'd, 419 F.2d 1034 7th Cir. 1969), cert. denied, 398 U.S. 937 (1970). Being a father and a grandfather (not to mention the employer of two long-haired clerks), I plead my constitutional right to remain silent.
76. 383 U.S. 131 (1966).
77. Id. at 139.
78. Id. at 142. See Schacht v. United States, 398 U.S. 58 (1970) (Government may not bar United States military uniforms in plays critical of the military). A recent denial of review by the Supreme Court deprived the legal profession of the opportunity to learn the limits of "appropriate action." Derrington v. City of Portland, 396 U.S. 901 (1969) (topless dancer).
79. 371 U.S. 415, 429 (1963).
80. Id. at 429–30.
81. There is another perspective from which to examine the problem of inherently disruptive media. Our thinking, channeled by case law, has been largely concerned with the rights accorded expression and dissemination of views. Consequently, we have usually directed our attention to the speaker and have ignored the audience. Is there a constitutional right for the audience—that undistributed mass, the public—to be informed? And if there is, what competing interests are there to be accommodated? May we assume that the press will always be a proper spokesman for the public's interest in information? What if the audience's interest in knowing what the speaker says conflicts with his desire to say it in a way that he deems most effective? Apart from a few quotations from the Founding Fathers, some statutory cases arising under the Administrative Procedure Act and the Freedom of Information Act there is surprisingly little guidance in this area. See Hennings, The People's Right to Know, 45 A.B.A.J. 667 (1959); O'Leary, The Right To Be Informed, 54 Mass. L.Q. 63 (1969). See also In re Caldwell, 311 F. Supp. 358 (N.D. Cal. 1970) (reporter entitled to have confidential asso-

ciation with Black Panther Party protected until "compelling and overriding national interests" are shown).

Two recent events illustrate the possible conflict between the rights of a speaker and the rights of the audience. Mayor Lindsay initiated a short-lived (and some would add, ill-starred) system of dual press conferences. Feeling that the informal give-and-take with the daily press was inhibited by the presence of television cameras, he held two conferences, one to which only the papers were invited, and one in which television cameras were permitted. We will never know if the "cultural wasteland's" right to some off-the-cuff wit has constitutional proportions in City Hall: a boycott of both conferences by several television stations forced the mayor to back down. See N.Y. Times, Jan. 22, 1970, at 1, col. 2; N.Y. Times, Jan. 27, 1970, at 34, col. 5. In February Chief Justice Burger spoke at the midyear meeting of the American Bar Association in Atlanta, Georgia. Finding that the persistent glare of television lights would inhibit his delivery and concerned that the ten-second clips drawn out of context from an extensive message would be misleading, he barred all but the press from the auditorium. Television stations were incensed and promised that they would in the future expect to be received on equal terms with the newspapers. N.Y. Times, Feb. 23, 1970, at 43, col. 2.

For our purposes, the most instructive aspect of both of these examples is that they indicate some of the more subtle ways in which particular media may prove disruptive—to the speaker as well as his audience. They also suggest the weakness of the usual dualistic analysis, which pits freedom of speech against some other governmental interest. Here the speaker's right to talk where and how he pleases contends with the public's right to know. I can say no more on the issue than to suggest that the speaker's right to present his message in a form he deems most effective is not one lightly to be pushed aside—by government or by the media.

82. 307 U.S. 496 (1939).
83. Id. at 515–16; see Amalgamated Food Employees Local 590 v. Logan Valley Plaza, Inc., 391 U.S. 308 (1968). Among the speech activities for which these public places are available are hand distribution of literature, Jamison v. Texas, 318 U.S. 413 (1943); Schneider v. State, 308 U.S. 147 (1939); public meetings, Kunz v. New York, 340 U.S. 290 (1951); Niemotko v. Maryland, 340 U.S. 268 (1951); Hague v. CIO, 307 U.S. 496 (1939); parades and demonstrations, Shuttlesworth v. City of Birmingham, 394 U.S. 147 (1969).
84. E.g., Edwards v. South Carolina, 372 U.S. 229 (1963). Cf. A Quaker Action Group v. Hickel, 421 F.2d 1111 (D.C. Cir. 1969) (a court test of regulations governing picketing at the White House).
85. 385 U.S. 39 (1966).
86. Id. at 50–51.
87. 379 U.S. 559 (1965).
88. 310 U.S. 88 (1940).
89. Id. at 106. See also Bakery Drivers Local 802 v. Wohl, 315 U.S. 769, 775 (1942) (Douglas, J., concurring).
90. 326 U.S. 501 (1946).
91. 391 U.S. 308 (1968).

92. The Court in Taggart v. Weinacker's, Inc., 397 U.S. 233 (1970) (per curiam) may have retreated a step or two even from *Logan Valley Plaza.* In the course of dismissing certiorari as improvidently granted, the Court seems to have indicated in dicta that the state courts could enjoin labor picketing on privately owned sidewalks, where "obstruction" of a narrow passageway was urged.
93. 393 U.S. 503 (1969).
94. See Scoville v. Board of Educ., 425 F.2d 10, 14 (7th Cir. 1970) (en banc) (school must make "affirmative showing" that it could reasonably forecast "substantial disruption").
95. See Burnside v. Byars, 363 F.2d 744 (5th Cir. 1966); Breen v. Kahl, 296 F. Supp. 702 (W.D. Wis.), aff'd, 419 F.2d 1034 (7th Cir. 1969), cert. denied, 398 U.S. 937 (1970). See also Hammond v. South Carolina State College, 272 F. Supp. 947 (D.S.C. 1967). A district court, relying on due process rather than First Amendment grounds, condemned suspension of a student for possession of obscene literature as "rank inconsistency," and "preposterous on its face." Vought v. Van Buren Pub. Schools, 306 F. Supp. 1388, 1396 (E.D. Mich. 1969).
96. Address by Judge Learned Hand, Meeting of the Legal Aid Society of New York City, Feb. 16, 1951, in Notable Quotes from a Great Judge, 1961 N.Y.S.B.J. 419, 423.
97. I. Dilliard, Learned Hand, The Spirit of Liberty 284 (3d ed. 1960).

David L. Bazelon

1. 214 F.2d 862 (D.C. Cir. 1954).
2. United States v. Brawner, No. 22–714 (D.C. Cir., Jan. 9, 1969).
3. McDonald v. United States, 312 F.2d 847, 851 (D.C. Cir. 1962) (en banc).
4. Washington v. United States, 390 F.2d 444 (D.C. Dir. 1962).
5. United States v. Eichberg, 439 F.2d 620 (D.C. Cir. 1971); Adams v. United States, 413 F.2d 411 (D.C. Cir. 1969); King v. United States, 372 F.2d 383 (D.C. Cir. 1967).
6. See, e.g., Model Penal Code § 4.01 (Proposed Official Draft 1962).
7. See N.Y. Times, July 19, 1971, at 14, cols. 3–8.
8. One of the proposals—that juries be permitted to convict or acquit in criminal cases upon a less than unanimous vote—is presently under constitutional review by the Supreme Court.*
9. For recent examples, see Cohen v. California, 403 U.S. 15, 27 (1971) (Blackmun, J.); Rogers v. Bellei, 401 U.S. 815, 845 (1971) (Brennan, J.).
10. In some cases of postconviction review, of course, the claim will be that although the decision was right under governing standards when made, the law has since changed. But the present retroactivity standards of the Supreme Court, see, e.g., Williams v. United States, 401 U.S. 646 (1971), are essentially that decisions will be retroactively applied only if they create a substantial possibility that the question of guilt was never

---

* Since Judge Bazelon's lecture, the Supreme Court upheld the constitutionality of an Oregon law requiring the vote of at least ten out of twelve jurors in noncapital cases. Apodaca v. Oregon, 406 U.S. 404 (1972). But it later held that a six-person jury had to be unanimous to convict constitutionally. Burch v. Louisiana, 441 U.S. 130 (1979). EDITOR'S NOTE.

reliably determined to begin with. In such a case, of course, it is hardly possible to say that the defendant was in fact shown to be guilty beyond a reasonable doubt.

11. ABA Project on Minimum Standards for Criminal Justice, Standards Relating to Pleas of Guilty (Approved Draft 1968).
12. See, e.g., Scott v. United States, 419 F.2d 264 (D.C. Cir. 1969).
13. "I Have Nothing to Do with Justice," Life, Mar. 12, 1971, at 57, 62.
14. D. Newman, Conviction: The Determination of Guilt or Innocence Without Trial 3 (1966).
15. Specter, Book Review, 76 Yale L.J. 604, 605 (1967).
16. Report of the President's Comm'n on Crime in the District of Columbia Table 4, at 242 (1966).
17. Watson v. United States, 439 F.2d 442 (D.C. Cir. 1970).
18. 399 U.S. 267 (1970).
19. Scott v. United States, 427 F.2d 609, 610 (D.C. Cir. 1970).
20. R. Traynor, The Riddle of Harmless Error (1970).
21. B. Cardozo, Law and Literature 130 (1931).

Shirley M. Hufstedler

1. See, e.g., Frank, Historical Bases of the Federal Judicial System, 13 Law & Contemp. Prob. 1, 9–28 (1948).
2. U.S. Const. art. III, § 1.
3. Frankfurter, Distribution of Judicial Power Between United States and State Courts, 13 Cornell L. Rev. 499, 514–15 (1928).
4. See, e.g., W. Murphy, Congress and the Court (1962); Elliott, Court-Curbing Proposals in Congress, 33 Notre Dame Law. 597 (1958); McKay, Court, Congress, and Reapportionment, 63 Mich. L. Rev. 255 (1964); Warren, Legislative and Judicial Attacks on the Supreme Court of the United States—A History of the Twenty-Fifth Section of the Judiciary Act, 47 Am. L. Rev. 1 (1913).
5. Act of Sept. 24, 1789, ch. 20, § 9, 1 Stat. 76.
6. Id. § 11, 1 Stat. 78; see id. § 12, 1 Stat. 79 (also allowed removal to the federal courts of diversity actions and those actions in which an alien was a party, if the action might have been commenced there and satisfied the $500 jurisdictional amount requirement).
7. Id. § 14, 1 Stat. 81. See generally Warren, New Light on the History of the Federal Judiciary Act of 1789, 37 Harv. L. Rev. 49, 62–71 (1923).
8. Act of Mar. 2, 1793, ch. 22, § 5, 1 Stat. 334 (now 28 U.S.C. § 2283 (1970)).
9. Act of Feb. 13, 1801, ch. 4, § 11, 2 Stat. 92.
10. Act of Mar. 8, 1802, ch. 8, § 1, 2 Stat. 132.
11. Act of Mar. 3, 1815, ch. 94, § 6, 3 Stat. 233, and Act of Feb. 4, 1815, ch. 31, § 8, 3 Stat. 198 (now 28 U.S.C. § 1442 (1970)).
12. Act of Mar. 2, 1833, ch. 57, § 3, 4 Stat. 633 (now 28 U.S.C. § 1442 (1970)).
13. Act of Mar. 2, 1833, ch. 57, § 7, 4 Stat. 634.
14. Based on reported decisions, Warren suggests that less than 10 cases were removed from state courts under the 1833 Act. Warren, Federal and State Court Interference, 43 Harv. L. Rev. 345, 370 n.122 (1930).
15. In response to state court interference with political prisoners during

the Civil War, Congress empowered the president to suspend the writ of habeas corpus and to detain certain political prisoners without charge or trial, and to permit removal to federal courts of state court proceedings that attempted to thwart exercise of this extraordinary power. Act of Mar. 3, 1863, ch. 81, §§ 1, 5, 12 Stat. 755, 756. Congress gave the lower federal courts habeas jurisdiction over state prisoners in 1867. Act of Feb. 5, 1867, ch. 27, ch. 28, § 1, 14 Stat. 385, 386 (now 28 U.S.C. § 2241 (1970)).

16. Act of Apr. 9, 1866, ch. 31, § 3, 14 Stat. 27 (now 28 U.S.C. § 1443 (1970)).

17. Act of Feb. 28, 1871, ch. 99, §§ 15, 16, 16 Stat. 438 (repealed, Act. of Feb. 8, 1894, ch. 25, 28 Stat. 36). In 1868, removal from state courts to lower federal courts was authorized in actions against all corporations (except banks) organized under federal law where the defense was based on the Constitution, treaties or laws of the United States. Act of July 27, 1868, ch. 255, § 2, 15 Stat. 227.

18. Act of Mar. 3, 1875, ch. 137, §§ 1, 2, 18 Stat. 470 (now 28 U.S.C. §§1331, 1332, 1441 (1970)). The act gave federal courts concurrent jurisdiction with state courts and removal jurisdiction in actions commenced in state courts over all litigation "arising under the Constitution or laws of the United States." For the first time since the period 1801–02, the lower federal courts were given general federal question jurisdiction.

19. E.g., Federal Reserve Act, ch. 6, § 2, 38 Stat. 251 (1913), as amended 12 U.S.C. § 502 (1970); Banking Act of 1933 (Federal Deposit Insurance Corporation Act), ch. 89, § 8, 48 Stat. 168, as amended 12 U.S.C. § 1818 (1970); Clayton Act, ch. 323, §§ 4, 11, 15, 16, 38 Stat. 731, 734, 736, 737 (1914), as amended 15 U.S.C. §§ 15, 21, 25, 26 (1970); Federal Trade Commission Act, ch. 311, §§ 5, 9, 38 Stat. 719, 722 (1914), as amended 15 U.S.C. §§ 45(c), 45(d), 49 (1970); Federal Food, Drug, and Cosmetic Act, ch. 675, § 302, 52 Stat. 1043 (1938), as amended 21 U.S.C. § 332 (1970); Fair Labor Standards Act of 1938, ch. 676, §§ 10, 17, 52 Stat. 1065, 1069, as amended 29 U.S.C. §§ 210, 217 (1970); Communications Act of 1934 (Federal Communications Commission Act), ch. 652, § 401, 48 Stat. 1092, as amended 47 U.S.C. § 401 (1970).

20. See text accompanying notes 16–17 supra. Several other pieces of post–Civil War civil rights legislation augmented the jurisdiction of federal courts. E.g., Act of May 31, 1870, ch. 114, § 1, 16 Stat. 140, as amended 42 U.S.C. § 1971 (1970) (injunctive action to protect voting rights); Act of Apr. 9, 1866, ch. 31, § 1, 14 Stat. 27, as amended 42 U.S.C. § 1982 (1970) (equal property rights of citizens); Act of April 20, 1871, ch. 22 §§ 1, 6, 17 Stat. 13, 15, as amended 42 U.S.C. §§ 1983, 1986 (1970) (civil action for deprivation of civil rights and for failure to prevent conspiracy to interfere with civil rights); id. § 2, 17 Stat. 13, as amended 42 U.S.C. § 1985 (1970) (civil action for conspiracy to interfere with civil rights). At the present, 28 U.S.C. § 1343 (1970) is the codified basis for jurisdiction of civil rights actions in federal district courts.

21. The advent and growth of specialized administrative agencies of varying kinds, created with a mandate to address particularized social and economic ills, resulted in at least some initial removal of litigation from the federal courts.

A classic manifestation of congressional antipathy toward judicial

tinkering with its reform measures is the Norris-LaGuardia Act, Act of
Mar. 23, 1932, ch. 90, §§ 1–10, 47 Stat. 70, as amended 29 U.S.C.
§§101–10 (1970). The law enunciates a general jurisdictional standard:

> No court of the United States, as defined in this chapter, shall have jurisdiction to
> issue any restraining order or temporary or permanent injunction in a case in-
> volving or growing out of a labor dispute, except in strict conformity with the
> provisions of this chapter; nor shall any such restraining order or temporary or
> permanent injunction be issued contrary to the public policy declared in this
> chapter.

29 U.S.C. § 101 (1970). Congress's expression of this policy indicates its
evident concern that federal courts might not be favorably disposed
toward the plight of "the individual unorganized worker [who] is commonly helpless to exercise actual liberty of contract and to protect his
freedom of labor, and thereby to obtain acceptable terms and conditions
of employment." Id. § 102. The statute sets out in great detail in several
sections specific acts that shall not be the subject of equitable relief
against workers in federal courts. Id. §§ 103–05.

22. E.g., Act of July 25, 1958, Pub. L. No. 85–554, §§ 1, 2, 72 Stat. 415,
amending 28 U.S.C. §§ 1331, 1332 (1952) (raising the amount in controversy from $3,000 to $10,000); Act of Dec. 29, 1950, ch. 1189, 64
Stat. 1129, as amended 28 U.S.C. §§ 2341–51 (1970) (formerly 5 U.S.C.
§§ 1031–42 (1964)) (restricting three-judge district courts and substituting court of appeals review of almost all federal administrative decisions).

The Johnson Act of 1937, Act of Aug. 21, 1937, ch. 726, § 1, 50 Stat.
738, as amended 28 U.S.C. § 1341 (1970), stripped federal courts of
"jurisdiction of any suit to enjoin, suspend, or restrain the assessment,
levy, or collection of any tax imposed by or pursuant to the laws of any
State." The sensitive economic problems faced by a nation at war gave
rise to the Emergency Price Control Act of January 30, 1942, ch. 26, 56
Stat. 23. The act established an Emergency Court of Appeals to review
all challenges to actions of the Office of Price Administration (OPA).
Section 204(d) of the act limited judicial determinations of the validity
of OPA regulations to the specially constituted Emergency Court of
Appeals and the Supreme Court on certiorari. All other federal courts
were expressly deprived of jurisdiction to consider the validity of OPA
regulations or actions. The price control legislation was upheld in Yakus
v. United States, 321 U.S. 414 (1944).

Many of the result-oriented proposals to cut back federal jurisdiction
were defeated in Congress. These included Senator Jenner's bills to
limit federal jurisdiction in cases involving state subversive control legislation and state bar admissions. S. 3386, 85th Cong., 2d Sess. (1958);
S. 2646, 85th Cong., 1st Sess. (1957). Early versions of the Omnibus
Crime Control and Safe Streets Act of 1968 were designed to overturn
Miranda v. Arizona, 384 U.S. 436 (1966), and the McNabb–Mallory exclusionary rule (McNabb v. United States, 318 U.S. 332 (1943); Mallory
v. United States, 354 U.S. 449 (1957)). See Title II of amended S. 917,
90th Cong., 2d Sess. (1968); S. Rep. No. 1097, 90th Cong., 2d Sess.
(1968). The statute as enacted did not cut back jurisdiction, but it did try
to soften the impact of those decisions. See, e.g., 18 U.S.C. § 3501(c)
(1970). See also text accompanying note 4 supra.

Some commentators have argued that the Constitution acts as a check on Congress' power to withdraw federal court jurisdiction since there is a constitutionally prescribed minimum of federal jurisdiction. E.g., Hart, The Power of Congress to Limit the Jurisdiction of Federal Courts: An Exercise in Dialectic, 66 Harv. L. Rev. 1362 (1953). It would seem, however, that this proposition has not been put to a clear-cut test. 1 W. Barron & A. Holtzoff, Federal Practice and Federal Procedure § 21, at 91 (rev. ed. 1960).

23. In Chisolm v. Georgia, 2 U.S. (2 Dall.) 419 (1793), the Supreme Court gave the lower federal courts the power to assert their jurisdiction over unwilling state governments. At issue was whether the federal courts might force the state to pay compensation for certain property expropriated from Loyalist sympathizers during the Revolution. The adoption of the Eleventh Amendment in 1798 quickly repealed the authority to do so.

Shortly after the turn of the nineteenth century, the Court decided Osborn v. United States Bank, 22 U.S. (9 Wheat.) 738, 816 (1824), in which it interpreted the Bank's authority " 'to sue and be sued . . . in all state courts . . . and in any circuit court in the United States.' " The provision was included in the legislation incorporating the Bank of the United States in an amendment to the Judiciary Act. The chartering law gave the federal courts jurisdiction to enjoin the collection of state taxes on the Bank. In *Osborn* the Court avoided the Eleventh Amendment on the theory that the state officials who sought to collect the unconstitutional tax were being sued in their individual capacity. In 1824, Andrew Jackson campaigned for president against the Bank of the United States and in 1826, the case of the Governor of Georgia v. Juan Madrazo, 26 U.S. (1 Pet.) 110 (1828), repudiated the notion that state officials acting in their official capacity might be personally subject to suit in federal courts despite the Eleventh Amendment.

24. 62 U.S. (21 How.) 506 (1859). The popular name is a misnomer. Booth was not a fugitive slave; he was a person who had been convicted for aiding and abetting the escape of a slave. Booth had been granted habeas relief by the Wisconsin Supreme Court.

25. Id. at 514–26.

26. The following cases are illustrative:

In Gelpcke v. City of Dubuque, 68 U.S. (1 Wall.) 175 (1864), the lower federal courts were authorized to enforce bonds issued by a city to finance railroad construction despite the state supreme court's declaration that the bonds were void under state law, State ex rel. Burlington & M.R.R.R. v. County of Wapello, 13 Iowa 388 (1862). *Gelpcke* was a diversity action brought in the Iowa District Court by a New York citizen to enforce bonds issued in the interim; the Supreme Court held the bonds valid and enforceable by the district court. The Court's reasoning is not entirely clear. Portions of the opinion seem to indicate that reversal by the Iowa Supreme Court was a violation of the contract clause of the Constitution. 68 U.S. (1 Wall.) at 206. Subsequent decisions by the Supreme Court have interpreted *Gelpcke* as an exercise in federal common law under Swift v. Tyson, 41 U.S. (16 Pet.) 1 (1842), or as an attempt to divine state law in an unsettled area. See Tidal Oil Co. v. Flanagan, 263 U.S. 444, 451–52 (1924), and Quirk & Wein, A Short

Constitutional History of Entities Commonly Known as Authorities, 56 Cornell L. Rev. 521, 548–50 (1971). *Gelpcke* did not explain how the district court could compel the city to honor the bonds.

In Tennessee v. Davis, 100 U.S. 257 (1879), the constitutionality of removing state criminal prosecutions against federal officers for acts committed in the course of executing federal law was upheld, and the lower federal courts were empowered to conduct a criminal trial applying state law. In the Pacific Railroad Removal Cases, 115 U.S. 1 (1885), the Court held that every action by or against a federally chartered corporation arose under the laws of the United States and was thus within federal question jurisdiction granted the federal courts in 1875.

27. 209 U.S. 123 (1908).
28. Mr. Justice Frankfurter has been credited with originating the phrase. See Note, The Chilling Effect in Constitutional Law, 69 Colum. L. Rev. 803 n.1 (1969). In fact, "chilling effect" is a paraphrase of Mr. Justice Frankfurter's expression in Wieman v. Updegraff, 344 U.S. 183, 195 (1952) (concurring opinion): "[A]n unmistakable tendency to chill that free play of the spirit which all teachers ought especially to cultivate and practice."
29. North Carolina Senator Overman was one of the most outspoken, vociferous opponents of "allowing one little federal judge to stand up against the governor and the legislature and the attorney-general of the State and say, 'This act is unconstitutional.' " 45 Cong. Rec. 7256 (1910); see also 42 Cong. Rec. 4847, 4853 (1908) (Senators Overman and Bacon). Senator Overman introduced in 1908 a bill to forbid all federal injunctions against the enforcement of state laws. 42 Cong. Rec. 4848–49 (1908). Two years later the House passed a very similar bill. 46 Cong. Rec. 313, 316 (1910); cf. S. 3732, 60th Cong., 1st Sess., 42 Cong. Rec. 4846–59 (1908). A general discussion of the historical backdrop for the passage of three-judge court legislation can be found in Currie, The Three-Judge District Court in Constitutional Litigation, 32 U. Chi. L. Rev. 1, 3–12 (1964).
30. Act of June 18, 1910, ch. 309 § 17, 36 Stat. 557 (now 28 U.S.C. §§ 1257, 2283, 2284 (1970)).
31. Klinger v. Missouri, 80 U.S. (13 Wall.) 257 (1872). Three years later the Court decided Murdock v. City of Memphis, 87 U.S. (20 Wall.) 590 (1875), holding that it would not decide state issues when it reviewed federal questions determined by state courts. Although *Murdock* has been criticized as misinterpreting the Judiciary Act of 1867, it is generally conceded that the conclusion was administratively necessary to permit the Court to handle its workload. See Note, Evasion of Supreme Court Mandates in Cases Remanded to State Courts Since 1941, 67 Harv. L. Rev. 1251, 1252 (1954).
32. 100 U.S. 313 (1879).
33. The Warren Court could hardly be said to have been insensitive to civil rights causes. Its refusal to accept Congress' invitation to expand civil rights removal jurisdiction (Act of July 2, 1964, Pub. L. No. 88–352, § 901, 78 Stat. 266 (codified at 28 U.S.C. § 1447(d) (1970)); see 110 Cong. Rec. 2770, 6551 (1964) and its adherence to the restrictive reading of the Removal Act begun in *Rives* is largely attributable to its concern about overloading its own docket and that of lower federal courts.

As Mr. Justice Stewart said, writing for the majority in City of Greenwood v. Peacock, 384 U.S. 808 (1966):

> It is worth contemplating what the result would be if the strained interpretation of § 1443(1) urged by the individual petitioners were to prevail. In the fiscal year 1963 there were 14 criminal removal cases of all kinds in the entire Nation; in fiscal 1964 there were 43. The present case was decided by the Court of Appeals for the Fifth Circuit on June 22, 1965, just before the end of the fiscal year. In that year, fiscal 1965, there were 1,079 criminal removal cases in the Fifth Circuit alone. But this phenomenal increase is no more than a drop in the bucket of what could reasonably be expected in the future.

384 U.S. at 832 (footnote omitted).

34. See, e.g., Prentis v. Atlantic Coast Line Co., 211 U.S. 210 (1908) (exhaustion of state administrative remedies); Barney v. City of New York, 193 U.S. 430 (1904) (abstention); Ex parte Royall, 117 U.S. 241 (1886) (exhaustion of state remedies prior to federal habeas). See also C. Wright, Law of Federal Courts § 49, at 186–88 (2d ed. 1970); Wright, The Abstention Doctrine Reconsidered, 37 Texas L. Rev. 815 (1959); Note, The Abstention Doctrine: Some Recent Developments, 46 Tul. L. Rev. 762, 762–65 (1972); Note, The Abstention Doctrine, 40 Tul. L. Rev. 578 (1966).

35. Act of Mar. 3, 1891 (Evarts Act), ch. 517, 26 Stat. 826.

36. Act of Feb. 13, 1925, ch. 229, 43 Stat. 936; see Frankfurter, supra note 3, at 503–04.

37. Address by Chief Justice Warren E. Burger, Report on Problems of the Judiciary, before The American Bar Ass'n, Aug. 14, 1972, in 58 A.B.A.J. 1049 (1972) [hereinafter Burger Address]; see New Ways to Speed Up Justice: Interview with Chief Justice Warren E. Burger, U.S. News & World Report, Aug. 21, 1972, at 38–39 [hereinafter Burger Interview]; N.Y. Times, Aug. 15, 1972, § 1, at 1, col. 1.

38. Burger Address, supra note 37, at 1053; see Burger Interview, supra note 37.

39. See F. Frankfurter & J. Landis, The Business of the Supreme Court 107 (1927); Carrington, Crowded Dockets and the Courts of Appeals: The Threat to the Function of Review and the National Law, 82 Harv. L. Rev. 542, 552–53 (1969); Hart, Foreword: The Time Chart of the Justices, The Supreme Court, 1958 Term, 73 Harv. L. Rev. 84 (1959); Wechsler, Toward Neutral Principles of Constitutional Law, 73 Harv. L. Rev. 1 (1959).

40. E.g., Burger Address, supra note 37, at 1049–50; Carrington, supra note 39, at 543–49; Hufstedler, New Blocks for Old Pyramids: Reshaping the Judicial System, 44 S. Cal. L. Rev. 901, 908–09 (1971); R. Kirks, Director, Administrative Office of the U.S. Courts, Management Statistics for the United States Courts (1972) (particularly the final chart, "United States District Courts: National Statistics Profile"); Administrative Office of the U.S. Courts, Annual Report of the Director, A-1 (1972) [hereinafter 1972 Annual Report].

Fiscal year 1972 witnessed a continued expansion of the caseload of the United States Courts of Appeals. With the number of cases filed and terminated reaching new highs, the backlog of pending cases also rose to a record level as filings exceeded terminations by 707 cases. During the 11-year period ending in fiscal year 1972, the number of cases filed, terminated and pending each increased by at least 200 percent, with pending cases rising almost 228 percent. 1972 Annual Report, supra at II-1.

41. 1972 Annual Report, supra note 40, at A-12 to A-21, A-92.

42. Chief Justice Burger urged the abolition of three-judge courts in his 1972 American Bar Association Address. Burger Address, supra note 37, at 1053. The American Law Institute has endorsed a proposal that would narrow the availability of such courts, but would not abolish them. ALI, Study of the Division of Jurisdiction Between State And Federal Courts § 1374, at 53–54, 316–26 (1969). During the 1971 term (through February 1972), slightly less than 5% of the cases docketed with the Supreme Court were appeals from three-judge district courts. Letter to the author from the Federal Judicial Center, Aug. 25, 1972.

43. Through February 10, 1972, of the 1971 term, a total of 2,926 cases were docketed with the Court. Of these, 539 were appeals or petitions for certiorari from state courts in criminal cases and 97 were petitions to review state court habeas decisions. (Statistics furnished to the author by the Federal Judicial Center.)

44. See, e.g., R. Sokol, A Handbook of Federal Habeas Corpus (1965); Bator, Finality in Criminal Law and Federal Habeas Corpus for State Prisoners, 76 Harv. L. Rev. 441, 483–84 (1963); Reitz, Federal Habeas Corpus: Impact of An Abortive State Proceeding, 74 Harv. L. Rev. 1315 (1961).

45. The Federalist No. 82, at 556–57 (J. Cooke ed. 1961) (A. Hamilton).

46. See text accompanying note 40 supra.

47. The Supreme Court has been criticized for its opaque pronouncements summarily affirming and reversing cases. See, e.g., Bickel & Wellington, Legislative Purpose and the Judicial Process: The Lincoln Mills Case, 71 Harv. L. Rev. 1, 3 (1957); Brown, Foreword: Process of Law, The Supreme Court, 1957 Term, 72 Harv. L. Rev. 77 (1958); Harper & Etherington, What the Supreme Court Did Not Do During the 1950 Term, 100 U. Pa. L. Rev. 354, 355–56 (1951); Harper & Rosenthal, What the Supreme Court Did Not Do In the 1949 Term—An Appraisal of Certiorari, 99 U. Pa. L. Rev. 293, 297–99 (1950); Kurland, Foreword: "Equal in Origin and Equal in Title to the Legislative and Executive Branches of the Government," The Supreme Court, 1963 Term, 78 Harv. L. Rev. 143, 175 (1964); Note, Supreme Court Per Curiam Practice: A Critique, 69 Harv. L. Rev. 707 (1956).

Although there is justification for the criticism, it is hard to see what the Court can do about it given its staggering caseload. A new national court will be faced with the same dilemma unless it has a sufficiently manageable burden to permit it time to articulate the bases for its decisions.

48. Carrington, supra note 39, at 612–17. Many of the proposals envision creation of specialized national courts. See, e.g., Friendly, A Federal Court of Administrative Appeals?, 74 Case & Com., Mar.–Apr. 1969, at 23; Griswold, The Need for a Court of Tax Appeals, 57 Harv. L. Rev. 1153 (1944); Wiener, Federal Regional Courts: A Solution for the Certiorari Dilemma, 49 A.B.A.J. 1169 (1963).

49. Unlike the existing certification procedure under 28 U.S.C. § 1254(3) (1970) (authorizing certification from a United States court of appeals to

the Supreme Court), the proposal contemplates certification of the entire case rather than certification of one or more legal issues in the case; and acceptance of certification is discretionary rather than obligatory.

50. See Hufstedler, supra note 40, at 909–10; cf. Hufstedler & Hufstedler, Improving the California Appellate Pyramid, 46 L.A.B. Bull. 275 (1971).

51. See, e.g., R. Jackson, The Supreme Court in the American System of Government 38 (1955); Currie, The Federal Courts and the American Law Institute (Pt. 1), 36 U. Chi. L. Rev. 1 (1968); Frankfurter, A Note on Diversity Jurisdiction—In Reply to Professor Yntema, 79 U. Pa. L. Rev. 1097 (1931); Frankfurter, supra note 3; Wechsler, Federal Jurisdiction and the Revision of the Judicial Code, 13 Law & Contemp. Prob. 216, 234 (1948).

The opinion is not unanimous. See, e.g., Moore & Weckstein, Diversity Jurisdiction: Past, Present and Future, 43 Texas L. Rev. 1 (1964); Wright, The Federal Courts and the Nature and Quality of State Law, 13 Wayne L. Rev. 317 (1967); Yntema, The Jurisdiction of the Federal Courts in Controversies Between Citizens of Different States, 19 A.B.A.J. 71 (1933). (These writers argue for retention and even expansion of diversity jurisdiction.)

The American Law Institute's proposal splits the difference, cutting diversity in half. See Wright, Restructuring Federal Jurisdiction: The American Law Institute Proposals, 26 Wash. & Lee L. Rev. 185 (1969).

52. See Friendly, The Historic Basis of Diversity Jurisdiction: 41 Harv. L. Rev. 483 (1928); Summers, Analysis of Factors That Influence Choice of Forum in Diversity Cases, 47 Ia. L. Rev. 933 (1962).

53. 41 U.S. (16 Pet.) 1 (1842).

54. See Kennedy, Federal Diversity Jurisdiction, 10 Kan. L. Rev. 47 (1961).

55. See, e.g., C. Wright, Law of Federal Courts § 23, at 78 (2d ed. 1970).

56. See 18 U.S.C. § 3771 (1970).

57. A useful overview of the draft of the new Federal Criminal Code appears in National Commission on Reform of Federal Criminal Laws, Study Draft of a New Criminal Code xxvi–xxxii (1970).

58. Id. at xlvii–lix; Schwartz, Federal Criminal Jurisdiction and Prosecutors' Discretion, 13 Law & Contemp. Prob. 64, 73–77 (1948).

59. Warren, Federal Criminal Laws and the State Courts, 38 Harv. L. Rev. 545 (1925). The following observation, made over 47 years ago, must appear ironic in light of the burgeoning caseload that overwhelms the federal courts today:

> The present congested condition of the dockets of the Federal Courts and the small prospect of any relief to the heavily burdened Federal Judiciary, so long as Congress continues, every year, to expand the scope of the body of Federal crimes, renders it desirable that consideration be given to the possibility of a return to the practice which was in vogue in the early days of the Federal judicial system [state court trials of federal crimes].

Id. Mr. Justice Story's dictum in Prigg v. Pennsylvania, 41 U.S. (16 Pet.) 539, 622 (1842), that federal law could not require state courts to enforce the Federal Fugitive Slave Act, Act of Feb. 12, 1793, ch. 7, 1 Stat. 302, has since been thoroughly undermined. In Mondou v. New York, N.H. & H.R.R., 223 U.S. 1 (1912), the Court held that Congress could require the state court to enforce federal rights arising under the Federal Employers' Liability Act, Act of Apr. 22, 1908, ch. 149, 35 Stat. 65, as amended 45 U.S.C. §§ 51–60 (1970), and in Testa v. Katt, 330 U.S. 386 (1947), the Court held that the states were required to enforce the penal damages provisions of the Federal Emergency Price Control Act, Act of June 30, 1942, ch. 26, § 205(e), 56 Stat. 34, as amended Act of June 30, 1944, ch. 325, § 108, 58 Stat. 640. The Court's opinion by Mr. Justice Black in *Testa* specifically pointed out that under the supremacy clause state courts could be required to enforce federal law whether the relief sought was deemed civil or penal in nature. 330 U.S. at 391.

Of course, practical problems would arise if a federal trial were conducted in a state court, but none is more complex than the problems inherent in a state prosecution removed to the federal courts under the Civil Rights Removal Act, 28 U.S.C. § 1443 (1970).

60. For example, the primary purpose of the Federal Fugitive Felon Act, 18 U.S.C. § 1073 (1970), was to provide a jurisdictional basis for federal law enforcement agencies to assist state authorities in capturing accused felons who flee from state jurisdiction. When the fugitives are captured, they are usually turned over to state authorities for prosecution. Schwartz, supra note 58, at 74.

61. 1972 Annual Report, supra note 40, at II-63 to II-64.

62. ABA Project on Minimum Standards for Criminal Justice, Standards Relating to Discovery and Procedure Before Trial 114–23, 135–37 (1969); see Preliminary Draft of Proposed Amendments to the Federal Rules of Criminal Procedure for United States District Courts 31–32 (1970); cf. 18 U.S.C. § 3500 (1970); Fed. R. Crim. P. 12, 16, 17.1; Miller, The Omnibus Hearing—An Experiment in Federal Criminal Discovery, 5 San Diego L. Rev. 293 (1968).

63. 28 U.S.C. § 2255 (1970).

64. If the procedure proved effective in federal criminal cases, it could be adapted to federal habeas review of state criminal proceedings.

65. Bator, supra note 44, at 444–53.

66. 312 U.S. 496 (1941).

67. Rooker v. Fidelity Trust Co., 263 U.S. 413 (1923). Mr. Justice Van Devanter, writing for the Court, said:

> If the constitutional questions stated in the [complaint] actually arose in the cause, it was the province and duty of the state courts to decide them; and their decision, whether right or wrong, was an exercise of jurisdiction. If the decision was wrong, that did not make the judgment void, but merely left it open to reversal or modification in an appropriate and timely appellate proceeding. Unless and until so reversed or modified, it would be an effective and conclusive adjudication. . . . Under the legislation of Congress, no court of the United States other than this Court could entertain a proceeding to reverse or modify the judgment for errors of that character. . . . To do so would be an exercise of appellate jurisdiction. The jurisdiction possessed by the District Courts is strictly original. . . .

Compare Louisiana Power & Light Co. v. Thibodaux, 360 U.S. 25 (1959) (an eminent domain case in which the district court was directed to abstain and to retain jurisdiction), with Martin v. Creasy, 360 U.S. 219 (1959) (an eminent domain case in which the district court was directed to abstain and to dismiss). Also compare Askew v. Hargrave, 401 U.S. 476 (1971) (a challenge to state school financing in which the district court was directed to defer and to retain jurisdiction), with Stainback v. Mo Hock Ke Lok Po, 336 U.S. 368 (1949) (a challenge to local law forbidding foreign language education in which the district court was directed to defer and to dismiss). See generally Note, Judicial Abstention from the Exercise of Federal Jurisdiction, 59 Colum. L. Rev. 749, 772–76 (1959).

68. See Florida ex rel. Hawkins v. Board of Control, 355 U.S. 839 (1957), a case arising from a black student's denial of admission to the University of Florida Law School solely because of his race. He unsuccessfully sought mandamus in the Florida Supreme Court. He then petitioned the United States Supreme Court for certiorari. The Court denied certiorari "without prejudice to the petitioner's seeking relief in an appropriate United States District Court." He was finally granted some relief in a civil rights action brought in a district court in Florida. The possible res judicata effect of the Florida state court decision was not mentioned. Hawkins v. Board of Control, 162 F. Supp. 851 (N.D. Fla. 1958).

If the district court retains jurisdiction and if the litigant adequately protests state court decision of his federal questions, the litigant is not foreclosed by a state decision of his federal questions from litigating those questions upon his return to the abstaining federal court. England v. Louisiana State Bd. of Medical Examiners, 375 U.S. 411, 415–17 (1964).

69. The nine-year federal–state badminton match played in the courts by the *Spector* litigants is a well-known example. See Spector Motor Service, Inc. v. O'Connor, 340 U.S. 602, 603–05 (1951). *Spector* is not a rare phenomenon. See C. Wright, Law of Federal Courts § 52, at 198 (2d ed. 1970).

70. 400 U.S. 433 (1971).

71. 380 U.S. 479 (1965).

72. 42 U.S.C. § 1983 (1970).

73. 389 U.S. 241 (1967).

74. 401 U.S. 37 (1971).

75. Id. at 43.

76. Id. at 44.

77. Id. at 55 (footnote omitted).

78. Id. at 55 n. 2.

79. See Rooker v. Fidelity Trust Co., 263 U.S. 413 (1923). See also the history of England v. Louisiana State Bd. of Medical Examiners, 375 U.S. 411 (1964), recited in the opinion of the three-judge district court. 194 F. Supp. 521, 521–22 (E.D. La. 1961).

80. If the litigant remitted to state court yields his federal claims to state adjudication without express protest, he can be deemed to have elected to forgo his right to return to the district court. See England v. Louisiana State Bd. of Medical Examiners, 375 U.S. 411, 417–22 (1964).

81. Osborn v. United States Bank, 22 U.S. (9 Wheat.) 738, 822 (1824). Mr. Justice Story recognized the same dangers in Martin v. Hunter's Lessee, 14 U.S. (1 Wheat.) 304, 348–49 (1816).

82. 401 U.S. 66 (1971).

83. Id. at 69–71, citing Great Lakes Dredge & Dock Co. v. Huffman, 319 U.S. 293 (1943).

84. When a federal court is deciding whether to abstain, it is making an explicit, although often unarticulated, choice about the appropriate allocation of judicial workload. If any rational basis exists for shifting particular cases between federal and state courts, it must be that, on balance, there is something about the facts or issues of the controversy that is more conducive to determination by a given system. Otherwise, we would be distributing cases without any assurance that a more satisfactory allocation of scarce judicial resources will result. What is needed is a more refined analysis of the crucial differences between federal and state courts and the kinds of cases that are best matched with these functional differences.

Obviously, no self-executing formula can be devised; conflicting factors can be expected to pull each way within a given case. Furthermore, different factors require varying weights or coefficients. For now, we can sketch only some of the considerations involved in the equation. Those favoring transfer to a state court system may include: state court expertise to resolve novel or unsettled state law questions; familiarity with local needs and policies—e.g., natural resources, transportation and health care; involvement of state administrative agencies or process (cf. 28 U.S.C. §§ 1341, 1342 (1970)); undisputed facts not requiring federal fact-finding to protect federal rights; and predominance of state law issues.

Factors favoring federal court disposition may include: immediacy or urgency of the situation, such as a pending election; pressing necessity for interim relief; public as opposed to private suit—e.g., where the state is a party; predominance of federal issues, especially constitutional ones; federal expertise; and protection of important federal policies, especially where uniformity is necessary and a broad class of persons is allegedly affected or swift enforcement of federal rights is required—e.g., first amendment liberties and equal protection.

85. Immediacy suggests several different lines of inquiry. It might include Mr. Justice Brennan's distinction between threatened and pending state court proceedings. Younger v. Harris, 401 U.S. 37, 56–58 (1971) (concurring opinion). It might involve injunctive versus declaratory relief. In some instances, the question will be the appropriateness of federal grants of preconduct review. Likewise, as Mr. Justice Stewart suggests, the propriety of federal intrusion may be determined largely by whether a civil or criminal case is involved. Id. at 55 (concurring opinion).

The substantiality prong of the inquiry focuses on the effect of the challenged law (e.g., for overbreadth) on the individual parties rather than on the status (timeframe) of the proceedings. This may be compared to what has been termed the "conduct" test. See The Supreme Court, 1970 Term, 85 Harv. L. Rev. 3, 309–10 (1971). This would most often arise in the setting of a challenge to the constitutionality of a statute "as applied" to the individual litigant.

Substantiality can also be measured on a societal level, i.e., in terms of the interests of nonparties. A challenge grounded in an unconstitutional "on its face" analysis poses, for example, serious questions of a societal chilling effect inhibiting the exercise of rights other than merely those of the immediate parties.

Substantiality should also take account of the admitted differences between criminal and civil proceedings. Although any per se rule in this entire analytical process should be eschewed, the invocation of federal power in a state civil proceeding would, in most instances, carry a much heavier burden of justification.

A key consideration here is to recognize there is necessary interplay between the immediacy and substantiality factors. Thus, although state action may be only threatened (as opposed to preconduct or pending), there may be a heightened need for federal intervention if the threatened proceeding is criminal and involves interests of a community-wide or national nature such as racial discrimination in housing or education.

86. Our concepts of ordered liberty and fundamental fairness necessarily change over time. This factor acknowledges the importance attached to the amenities of procedural due process in the development and adjudication of basic constitutional issues. In many instances, it will border on divining the intangible, although there are admittedly some objective criteria for gauging this factor (e.g., past state judicial treatment of this or related issues and state doctrines of appellate review and collateral attack).

If, on balance, the federal court concludes that a full, fair and expeditious opportunity to air the federal constitutional issues will not be provided, this should terminate the investigation for several reasons: (1) Federal constitutional rights cannot be adequately presented if the state processes for their resolution are fatally defective; (2) there is no value to postponement because it is more likely than not that the issues will again be presented to the federal courts; and (3) in terms of the cost/benefit analysis implicit in the balancing of state and federal interests, rarely will there be a situation in which any supposed state interests will overshadow the federal concern in checking diminution of constitutional rights and preventing potential loss of a federal forum.

87. This cost/benefit assessment may require a threshold articulation of several paramount policy considerations underlying the balancing process. For example, there is a federal judicial interest calling for special vigilance in the protection of civil rights. However, there is also a potentially seductive pitfall here: exclusively bottoming the analysis on some hierarchy of constitutional rights (e.g., that First Amendment rights are more important than others). Such per se rules should be steadfastly avoided.

There is also a federal interest in affording an efficient, responsive forum for adjudicating cases truly national in scope of interest that affect basic constitutional rights. Likewise, if there is no guaranty of a later federal forum, the federal court should not abstain.

There is an obvious state interest in prosecuting ordinary local crimes. Conversely, the offense to state interests is likely to be less in a civil proceeding where the state is not a party. A state, however, has no legitimate interest in bad faith prosecution or harassment aimed solely at discouraging the exercise or vindication of federal constitutional rights.

If, on balance, the net result is a minimal or attenuated clash between the interests—a false conflicts situation—the state interest should predominate. Thus, absent any other considerations, abstention would be appropriate. When the federal–state collision is obvious or inevitable, the scale must tip in favor of finding no overwhelming policy for federal abstention. There would most likely be no net saving of federal judicial resources and the very real prospect of vitiation of constitutional liberties.

James L. Oakes

1. See, e.g., R. Berger, Government by Judiciary 249–418 (1977); Hazard, The Supreme Court as a Legislature, 64 Cornell L. Rev. 1 (1978); Jones, The Brooding Omnipresence of Constitutional Law, 4 Vt. L. Rev. 1 (1979).
2. The terms are constantly used, however. See Glekel, The Burger Court and Traditional Activism, N.Y.L.J., Oct. 16, 1978, at 1, col. 2 ("the Burger Court, although dominated by very different ideological predilections, is no less interventionist than the Warren Court"). Ronald Dworkin has demonstrated how the terminology of "strict" and "liberal" construction fails to distinguish the separate issues of (1) faithfulness in adhering to the intent of the Founders and (2) breadth of view of the moral rights of individuals against societies. R. Dworkin, Taking Rights Seriously 133 (1977).
3. G. Wood, The Creation of the American Republic, 1776–1787, at 152 (1969) (quoting 1 C. Montesquieu. The Spirit of Laws 174 (T. Nugent trans. 1873) (1st French ed. Geneva 1748)).
4. B. Bailyn, The Ideological Origins of the American Revolution 58 (1967).
5. Id. at 55.
6. The Federalist No. 10 (J. Madison), at 129, 135 (B. Wright ed. 1961).
7. R. Neustadt, Presidential Power 101 (1976) (emphasis in original); see Jones, supra note 1, at 29–33; Nelson, The Eighteenth Century Background of John Marshall's Constitutional Jurisprudence, 76 Mich. L. Rev. 893, 902–04 (1978).
8. My own statement of that role is more fully set forth in an unpublished manuscript, J. Oakes, The Role of Courts in Government Today (Arthur E. Whittemore Lecture, Marlboro, Vt., Apr. 27, 1978) (on file at New York University Law Review).
9. Letter from Thomas Jefferson to James Madison (Mar. 15, 1789), reprinted in 5 The Writings of Thomas Jefferson 81 (P. Ford ed. 1895).
10. Id.
11. Address by James Madison, House of Representatives (June 8, 1789), reprinted in Mind of the Founder 224 (M. Meyers ed. 1973) [hereinafter Madison Address].
12. Other institutions were also to exercise "checking" functions. See Blasi, The Checking Value in First Amendment Theory, 1977 Am. B. Foundation Research J. 521, 527, 531–44.
13. The Federalist No. 78 (A. Hamilton), at 491 (B. Wright ed. 1961). Hamilton was referring directly to Montesquieu's statement. "Of the three powers above mentioned, the judiciary is in some measure next to nothing." 1 C. Montesquieu, supra note 3, at 178, quoted in The Federalist No. 78 (A. Hamilton), at 491 n. * (B. Wright ed. 1961).

14. The Federalist No. 78 (A. Hamilton), at 491 (B. Wright ed. 1961). This sentiment was echoed by Madison in his letter of May 6, 1821, to Judge Spencer Roane of the Virginia Supreme Court of Appeals in respect to McCulloch v. Maryland, 17 U.S. (4 Wheat.) 316 (1819). Mind of the Founder, supra note 11, at 464 ("whatever may be the latitude of Jurisdiction assumed by the Judicial Power of the U.S. it is less formidable to the reserved sovereignty of the States than the latitude of power which it has assigned to the National Legislature"). Judge, later Justice, Roane was Marshall's Virginia nemesis who opposed judicial review at the time of McCulloch v. Maryland. See G. Gunther, John Marshall's Defense of McCulloch v. Maryland 106–54 (1969).
15. The Federalist No. 78 (A. Hamilton), at 491 (B. Wright ed. 1961).
16. U.S. Const. art. III, § 1; see The Federalist No. 79 (A. Hamilton), at 497–99 (B. Wright ed. 1961).
17. See Marbury v. Madison, 5 U.S. (1 Cranch) 137, 177–80 (1803).
18. See J. Main, The Antifederalists 124–25 (1961). Their concerns were to some extent justified by McCulloch v. Maryland, 17 U.S. (4 Wheat.) 316 (1819). See Mind of the Founder, supra note 11, at 456–69; G. Gunther, supra note 14, at 52–77, 106–54.
19. Compare Thayer, The Origin and Scope of the American Doctrine of Constitutional Law, 7 Harv. L. Rev. 129, 136–37 (1893) and Bickel, The Original Understanding and the Segregation Decision, 69 Harv. L. Rev. 1, 3–4, 58–59 (1955) with L. Levy, Judicial Review, History, and Democracy, in Judgments 24, 35 (1972) [hereinafter Levy, Judicial Review] and Rostow, The Democratic Character of Judicial Review, 66 Harv. L. Rev. 193, 193–210 (1952).
20. The Federalist No. 78 (A. Hamilton), at 494 (B. Wright ed. 1961).
21. See J. Main, supra note 18, at 125, 158–60.
22. Id. at 160.
23. Id. at 160–61.
24. Madison had previously expressed doubts about the value of enumerating rights. See Letter from James Madison to Thomas Jefferson (Oct. 17, 1788), reprinted in 5 Writings of James Madison 271–72 (G. Hunt ed. 1904); B. Bailyn, supra note 4, at 189 n.30.
25. Madison Address, supra note 11, at 220.
26. Id. at 221.
27. See Goldberg v. Kelly, 397 U.S. 254, 266 (1970).
28. Compare Village of Belle Terre v. Boraas, 416 U.S. 1, 7 (1974) with id. at 15–17 (Marshall, J., dissenting).
29. See R. Dworkin, supra note 2, at 131–49.
30. The Federalist No. 10 (J. Madison), at 133 (B. Wright ed. 1961). Justice Jackson, in his colorful way, wrote perhaps the ultimate judicial formulation of this idea in West Virginia State Bd. of Educ. v. Barnette, 319 U.S. 624 (1943), in which the Court held that requiring public school students to salute the flag violates the First Amendment:

> The very purpose of a Bill of Rights was to withdraw certain subjects from the vicissitudes of political controversy, to place them beyond the reach of majorities and officials and to establish them as legal principles to be applied by the courts. One's right to life, liberty, and property, to free speech, a free press, freedom of worship and assembly, and other fundamental rights may not be submitted to vote; they depend on the outcome of no elections.

Id. at 638.

31. Here it may be worthwhile to acknowledge my own awareness of the importance of property rights, not only in the minds of the framers, but also in the Constitution itself. Overreaction, perhaps, to the reasoning employed in Lochner v. New York, 198 U.S. 45, 53 (1905), see Note, Fornication, Cohabitation, and the Constitution, 77 Mich. L. Rev. 252, 257–59 (1978), for too long resulted in a failure to clarify their importance in an actual decision, see L. Tribe, American Constitutional Law § 8-2, at 435 (1978). This failure was remedied in Lynch v. Household Fin. Corp., 405 U.S. 538, 551–52 (1972), followed by the opinion in McClendon v. Rosetti, 460 F.2d 111, 112–13 (2d Cir. 1972) (Oakes, J.).

32. See Walzer, Nervous Liberals, N.Y. Rev. Books, Oct. 11, 1979, at 5.

33. Black, The Bill of Rights, 35 N.Y.U.L. Rev. 865, 880 (1960).

34. Letter from James Madison to Spencer Roane (Sept. 2, 1819), reprinted in Mind of the Founder 458 (M. Meyers ed. 1973).

35. Geoffrey Hazard has hazarded the political and epistemological arguments against case-by-case legal decisionmaking, as opposed to the process of generalization involved in legislation. Hazard, supra note 1, at 11–12, but answers them in his own moderate way, directing us to the "Scylla of undue breadth" and "the Charybdis of merely ad hoc decisions," id. at 13.

36. Ashwander v. TVA, 297 U.S. 288, 346–48 (1936) (Brandeis, J., concurring). The seven rules are refusing to decide constitutional issues (1) in "friendly" litigation, (2) before resolution of the issue is necessary, (3) in a broader manner than the facts warrant, (4) when the case may be decided on other grounds, (5) when the plaintiff has failed to show injury, (6) when the plaintiff has benefited from the statute at issue, or (7) when the constitutional issue may be avoided by statutory construction.

37. See Railroad Comm'n v. Pullman Co., 312 U.S. 496, 500–01 (1941); Hufstedler, Comity and the Constitution, 47 N.Y.U.L. Rev. 841, 860–66.

38. See B. Cardozo, The Nature of the Judicial Process, in Selected Writings of Benjamin Nathan Cardozo 107, 168–83 (1967) [hereinafter Cardozo, The Judicial Process].

39. See Chayes, The Role of the Judge in Public Law Litigation, 89 Harv. L. Rev. 1281, 1282–83, 1302–04 (1976); text accompanying notes 209–37 infra.

40. See, e.g., Gladstone Realtors v. Village of Bellwood, 441 U.S. 91, 100, 113–15 (1979); Singleton v. Wulff, 428 U.S. 106, 113–19 (1976) (plurality opinion); United States v. Scrap, 412 U.S. 669, 686–88 (1973). But see Warth v. Seldin, 422 U.S. 490, 500 (1975); Sierra Club v. Morton, 405 U.S. 727, 738–40 (1972).

41. See Cascade Natural Gas Corp. v. El Paso Natural Gas Co., 386 U.S. 129, 133–36 (1967). For broadened concepts of the importance of the intervenor's role, see United States v. Board of Educ., 605 F.2d 573, 576–77 (2d Cir. 1979).

42. See Miller, Of Frankenstein Monsters and Shining Knights: Myth, Reality, and the "Class Action Problem", 92 Harv. L. Rev. 664, 668 & n.21 (1979).

43. See Elrod v. Burns, 427 U.S. 347, 351–53 (1976) (plurality opinion); Baker v. Carr, 369 U.S. 186, 210–17 (1962).

44. See Chayes, supra note 39, at 1288–302.

45. See Walzer, supra note 32, at 5. Norman Dorsen's collection of essays, The Rights of Americans (N. Dorsen ed. 1970), collates those burgeoning demands from "widely disparate groups"—demands which demonstrate that "the security of individual rights is, or should be, of universal concern." Dorsen, Introduction to id. at xii–xiii.

46. For this brief capsulation I have drawn on the extraordinary L. Levy, Origins of the Fifth Amendment 150–70 (1968) [hereinafter L. Levy, Origins]. His historical expositions of the Fifth Amendment, see id., and of the First Amendment, see L. Levy, Legacy of Suppression (1960) [hereinafter L. Levy, Legacy] are, in my view, required reading for any basic comprehension of those amendments or the Bill of Rights generally.

47. U.S. Const. amend. V ("No person shall be . . . deprived of life, liberty, or property, without due process of law. . . .").

48. Id. amend. VI ("In all criminal prosecutions, the accused shall enjoy the right to a speedy and public trial, by an impartial jury of the State and district wherein the crime shall have been committed . . . and to have the assistance of counsel for his defence.").

49. Id. amend. V ("No person . . . shall be compelled in any criminal case to be a witness against himself. . . .").

50. Id. amend. VI ("In all criminal prosecutions, the accused shall enjoy the right . . . to be confronted with the witnesses against him. . . .").

51. Id. amend. I ("Congress shall make no law . . . abridging the freedom of speech. . . .").

52. Trial of John Peter Zenger, 17 Howell's State Trials 675 (N.Y. Sup. Ct. of Judicature 1735); see Trial of Harry Croswell, 17 Howell's State Trials 46 (N.Y. Sup. Ct. 1803) (argument of Alexander Hamilton).

53. The power of a jury in Anglo-American law to acquit against the weight of the evidence has been clear at least since Bushell's Case, 124 Eng. Rep. 1006, 1009 (C.P. 1670). The power to acquit against a directed verdict of guilty, as in Zenger's case, is of more recent origin. See generally 1 L. Radzinowicz, A History of English Criminal Law 91–97 (1948).

54. See B. Bailyn, supra note 4, at 110–15.

55. See Mooney v. Holohan, 294 U.S. 103 (1935); R. Frost, The Mooney Case (1968).

56. See Powell v. Alabama, 287 U.S. 45 (1932); D. Carter, Scottsboro (1969).

57. See R. Stern, The Oppenheimer Case (1969).

58. See United States v. Dellinger, 472 F.2d 340 (7th Cir. 1972); cert. denied, 410 U.S. 970 (1973); United States v. Seale, 461 F.2d 345 (7th Cir. 1972); The Conspiracy Trial (J. Clavir & J. Spitzer eds. 1970).

59. 95 Eng. Rep. 807, 817–18 (K.B. 1765) (citing Wilkes v. Wood, 98 Eng. Rep. 489, 498–99 (C.P. 1763) (£ 1000 damages awarded plaintiff; general warrants held illegal)); D. Hutchinson, Foundations of the Constitution 293–98 (1975). For a modern application of Entick v. Carrington, see Birnbaum v. United States, 588 F.2d 319, 323–24 (2d Cir. 1978) (CIA illegal mail openings violate right to privacy).

60. Boyd v. United States, 116 U.S. 616, 626 (1886). It is interesting that Zurcher v. Stanford Daily, 436 U.S. 547 (1978), involving somewhat analogous facts, cites neither Entick nor Boyd. However, Stanford v. Texas, 379 U.S. 476, 481–85 (1965), cited in Zurcher v. Stanford Daily, 436 U.S. 564, did rely heavily on both cases.

61. Boyd v. United States, 116 U.S. 616, 626–27 (1886).
62. See Stanford v. Texas, 379 U.S. 476, 481–85 (1965); L. Levy, Legacy, supra note 46, at 145–48.
63. E.g., Zurcher v. Stanford Daily, 436 U.S. 547, 563–66 (1978) (exploring relationship between First and Fourth Amendments in the search of a newspaper office); Griswold v. Connecticut, 381 U.S. 479, 484–85 (1965) (extracting right of privacy from First, Third, Fourth, Fifth, and Ninth Amendments); Escobedo v. Illinois, 378 U.S. 478, 485–92 (1964) (construing Sixth Amendment right to counsel with sensitivity to Fifth Amendment right against self-incrimination).
64. See Shapiro v. Thompson, 394 U.S. 618, 629–31 (1969).
65. See Roe v. Wade, 410 U.S. 113, 152–54 (1973); Griswold v. Connecticut, 381 U.S. 479, 484–85 (1965); Redlich, Are There "Certain Rights . . . Retained by the People"?, 37 N.Y.U.L. Rev. 787, 804–10 (1962), cited in Griswold v. Connecticut, 381 U.S. at 490 n.6 (Goldberg, J., concurring). See generally 1 N. Dorsen, P. Bender & B. Neuborne, Emerson, Haber, and Dorsen's Political and Civil Rights in the United States 735–846 (4th ed. 1976) [hereinafter N. Dorsen].
66. Craven, Personhood: The Right to Be Let Alone, 1976 Duke L.J. 699, 701–02; see, e.g., East Hartford Educ. Ass'n v. Board of Educ., 562 F.2d 838, 840–42 (2d Cir. 1977) (teacher dress code), rev'd en banc, id. at 856; Bishop v. Colaw, 450 F.2d 1069, 1075 (8th Cir. 1971) (student dress code).
67. See B. Patterson, The Forgotten Ninth Amendment 19 (1955); Redlich, supra note 65, at 800.
68. I am partially indebted for this insight to Marvin Meyers' greater insight into Madison's thinking as a whole. See Meyers, Introduction to Mind of the Founder, supra note 34, at xvii–xx.
69. I speak here of humanism as involving freedom, tolerance, and a degree of naturalism, recognizing the value and dignity of man. See 4 Encyclopedia of Philosophy 69 (1967). Pico della Mirandola, see id. at 70, finds his modern counterpart in John Rawls:

> Each person possesses an inviolability founded on justice that even the welfare of society as a whole cannot override. . . . Therefore in a just society the liberties of equal citizenship are taken as settled; the rights secured by justice are not subject to political bargaining or to the calculus of social interests.

J. Rawls, A Theory of Justice 3–4 (1971). See also Karst, The Supreme Court, 1976 Term—Foreword: Equal Citizenship Under the Fourteenth Amendment, 91 Harv. L. Rev. 1, 5–11 (1977).
70. See L. Tribe, supra note 31, § 11-1, at 565.
71. But see Zurcher v. Stanford Daily, 436 U.S. 547, 559, 565–67 (1978) (search based on warrant does not infringe First Amendment; state need not rely on subpoena).
72. E.g., United States v. Albarado, 495 F.2d 799, 805–06 (2d Cir. 1974); United States v. Davis, 482 F.2d 893, 909 & n.43 (9th Cir. 1973).
73. See L. Levy, Origins, supra note 46, at 83–108, 136–72, for the religious "heresy" origins of the Fifth Amendment. For the political heresy origins of the First Amendment, see Dennis v. United States, 341 U.S. 494, 583–85 (1951) (Douglas, J., dissenting).
74. 198 U.S. 45, 57 (1905).
75. See L. Tribe, supra note 31, §§ 8-5 to 8-7.

76. See Karst, supra note 69, at 26–27.
77. See Craven, supra note 66, at 701–02.
78. Whalen v. Roe, 429 U.S. 589, 599–600 (1977). See generally, L. Tribe, supra note 31, §§ 15-1 to 15-3.
79. See Dieffenbach c. Attorney Gen., 604 F.2d 187, 195–98 (2d Cir. 1979); Image Carrier Corp. v. Beame, 567 F.2d 1197, 1202–03 (2d Cir. 1977) ("Just as the Due Process clause of the Fourteenth Amendment did not 'enact Mr. Herbert Spencer's Social Statics,' the Equal Protection [c]lause of the same amendment did not enact Professor Milton Friedman's economics of the marketplace.") (footnotes omitted), cert. denied, 440 U.S. 979 (1979).

The view that the Due Process Clause does not impose *substantive* limitations on governmental action in the economic arena does not, of course, eliminate constitutional protections for property. Property is itself a personal right. See L. Hand, Chief Justice Stone's Concept of the Judicial Function, in The Spirit of Liberty 201, 206 (3d ed. 1960). Procedural due process must still be observed in individual cases and, when regulations become too restrictive, compensation may be required because courts will find a "taking." The fact that more extensive substantive protections are accorded to individual *liberties* of various kinds is based on a recognition that governmental actions in these areas may intrude on individual integrity more severely than do "economic" regulations. Whether, and the extent to which, there is a distinction that makes a difference between individual property rights and the rights of business entities is a further question that is moot for present purposes. The philosophical implications as well as the limitations of a legal/social property distinction are brilliantly explored in Soper, On the Relevance of Philosophy to Law: Reflections on Ackerman's Private Property and the Constitution, 79 Colum. L. Rev. 44, 56–63 (1979).

80. See Bivens v. Six Unknown Named Agents of Fed. Bureau of Narcotics, 403 U.S. 388, 389 (1971).
81. See Hernandez v. Lattimore, 612 F.2d 61, 67–68 (2d Cir. 1979).
82. See Goldberg v. Kelly, 397 U.S. 254, 255–56 (1970).
83. W. Shirer, The Rise and Fall of the Third Reich 194 (1960).
84. Id.
85. N.Y. Times, Aug. 22, 1979, at 1, col. 1.
86. See P. Murphy, The Meaning of Freedom of Speech 67–100 (1972).
87. Korematsu v. United States, 323 U.S. 214, 219 (1944).
88. See, e.g., R. Griffith, The Politics of Fear 131–51 (1970); E. Latham, The Communist Controversy in Washington 319–416 (1966).
89. See Watergate Special Prosecution Force, Report 50–70 (1975); P. Kurland, Watergate and the Constitution 1–15 (1978); A Miller, Social Change and Fundamental Law 267–311 (1979); D. Rather & G. Gates, The Palace Guard 293 (1974).
90. L. Hand, The Spirit of Liberty, in The Spirit of Liberty, supra note 79, at 189, 190.
91. Douglas, The Bill of Rights is Not Enough, 39 N.Y.U.L. Rev. 207, 207 (1963).
92. See R. Dworkin, supra note 2, at 131–49.
93. Cardozo, The Judicial Process, supra note 38, at 182–83.
94. Id. at 182.

95. I do not know whether this term is my own; I tend to think it is not.
96. 1 A. de Tocqueville, Democracy in America 280 (1956) (1st ed. London 1835) (1st French ed. Paris 1835), quoted in A. Cox, The Role of the Supreme Court in American Government 1 (1976).
97. See Johnson, The Alabama Punting Syndrome, Judges' J., Spring 1979, at 4, 53–54.
98. See West Virginia State Bd. of Educ. v. Barnette, 319 U.S. 624, 640–42 (1943) (invalidating flag salute requirement).
99. See Moore v. Dempsey, 261 U.S. 86, 91 (1923).
100. See Near v. Minnesota ex rel. Olson, 283 U.S. 697, 720–23 (1931).
101. See New York State Ass'n for Retarded Children v. Carey, 596 F.2d 27, 29 (2d Cir.), cert. denied, 100 S. Ct. 70 (1979).
102. See Wooley v. Maynard, 430 U.S. 705, 713–17 (1977).
103. See Moore v. City of E. Cleveland, 431 U.S. 494, 498–500 (1977) (plurality opinion).
104. Brown v. Board of Educ., 349 U.S. 294, 301 (1955).
105. Letter from James Madison to Spencer Roane (Sept. 2, 1819), reprinted in Mind of the Founder, supra note 34, at 458.
106. DeFunis v. Odegaard, 416 U.S. 312, 317–20 (1974).
107. United Jewish Organizations v. Carey, 430 U.S. 144, 155–62 (1977) (plurality opinion).
108. Regents of the Univ. of Cal. v. Bakke, 438 U.S. 265, 315–20 (1978) (Powell, J., announcing the judgment of the Court).
109. United Steelworkers v. Weber, 99 S. Ct. 2721, 2730 (1979).
110. Board of Educ. v. Harris, 100 S. Ct. 363, 368–70 (1979).
111. Fullilove v. Kreps, 584 F.2d 600, 601 (2d Cir. 1978), cert. granted, 441 U.S. 960 (1979) (No. 78–1007).
112. See Green v. United States, 356 U.S. 165, 195 (1958) (Black, J., dissenting).
113. The exception that proves this "rule" is, of course, the Civil War, which was precipitated in part by Scott v. Sandford, 60 U.S. (19 How.) 393 (1857), where the Court determined that because Dred Scott was not a citizen of Missouri he had no standing to sue and the court had no jurisdiction, id. at 406, but inexplicably went on to decide that the Missouri Compromise was unconstitutional insofar as it prohibited slaveholding in the Louisiana Purchase north of 36°30′, except in Missouri, id. at 432, 451–52. See Speech by Abraham Lincoln at Springfield, Ill. (June 17, 1858), reprinted in 3 The Writings of Abraham Lincoln 1–13 (A. Lapsley ed. 1905).
114. Mr. Justice Jackson stated in West Virginia Bd. of Educ. v. Barnette, 319 U.S. 624 (1943):

> Nor does our duty to apply the Bill of Rights to assertions of official authority depend upon our possession of marked competence in the field where the invasion of rights occurs. True, the task of translating the majestic generalities of the Bill of Rights, conceived as part of the pattern of liberal government in the eighteenth century, into concrete restraints on officials dealing with the problems of the twentieth century, is one to disturb self-confidence. These principles grew in soil which also produced a philosophy that the individual was the center of society, that his liberty was attainable through mere absence of governmental restraints, and that government should be entrusted with few controls and only the mildest supervision over men's affairs. We must transplant these rights to a soil in which the *laissez-faire* concept or principle of non-interference has withered at

least as to economic affairs, and social advancements are increasingly sought through closer integration of society and through expanded and strengthened governmental controls. These changed conditions often deprive precedents of reliability and cast us more than we would choose upon our own judgment. But we act in these matters not by authority of our competence but by force of our commissions. We cannot, because of modest estimates of our competence in such specialties as public education, withhold the judgment that history authenticates as the function of this Court when liberty is infringed.

Id. at 639–40.

115. Equity is A Roguish thing, for Law wee have a measure know what to trust too. Equity is according to ye conscience of him y^t is Chancell^{or}, and as y^t is larger or narrower soe is equity[.] Tis all one as if they should make ye Standard for ye measure wee call A foot, to be ye Chancellors foot; what an uncertain measure would this be; One Chancello^r ha's a long foot another A short foot a third an indifferent foot; tis ye same thing in ye Chancello^{r}s Conscience.

Table Talk of John Selden 43 (F. Pollock ed. 1927) (1st ed. n.p. 1689) (footnotes omitted).

116. 28 U.S.C. § 453 (1976).
117. See Wechsler, Toward Neutral Principles of Constitutional Law, 73 Harv. L. Rev. 1, 16 (1959).
118. Miller & Howell, The Myth of Neutrality in Constitutional Adjudication, 27 U. Chi. L. Rev. 661, 664 (1960).
119. Cf. M. Cohen, Law and the Social Order 380 n.86 (1933) ("I have an abiding conviction that to recognize the truth and adjust oneself to it is in the end the easiest and most advisable course."), quoted in Miller & Howell, supra note 118, at 695.
120. For example, my opinion in Board of Educ. v. Califano, 584 F.2d 576, 588 n.39 (2d Cir. 1978), aff'd sub nom. Board of Educ. v. Harris, 100 S. Ct. 363 (1979).
121. See generally Cardozo, The Judicial Process, supra note 38, at 160 ("We shall have a false view of the landscape if we look at the waste spaces only, and refuse to see the acres already sown and fruitful.").
122. See Bell v. Wolfish, 441 U.S. 520, 558–60 (1979).
123. See East Hartford Educ. Ass'n v. Board of Educ., 562 F.2d 838, 840–42 (2d Cir. 1977), rev'd en banc, id. at 856.
124. See Brown v. Thomson, 435 U.S. 938 (1978) (order granting stay).
125. Cardozo, The Judicial Process, supra note 38, at 164.
126. See Warren, The Bill of Rights and the Military, 37 N.Y.U.L. Rev. 181, 200 (1962).
127. See Brewer v. Williams, 430 U.S. 387, 420–24 (1977) (Burger, C.J., dissenting).
128. Warren, supra note 126, at 200.
129. E.g., United States v. Albarado, 495 F.2d 799, 808–09 (2d Cir. 1974); United States v. Davis, 482 F.2d 893, 906–07 (9th Cir. 1973). See generally Andrews, Screening Travelers at the Airport to Prevent Hijacking: A New Challenge for the Unconstitutional Conditions Doctrine, 16 Ariz. L. Rev. 657, 666, 738–42 (1975).
130. Douglas, supra note 91, at 240.
131. The late, great Professor Wigmore and his latter-day adherents on the Supreme Court would probably disagree with this statement. The greatest obeisance to the truth-finding process is contained in the argu-

ments questioning the soundness of the exclusionary rule, where the evidence illegally obtained is often highly probative of the defendant's guilt. See Wigmore, Using Evidence Obtained by Illegal Search and Seizure, 8 A.B.A.J. 479, 482, 484 (1922); Brewer v. Williams, 430 U.S. 387, 422–24 (1977) (Burger, C.J., dissenting); Stone v. Powell, 428 U.S. 465, 485, 489–91 (1976) (Powell, J.).

132. Damaška, Evidentiary Barriers to Conviction and Two Models of Criminal Procedure: A Comparative Study, 121 U. Pa. L. Rev. 506, 578–89 (1973).

133. Id. at 581.

134. See Trial of John Peter Zenger, 17 Howell's State Trials 675 (N.Y. Sup. Ct. of Judicature 1735); Bushell's Case, 124 Eng. Rep. 1006 (C.P. 1670).

135. Oakes, The Exclusionary Rule—A Relic of the Past?, in Constitutional Government in America (R. Collins ed. forthcoming) [herinafter Oakes, The Exclusionary Rule].

136. While this accommodation is viewed by some as a very costly one, I found it fascinating, while preparing for this lecture, to note the analysis by the General Accounting Office of Fourth Amendment suppression motions made in some 2,804 federal cases brought in 1978. Comptroller General of the United States, The Impact of the Exclusionary Rule on Federal Criminal Prosecutions (1979). Less than half the defendants made suppression motions even where search and seizure was an element in the case. Id. at 9. In only 1.3% of the 2,804 cases was evidence excluded as a result of the motion. Id. at 11. In more than half of these cases the defendants were found guilty anyway. Id. at 13. In the remaining approximately ½ of 1% of acquittals or dismissals, it does not appear whether the inadmissibility was the sole and exclusive cause of the acquittal or dismissal. Id. This closely parallels my own experience as attorney general of Vermont.

137. 430 U.S. 387, 416 (1977) (Burger, C.J., dissenting).

138. Id. at 417.

139. Id.

140. Id. at 415.

141. See Haynes v. Washington, 373 U.S. 503, 515–18 (1963).

142. See North Carolina v. Butler, 441 U.S. 369, 372–76 (1979); Stone, The Miranda Doctrine in the Burger Court, 1977 Sup. Ct. Rev. 99, 100–01 & nn.6–7 (discussing the 11 other decisions). See generally Kamisar, Brewer v. Williams, Massiah, and Miranda: What Is "Interrogation"? When Does It Matter?, 67 Geo. L.J. 1 (1978).

143. U.S. Const. art. VI, cl. 3.

144. Id. amend. I.

145. Freedom of the Press from Zenger to Jefferson 226–27 (L. Levy ed. 1966) (extract of The Virginia Report of 1799–1800, Touching the Alien and Sedition Laws 228 (Philadelphia 1850)).

146. Madison's original proposal of June 8, 1789, was: "'The people shall not be deprived or abridged of their right to speak, to write, or to publish their sentiments; and the freedom of the press, as one of the great bulwarks of liberty, shall be inviolable.'" Levy, Introduction to id. at liv n.87.

147. See 4 Annals of Cong. 934 (1794) (remarks of Rep. Madison) ("If we advert to the nature of Republican Government, we shall find that the

censorial power is in the people over the Government, and not in the Government over the people."), quoted in New York Times Co. v. Sullivan, 376 U.S. 254, 275 (1964).

148. 376 U.S. 254, 265 (1964).
149. Nebraska Press Ass'n v. Stuart, 427 U.S. 539, 569–70 (1976) (judicial action); New York Times Co. v. United States, 403 U.S. 713, 714 (1971) (per curiam) (executive action).
150. United States v. Calandra, 414 U.S. 338, 348 (1974).
151. United States v. Janis, 428 U.S. 433, 447–49, 453–54 (1976); United States v. Calandra, 414 U.S. 338, 349–52 (1974). But see Kamisar, Is the Exclusionary Rule an 'Illogical' or 'Unnatural' Interpretation of the Fourth Amendment?, 62 Judicature 66, 81–84 (1978); Oakes, The Exclusionary Rule, supra note 135.
152. 232 U.S. 383 (1914).
153. Id. at 398.
154. Id. at 391–92.
155. Silverthorne Lumber Co. v. United States, 251 U.S. 385, 392 (1920).
156. See Olmstead v. United States, 277 U.S. 438, 469–71 (1928) (Holmes, J., dissenting); id. at 478–79 (Brandeis, J., dissenting).
157. See California v. Minjares, 100 S. Ct. 9, 11–12 (Rehnquist, J., dissenting from denial of stay), cert. denied, 100 S. Ct. 181 (1979).
158. 287 U.S. 45, 71 (1932).
159. 372 U.S. 335, 336–37, 342–45 (1963).
160. 407 U.S. 25, 37 (1972).
161. See Burger, The Special Skills of Advocacy: Are Specialized Training and Certification of Advocates Essential to Our System of Justice?, 42 Fordham L. Rev. 227, 234 (1973); Oakes, Lawyer and Judge: The Ethical Duty of Competency, in Ethics and Advocacy 57–58 (1978) (background paper to the Final Report of the Annual Chief Justice Earl Warren Conference on Advocacy in the United States, June 23–24, 1978).
162. See, e.g., United States v. Bubar, 567 F.2d 192, 201–04 (2d Cir.), cert. denied, 434 U.S. 872 (1977); Rickenbacker v. Warden, 550 F. 2d 62, 65 (2d Cir. 1976), cert. denied, 434 U.S. 826 (1977). But see, e.g., Boyer v. Patton, 579 F.2d 284, 286–89 (3d Cir. 1978); United States v. Lucas, 513 F.2d 509, 511–12 (D.C. Cir. 1975). See generally Maryland v. Marzullo, 435 U.S. 1011, 1011–12 (1978) (White, J., dissenting from denial of certiorari) (reviewing conflicting standards among the circuit courts concerning what constitutes adequate counsel).
163. Herbert v. Lando, 441 U.S. 153, 169–77 (1979).
164. Id. at 156.
165. Branzburg v. Hayes, 408 U.S. 665, 704 (1972).
166. Id. at 690–91.
167. Gannett Co. v. DePasquale, 99 S. Ct. 2898, 2908–12 (1979); see Goodale, Gannett Means What It Says; But Who Knows What It Says?, Nat'l L. J., Oct. 15, 1979, at 20, col. 1.
168. See Gannett Co. v. DePasquale, 99 S. Ct. 2898, 2918 (1979) (Rehnquist, J., concurring); Rapid City Journal Co. v. Circuit Court, 283 N.W.2d 563, 566–68 (S.D. 1979); Richmond Newspapers, Inc. v. Virginia, 448 U.S. 555 (1980) (reversing Virginia Supreme Court's unreported decision that Gannett allowed trial court to bar press and public from courtroom during capital murder trial).

169. United States v. Barnes, 604 F.2d 121, 140–43 (2d Cir. 1979), cert. denied, 446 U.S. 907 (1980). Along with Judges Meskill and Timbers, I dissented from the denial of a petition for rehearing en banc. See id. at 175.

170. Structural due process is not, strictly speaking, a remedy but an expanded recognition of constitutionally protected rights. See text accompanying notes 173–83 infra.

171. 42 U.S.C. § 1983 (1976); see text accompanying notes 184–208 infra.

172. See text accompanying notes 209–26 infra.

173. It is a well-settled proposition that corporations are persons within the meaning of the due process and Equal Protection Clauses of the Fourteenth Amendment. See Covington & Lexington Turnpike Rd. Co. v. Sandford, 164 U.S. 578, 592 (1896); Santa Clara County v. Southern Pac. R.R., 118 U.S. 394, 396 (1886); cf. First Nat'l Bank of Boston v. Bellotti, 435 U.S. 765, 776–78 (1978) (speech by corporation enjoys First Amendment protection).

174. See Friendly, "Some Kind of Hearing", 123 U. Pa. L. Rev. 1267, 1275–77 (1975).

175. E.g., Mathews v. Eldridge, 424 U.S. 319, 335 (1976); Goldberg v. Kelly, 397 U.S. 254, 263 (1970).

176. See Cafeteria & Restaurant Workers Local 473 v. McElroy, 367 U.S. 886, 894–95 (1961); Buck v. Board of Educ., 553 F.2d 315, 318 (2d Cir. 1977), cert. denied, 438 U.S. 904 (1978); id. at 323 (Oakes, J., dissenting).

177. See Goldberg v. Kelly, 397 U.S. 254, 267–68 (1970).

178. See United States Dep't of Agriculture v. Murry, 413 U.S. 508, 517–19 (1973) (Marshall, J., concurring); L. Tribe, supra note 31, §§ 17-1 to 17-3; Tribe, Structural Due Process, 10 Harv. C.R.-C.L. L. Rev. 269 (1975).

179. To illustrate the limitations on government action imposed by structural due process, Professor Tribe presents the dilemma of a young woman dismissed from a public high school during her senior year pursuant to a regulation "which calls for the immediate exclusion of any student who has completed at least the tenth grade and is an unwed mother." Tribe, supra note 178, at 270. If an attack on the substantive policies supporting the exclusion (reducing commotion, discouraging premarital sex, and encouraging better care for the children of teenage unwed mothers) and on the procedures used to implement those policies (providing a hearing to verify a girl's status as an unwed mother) were to fail, the exclusion could be contested as a violation of structural due process. Such an attack would focus on the very existence of the flat rule and would require that an individual hearing be provided to consider a student's personal situation as part of any disposition. In effect, the court would hold *that the area in question is one where governmental policy-formation and/or application are constitutionally required to take a certain form, to follow a process with certain features, or to display a particular sort of structure.* Id. at 291 (emphasis in original).

180. 531 F.2d 1114, 1124–26 (2d Cir. 1976).

181. Some were already in the process of adjusting. Id. at 1123 & n.11.

182. Beazer v. New York City Transit Auth., 558 F.2d 97, 99 (2d Cir. 1977), rev'd, 440 U.S. 568 (1979).

183. New York City Transit Auth. v. Beazer, 440 U.S. 568, 587–94 (1979).
184. See Developments in the Law—Section 1983 and Federalism, 90 Harv. L. Rev. 1133, 1172 (1977) [hereinafter Developments—Section 1983].
185. See, e.g., Paul v. Davis, 424 U.S. 693, 699–701 (1976); Atkins v. Lanning, 556 F.2d 485, 489 (10th Cir. 1977); Smith v. Spina, 477 F.2d 1140, 1143, 1144 (3d Cir. 1973); Wells v. Ward, 470 F.2d 1185, 1187 (10th Cir. 1972): 1 N. Dorsen, supra note 65, at 1551–52.
186. See Meachum v. Fano, 427 U.S. 215, 226 (1976); Bishop v. Wood, 426 U.S. 341, 344 & n.7 (1976); Paul v. Davis, 424 U.S. 693, 710–11 (1976).
187. See Glennon, Constitutional Liberty and Property: Federal Common Law and Section 1983, 51 S. Cal. L. Rev. 355, 359–63 (1978).
188. See, e.g., Stump v. Sparkman, 435 U.S. 349, 355–57 (1978) (immunity for state judges); Imbler v. Pachtman, 424 U.S. 409, 424–31 (1976) (immunity for state prosecutors); Scheuer v. Rhodes, 416 U.S. 232, 247–49 (1974) (good faith defense for state executive officers); Pierson v. Ray, 386 U.S. 547, 555–58 (1967) (good faith defense for state police officers); 2 N. Dorsen, supra note 65, at 543–44.
189. 436 U.S. 658, 690 (1978). This holding was to some extent anticipated in Brault v. Town of Milton, 527 F.2d 736, 744 n.6 (2d Cir. 1975) (en banc) (Oakes, J., dissenting).
190. 365 U.S. 167, 187–92 (1961); see 436 U.S. at 663.
191. 436 U.S. at 694. There are indications that the courts will hold plaintiffs to a high threshold in determining whether a municipal "policy" or "custom" exists. See Dominquez v. Beame, 603 F.2d 337, 341–42 (2d Cir. 1979); Owens v. Haas, 601 F.2d 1242, 1246–47 (2d Cir.), cert. denied, 100 S. Ct. 483 (1979). But see Oshiver v. Court of Common Pleas, 469 F. Supp. 645, 648 (E.D. Pa. 1979).
192. This question was left open in Monell, 436 U.S. at 701; see 2 N. Dorsen, supra note 65, at 543. Sala v. County of Suffolk, 604 F.2d 207, 209–11 (2d Cir. 1979), appears to allow a good faith defense to a municipality in a situation where the individual officer did not act in bad faith and the prior case law did not suggest that the conduct (strip-searching) was unconstitutional. Accord, Owen v. City of Independence, 589 F.2d 335, 337–38 (8th Cir. 1978), reversed, 445 U.S. 622 (1980); Ohland v. City of Montpelier, 467 F. Supp. 324, 344–48 (D. Vt. 1979). Contra, Shuman v. City of Philadelphia, 470 F. Supp. 449, 464 (E.D. Pa. 1979).
193. McCabe v. Atchison, T. & S.F. Ry., 235 U.S. 151, 160–64 (1914), held that an Oklahoma law permitting railroads to provide separate dining, sleeping, and chair cars for whites, but not blacks, was unconstitutional; it also held that the plaintiffs had no remedy.
194. 435 U.S. 247 (1978).
195. Id. at 254–57.
196. Id. at 257–59.
197. Carey involved the right of public school students to collect substantial "nonpunitive damages," id. at 248, as a result of their suspension from school without due process. The Court held that the students were not entitled to damages absent proof of actual injury caused by the denial of due process. Id. at 260–64.
198. See id. at 266–67.
199. See Aldisert, Judicial Expansion of Federal Jurisdiction: A Federal

Judge's Thoughts on Section 1983, Comity and the Federal Caseload, 1973 Law & Soc. Ord. 557.

200. See, e.g., Edelman v. Jordan, 415 U.S. 651, 660–63 (1974); Employees of the Dep't of Pub. Health & Welfare v. Department of Pub. Health & Welfare, 411 U.S. 279, 291–94 & n.8 (1973) (Marshall, J., concurring in the result).

201. See, e.g., Huffman v. Pursue, Ltd., 420 U.S. 592, 599–607 (1975); Younger v. Harris, 401 U.S. 37, 44–45, 53–54 (1971).

202. See Turco v. Monroe County Bar Ass'n, 554 F.2d 515, 520–21 (2d Cir.), cert. denied, 434 U.S. 834 (1977); Thistlethwaite v. City of New York, 497 F.2d 339, 341–42 (2d Cir.), cert. denied, 419 U.S. 1093 (1974); Restatement (Second) of Judgments §§ 47–48, 68 (Tent. Draft No. 1, 1973).

203. See Scoggin v. Schrunk, 522 F.2d 436, 437 (9th Cir. 1975), cert. denied, 423 U.S. 1066 (1976). But see New Jersey Educ. Ass'n v. Burke, 579 F.2d 764, 773–74 (3d Cir.), cert. denied, 439 U.S. 894 (1978). See generally Developments—Section 1983, supra note 184, at 1330–54.

204. See Mitchell v. National Broadcasting Co., 553 F.2d 265, 276 (2d Cir. 1977).

205. See Huffman v. Pursue, Ltd., 420 U.S. 592, 605–07 (1975). Prospective § 1983 plaintiffs may also face another hurdle in having their federal claims heard in federal court: a requirement that they exhaust state nonjudicial remedies. Although the general rule has been that exhaustion is not required in § 1983 actions, see Damico v. California, 389 U.S. 416, 417 (1967) (per curiam), there are indications that in the future, exhaustion of administrative remedies may be imposed as a predicate to § 1983 actions. See Runyon v. McCrary, 427 U.S. 160, 186 n.* (1976) (Powell, J., concurring); Comment, Exhaustion of State Administrative Remedies in Section 1983 Cases, 41 U. Chi. L. Rev. 537, 554–55 (1974). Compare Gibson v. Berryhill, 411 U.S. 564, 574–75 (1973) with id. at 581 (Marshall, J., concurring) (rejecting suggestion of majority opinion "that the question remains open whether plaintiffs in some suits brought under 42 U.S.C. § 1983 may have to exhaust administrative remedies"). The majority of lower federal courts still do not require exhaustion, see e.g., Wells Fargo Armored Serv. Corp. v. Georgia Pub. Serv. Comm'n, 547 F.2d 938, 939 n.1 (5th Cir. 1977); Wolder v. Rahm, 549 F.2d 543, 544 (8th Cir. 1977); Strong v. Collatos, 450 F. Supp. 1356, 1359 n.8 (D. Mass. 1978), aff'd on other grounds, 593 F.2d 420 (1st Cir. 1979), although the Second Circuit has adopted a contrary rule, see Mitchell v. National Broadcasting Co., 553 F.2d 265, 276 (2d Cir. 1977); Doe v. Anker, 451 F. Supp. 241, 248 (S.D.N.Y. 1978).

206. See Stone v. Powell, 428 U.S. 465, 493 n.35 (1976). But see Gibbons, Hague v. CIO: A Retrospective, 52 N.Y.U.L. Rev. 731, 741–44 (1977); Neuborne, The Myth of Parity, 90 Harv. L. Rev. 1105, 1105–06, 1115–16 (1977).

207. H. Friendly, Federal Jurisdiction: A General View 90 (1973).

208. See Levy, Judicial Review, supra note 19, at 34–36.

209. The structural injunction differs fundamentally from classic injunctive relief, which requires a threat of irreparable harm, is aimed at preventing discrete injury-producing acts, and is usually framed as a negative command. See Leubsdorf, The Standard for Preliminary Injunctions, 91 Harv. L. Rev. 525, 525–26 (1978). The premise underlying structur-

al injunctive relief is that "the constitutional wrong is the structure itself; the reorganization is designed to bring the structure within constitutional bounds." O. Fiss, The Civil Rights Injunction 11 (1978). Structural injunctions contemplate close and continuing scrutiny by the court. See text accompanying notes 217–19 infra.

210. 347 U.S. 483, 495 (1954); see Brown v. Board of Educ. (Brown II), 349 U.S. 294, 299–301 (1955).

211. Morgan v. McDonough, 540 F.2d 527, 533–35 (1st Cir. 1976) (appeal from order designating temporary receiver), cert. denied, 429 U.S. 1042 (1977); Morgan v. Kerrigan, 530 F.2d 401, 425 (1st Cir.) (city-wide desegregation plan promulgated by district court upheld), cert. denied, 426 U.S. 935 (1976); Morgan v. Kerrigan, 509 F.2d 580, 598 (1st Cir. 1974) (findings of intentional segregation upheld), cert. denied, 421 U.S. 963 (1975).

212. Dayton Bd. of Educ. v. Brinkman, 99 S. Ct. 2971, 2977, 2980–81 (1979).

213. E.g., Detainees of the Brooklyn House of Detention for Men v. Malcolm, 520 F.2d 392, 399 (2d Cir. 1975) (overcrowding and excessive confinement); Rhem v. Malcolm, 371 F. Supp. 594, 621–22 (S.D.N.Y.) (same), aff'd, 507 F.2d 333 (2d Cir. 1974).

214. Wyatt v. Stickney, 344 F. Supp. 373, 376–77 (M.D. Ala. 1972), aff'd in part, remanded in part, and decision reserved in part sub nom. Wyatt v. Aderholt, 503 F.2d 1305 (5th Cir. 1974).

215. E.g., New York State Ass'n for Retarded Children, Inc. v. Carey, 596 F.2d 27 (2d Cir. 1979), cert. denied, 100 S. Ct. 70 (1979); Wyatt v. Stickney, 344 F. Supp. 387, 392–94 (M.D. Ala. 1972), aff'd in part, remanded in part, and decision reserved in part sub nom. Wyatt v. Aderholt, 503 F.2d 1305 (5th Cir. 1974); cf. Pennsylvania Ass'n for Retarded Children v. Pennsylvania, 343 F. Supp. 279, 302–16 (E.D. Pa. 1972) (three-judge court) (retarded children's attendance at public school).

216. The literature on structural injunctions and institutional relief is quite substantial. E.g., O. Fiss, supra note 209; M. Harris & D. Spiller, Jr. After Decision: Implementation of Judicial Decrees in Correctional Settings (1977); H. Kalodner & J. Fishman, Limits of Justice: The Courts' Role in School Desegregation (1978); Berger, Away from the Courthouse and into the Field: The Odyssey of a Special Master, 78 Colum. L. Rev. 707 (1978); Chayes, supra note 39; Diver, The Judge as Political Powerbroker: Superintending Structural Change in Public Institutions, 65 Va. L. Rev. 43 (1979); Harris, The Title VII Administrator: A Case Study in Judicial Flexibility, 60 Cornell L. Rev. 53 (1974); Special Project, The Remedial Process in Institutional Reform Litigation, 78 Colum. L. Rev. 784 (1978) [hereinafter Special Project, Institutional Reform]. I have particularly relied on Professor Chayes's article.

217. See Chayes, supra note 39, at 1289–92. See generally Developments in the Law—Class Actions, 89 Harv. L. Rev. 1318 (1976).

218. The Wyatt case illustrates well the continuing involvement of a federal court and the parties in the fashioning of structural remedies. See Wyatt v. Stickney, 344 F. Supp. 387 (M.D. Ala. 1972) (school for the mentally retarded), aff'd in relevant part, remanded in part, and decision reserved in part sub nom. Wyatt v. Aderholt, 503 F.2d 1305 (5th Cir. 1974); Wyatt v. Stickney, 344 F. Supp. 373 (M.D. Ala. 1972) (mental hospitals), aff'd in relevant part, remanded in part, and decision re-

served in part sub nom. Wyatt v. Aderholt, 503 F.2d 1305 (5th Cir. 1974); Note, The Wyatt Case: Implementation of a Judicial Decree Ordering Institutional Change, 84 Yale L.J. 1338 (1975) [hereinafter Note, The Wyatt Case].

219. See Special Project, Institutional Reform, supra note 216, at 826–37; Note, The Wyatt Case, supra note 218.

220. See O. Fiss, supra note 209.

221. See Chayes, supra note 39.

222. See Holt v. Sarver, 309 F. Supp. 362, 372–81 (E.D. Ark. 1970), aff'd, 442 F.2d 304 (8th Cir. 1971).

223. See New York State Ass'n for Retarded Children v. Carey, 596 F.2d 27 (2d Cir. 1979), cert. denied, 100 S. Ct. 70 (1979).

224. See R. Kluger, Simple Justice (1976).

225. The Rights of Americans, supra note 45, is as good a compendium of what those rights are or should be as I know. One does not have to agree that all of the suggested rights should be immediately judicially enforceable to recognize the affirmative side of the Bill of Rights.

226. See Bell, Waiting on the Promise of Brown, 39 Law & Contemp. Prob. 341, 357–58, 372 (1975).

227. Dworkin views Learned Hand as taking this position of extreme skepticism about rights. R. Dworkin, supra note 2, at 140. So does Frank, Some Reflections on Judge Learned Hand, 24 U. Chi. L. Rev. 666, 697–98 (1957).

228. See R. Dworkin, supra note 2, at 140–47.

229. My brother Leonard Moore regularly makes it. E.g., Evans v. Lynn, 537 F.2d 571, 598 (2d Cir. 1976) (en banc), cert. denied, 429 U.S. 1066 (1977); Crawford v. Cushman, 531 F.2d 1114, 1127 (2d Cir. 1976) (Moore, J., dissenting) ("Increasingly has this Court embroiled itself in the daily affairs of our society's many walks of life. Schools, prisons, hospitals—all are supervised in various aspects by our Olympian pronouncements.").

230. Professor Sandalow has suggested a sliding scale of judicial deference dependent on the body to which the matter has been referred. On his scale, careful consideration by the Congress calls for the greatest deference, while hasty action by a local school board calls for the least. Sandalow, Judicial Protection of Minorities, 75 Mich. L. Rev. 1162, 1186–90 (1977). One has the feeling that this is done, subconsciously at least, by many judges, though they may not openly acknowledge Professor Sandalow's model.

231. Douglas, supra note 91, at 232.

232. R. Dworkin, supra note 2, at 142–44.

233. L. Tribe, supra note 31, §§ 1-7 to 1-9.

234. See Schwartz, Of Administrators and Philosopher-Kings: The Republic, the Laws, and Delegation of Power, 72 Nw. U.L. Rev. 443, 460 (1978).

235. See Communications Act, 47 U.S.C. §§ 151–609 (1976).

236. See National Environmental Policy Act of 1969, 42 U.S.C. §§ 4321–4361 (1976).

237. See Occupational Safety and Health Act of 1970, 29 U.S.C. §§ 651–678 (1976).

238. See Oakes, The Judicial Role in Environmental Law, 52 N.Y.U.L. Rev. 498 (1977).

239. The Eleventh Amendment was passed in response to the Court's decision in Chisolm v. Georgia, 2 U.S. (2 Dall.) 419 (1793), that a state is liable to suit in federal court by a citizen of another state. The Court's decision that an unapportioned federal income tax is unconstitutional, Pollack v. Farmers' Loan & Trust Co., 157 U.S. 429, 583 (1895), was overturned by the Sixteenth Amendment.

I do not forget that one decision was overturned by the Civil War. See note 113 supra.

John Paul Stevens

1. The doctrine of *stare decisis et non quieta movere*, "to stand by the decisions and not to disturb settled points," developed during "the infancy of our law." Historians agree that Bracton's *Note Book*, containing one of the first collections of English decisions, gave early impetus to the doctrine. Bracton did not understand the modern implications of stare decisis, but he directed the attention of the legal profession to past decisions in "an attempt to bring back the law to its ancient principles." The first comprehensive law reports, the *Year Books*, not only constituted in and of themselves evidence of the importance of prior decisions, but they also contained progressively frequent reference to earlier cases and often a direct statement that certain cases were of some authority, such as the words of Chief Justice Priscot in 1454: "If this plea were now adjudged bad, as you maintain, it would assuredly be a bad example to the young apprentices who study the *Year Books*, for they would never have confidence in their books if now we were to adjudge the contrary of what has been so often adjudged in the Books."

Sprecher, The Development of the Doctrine of Stare Decisis and the Extent to Which It Should Be Applied, 31 A.B.A. J. 501–02 (1945) (footnotes omitted).
2. The Latin phrase was translated by Justice Goldberg to mean "let the decision stand and do not disturb things which have been settled." A. Goldberg, Equal Justice 74 (1971). Justice Reed's rendition was: "stand by the precedents and do not disturb the calm." Reed, *Stare Decisis* and Constitutional Law, 35 Pa. B.A.Q. 131, 131 (1938) (then Solicitor General of the United States).
3. Reed, supra note 2.
4. Jackson, Decisional Law and Stare Decisis, 30 A.B.A. J. 334 (1944).
5. W.O. Douglas, Stare Decisis (1949).
6. A. Goldberg, supra note 2, at 74–97.
7. Schaefer, New Ways of Precedent, 2 Manitoba L.J. 255 (1967); Schaefer, Precedent and Policy, 34 U. Chi. L. Rev. 3 (1966).
8. Sprecher, supra note 1. This remarkable essay was, of course, written many years before its author became a judge.
9. B. Cardozo, The Nature of the Judicial Process 149 (1921).
10. There is therefore a certain complexity in the structure of the idea of justice. We may say that it consists of two parts: a uniform or constant feature, summarized in the precept "Treat like cases alike" and a shifting or varying criterion used in determining when, for any given purpose, cases are alike or different. In this respect justice is like the notions of what is genuine, or tall, or warm, which contain an implicit reference to a standard which varies with the classification of the thing to which they are applied. A tall child may be the same height as a short man, a warm winter the same temperature as a cold summer, and a fake diamond may be a genuine antique. But justice is far more complicated than these notions because the shifting standard of relevant resemblance between different cases in-

corporated in it not only varies with the type of subject to which it is applied, but may often be open to challenge even in relation to a single type of subject.

H.L.A. Hart, The Concept of Law 156 (1961).

11. "[S]tare decisis foster[s] public confidence in the judiciary and public acceptance of individual decisions by giving the appearance of impersonal, consistent, and reasoned opinions." Goldberg, supra note 2, at 75 (footnote omitted). See Mahnich v. Southern S.S. Co., 321 U.S. 96, 113 (1944) (Roberts, J., dissenting) ("Respect for tribunals must fall when the bar and the public come to understand that nothing that has been said in prior adjudication has force in a current controversy.").

12. Uniformity and continuity in law are necessary to many activities. If they are not present, the integrity of contracts, wills, conveyances and securities is impaired. (See United States v. Title Ins. Co., 265 U.S. 472, 486–87.) And there will be no equal justice under law if a negligence rule is applied in the morning but not in the afternoon. *Stare decisis* provides some moorings so that men may trade and arrange their affairs with confidence. *Stare decisis* serves to take the capricious element out of law and to give stability to a society. It is a strong tie which the future has to the past.

W.O. Douglas, supra note 5, at 8.

13. See text accompanying notes 16–26 infra.

14. See text accompanying notes 27–47 infra.

15. See text accompanying notes 48–84 infra.

16. United States v. South-Eastern Underwriters Ass'n, 322 U.S. 533, 539–53 (1944) (overruling Paul v. Virginia, 75 U.S. (8 Wall.) 168 (1868)); Smith v. Allwright, 321 U.S. 649, 664–66 (1944) (overruling Grovey v. Townsend, 295 U.S. 45 (1935)); Mahnich v. Southern S.S. Co., 321 U.S. 96, 105 (1944) (overruling Plamals v. Pinar Del Rio, 277 U.S. 151 (1928)); Mercoid Corp. v. Mid-Continent Inv. Co., 320 U.S. 661, 668 (1944) (overruling Leeds & Catlin Co. v. Victor Talking Machine Co. (No. 2), 213 U.S. 325 (1909)); Federal Power Comm'n v. Hope Natural Gas Co., 320 U.S. 591, 606–07 (1944) (overruling United Railways v. West, 280 U.S. 234 (1930)).

17. In his dissenting opinion in Mahnich v. Southern S.S. Co., he stated:

The tendency to disregard precedents in the decision of cases like the present has become so strong in this court of late as, in my view, to shake confidence in the consistency of decision and leave courts below on an uncharted sea of doubt and difficulty without any confidence that what was said yesterday will hold good tomorrow . . . .

321 U.S. 96, 113 (1944) (Roberts, J., dissenting). See also Justice Roberts's dissenting opinion in Smith v. Allwright, 321 U.S. 649, 669 (1944):

The reason for my concern is that the instant decision, overruling that announced about nine years ago, tends to bring adjudications of this tribunal into the same class as a restricted railroad ticket, good for this day and train only. I have no assurance, in view of current decisions, that the opinion announced to-day may not shortly be repudiated and overruled by justices who deem they have new light on the subject. In the present term the court has overruled three cases.

Id.

18. In remarks to the American Law Institute, Justice Jackson described the doctrine of *stare decisis* as "an old friend of the common lawyer, who is

now much concerned about its anemic condition." Jackson, supra note
4, at 334.

19. These figures are based on Professor Maltz's compilation of cases in
which the Supreme Court overruled itself on constitutional issues during the period from 1960 to 1979. See Maltz, Some Thoughts on the
Death of Stare Decisis in Constitutional Law, 1980 Wis. L. Rev. 467,
494–96 (appendix). For a collection of earlier similar compilations, see
id. at 494 n.125.

20. After summarizing the number of overrulings of cases involving constitutional issues in the two decades subsequent to 1959, and comparing
them with the number of reversals preceding this period, Professor
Maltz concludes that it seemed "fair to say that if a majority of the Warren or Burger Court has considered a case wrongly decided, no constitutional precedent—new or old—has been safe." See id. at 467.

21. B. Cardozo, supra note 9, at 129.

22. See Mahnich v. Southern S.S. Co., 321 U.S. 96, 107–11 (1944) (Roberts,
J. dissenting).

23. After noting that the Constitution had "successfully functioned in the
frontier society of 1800, in the lusty and uncontrolled capitalism of
1900, and in the rapidly coalescing industral society of 1930," Justice
Reed concluded that our people would not

> tolerate a fixity in constitutional decisions which the framers wisely eliminated
> from the Constitution itself. If, for example, the Constitution itself sedulously re-
> frains from defining the power "to regulate commerce *** among the several
> States", we would seriously have breached our constitutional philosophy, if a de-
> cision of the Supreme Court were to engraft a frozen rigidity into these living
> words.
>   Our assurance that our children will live, as have we, under a constitutional
> democracy rests, in the last analysis, upon the power of that form of government
> to adjust itself to the crises, the changing economy, and the changing temper of
> the people. The position of the Supreme Court on *stare decisis* makes that adjust-
> ment possible.

Reed, supra note 2, at 149–50.

24. Sprecher, supra note 1, at 503 & n.24 (quoting Mirehouse v. Rennell, 36
Rev. Rep. 179, 180, 1 Cl. & Fin. 527, 546 (1833) (Parke, J.)).

25. Although the legitimacy of judicial lawmaking is a necessary predicate
for an overruling decision, it is not necessarily a sufficient justification
inasmuch as the necessity for interstitial lawmaking—a power that
"must be lodged somewhere," B. Cardozo, supra note 9, at 135—might
justify the first exercise of judicial power without providing the same
justification for the second. In most overruling situations, however, it is
by no means clear that the precedent is exactly like the case before the
Court, cf. note 10 supra; rather, it is merely one of the significant guide-
posts that circumscribe judges' action. See note 26 and accompanying
text infra. "[T]he Court then facing the issue may have before it different facts and may also have the benefit of the additional precedent
and wisdom that often come with the passage of time." Owen v. Lash,
682 F.2d 648, 659 (7th Cir. 1982) (Stewart, J. writing for the Seventh
Circuit).

26. Even within the gaps, restrictions not easy to define, but felt, however impalpable
they may be, by every judge and lawyer, hedge and circumscribe his action. They

are established by the traditions of the centuries, by the example of other judges, his predecessors and his colleagues, by the collective judgment of the profession, and by the duty of adherence to the pervading spirit of the law.

B. Cardozo, supra note 9, at 114.

27. Southern Pac. Co. v. Jensen, 244 U.S. 204 (1917).
28. See id. at 218–23 (Holmes, J., dissenting). Justice Holmes stated:

I recognize without hesitation that judges do and must legislate, but they can do so only interstitially; they are confined from molar to molecular motions. A common-law judge could not say I think the doctrine of consideration a bit of historical nonsense and shall not enforce it in my court. No more could a judge exercising the limited jurisdiction of admiralty say I think well of the common-law rules of master and servant and propose to introduce them here *en bloc*. Certainly he could not in that way enlarge the exclusive jurisdiction of the District Courts and cut down the power of the States.
. . .
    The common law is not a brooding omnipresence in the sky but the articulate voice of some sovereign or quasi-sovereign that can be identified; although some decisions with which I have disagreed seem to me to have forgotten the fact.

Id. at 221–22 (Holmes, J., dissenting).

29. Act of Oct. 6, 1917, ch. 97, §§ 1, 2, 40 Stat. 395 (repealed by Act of June 25, 1948, ch. 646, 62 Stat. 869, 931).
30. Knickerbocker Ice Co. v. Stewart, 253 U.S. 149 (1920) (unlawful delegation of congressional legislative power in derogation of constitutional command for uniformity of maritime law).
31. Id. at 167 (Holmes, J., dissenting).
32. Act of June 10, 1922, ch. 216, §§ 1, 2, 42 Stat. 634–35 (repealed by Act of June 25, 1948, ch. 646, 62 Stat. 869, 931).
33. 264 U.S. 219 (1924).
34. Id. at 228.
35. Id. at 229–35 (Brandeis, J., dissenting).
36. To hold that Congress can effect this result by sanctioning the application of state workmen's compensation laws to accidents to any other class of employees occurring on the navigable waters of the State would not, in my judgment, require us to overrule any of these cases. It would require merely that we should limit the application of the rule therein announced, and that we should declare our disapproval of certain expressions used in the opinions. Such limitation of principles previously announced, and such express disapproval of *dicta*, are often necessary. It is an unavoidable incident of the search by courts of last resort for the true rule. The process of inclusion and exclusion, so often applied in developing a rule, cannot end with its first enunciation. The rule as announced must be deemed tentative. For the many and varying facts to which it will be applied cannot be foreseen. Modification implies growth. It is the life of the law.

Id. at 236 (Brandeis, J., dissenting) (footnote omitted).

37. If the Court is of opinion that this act of Congress is in necessary conflict with its recent decisions, those cases should be frankly overruled. The reasons for doing so are persuasive. Our experience in attempting to apply the rule, and helpful discussions by friends of the Court, have made it clear that the rule declared is legally unsound; that it disturbs legal principles long established; and that if adhered to, it will make a serious addition to the classes of cases which this Court is required to review. Experience and discussion have also made apparent how unfortunate are the results, economically and socially. It has, in part, frustrated a promising attempt to alleviate some of the misery, and remove some of the injustice, incident to the conduct of industry and commerce. These farreaching and

unfortunate results of the rule declared in Southern Pacific Co. v. Jensen cannot have been foreseen when the decision was rendered. If it is adhered to, appropriate legislative provision, urgently needed, cannot be made until another amendment of the Constitution shall have been adopted. For no federal workmen's compensation law could satisfy the varying and peculiar economic and social needs incident to the diversity of conditions in the several States.

Id. at 236–37 (Brandeis, J., dissenting) (footnotes omitted).

38. Id. at 238 (footnote omitted).
39. See notes 3–8 supra.
40. Davis v. Department of Labor and Indus., 317 U.S. 249 (1942).
41. Id. at 256.
42. "Only if the Court were to overrule the Jensen case in its constitutional aspects could I join in reversal of the judgment here." Id. at 263 (Stone, C.J., dissenting).
43. Id. at 258–59 (Frankfurter, J., concurring).
44. Such a desirable end cannot now be achieved merely by judicial repudiation of the Jensen doctrine. Too much has happened in the twenty-five years since that ill-starred decision. Federal and state enactments have so accommodated themselves to the complexity and confusion introduced by the Jensen rulings that the resources of adjudication can no longer bring relief from the difficulties which the judicial process itself brought into being. Therefore, until Congress sees fit to attempt another comprehensive solution of the problem, this Court can do no more than bring some order out of the remaining judicial chaos as marginal situations come before us. Because it contributes to that end, I join in the Court's opinion.

Id. at 259 (Frankfurter, J., concurring).

45. In this respect the Jensen case is not unique. See Runyon v. McCrary, 427 U.S. 160, 189–92 (1976) (Stevens, J., concurring).
46. For example, regardless of the propriety of the original determination that voting in state elections is an interest protected by section one of the Fourteenth Amendment or that the provision imposes the substance of the First Amendment upon the states, each of these determinations is far too deeply embedded in the constitutional order to admit of reassessment. I do not think that an individual appointed to the Court could responsibly base his vote, in relevant cases, on the theory that only the national government is bound to respect free expression or the theory that the Fourteenth Amendment was never intended to reach suffrage qualifications. Nor—although this is a different issue—could *five* justices responsibly so decide, although a solid case on the merits could be made if these matters were considered de novo. History has its claims, at least where settled expectations of the body politic have clustered around constitutional doctrine.

Monaghan, Taking Supreme Court Opinions Seriously, 39 Md. L. Rev. 1, 7 (1979) (footnotes omitted).

47. See Florida Dep't. of Health & Rehabilitation Servs. v. Florida Nursing Home Ass'n, 450 U.S. 147, 151 (1981) (Stevens, J., concurring).
48. See Leiman, The Rule of Four, 57 Colum. L. Rev. 975, 981–82 (1957).
49. The Judiciary Act of 1925 is often referred to as the Judges' Bill because it was drafted by a committee of Supreme Court Justices. See Hellman, The Business of the Supreme Court Under the Judiciary Act of 1925: The Plenary Docket in the 1970's, 91 Harv. L. Rev. 1711, 1712 (1978).
50. Act of Feb. 13, 1925, ch. 229, 43 Stat. 936 (current version at 28 U.S.C. §§ 1251–1294 (1976)). On the historical precursors to this expansion of the Supreme Court's discretionary appellate jurisdiction, see notes 53–54 infra.

51. On December 18, 1924, Justice McReynolds testified before the Committee on the Judiciary of the House of Representatives as follows:

> Every year now Congress is passing many acts and every act that is passed probably sooner or later will come to us in some one or other of its aspects. The more Federal acts there are the more opportunities there are of bringing cases to us, and it has been growing and growing until it is utterly impossible for us to try every case in which there is a Federal question involved. So it must be determined whether the court will slip behind and delays will increase or whether the number of cases presented to the court shall be restricted.

Hearings on H.R. 8206 Before the Committee on the Judiciary, 68th Cong., 2d Sess. 20 (1924) [hereinafter House Hearings].

52. "For the three terms preceding the [1925] Act . . . eighty per cent of the cases came to the Court as a matter of course, regardless of the Court's judgment as to the seriousness of the questions at issue. In less than twenty per cent did the Court exercise discretion in assuming jurisdiction." Frankfurter & Landis, The Supreme Court Under the Judiciary Act of 1925, 42 Harv. L. Rev. 1, 10–11 (1928). The Judiciary Act of 1925, note 50 supra, altered the nature of the Supreme Court's appellate review by reallocating many classes of cases from obligatory review by appeal or writ of error to discretionary review by writ of certiorari.

53. William Howard Taft described the background of the 1891 Act as follows:

> At the centenary celebration of the launching of the Federal Constitution in Philadelphia, the addresses of the Justices of the Supreme Court and of the distinguished members of the Bar contained urgent appeals to Congress to relieve the Court, which was then considerably more than three years behind.
>
> Congress sought to remove congestion by the Act of March 3d, 1891. [Circuit Court of Appeals Act of 1891, ch. 517, 26 Stat. 826 (current version at 28 U.S.C. §§ 1251–1294 (1976))]. It created nine Circuit Courts of Appeals as intermediate courts of review. . . .
>
> In the Act of 1891, Congress for the first time conferred upon the Supreme Court, in extensive classes of litigation, discretion to decline to review cases if they did not seem to the Court to be worthy of further review. In this discretionary jurisdiction the most numerous class of cases was of those which depended upon the diverse citizenship of the parties as the basis of federal jurisdiction.

Taft, The Jurisdiction of the Supreme Court Under the Act of February 13, 1925, 35 Yale L.J. 1, 1-2 (1925).

54. Justice Van Devanter testified:

> Then, we have the cases coming from the State courts. For a great many years cases came from the State courts on writ of error only to the Supreme Court, the cases being those in which there were Federal questions which were decided adversely to the litigant asserting the Federal right. The statute was changed about 1914 so as to permit the Supreme Court to take cases on petitions for certiorari where the Federal question was decided in favor of the Federal right. That situation continued until 1916, when a statute was enacted which enlarged the number of cases that could come on petition for certiorari from State courts, and decreased accordingly the number that could come on writ of error.

Hearings on S. 2060 and 2061 Before a Subcomm. of the Committee on the Judiciary, 68th Cong., 1st Sess. 34 (1924) [hereinafter Senate Hearings].

The Court's discretionary docket was substantially enlarged with the enactment of the Act of Sept. 6, 1916, Pub. L. No. 64–258, § 3, 39 Stat. 726, 727 (repealed by Act of Feb. 13, 1925, Pub. L. No. 68–415, § 13, 43 Stat. 936, 941), which removed cases arising under the Federal Employers Liability Act from those which the Court was statutorily required to hear. Nevertheless, prior to the enactment of the Judiciary Act of 1925, over 80% of the Court's docket was obligatory rather than discretionary. See Frankfurter & Landis, supra note 52, at 10–11.

55. For example, Chief Justice Taft testified:

> I heard the late Philander Knox, with whom I was on intimate terms, say either to me or to some one in my hearing, a word or two indicating that he thought the question of whether a case got in by certiorari or not was governed by the temperament, the digestion and the good nature of the particular person in the court to whom the question was referred, that it was distributed in some way so that each member of the court had two or three certioraris that it could let in.
> . . .
> Now, the truth is, and I want to emphasize that because I think perhaps I have more to do with certioraris in one way than any other member of the court, because I have to make the first statement of the case when a certiorari comes up for disposition; I write out every case that comes up for certiorari and I read it to the court. I think the members of the court are a little impatient sometimes because I give too much detail. Perhaps that is because I am a new member, or was a new member. And then having stated the case I go around and ask each member of the court, who has his memorandum, as to what view he takes. Then having discussed the case we vote on it.

House Hearings, supra note 51, at 26–27.

56. Justice Van Devanter testified:

> The petition and brief are required to be served on the other party, and time is given for the presentation of an opposing brief. When this has been done copies of the printed record as it came from the circuit court of appeals and of the petition and briefs are distributed among the members of the Supreme Court. . . .

House Hearings, supra note 51, at 8.

57. Justice Van Devanter unequivocally stated that "each judge examines them and prepares a memorandum or note indicating his view of what should be done." Id.

58. In conference these cases are called, each in its turn, and each judge states his views in extenso or briefly as he thinks proper; and when all have spoken any difference in opinion is discussed and then a vote is taken. I explain this at some length because it seems to be thought outside that the cases are referred to particular judges, as, for instance, that those coming from a particular circuit are referred to the justice assigned to that circuit, and that he reports on them, and the others accept his report. That impression is wholly at variance with what actually occurs.

Id. Chief Justice Taft also elaborated on the procedure, see note 55 supra.

59. Reading the legislative history in its entirety, I gain the impression that the principal emphasis in the presentation made by the justices concentrated on the individual attention given to every petition by every justice and the full discussion of every petition at conference, and that significantly less emphasis was placed on the Rule of Four. See House Hearings, supra note 51, at 8.

60. Id. at 13. In Southern Power Co. v. North Carolina Public Serv. Co., 263

U.S. 508, 509 (1924), the Court noted that 420 petitions for certiorari had been filed during the 1922 Term. However the difference between this figure and the figures mentioned by Justice Van Devanter may be explained (possibly by difference between filings and dispositions), it is plain that the Court was required to deal with relatively few petitions each week.

61. Shortly after the enactment of the 1925 Act, Chief Justice Taft wrote:

A question has been under consideration by the Court as to whether it would be practical to give oral hearings to applications for certioraris. The changes in the new Act will doubtless increase the number of these applications, and if the Court could be relieved by short oral statements of the burden of close examination of briefs and records, it might help its disposition of the business and at the same time give assurance to counsel of the fact, which seems sometimes to have been doubted, that the full Court seriously considers every application for a certiorari and votes upon it as a real issue to be judicially determined. If there are to be five hundred applications for certiorari a year (a conservative estimate), and ten minutes should be allowed to a side, this would consume, if all the applications were orally presented and opposed, eight weeks of the oral sessions of the Court. The Court gives about eighteen weeks to oral sessions during an annual term, so that it would take a little less than one-half of the oral sessions devoted by the Court to argument. Of course it is suggested that even if argument were permitted, advantage would not be taken in many cases in which briefs would be solely relied on. An experiment of a week or two at the beginning of the term might possibly enable the Court to judge more safely as to this. I fear, however, that the experiment would show to be true what Senator Cummins said upon the floor of the Senate, when it was proposed to require oral hearings of certiorari applications, that we might just as well not pass the law at all.

Taft, supra note 53, at 12.

62. Current debate over proposals for reducing the Court's overcrowded docket has generated many compilations of this geometric expansion. See, e.g., Federal Judicial Center, Report of the Study Group on the Caseload of the Supreme Court 1–9 (1972), reprinted in 57 F.R.D. 573, 577–84 (1972) [hereinafter Freund Study Group]; Griswold, Rationing Justice—The Supreme Court's Caseload and What the Court Does Not Do, 60 Cornell L. Rev. 335, 336–38 (1975).

63. I have previously commented on this "totally unnecessary" use of the Court's scarce resources. See Singleton v. Commissioner, 439 U.S. 940, 942–46 (1978) (opinion of Stevens, J., respecting the denial of the petition for writ of certiorari).

64. After reviewing the congressional hearings and debates, one commentator notes that although "[t]here is ample indication that Congress had the rule of four in mind when it approved the Judges Bill," Leiman, supra note 48, at 985, "[t]here is no evidence that Congress intended the Court to transfer to the hands of a minority of its membership the power to determine what cases the Court will decide." Id. at 987–88. See also note 59 supra.

The comment that comes closest to suggesting that a legislative limitation should be placed upon the Court's discretionary control over its certiorari docket is found in the following colloquy during the Senate Hearings:

Senator Spencer. What would be your judgment as to the advisability of placing any legislative limitation upon the discretionary power to grant the writ, as,

for example, when the decision of the circuit court of appeals is different from
that of the district court, or when in the judgment of two or three of the justices
of the Supreme Court the writ ought to be granted?

Mr. Justice Van Devanter. I believe it better to make no limitation along either
line. The circuit court of appeals may have differed from the district court because there had been an intervening decision on the question by our court, or, if
the question was one of State law, because there had been an intervening decision
thereon by the supreme court of the State. In such a situation, and in some
others, the fact that the district court and the circuit court of appeal differed
would not be of much importance. Again, the circuit court of appeal is an appellate court presided over by three judges, and while, as you will see, we sometimes
reverse the circuit court of appeal and affirm the district court, I think the matter
would better be left without the limitation suggested.

When I speak of a discretionary jurisdiction on certiorari I do not mean, of
course, that the Supreme Court merely exercises a choice or will in granting or
refusing the writ, but that it exercises a sound judicial discretion, gives careful
thought to the matter in the light of the supporting and opposing briefs, and re-
solves it according to recognized principles.

Senate Hearings, supra note 54, at 32. Justice Van Devanter apparently
put an end to any consideration of such a legislative limitation.

65. This is not to suggest that the problem has only recently surfaced. As
early as 1928, Frankfurter and Landis detected "the seeds of competition between the task of deciding cases and the necessity of disposing of
petitions for certiorari." Frankfurter & Landis, supra note 52, at 11.

66. We once thought that substitution of discretionary in place of mandatory jurisdiction would cure overloading. It has helped greatly. But the burden of passing
on petitions invoking discretion is considerable, and the temptation to judges is
great to take hold of any result that strikes them as wrong or any question that is
interesting, even if not of general importance. The fact is that neither the judges
nor the profession have wholeheartedly and consistently accepted the implications of discretionary jurisdiction in courts of last resort.

Jackson, supra note 4, at 335.

67. Letter from Chief Justice Charles Evans Hughes to Senator Burton K.
Wheeler (Mar. 21, 1937). This celebrated letter was sent to the senator
during congressional consideration of President Roosevelt's court-
packing plan of 1937. For a reprint of the letter, see Sen. Rep. No. 711,
75th Cong., 1st Sess. 38–40 (1937). On the circumstances surrounding
the writing of this letter, see Freund, Charles Evans Hughes as Chief
Justice, 81 Harv. L. Rev. 4, 21–34 (1967).

68. Letter from Paul A. Freund to John Paul Stevens (Aug. 24, 1982). I
found that comment of particular interest because one of the points
made in Justice Brandeis' criticism of the Jensen rule in his dissent in
Washington v. W.C. Dawson & Co., 264 U.S. 219, 237 (1924)—an opinion that was written while the Judges' Bill was under consideration—was
that adherence to the Jensen rule would "make a serious addition to the
classes of cases which this Court is required to review." 264 U.S. at 237
(footnote omitted).

69. Harold Burton Papers, Manuscript Division, Library of Congress.

70. I am indebted to my law clerks, Carol Lee and Jeffrey Lehman, for
assembling this data from Justice Burton's records and from my docket
sheets, for identifying the cases listed in notes 72 and 73 infra, and for
making a number of valuable criticisms of the text of these remarks. I

am also indebted to my former law clerk Matthew Verschelden for valuable research assistance concerning the doctrine of *stare decisis*.

71. It is interesting to note that the impression gained by Judge Henry J. Friendly "from thumbing the volumes of 'a generation ago' is that the Court was deciding a good many cases not meriting its attention—as several Justices thought." H. Friendly, Federal Jurisdiction: A General View 51 (1973).

72. Wade v. Mayo, 334 U.S. 672 (1948), rev'g 158 F.2d 614 (5th Cir. 1946); Price v. Johnston, 334 U.S. 266 (1948), rev'g (5–4) 159 F.2d 234 and 161 F.2d 705 (9th Cir. 1947); Oyama v. California, 332 U.S. 633 (1948), rev'g 29 Cal. 2d 164, 173 P.2d 794 (1946); Haley v. Ohio, 332 U.S. 596 (1948), rev'g147 Ohio St. 340, 70 N.E. 2d 905 (1947); Blumenthal v. United States, 332 U.S. 539 (1947), aff'g 158 F.2d 883 (9th Cir. 1946); United States v. Standard Oil Co., 332 U.S. 301 (1947), aff'g 153 F.2d 958 (9th Cir. 1946); Fay v. New York, 332 U.S. 261 (1947), aff'g (5-4) 296 N.Y. 510, 68 N.E.2d 453 (1946); Foster v. Illinois, 332 U.S. 134 (1947), aff'g (5-4) 394 Ill. 194, 68 N.E. 2d 252 (1946); Oklahoma v. United States, 331 U.S. 788 (1947), aff'g per curiam United States v. Champlin Ref. Co., 156 F.2d 769 (10th Cir. 1946); Bazley v. Commissioner 331 U.S. 737 (1947), aff'g 155 F.2d 237 (3rd Cir. 1946) and 155 F.2d 246 (3rd Cir. 1946); Mexican Light & Power Co. v. Texas Mexican Ry., 331 U.S. 731 (1947), aff'g (7–2) 145 Tex. 50, 193 S.W.2d 964 (1946); Rutherford Food Corp. v. McComb, 331 U.S. 722 (1947), aff'g as modified Walling v. Rutherford Food Corp., 156 F.2d 513 (10th Cir. 1946); Interstate Natural Gas Co. v. FPC, 331 U.S. 682 (1947), aff'g 156 F.2d 949 (5th Cir. 1946); United States v. Bayer, 331 U.S. 532 (1947), rev'g 156 F. 2d 964 (2d Cir. 1946); NLRB v. Jones & Laughlin Steel Corp., 331 U.S. 416 (1947), rev'g (5–4) 154 F.2d 932 (6th Cir. 1946); Champion Spark Plug Co. v. Sanders, 331 U.S. 125 (1947), aff'g 156 F.2d 488 (2d Cir. 1946); McCullough v. Kammerer Corp., 331 U.S. 96 (1947), rev'g 156 F.2d 343 (9th Cir. 1946); Land v. Dollar, 330 U.S. 731 (1947), aff'g 154 F.2d 307 (D.C. Cir. 1946); Penfield Co. v. SEC, 330 U.S. 585 (1947), aff'g in part 157 F.2d 65 (9th Cir. 1946); Confederated Bands of Ute Indians v. United States, 330 U.S. 169 (1947), aff'g 64 F. Supp. 569 (Ct. Cl. 1946); Ellis v. Union Pac. R.R., 329 U.S. 649 (1947), rev'g (8–1) 147 Neb. 18, 22 N.W.2d 305 (1946); Transparent-Wrap Mach. Corp. v. Stokes & Smith Co., 329 U.S. 637 (1947), rev'g 156 F.2d 198 (2d Cir. 1946); Albrecht v. United States, 329 U.S. 599 (1947), aff'g 155 F.2d 77 (8th Cir. 1946); Local 2880 v. NLRB, 158 F.2d 365 (9th Cir. 1946), cert. granted, 331 U.S. 798 (1947), dismissed voluntarily on motion, 332 U.S. 845 (1948); United States v. Fried, 161 F.2d 453 (2d Cir.), cert. granted, 331 U.S. 804, dismissed voluntarily on motion, 332 U.S. 807 (1947).

73. Minnick v. California Dep't of Corrections, 452 U.S. 105 (1981), dismissing writ of cert., 95 Cal. App. 3d 506, 157 Cal. Rptr. 260 (Ct. App. 1979); City of Memphis v. Greene, 451 U.S. 100 (1980), aff'g 592 F.2d 1133 (10th Cir. 1979); Northwest Airlines, Inc. v. Transport Workers Union, 451 U.S. 77 (1981), aff'g in part and vacating in part 606 F.2d 1350 (D.C. Cir. 1979); Michael M. v. Superior Court, 450 U.S. 464 (1981), aff'g 25 Cal. 3d 608, 601 P.2d 572, 159 Cal. Rptr. 340 (1979); Sears, Roebuck & Co. v. County of Los Angeles, 449 U.S. 1119 (1981),

aff'g by an equally divided court Zee Toys, Inc. v. County of Los Angeles, 85 Cal. App. 3d 763, 149 Cal. Rptr. 750 (1978); Fedorenko v. United States, 449 U.S. 490 (1981), aff'g 597 F.2d 946 (5th Cir. 1979); Cuyler v. Adams, 449 U.S. 433 (1981), aff'g 592 F.2d 720 (3d Cir. 1979); United States v. Cortex, 449 U.S. 411 (1981), rev'g 595 F.2d 505 (9th Cir. 1979); Firestone Tire & Rubber Co. v. Risjord, 449 U.S. 368 (1981), vacating and remanding 612 F.2d 377 (8th Cir. 1980); Watkins v. Sowders, 449 U.S. 341 (1981), aff'g Summitt v. Bordenkircher, 608 F.2d 247 (6th Cir. 1979); EPA v. National Crushed Stone Ass'n, 449 U.S. 64 (1980), rev'g 601 F.2d 111 and 604 F.2d 239 (4th Cir. 1979); Republic Steel Corp. v. OSHA, 448 U.S. 917 (1980) (dismissed pursuant to Rule 53); United States v. Sioux Nation of Indians, 448 U.S. 371 (1980), aff'g 601 F.2d 1157 (Ct. Cl. 1979); Thomas v. Washington Gas Light Co., 448 U.S. 261 (1980), rev'g 598 F.2d 617 (4th Cir. 1979); Dawson Chem. Co. v. Rohm & Hass Co., 448 U.S. 176 (1980), aff'g 599 F.2d 685 (5th Cir. 1979); Maher v. Gagne, 448 U.S. 122 (1980), aff'g 594 F.2d 336 (2d Cir. 1979); Rawlings v. Kentucky, 448 U.S. 98 (1980), aff'g 581 S.W.2d 348 (Ky. 1979); Maine v. Thiboutot, 448 U.S. 1 (1980), aff'g 405 A.2d 230 (Me. 1979); Roadway Express, Inc. v. Piper, 447 U.S. 752 (1980), aff'g and remanding Monk v. Roadway Express, Inc., 599 F.2d 1378 (5th Cir. 1979); Walter v. United States, 447 U.S. 649 (1980), dismissing cert. in part and rev'g 592 F.2d 788 and 597 F.2d 63 (5th Cir. 1979); Reeves, Inc. v. Stake, 447 U.S. 429 (1980), aff'g Reeves, Inc. v. Kelley, 603 F.2d 736 (8th Cir. 1979); Diamond v. Chakrabarty, 447 U.S. 303 (1980), aff'g 596 F.2d 952 (C.C.P.A. 1979); United States v. Henry, 447 U.S. 264 (1980), aff'g 590 F.2d 544 (4th Cir. 1979); New York Gaslight Club, Inc. v. Carey, 447 U.S. 54 (1980), aff'g 598 F.2d 1253 (2d Cir. 1979); Standefer v. United States, 447 U.S. 10 (1980), aff'g 610 F.2d 1076 (3d Cir. 1979); Walker v. Armco Steel Corp., 446 U.S. 740 (1980), aff'g F.2d 1133 (10th Cir. 1979); Andrus v. Shell Oil Co., 446 U.S. 657 (1980), aff'g 591 F.2d 597 (10th Cir. 1979); Andrus v. Glover Constr. Co., 446 U.S. 608 (1980), aff'g 591 F.2d 554 (10th Cir. 1979); Andrus v. Utah, 446 U.S. 500 (1980), rev'g State of Utah v. Kleppe, 586 F.2d 756 (10th Cir. 1979); Busic v. United States, 446 U.S. 398 (1980), rev'g and remanding 587 F.2d 577 (3d Cir. 1978); Nachman Corp. v. Pension Benefit Guar. Corp., 446 U.S. 359 (1980), aff'g 592 F.2d 947 (7th Cir. 1979); Cuyler v. Sullivan, 446 U.S. 335 (1980), vacating and remanding 593 F.2d 512 (3d Cir. 1979); Roberts v. United States, 445 U.S. 552 (1980), aff'g 600 F.2d 815 (D.C. Cir. 1978); United States v. Clarke, 445 U.S. 253 (1980), rev'g 590 F.2d 765 (9th Cir. 1979); California Retail Liquor Dealers Ass'n v. Midcal Alum., Inc., 445 U.S. 97 (1980), aff'g 90 Cal. App. 3d 979, 153 Cal. Rptr. 757 (1979); Massachusetts v. Meehan, 445 U.S. 39 (1980) (per curiam), dismissing writ of cert. as improvidently granted, 377 Mass. 522, 387 N.E.2d 527 (1979).

The fact that there may be significant cases listed supra and in note 72 supra does not necessarily demonstrate the value of the Rule of Four, because the significant issues decided in these cases might well have come before the Court in other litigation in due course. The frequency with which an issue arises, of course, is one measure of its significance.

74. See House Hearings, supra note 51, at 8.
75. It is of interest to note that another distinguished tribunal with a compa-

rable volume of business and comparable discretionary control over its docket follows a majority vote case selection rule. Over 3,000 petitions for review are filed in the California Supreme Court each year. Judicial Council of Cal., Annual Report of the Administrative Office 69–72 (1981). I am told that that court follows a selection process of dividing the petitions into an "A" list and a "B" list, and that only the cases on one of those lists are discussed in conference. They also follow a Rule of Four, but since there are only seven justices on that court, that number represents a majority.

76. In an uncharacteristic slip during the interval between his service as an associate justice and his service as chief justice, Charles Evans Hughes inadvertently "observed that in the Supreme Court, aside from administrative matters of the merest routine, every action of the Court is taken on the concurrence of a majority of its members." C. Hughes, The Supreme Court of the United States 56–57 (1928). I wonder if subconsciously the chief justice regarded the processing of certiorari petitions as a form of "second class work." Cf. Stevens, Some Thoughts on Judicial Restraint, 66 Judicature 177, 182 (1982) (suggesting that present Court does a poor job of selecting cases on merits).

77. A question raised in 1959 by Professor Henry M. Hart, Jr. puts the problem of numbers in proper perspective:

> Does a nation of 165 millions realize any significant gain merely because its highest judicial tribunal succeeds in deciding 127 cases by full opinion instead of 117? 137 cases? 147 cases? Or even 157 cases? The hard fact must be faced that the Justices of the Supreme Court of the United States can at best put their full minds to no more than a tiny handful of the trouble cases which year by year are tossed up to them out of the great sea of millions and even billions of concrete situations to which their opinions relate. When this fact is fully apprehended, it will be seen that the question whether this handful includes or excludes a dozen or so more cases is unimportant. It will be seen that what matters about Supreme Court opinions is not their quantity but their quality.

Hart, The Supreme Court, 1958 Term—Foreword: The Time Chart of the Justices, 73 Harv. L. Rev. 84, 96 (1959).

78. There have been two major proposals to create a new National Court of Appeals. See U.S. Commission on Revision of the Federal Court Appellate System, Structure and Internal Procedures: Recommendations for Change (1975) [hereinafter Hruska Commission Report]; Freund Study Group, supra note 62. The "Freund" National Court would screen all of the applications for review filed in the Supreme Court and either deny review or certify to the Supreme Court for final review. Freund Study Group, supra note 62, at 20–23, 57 F.R.D. at 592–94. The "Hruska" National Court would not screen cases, but rather provide authoritative decisions on cases referred to it by the Supreme Court. Hruska Commission Report, supra, at 32–34, 39.

The proposals have generated a wealth of literature by their principal drafters as well as by outside commentators. See, e.g., Alsup, A Policy Assessment of the National Court of Appeals, 25 Hastings L.J. 1313 (1974); Black, The National Court of Appeals: An Unwise Proposal, 83 Yale L.J. 883 (1974); Freund, A National Court of Appeals, 25 Hastings L.J. 1301 (1974); Hruska, The Commission on Revision of the Federal Court Appellate System: A Legislative History, 1974 Ariz. St. L.J. 579.

79. See Griswold, supra note 62, at 339–41; see also, Hruska Commission Report, supra note 78, at 5–10.
80. As Professor Hellman demonstrated, "the important question is not how the present compares with the past, but whether the number of plenary decisions today is adequate to meet current needs." Hellman, supra note 49, at 1736.

Although reflection about the Rule of Four lends no support to the argument that a new court should be created to enlarge our decision-making capacity, it does indicate that if a new court were created to control our docket—assuming that court acted only by majority vote—it would grant review in a smaller number of cases than our present Court does. But cf. Freund Study Group, supra note 62, at 21, 57 F.R.D. at 592 (recommending that a National Court of Appeals propose cases for Supreme Court review whenever three of the seven members agree).

It also follows, I believe, that if Congress should create a new National Court of Appeals to enlarge the federal judiciary's lawmaking power by deciding cases referred to it by the Supreme Court, see Hruska Commission Report, supra note 78, at 32–34, 39, special attention should be given to the question whether the decision to refer should require a majority vote or merely a new Rule of Four.
81. The members of the Court have unanimously endorsed legislation that would convert the Court's remaining mandatory jurisdiction. The House passed H.R.6872 on September 20, 1982, 128 Cong. Rec. H7269–75 (daily ed. Sept. 20, 1982). See 69 A.B.A. J. 153 (1983). Both bills have been reintroduced in the 98th Congress. S. 645, 98th Cong., 1st Sess. (1983), 129 Cong. Rec. S1845 (daily ed. Mar. 1, 1983); H.R. 1968, 98th Cong., 1st Sess. (1983), 129 Cong. Rec. H940 (daily ed. Mar. 8, 1983). The enactment of these pending bills would have a substantial impact on the Court's workload. During the 1981 Term, the Court voted to hear 207 cases on the merits, of which 58 were appeals. A significant number of these appeals did not present questions of sufficient importance to merit discretionary review.
82. See Stevens, supra note 76.
83. Another luxury whose days are surely numbered is the pleasant custom of admitting large numbers of new members of the bar in open Court.
84. See note 78 supra. See also the editor's note at p. 157 supra.

Wilfred Feinberg

1. P. Bator, P. Mishkin, D. Shapiro & H. Wechsler, Hart and Wechsler's The Federal Courts and the Federal System 11–12 (2d ed. 1973).
2. The literature on the constitutionality of court-stripping bills is extensive. Recent articles include Bator, Congressional Power Over the Jurisdiction of the Federal Courts, 27 Vill. L. Rev. 1030 (1982); Brilmayer & Underhill, Congressional Obligation to Provide a Forum for Constitutional Claims: Discriminatory Jurisdictional Rules and the Conflict of Laws, 69 Va. L. Rev. 819 (1983); Sager, The Supreme Court, 1980 Term—Foreword: Constitutional Limitations on Congress' Authority to Regulate the Jurisdiction of the Federal Courts, 95 Harv. L. Rev. 17 (1981). For a classic treatment of this issue, see Hart, The Power of Con-

gress to Limit the Jurisdiction of Federal Courts: An Exercise in Dialectic, 66 Harv. L. Rev. 1362 (1953).

3. Address by David R. Brink, The Separation of Powers: Whose Ox Is Being Gored?, National Press Club 13 (Apr. 28, 1982) (on file at New York University Law Review).

4. S. 3018, 97th Cong., 2d Sess. (1982) (on file at New York University Law Review).

5. Judge Leonard I. Garth, of the United States Court of Appeals for the Third Circuit, stated recently that congressional respect for federal court jurisdiction "may come to be regarded during the years of our lifetime as the most vital item on this Nation's agenda." Address by Judge Leonard I. Garth, Pruning the Least Dangerous Branch: Congressional Intrusions on the Federal Judicial Power, The Arthur T. Vanderbilt Lecture, Harvard Law School Association of New Jersey 29 (Feb. 10, 1982) (on file at New York University Law Review). For our titles, Judge Garth and I independently borrowed Alexander Bickel's phrase, see A. Bickel, The Least Dangerous Branch (1962), borrowed in turn from Alexander Hamilton, see The Federalist No. 78, at 483 (A. Hamilton) (H.C. Lodge ed. 1888) ("[T]he judiciary, from the nature of its functions, will always be the least dangerous to the political rights of the Constitution.").

6. 1 J. Goebel, History of the Supreme Court of the United States: Antecedents and Beginnings to 1801, at 724 (1971).

7. Id. at 724–25.

8. Id. at 725–28.

9. 2 U.S. (2 Dall.) 419 (1793).

10. J. Goebel, supra note 6, at 734–36.

11. Warren, Legislative and Judicial Attacks on the Supreme Court of the United States—A History of the Twenty-Fifth Section of the Judiciary Act (pts. 1 & 2), 47 Am. L. Rev. 1, 161, 166 (1913).

12. J. Goebel, supra note 6, at 736.

13. Id. at 736–41. In February 1798, the Supreme Court decided that after the ratification of the Eleventh Amendment, the federal courts had no jurisdiction over cases in which a state was sued by citizens of another state or by the citizens or subjects of a foreign state. See Hollingsworth v. Virginia, 3 U.S. (3 Dall.) 378 (1798).

14. 2 G. Haskins & H. Johnson, History of the Supreme Court of the United States: Foundations of Power: John Marshall, 1801–15, at 110–22 (1981).

15. Id. at 111–15.

16. Id. at 115–16.

17. Id. at 122–26.

18. Id. at 117 (quoting Edmund Randolph).

19. Id. at 108.

20. Id. at 108–09, 138–39.

21. Id. at 139.

22. Id. at 140.

23. Id. at 159–60.

24. Id. at 153.

25. Id. at 209.

26. Id. at 184.

27. Id. at 205–11.
28. R. Morris, Seven Who Shaped Our Destiny: The Founding Fathers as Revolutionaries (1973).
29. Id. at 126–27.
30. G. Haskins & H. Johnson, supra note 14, at 205.
31. Id. at 211.
32. Id. at 211–12.
33. Id. at 217–19.
34. See id. at 217 n. 60.
35. Id. at 245.
36. These powers had been established in Martin v. Hunter's Lessee, 14 U.S. (1 Wheat.) 304 (1816). See generally G. Haskins & H. Johnson, supra note 14, at 312–65.
37. Warren, supra note 11, at 9–12, 22–23, 166–71, 174, 182–84.
38. See, e.g., id. at 5, 166, 169; see text accompanying note 42 infra.
39. Warren, supra note 11, at 175.
40. G. Haskins & H. Johnson, supra note 14, at 322–31.
41. Id. at 322–23.
42. Morris, The Forging of the Union Reconsidered: A Historical Refutation of State Sovereignty over Seabeds, 74 Colum. L. Rev. 1056, 1079–80 (1974).
43. G. Haskins & H. Johnson, supra note 14, at 324 & n. 46.
44. Id. at 323–24.
45. United States v. Peters, 9 U.S. (5 Cranch) 115 (1809). The Court skirted the potential Eleventh Amendment problem by stating that the money in question "was in possession, not of the state of Pennsylvania, but of David Rittenhouse [the Treasurer of the Commonwealth] as an individual." Id. at 141; see G. Haskins & H. Johnson, supra note 14, at 326–27
46. G. Haskins & H. Johnson, supra note 14, at 327–31.
47. Huidekoper's Lessee v. Douglass, 7 U.S. (3 Cranch) 1 (1805); see G. Haskins & H. Johnson, supra note 14, at 317–21.
48. Huidekoper's Lessee, 7 U.S. at 70–71; G. Haskins & H. Johnson, supra note 14, at 320–21.
49. G. Haskins & H. Johnson, supra note 14, at 321.
50. Id.
51. Id. at 322.
52. Warren, supra note 11, at 22, 27–28, 30–34.
53. Id. at 26; see also id. at 168.
54. Id. at 164.
55. Id. at 29.
56. Mayor of New York v. Miln, 33 U.S. (8 Pet.) 118, 122 (1834) (Marshall, C.J.); see Warren, supra note 11, at 165.
57. H. Hyman & W. Wiecek, Equal Justice Under Law: Constitutional Development 1835–1875, at 194–97, 201–02 (1982).
58. Id. at 196–97.
59. 60 U.S. (19 How.) 393 (1857); see H. Hyman & W. Wiecek, supra note 57, at 172–90.
60. 60 U.S. at 404–05.
61. Id. at 452.
62. H. Hyman & W. Wiecek, supra note 57, at 191.

63. Id. at 191–92.
64. Id. at 192.
65. Id. at 195–96.
66. 6 C. Fairman, History of the Supreme Court of the United States: Reconstruction and Reunion 1864–88, at 437 (1971).
67. Id. at 438.
68. Id. at 448–49.
69. Id. at 448.
70. See id. at 437–38.
71. Id. at 449–51.
72. Id. at 459, 467–69.
73. 74 U.S. (7 Wall.) 506, 514–15 (1869).
74. C. Fairman, supra note 66, at 440–44.
75. 74 U.S. at 515.
76. C. Fairman, supra note 66, at 471, 475–78.
77. 75 U.S. (8 Wall.) 85, 105–06 (1869).
78. See Van Alstyne, A Critical Guide to Ex Parte McCardle, 15 Ariz. L. Rev. 229, 249 & n.75 (1973) (discussing view of commentators that McCardle curtailed none of the Court's "essential" functions). For a discussion and criticism of the "essential functions" thesis, see Gunther, Congressional Power to Curtail Federal Court Jurisdiction: An Opinionated Guide to the Ongoing Debate, in The Courts: Separation of Powers 15, 21–22 (B. Goulet ed. 1984).
79. See Van Alstyne, supra note 78, at 257–60.
80. 75 U.S. (8 Wall.) 603 (1870).
81. See Knox v. Lee, 79 U.S. (12 Wall.) 457, 530 (1871).
82. 79 U.S. (12 Wall.) 457 (1871).
83. See Ratner, Was the Supreme Court Packed by President Grant?, 50 Pol. Sci. Q. 343 (1935).
84. 157 U.S. 429 (1895).
85. The Sixteenth Amendment was adopted in 1913. Since then, only one Supreme Court decision has been overruled by a constitutional amendment: the Twenty-sixth Amendment, which lowered the voting age to eighteen, overruled Oregon v. Mitchell, 400 U.S. 112 (1970).
86. 157 U.S. at 607 (Field, J.).
87. Id. at 443–44 (argument for appellants).
88. P. Murphy, The Constitution in Crisis Times 1918–1969, at 141 (1972).
89. Id. at 146–48.
90. Id. at 155 n.82.
91. Elliott, Court-Curbing Proposals in Congress, 33 Notre Dame Law, 597, 605–06 (1958).
92. P. Murphy, supra note 88, at 152.
93. Id. at 152–53; Elliott, supra note 91, at 605.
94. P. Murphy, supra note 88, at 153; Elliott, supra note 91, at 605.
95. W. Leuchtenburg, Franklin D. Roosevelt and the New Deal 1932–1940, at 236 (1963).
96. Id. at 237.
97. Id. at 237–38. See generally Leuchtenburg, The Origins of Franklin D. Roosevelt's "Court-Packing" Plan, 1966 Sup. Ct. Rev. 347.
98. Id. at 238.
99. Id. at 239.
100. See P. Murphy, supra note 88, at 294–306.

101. Pennsylvania v. Nelson, 350 U.S. 497 (1956).
102. Communist Party v. Subversive Activities Control Bd., 351 U.S. 115 (1956).
103. Cole v. Young, 351 U.S. 536 (1956).
104. Slochower v. Board of Higher Educ., 350 U.S. 551 (1956).
105. Konigsberg v. State Bar, 353 U.S. 252 (1957); Schware v. Board of Bar Examiners, 353 U.S. 232 (1957).
106. See P. Murphy, supra note 88, at 328.
107. See Yates v. United States, 354 U.S. 298 (1957).
108. Service v. Dulles, 354 U.S. 363 (1957).
109. Sweezy v. New Hampshire, 354 U.S. 234 (1957); Watkins v. United States, 354 U.S. 178 (1957).
110. See P. Murphy, supra note 88, at 330–33.
111. Elliott, supra note 91, at 598, 600–02.
112. Id. at 598 (discussing S. 2646, 85th Cong., 1st Sess. (1957)).
113. P. Murphy, supra note 88, at 332.
114. Elliott, supra note 91, at 598.
115. P. Murphy, supra note 88, at 332–33.
116. 347 U.S. 483 (1954).
117. Eisenberg, Congressional Authority to Restrict Lower Federal Court Jurisdiction, 83 Yale L.J. 498, 498–99 (1974).
118. Id. at 498 n.6 (discussing H.R. 1228, 85th Cong., 1st Sess. (1957)).
119. Id. (discussing S. 3467, 85th Cong., 2d Sess. 1958)).
120. Id. at 499 & n.13.
121. Id. at 499 n.13 (discussing H.R. 13915, 92d Cong., 2d Sess. (1972)).
122. See P. Murphy, supra note 88, at 386–91; Eisenberg, supra note 117, at 499 & n.10.
123. 377 U.S. 533 (1964).
124. P. Murphy, supra note 88, at 389.
125. Eisenberg, supra note 117, at 499 & n.10 (discussing H.R. 11926, 88th Cong., 2d Sess. (1964)).
126. See P. Murphy, supra note 88, at 389–91.
127. M.F. McNamara, 2,000 Famous Legal Quotations 550 (1967).
128. Committee on Federal Legislation, Jurisdiction-Stripping Proposals in Congress: The Threat to Judicial Constitutional Review, 36 Rec. A.B. City N.Y. 557, 559 (1981).
129. 116 Cong. Rec. 11,913 (1970).
130. See text accompanying note 31 supra.
131. Address by David R. Brink, supra note 3, at 5.
132. S. 3018, supra note 4.
133. Address by Senator Joseph R. Biden, The Radical Right and the Constitution: The Assault on Our Independent Federal Judiciary, Association of the Bar of the City of New York 2 (May 3, 1983) (on file at New York University Law Review).
134. S. 3018, supra note 4, § 161.
135. Id. §§ 111–112.
136. Id. §§ 121–123.
137. Id. § 171.
138. Id. § 131.
139. National Legal Center for the Public Interest, 2 Judicial/Legislative Watch Report No. 14, Nov. 5, 1982, at 3 (quoting memorandum of Staff of Senate Subcommittee on Separation of Powers).

140. S. 3018, supra note 4, §§ 141–142.
141. Id. § 151 (proposing to amend 42 U.S.C. § 1988).
142. Id. § 181. Former 28 U.S.C. §§ 2281–2282, repealed in 1976, imposed a similar requirement for injunctions against the enforcement of allegedly unconstitutional statutes, both state and federal.
143. S. 3018, supra note 4, § 191.
144. National Legal Center for the Public Interest, supra note 139, at 5 (quoting memorandum of Staff of Senate Subcommittee on Separation of Powers).
145. S. 3018, supra note 4, §§ 201–211.
146. Id. § 210.
147. Id. § 201.
148. Id. § 201(b) (1), (2).
149. Id. § 202(a).
150. Id. § 202(c).
151. Id. § 202(b).
152. Id.
153. Id. § 202(b) (4).
154. Id. § 202(b) (5).
155. The Federalist No. 78, supra note 5, at 488; see Kaufman, Chilling Judicial Independence, 88 Yale L.J. 681 (1979).
156. Address by Senator Joseph R. Biden, supra note 133, at 4.
157. Id. at 3.
158. Id. at 10–12.
159. Compare 1982 Annual Report of the Director of the Administrative Office of the United States Courts 4 (206,193 cases) [hereinafter 1982 Report] with 1962 Annual Report of the Director of the Administrative Office of the United States Courts 196 (61,836 cases) [hereinafter 1962 Report].
160. Compare 1982 Report, supra note 159, at 189 (5,311 cases) with 1962 Report, supra note 159, at 176 (2,185 cases).
161. Compare 1982 Report, supra note 159, at 190 (27,946 cases) with 1962 Report, supra note 159, at 180 (4,823 cases).
162. See 1982 Report, supra note 159, at 4 (total civil cases: 206,193; diversity cases: 50,555).
163. See 1982 Report, supra note 159, at 194–95 (total civil cases: 18,784; diversity cases: 3,217).
164. C. Fairman, supra note 66, at 469.

Harry A. Blackmun

1. 347 U.S. 483 (1954).
2. See, e.g., Pulliam v. Allen, 466 U.S. 522, 555–56, and n.16 (1984) (dissenting opinion); Maine v. Thiboutot, 448 U.S. 1, 27, and n.16 (1980) (dissenting opinion).
3. See, e.g., Aldisert, Judicial Expansion of Federal Jurisdiction: A Federal Judge's Thoughts on Section 1983, Comity and the Federal Caseload, 1973 Law and the Social Order 557; Whitman, Constitutional Torts, 79 Mich. L. Rev. 5, 6, 26, and nn.10, 115 (1980).
4. See, e.g., Patsy v. Florida Board of Regents, 457 U.S. 496, 516 (1982) (concurring opinion); H.R. 4412, 98th Cong., 1st Sess. (1983) (sugges-

tion for legislation to require state prisoners to exhaust all state remedies before bringing a § 1983 suit and to prevent relitigation of claims addressed in state proceedings); Whitman, supra note 3 (limit § 1983 to injunctive relief). See generally Federalism and the Federal Judiciary: Hearings before the Subcommittee on Separation of Powers of the Senate Committee of the Judiciary, 98th Cong., 1st Sess. (1983).

5. See Barron v. Mayor of Baltimore, 7 Pet. 243 (1833).
6. See, e.g., McCulloch v. Maryland, 4 Wheat. 316 (1819); Gibbons v. Ogden, 9 Wheat. 1 (1824); Cooley v. Board of Wardens, 12 How. 299 (1852).
7. See the Judiciary Act of 1789, § 12, 1 Stat. 79; P. Bator, P. Mishkin, D. Shapiro, & H. Wechsler, Hart and Wechsler's The Federal Courts and the Federal System 845, 1192–1193 (2d ed. 1973).
8. See, e.g., Calder v. Bull, 3 Dall. 386 (1798); McCulloch v. Maryland, supra note 6; Dartmouth College v. Woodward, 4 Wheat. 518 (1819); Gibbons v. Ogden, supra note 6; Cooley v. Board of Wardens, supra note 6. The Dred Scott case was the grim exception that proved the rule: the Court's disastrous encounter with the "peculiar institution" of slavery was part and parcel of a jurisdictional holding that Dred Scott was not a citizen of Missouri and hence could not bring a trespass action against his owner in federal court. See Scott v. Sandford, 19 How. 393, 454 (1857).
9. Act of Apr. 9, 1866, 14 Stat. 27, reenacted by § 18 of the Enforcement Act of 1870, 16 Stat. 144 (now codified at 42 U.S.C. §§ 1981 and 1982).
10. Act of May 31, 1870, 16 Stat. 140. See generally Lansford, Comment: Municipal Liability under the Ku Klux Klan Act of 1871—An Historical Perspective, in Section 1983, Sword and Shield, Civil Rights Violations: The Liability of Urban, State and Local Government 23 (R. Freilich & R. Carlisle eds. 1983).
11. Act of Apr. 20, 1871, 17 Stat. 13.
12. In 1874, the scope of the section was expanded to include deprivations of rights secured by the Constitution "and laws." Rev. Stat. § 1979. See Chapman v. Houston Welfare Rights Organization, 441 U.S. 600, 608 (1979).
13. Act of Mar. 1, 1875, ch. 144, 18 Stat. (part 3) 335.
14. See Act of Mar. 3, 1863, § 5, 12 Stat. 756; Act of Apr. 9, 1866, § 3, 14 Stat. 27; Act of July 13, 1866, § 67, 14 Stat. 171. See generally Developments in the Law, Section 1983 and Federalism, 90 Harv. L. Rev. 1133, 1148 (1977).
15. Act of Feb. 5, 1867, ch. 28, § 1, 14 Stat. 385.
16. Act of Mar. 3, 1875, §§ 1 and 2, 18 Stat. (part 3) 470.
17. See F. Frankfurter & J. Landis, The Business of the Supreme Court, A Study in the Federal Judicial System 65 (1928).
18. 407 U.S. 225 (1972).
19. Id., at 242, quoting Ex parte Virginia, 100 U.S. 339, 346 (1880).
20. Cong. Globe, 39th Cong., 1st Sess., 476 (1866) (remarks of Sen. Saulsbury).
21. Id., at 1293 (remarks of Rep. Bingham).
22. Id., at 478–479 (remarks of Sen. Saulsbury); id., at 598 (remarks of Sen. Davis); id., at 1778 (remarks of Sen. Johnson).
23. Id., at 602–603 (remarks of Sen. Lane); id., at 1124 (remarks of Rep. Cook); id., at 1833–1834 (remarks of Rep. Lawrence); id., at 1265 (re-

marks of Rep. Broomall). See generally Zeigler, A Reassessment of the Younger Doctrine in Light of the Legislative History of Reconstruction, 1983 Duke L.J. 987, 1000, and nn.87–91.

24. Cong. Globe, 42d Cong., 1st Sess., App. 258 (1871).
25. Id., at App. 260.
26. Id., at 365. See also id., at 352 (remarks of Rep. Beck); id., at App. 88 (remarks of Rep. Storm); id., at App. 50 (remarks of Rep. Kerr); id., at 365–366 (remarks of Rep. Arthur); id., at 373 (remarks of Rep. Archer); id., at 385 (remarks of Rep. Lewis); id., at 396 (remarks of Sen. Rice); id., at App. 91 (remarks of Rep. Duke); id., at App. 112 (remarks of Rep. Moore); id., at App. 117–118 (remarks of Sen. Blair); id., at App. 148 (remarks of Rep. Lamison); id., at App. 179 (remarks of Rep. Voorhees); id., at App. 304 (remarks of Rep. Slater). See generally Zeigler, supra note 23, at 1016–1017, and nn.187 and 188.
27. See, e.g., Cong. Globe, 42d Cong., 1st Sess., 337 (1871) (remarks of Rep. Whitthorne); id., at 361 (remarks of Rep. Swann); id., at 373 (remarks of Rep. Archer).
28. Id., at 366.
29. See, e.g., id., at App. 73 (remarks of Rep. Blair); id., at App. 85 (remarks of Rep. Bingham); id., at App. 141 (remarks of Rep. Shanks). See generally Carpenters and Joiners v. Scott, 463 U.S. 825, 840–47 (1983).
30. See id., at 842–44.
31. 16 Wall. 36.
32. 92 U.S. 542 (1876).
33. 106 U.S. 629 (1883).
34. 109 U.S. 3 (1883).
35. Id., at 57.
36. See, e.g., Benedict, Preserving Federalism: Reconstruction and the Waite Court, 1978 S. Ct. Rev. 39.
37. See R. Kluger, Simple Justice 59 (1976).
38. 2 Cong. Rec. 3411 (1874).
39. See R. Carr, Federal Protection of Civil Rights: Quest for a Sword 46 (1947).
40. See Davis, The Federal Enforcement Acts, in Studies in Southern History and Politics 223–224 (1914), cited in Lansford, supra note 10, at 28, n.27, and in Maslow & Robinson, Civil Rights Legislation and the Fight for Equality, 1862–1952, 20 U. Chi. L. Rev. 363, 370, n.29 (1953).
41. Act of Feb. 8, 1894, 28 Stat. 36.
42. See Kluger, supra note 37, at 68.
43. Ibid.
44. Myers v. Anderson, 238 U.S. 368 (1915); Guinn v. United States, 238 U.S. 347 (1915).
45. Buchanan v. Warley, 245 U.S. 60 (1917).
46. Nixon v. Herndon, 273 U.S. 536 (1927).
47. Nixon v. Condon, 286 U.S. 73 (1932).
48. Lane v. Wilson, 307 U.S. 268 (1939).
49. H. Aptheker, A Documentary History of the Negro People in the United States 907 (1951), quoted in C. Vose, Caucasians Only, The Supreme Court, the NAACP, and the Restrictive Covenant Cases 31 (1959).
50. See Kluger, supra note 37, at 166.

51. Exec. Order No. 8802, 3 CFR 957 (1938–1943 Comp.).
52. See 238 U.S., at 353.
53. See 245 U.S., at 69.
54. Moore v. Dempsey, 261 U.S. 86 (1923).
55. See Vose, supra note 49, at 40.
56. Shelley v. Kraemer, 334 U.S. 1 (1948); Hurd v. Hodge, 334 U.S. 24 (1948).
57. See Kluger, supra note 37, at 250–253.
58. Gressman, The Unhappy History of Civil Rights Legislation, 50 Mich. L. Rev. 1323, 1357–1358 (1952).
59. Carr, supra note 39, at 199.
60. 313 U.S. 299 (1941).
61. 325 U.S. 91 (1945).
62. Id., at 92–93.
63. Id., at 144.
64. Id., at 142.
65. Id., at 109.
66. Id., at 114, n.5.
67. Carr, supra note 39, at 106–107 (footnotes omitted).
68. 321 U.S. 649 (1944).
69. 365 U.S. 167(1961).
70. Id., at 203 (footnote omitted).
71. Cong. Globe, 42d Cong., 1st Sess., 390 (1871), quoted in Shapo, Constitutional Tort: Monroe v. Pape, and the Frontiers Beyond, 60 Nw. U.L. Rev. 277 (1965).
72. 365 U.S., at 242.
73. Id., at 180.
74. Id., at 179, quoting Mr. Voorhees of Indiana, Cong. Globe, 42d Cong., 1st Sess., App. 179 (1871).
75. Monell v. New York City Dept. of Social Services, 436 U.S. 658, 663 (1978).
76. Hague v. CIO, 307 U.S. 496 (1939).
77. Smith v. Allwright, 321 U.S. 649 (1944).
78. Shelton v. Tucker, 364 U.S. 479 (1960).
79. Mayor and City Council of Baltimore v. Dawson, 350 U.S. 877 (1955) (beaches); Gayle v. Browder, 352 U.S. 903 (1956) (buses).
80. Keyishian v. Board of Regents, 385 U.S. 589 (1967).
81. Tinker v. Des Moines School Dist., 393 U.S. 503 (1969).
82. Dombrowski v. Pfister, 380 U.S. 479 (1965).
83. NAACP v. Button, 371 U.S. 415 (1963).
84. Supreme Court of Virginia v. Consumers Union of United States, Inc., 446 U.S. 719 (1980); Village of Schaumburg v. Citizens for a Better Environment, 444 U.S. 620 (1980).
85. Goldberg v. Kelly, 397 U.S. 254 (1970).
86. Memphis Light, Gas & Water Div. v. Craft, 436 U.S. 1 (1978).
87. Board of Regents v. Roth, 408 U.S. 564 (1972); Perry v. Sindermann, 408 U.S. 593 (1972).
88. Logan v. Zimmerman Brush Co., 455 U.S. 422 (1982).
89. Fuentes v. Shevin, 407 U.S. 67 (1972); Lynch v. Household Finance Corp., 405 U.S. 538 (1972).
90. Cleveland Board of Education v. LaFleur, 414 U.S. 632 (1974).

91. Rosado v. Wyman, 397 U.S. 397 (1970); Shapiro v. Thompson, 394 U.S. 618 (1969).
92. E.g., Kramer v. Union Free School District, 395 U.S. 621 (1969); Harper v. Virginia Bd. of Elections, 383 U.S. 663 (1966); Reynolds v. Sims, 377 U.S. 533 (1964); Gray v. Sanders, 372 U.S. 368 (1963).
93. Craig v. Boren, 429 U.S. 190 (1976).
94. Zablocki v. Redhail, 434 U.S. 374 (1978).
95. O'Connor v. Donaldson, 422 U.S. 563 (1975); Estelle v. Gamble, 429 U.S. 97 (1976); Wolff v. McDonnell, 418 U.S. 539 (1974); Cruz v. Beto, 405 U.S. 319 (1972).
96. 404 F.2d 571 (CA 8 1968).
97. See, e.g., Lovell v. Brennan, 566 F. Supp. 672 (D. Me. 1983), aff'd, 728 F.2d 560 (CA1 1984). See generally Bronstein, Criminal Justice: Prison and Penology, in Our Endangered Rights 221 (N. Dorsen ed. 1984).
98. 451 U.S. 527 (1981).
99. 468 U.S. 517 (1984).
100. 465 U.S. 89 (1984).
101. 403 U.S. 388 (1971).
102. 347 U.S. 497 (1954).
103. See, e.g., 1 J. Moore, J. Lucas, H. Fink, D. Weckstein, & J. Wicker, Moore's Federal Practice ¶ 0.6[5] (1984). But cf. Tarble's Case, 13 Wall. 397 (1872).
104. I do not mean to gloss over the fact that there are still exceptions to this symmetry. The two most obvious are the federal removal statutes, which generally mean that § 1983 litigation remains in state courts only if both plaintiff and defendant want it there, and the federal criminal statutes, especially 18 U.S.C. §§ 241 and 242, which provide for federal prosecution of state officials in federal court alone. It is interesting to note with respect to the latter, however, that fewer than 450 federal prosecutions have taken place under §§ 241 and 242 since 1970—an average of less than one prosecution per state per year.
105. Quern v. Jordan, 440 U.S. 332 (1970).
106. Supreme Court of Virginia v. Consumers Union of United States, Inc., 446 U.S. 719 (1980). See also Pierson v. Ray, 386 U.S. 547 (1967), and Tenney v. Brandhove, 341 U.S. 367 (1951). But cf. Pulliam v. Allen, 466 U.S. 522 (1984).
107. Davis v. Scherer, 468 U.S. 183 (1984).
108. 451 U.S., at 546.
109. Id., at 545.
110. But see Hudson v. Palmer, 468 U.S., at 541, n.4 (Stevens, J., concurring in part and dissenting in part).
111. See id., at 533 ("the State's action is not complete until and unless it provides or refuses to provide a suitable postdeprivation remedy").
112. 454 U.S. 312 (1981).
113. 463 U.S. 825 (1983).
114. Younger v. Harris, 401 U.S. 37 (1971).
115. See, e.g., Gerstein v. Pugh, 420 U.S. 103 (1975); Dombrowski v. Pfister, 380 U.S. 479 (1965). See also Milliken v. Bradley, 433 U.S. 267 (1977); Swann v. Charlotte-Mecklenburg Bd. of Ed., 402 U.S. 1 (1971).
116. 414 U.S. 488 (1974).
117. 423 U.S. 362 (1976).

118. 461 U.S. 95 (1983).
119. Id., at 112.
120. Id., at 137.
121. Patsy v. Board of Regents, 457 U.S. 496 (1982).
122. Pulliam v. Allen, 466 U.S. 522 (1984).
123. Burnett v. Grattan, 468 U.S. 42 (1984).
124. Smith v. Robinson, 468 U.S. 992 (1984); Brown v. General Services Administration, 425 U.S. 820 (1976); Johnson v. Railway Express Agency, Inc., 421 U.S. 454 (1975); Adickes v. S.H. Kress & Co., 398 U.S. 144 (1970).
125. See Griffin v. Breckenridge, 403 U.S. 88 (1971).
126. Illinois Brick Co. v. Illinois, 431 U.S. 720, 736 (1977).
127. The Great Rights 11 (E. Cahn ed. 1963).

William J. Brennan, Jr.

1. Brennan, The Bill of Rights and the States, 36 N.Y.U.L. Rev. 761 (1961).
2. 347 U.S. 483 (1954).
3. 369 U.S. 186 (1962).
4. Schwartz, The Amendment in Operation: A Historical Overview, in The Fourteenth Amendment 29, 30 (B. Schwartz ed. 1970).
5. Brennan, State Constitutions and the Protection of Individual Rights, 90 Harv. L. Rev. 489, 490 (1977).
6. 1 Annals of Cong. 439 (J. Gales ed. 1789).
7. Id. at 435.
8. Id. at 440.
9. Id. at 755.
10. See generally I. Brant, James Madison, Father of the Constitution 271 (1950).
11. 32 U.S. (7 Pet.) 243 (1833).
12. Id. at 247.
13. L. Tribe, American Constitutional Law § 1–3, at 5 (1978).
14. U.S. Const. amend. XIV.
15. 18 Stat. 335 (1875).
16. Brennan, Landmarks of Legal Liberty, in The Fourteenth Amendment 1, 4 (B. Schwartz ed. 1970).
17. Slaughterhouse Cases, 83 U.S. (16 Wall.) 36, 79–81 (1873).
18. Brennan, supra note 1, at 769.
19. Twining v. New Jersey, 211 U.S. 78, 99 (1908).
20. Palko v. Connecticut, 302 U.S. 319, 326 (1937).
21. See Gitlow v. New York, 268 U.S. 652, 666 (1925).
22. See Chicago B. & Q. R.R. v. Chicago, 166 U.S. 226 (1897).
23. See Betts v. Brady, 316 U.S. 455 (1942).
24. See Wolf v. Colorado, 338 U.S. 25 (1949).
25. Brennan, supra note 1, at 776.
26. See Mapp v. Ohio, 367 U.S. 643, 655 (1961).
27. Brennan, supra note 1, at 777.
28. Id. (quoting Palko v. Connecticut, 302 U.S. 319, 325 (1937); Hurtado v. California, 110 U.S. 516, 535 (1884); and Snyder v. Massachusetts, 291 U.S. 97, 105 (1922)).

29. Duncan v. Louisiana, 391 U.S. 145, 148 (1968).
30. 367 U.S. 643 (1961).
31. 388 U.S. 25 (1949).
32. Allen, Federalism and the Fourth Amendment: A Requiem for Wolf, 1961 Sup. Ct. Rev. 1, 47.
33. Lewis, An Old Court Dispute: Search-Seizure Edict Revives Issue of Applying Bill of Rights to States, N.Y. Times, June 21, 1961, at 21, col. 1.
34. Schaefer, Federalism and State Criminal Procedure, 70 Harv. L. Rev. 1, 26 (1956).
35. Ohio ex. rel. Eaton v. Price, 364 U.S. 263, 275 (1956) (Brennan, J., dissenting from the judgment of an equally divided court).
36. 370 U.S. 660 (1962).
37. Id. at 666 (citation omitted).
38. Furman v. Georgia, 408 U.S. 238, 240 (1972).
39. 372 U.S. 335 (1963).
40. Answer to Respondent's Response to Petition for Writ of Certiorari at 2–3, Gideon v. Wainwright, 372 U.S. 335 (1963) (No. 155), quoted in R. Cortner, The Supreme Court and the Second Bill of Rights 195 (1981).
41. R. Cortner, supra note 40, at 199–200.
42. Gideon, 372 U.S. at 340 (quoting Betts v. Brady, 316 U.S. 455, 465 (1942)).
43. Id. at 352 (Harlan, J., concurring).
44. Id.
45. R. Cortner, supra note 40, at 196.
46. Brennan, supra note 5, at 494.
47. 378 U.S. 1 (1964).
48. 211 U.S. 78 (1908).
49. Malloy, 378 U.S. at 5.
50. R. Cortner, supra note 40, at 217.
51. Brennan, supra note 5, at 494.
52. See Pointer v. Texas, 380 U.S. 400 (1965).
53. See Klopfer v. North Carolina, 385 U.S. 213 (1967).
54. See Parker v. Gladden, 385 U.S. 363 (1966).
55. See Washington v. Texas, 388 U.S. 14 (1967).
56. 391 U.S. 145 (1968).
57. Id. at 149 n.14.
58. Id. at 150 n.14.
59. Id. at 171 (Black, J., concurring).
60. 395 U.S. 704 (1969).
61. Address by Attorney General Edwin Meese, American Bar Association (July 9, 1985).
62. R. Cortner, supra note 40, at 301.
63. 468 U.S. 897 (1984).
64. Id. at 922–25.
65. Id. at 972 (Stevens, J., dissenting).
66. Id. (Stevens, J., dissenting).
67. Id. at 978 (Stevens, J., dissenting).
68. United States v. Miller, 425 U.S. 435, 443 (1976).
69. Fisher v. United States, 425 U.S. 391, 408 (1976).
70. United States v. Watson, 423 U.S. 411, 423–24 (1976); Schneckloth v. Bustamonte, 412 U.S. 218, 247–48 (1973).
71. Apodaca v. Oregon, 406 U.S. 404, 410–14 (1972) (plurality opinion).

72. Hudgens v. NLRB, 424 U.S. 507, 521 (1976).
73. Rummel v. Estelle, 445 U.S. 263, 285 (1980).
74. Wilkes, The New Federalism in Criminal Procedure, 62 Ky. L.J. 421, 421 (1974).
75. Brennan, supra note 5, at 498 (citing Rizzo v. Goode, 423 U.S. 362, 380 (1976); Simon v. Eastern Ky. Welfare Rights Org., 426 U.S. 26, 41–46 (1976); Warth v. Seldin, 422 U.S. 490, 508–10 (1975); O'Shea v. Littleton, 414 U.S. 448, 502–04 (1974)).
76. Collins, Reliance on State Constitutions, in Developments in State Constitutional Law, 1, 4 (B. McGraw ed. 1985).
77. Id. at 2.
78. Robins v. Pruneyard, 23 Cal.3d 899, 910, 592 P.2d 341, 347, 153 Cal. Rptr. 854, 860 (1979), aff'd, 447 U.S. 74 (1980).
79. Batchelder v. Allied Stores Int'l, Inc., 388 Mass. 83, 87–93, 445 N.E.2d 590, 593–95 (1983); Western Pa. Socialist Workers 1982 Campaign v. Connecticut Gen. Life Ins. Co., 515 A.2d 1331, 1333–39 (Pa. 1986); Alderwood Assocs. v. Washington Envtl. Council, 96 Wash.2d 230, 237–46, 635 P.2d 108, 112–17 (1981).
80. Gustafson v. Florida, 414 U.S. 260, 266 (1973); United States v. Robinson, 414 U.S. 218, 235 (1973).
81. People v. Brisendine, 13 Cal. 3d 528, 551–52, 531 P.2d 1099, 1114–15, 119 Cal. Rptr. 315, 330–31 (1975); State v. Kaluna, 55 Haw. 361, 368–70, 52 P.2d 51, 58–60 (1974).
82. Compare South Dakota v. Opperman, 428 U.S. 364 (1976) (search of car impounded for parking violation not unreasonable, and therefore permissible under Fourth Amendment) with State v. Opperman, 247 N.W.2d 673 (S.D. 1976) (on remand, same search held not permissible under state constitution).
83. See Developments in State Constitutional Law, supra note 76, at 222–35.
84. See Brennan, supra note 5, at 503; see also cases cited in Developments in State Constitutional Law, supra note 76, at 24 n.13.
85. Sager, Fair Measure: The Legal Status of Underenforced Constitutional Norms, 91 Harv. L. Rev. 1212 (1978).
86. See id. at 1212–13; see also Utter, Swimming in the Jaws of the Crocodile: State Court Comment on Federal Constitutional Issues when Disposing of Cases on State Constitutional Grounds, 63 Tex. L. Rev. 1025, 1042–45 (1985).
87. Abrahamson, Criminal Law and State Constitutions: The Emergence of State Constitutional Law, 63 Tex. L. Rev. 1141, 1141 n.2 (1985) (quoting Crist v. Bretz, 437 U.S. 28, 39–40 (1978) (Burger, C.J., dissenting)).
88. Williams v. Florida, 399 U.S. 78, 136 (1970) (Harlan, J., concurring in result).
89. Trop v. Dulles, 356 U.S. 86, 101 (1970).
90. Collins, Plain Statements: The Supreme Court's New Requirement, A.B.A. J., Mar. 1984, at 92.
91. Florida v. Casal, 462 U.S. 637, 639 (1983) (Burger, C.J., concurring).
92. State v. Jackson, 672 P.2d 255, 264 (Mont. 1983) (Shea, J., dissenting).
93. Note, Michigan v. Long: Presumptive Federal Appellate Jurisdiction over State Cases Containing Ambiguous Grounds of Decision, 69 Iowa L. Rev. 1081, 1096–97 (1984) (footnote omitted).

94. Keyser, State Constitutions and Theories of Judicial Review: Some Variations on a Theme, 63 Tex. L. Rev. 1051, 1077 (1985).
95. See, e.g., Collins, supra note 90.
96. See Florida v. Casal, 462 U.S. 637, 639 (1983) (Burger, C.J., concurring); Colorado v. Nunez, 465 U.S. 324, 327 (1984) (White, J., concurring).
97. See Pollock, Adequate and Independent State Grounds as a Means of Balancing the Relationship Between State and Federal Courts, 63 Tex. L. Rev. 977, 993 (1985).
98. 463 U.S. 1032 (1983).
99. Mosk, The State Courts, in American Law: The Third Century 213, 216 (B. Schwartz ed. 1976).
100. Brennan, supra note 5, at 503.
101. 1 Annals of Cong. 439 (J. Gales ed. 1789).
102. Brennan, supra note 16, at 10.

Index

345